dictionary

of italian

painting

Tudor publishing company

New York

We wish to thank the following publishers for permission
to reproduce material in their possession:
Éditions Braun, Paris ('Les Siennois')
Éditions Minotaure, Paris ('Monsu Desiderio')
Edizioni Vallecchi, Florence ('Predelle')
the periodical 'l'Œil', Paris.

Ektachromes:
Epoca, Milan; Scala, Milan; Meyer, Vienna.
Photographs:
Albertina, Vienna.
Alinari, Florence.
Ashmolean Museum, Oxford.
Biblioteca Ambrosiana, Milan.
British Museum, London.
Lehman Collection, New York.
Galleria dell'Accademia, Venice.
Giraudon, Paris.
Isabella Stewart Gardner Museum, Boston.
Museo Correr, Venice.
Museo degli Uffizi, Florence.
Service de documentation de la réunion des Musées
Nationaux, Paris.

Printed by Imprimerie J.-M. Monnier, Paris.
Text set by Imprimerie Darantiere, Dijon.
Plates made by Clichés Union, Paris.
Translated from the French
DICTIONNAIRE DE LA PEINTURE ITALIENNE
© 1964 Fernand Hazan Éditeur, Paris
Printed in France

FOREWORD

3485

This book is not a dictionary of painters, but, as the title indicates, a dictionary of painting, in other words, it is intended as a vast historical panorama where the various periods and aspects of Italian painting are treated in the form of brief articles, in alphabetical order for easy reference.

The field has been limited to the period covering the Duecento to the end of the 18th century, from Cimabue and Cavallini to Tiepolo, Canaletto and Guardi. The early beginnings and modern times have been purposely omitted.

The names of some two hundred and fifty painters have been selected from these six centuries, all equally productive and each one the opening of a fresh chapter in the history of art. The articles on individual painters are not simply biographies followed by a list of their works: they are critical studies, based on the most recent research, in which reliability of information has not been sacrificed to the conciseness, required by the plan of the book. Doubtful attributions are discussed, major works analysed and characteristics of style described as far as possible, while taking into account individual temperaments and influences, the practices of studios and traditions of schools.

Other articles deal with subjects which, in a history of Italian painting, would be mentioned in marginal, but indispensable, comments, or developed in detail. Consequently, in addition to the names of artists there are those of the great popes (like Pius II, Julius II, Sixtus IV or Leo X), eminent personalities or noble families (the Medici, Gonzaga, Montefeltre, etc.) whose patronage contributed to the progress and flowering of the arts.

Place has been found, too, for cultural centres where the artistic life was particularly intense. Some of these towns acted as magnets, because they were historic capitals, residences of a splendid court or holy places: others became the seat of flourishing schools, during their golden ages, because they were the cradle of numerous artists. The two kinds were not necessarily distinct; Rome is the best example of their combination.

The great eras have not been forgotten either (Duecento, Quattrocento, Renaissance), nor the movements and styles to which posterity has given a name. Information on their essential characteristics and development will be found in articles like those on the Baroque and Mannerism.

LIST OF CONTRIBUTORS

Sylvie Béguin   S. B.
Conservateur au Musée du Louvre

André Chastel   A. C.
Professeur à la Sorbonne

Pierre du Colombier   P. C.

Michel Laclotte   M. L.
Inspecteur principal des Musées de Province

André Linzeler   A. L.
Conservateur honoraire à la Bibliothèque Nationale

Paul-Henri Michel   P.-H. M.
Conservateur honoraire à la Bibliothèque Mazarine

Peter Murray   P. M.
Ph.D., F.S.A. Lecturer in art, University of London

Jacques Thuillier   J. T.
Chargé d'enseignement à la Faculté des Lettres de Dijon

A

ABBATE Niccolò dell'. *See* Niccolò
dell'Abbate.

ACADEMICISM. This term, frequently
employed by art historians, has never
succeeded, like the expressions 'mannerism' and 'baroque' (*see* these words), in
changing from a derogatory epithet to
an accepted art-historical classification.
When applied to Italian art, in particular,
it serves to denote neither a period, nor a
clearly defined trend, nor a characteristic
artistic attitude.

'Academies', or assemblies of men of
letters or artists modelled on the Academy of Athens, sprang up in Italy at the
time of the Renaissance, and the term
was often used to distinguish the confraternities of artists from the corpora-
tions of artisan painters. Thus the
Accademia di San Luca at Rome, under the
presidency of a prince who was elected
to the office, retained the modest func-
tions that it had at the beginning: the
organisation of professional matters,
religious duties and mutual assistance.
Its assemblies were sometimes the scene
of professions of faith and even of doctrinal disputes, notably in the first half
of the 17th century and at the time of the
neo-classic reaction. The Accademia di
San Luca was not, however, regarded as
an institution of national importance, as
were the Royal Academy or the École des
Beaux-Arts in France, and one cannot
attribute to it any pretensions to 'academicism'. Nor can one do so in the case
of the academies which were created in
most of the capitals of Italy, such as the
Accademia del Disegno, founded in Florence in 1562, the *Accademia Ambrosiana*
founded in 1622 by St Charles Borromeo
in Milan, or the *Accademia di Belle Arti*
instituted in Parma in 1757 by Philip of

ANNIBALE CARRACCI. WOMAN CARRYING A
BASKET. DRAWING. STUDY FOR THE FRESCOES
IN THE PALAZZO FARNESE. LOUVRE, PARIS.

Bourbon under the direction of two
French artists.

Other 'academies', less official and
often short-lived, represented, on the
contrary, a particular trend in art. The
most famous of these was the *Accademia
degli Incamminati,* founded in 1585/86 by
the Carracci, as a reaction against the style
of painting in vogue in the mannerist
studios of Bologna. Its doctrine was
based on a repudiation of rhetorical
trends, a recourse to nature, and study

ANNIBALE CARRACCI. FAUN. DRAWING.
STUDY FOR THE FRESCOES IN THE PALAZZO
FARNESE. LOUVRE, PARIS.

directly from the nude. Now, by a
curious turn of Fate, the art of the
Carracci and their disciples, judged by
the work of their remote successors, was
during the 19th century profoundly
misunderstood and accused of consisting
solely of hollow rhetoric and conven-
tionality. Hence a confusion between
'academicism' in its vague sense and the
teaching of the Carracci, or the 'academic' art of Bologna. The essential
character of academicism has been taken
to lie in an eclecticism which rejected
individual inspiration in favour of a
slavish imitation of the great masters,
whose charter could be a sonnet which,

in the 17th century, was attributed by
Malvasia to Agostino Carracci, and
which recommends the painter to follow
'the awful path traced by Michelangelo; the true naturalism of Titian,
the pure and incomparable style of
Correggio, the perfect harmony of
Raphael . . .' Unfortunately, this sonnet may be pure invention on the part of
Malvasia. The art of the Carracci, now
better understood, is seen to be both
powerful and varied in its inspiration,
and the term 'academic' is as ill-suited to
the works of their pupils, Guido Reni
and Domenichino, now completely
rehabilitated in the eyes of the experts.
The word 'academicism' also tends
to be used in a third sense, wider and less
precise. 'Academicism' in this sense
describes the stage in the development of
a style when the artist, his creative urge
spent, is content to repeat the formulas of
his school. But when one attempts to
apply this definition to such or such a
period in Italian art, difficulties spring
up. As a result of the confusion of
terms described above, the first symp-
toms of ossification as represented by the
academy of the Carracci in Bologna at the
end of the 16th century, were eagerly
denounced. 'Bolognese academicism' it
was believed, progressively invaded the
whole of Italy, penetrating and then
destroying the naturalism of Caravaggio
and sparing only certain foreign geniuses
like Claude Lorrain and Poussin, and
some well guarded outposts such as the
Venice of Tiepolo and Guardi. Whilst
in Paris one healthy reaction succeeded
another (Watteau, Fragonard, Delacroix,
Courbet), Italian at was believed to have
sunk into a quagmire. This conception,
formerly accepted on all sides, can only
be regarded as a distorted picture. The
17th century in Italy is once more regarded as one of the most vigorous and
inspired in the history of painting. The
18th century in its turn appears rich in
original artists. Often described as
the triumph of academic formulas, the

neo-classic reaction at the end of the 18th century and the beginning of the 19th, is in fact the expression, more or less successful, but frequently elegant, given by Italy to a great European movement. Here again, the term 'academicism' is more appropriate to the vocabulary of the critic than that of the art historian.   J. T.

ALBANI Francesco (Bologna, 1578 - Bologna, 1660). It was after the death of Agostino Carracci (1602) that Albani arrived in Rome, where he assisted Annibale in decorating the Farnese palace, and was thereafter influenced by his style. He carried out a whole series of decorative works (the chapel in the choir of Santa Maria della Pace, 1611-1614, the ceiling in the Palazzo Verospi, etc.), and altarpieces (*Baptism of Christ,* Bologna, Pinacoteca); but he found his own particular talent lay in medium-sized pictures with mythological subjects (the four *tondi* of the *Story of Cupid,* 1622, Rome, Galleria Borghese). These show an ingenious, rather limited train of thought, and a flaccid style, but with a certain charm that brought him widespread fame from the 17th

through to the 18th century.   J. T.

ALBERTINELLI Mariotto (Florence, 1474 - Florence, 1515). Albertinelli was taught by Cosimo Rosselli at the same time as Fra Bartolomeo. The two pupils painted together several pictures signed with a cross between two rings, e.g. the *Annunciation* of 1497 in the Duomo at Volterra. They separated in 1500 when Bartolomeo became a Dominican. Albertinelli's manner can be said to sum up the practice of Florentine ateliers in narrative and construction at a time when, under the combined influence of Leonardo da Vinci and Perugino, interest was concentrating on subtle effects and airy composition. Thus the Uffizi *Visitation* of 1503 and the fresco with the Crucifixion in the Certosa of Val d'Ema offer rhythmically satisfying unities. The large *Annunciation* of 1510 (Florence, Accademia) is a good example of what classical sensibility, reduced to elegant formulas, which were occasionally insipid and always restrained, could become in his hands.   A. C.

ALLEGRI Antonio, *called* Correggio. *See* Correggio.

MARIOTTO ALBERTINELLI. ADORATION OF THE INFANT JESUS. DETAIL FROM THE PREDELLA OF THE 'VISITATION'. 1503. UFFIZI, FLORENCE.

ANDREA DEL CASTAGNO. PIPPO SPANO.
ABOUT 1450. CENACOLO DI SANT'APOLLONIA,
FLORENCE.

ALTICHIERO (born at Zevio, near Verona; active between 1369 and 1384). A fresco in Sant'Anastasia, painted in about 1390 at the end of his career, is the only remaining proof of Altichiero's activity at Verona, since the paintings executed in the Scaligeri Palace have disappeared. His most important works are preserved at Padua, where he lived for a long time: these are the monumental *Crucifixion* and the scenes from the *Life of St James* (the latter being painted with the assistance of his pupils)

in the Basilica of Sant'Antonio, completed before 1379, and the cycle of frescoes decorating the Oratorio di San Giorgio which he finished in 1384 and on which a certain Avanzo no doubt collaborated. These enormous works set Altichiero among the most original Italian artists in the second half of the 14th century. He retained Giotto's dignity in narrative, as well as his highly classical solidity of volume and the amplitude of space in his pictures. However, by imposing a touch of naturalism and a liking for local colour and individual portraiture, he broke new ground and emerged as a founder of a new school.   M. L.

ANDREA di BARTOLO Son of Bartolo di Fredi. *See* this name.

ANDREA del CASTAGNO Andrea di Bartolo di Bargilla, *called* (Corella, *ca* 1423 - Florence, 1457). The name derives from the township of Castagno where Andrea's father had settled down. From his modest peasant origins Andrea derived a certain harshness and great vigour. He worked probably with Filippo Lippi and had the opportunity of studying Masaccio before executing at the Palazzo del Podestà in Florence a *damnatio* of Cosimo's adversaries sentenced, after the battle of Anghiari (1440), to be hanged by their heels. These frescoes earned him the name of Andreino degl'Impiccati (of the hanged men) and obliged him perhaps to stay away from Florence for a time. In any case, in 1442 he was in Venice where, together with a certain Francesco da Faenza, he decorated the apse of the old church of San Zaccaria with energetic frescoes representing God the Father, the Four Evangelists, St Zacharias and St John the Baptist. His work for the Pazzi is thought to date from his return to Tuscany. In the chapel of the Castello del Trebbio, in the Val delle Sieci, he painted a fresco of the *Madonna and Child* with St John the Baptist and

St Jerome and the children of the donor against an extraordinary background of brocade (Florence, Contini Bonacossi Collection). In 1444 he made a cartoon for a stained glass window with the Resurrection intended for one of the *oculi* of the Duomo at Florence. Between 1445 and 1450 he decorated the Monastery of Sant'Apollonia with monumental frescoes which created a sensation: the *Last Supper* and three scenes from the *Passion*. Commissions now became numerous. In 1449 he did an altarpiece with the *Assumption* (Berlin) for the rector of San Miniato, Fra Le Torri. He also painted portraits —the *Portrait of a Man* (Washington, Mellon Collection) is no doubt by him— and gave a new impulse to secular painting. In a loggia of the Villa Carducci di Legnaia he depicted, under a painted frame, a series of over lifesize *Famous Men and Women* (they have been taken down and are now in the refectory of Sant'Apollonia). From 1451 onwards he continued the frescoes at Sant'Egidio abandoned five years earlier by Domenico Veneziano. But in 1454-1455 it is at the Annunziata that he gave the full measure of his force with the *St Julian,* which recalls a little the light tones of Veneziano, the *Trinity* represented in an extraordinary foreshortening, and in the Chapel of Ottaviano de' Medici, *Lazarus, Martha and Magdalen* (lost). In 1456 he executed for Santa Maria del Fiore an equestrian portrait of Niccolò da Tolentino as a pendant, on the same wall, to Uccello's fresco painted twenty years before. The portrait marks undoubtedly the apogee of his style, a late stage of which is exemplified in the tense and moving *Crucifixion* of the Convento degli Angeli (now at Sant' Apollonia). Castagno died in mid-career, struck down by the plague in 1457. The harshness of his temperament gave rise to the legend, propagated by Vasari, that he murdered Domenico Veneziano. He developed with greater

ANDREA DEL CASTAGNO. SIBYL OF CUMAE. ABOUT 1450. CENACOLO DI SANT'APOLLONIA, FLORENCE.

consistency than Uccello, though not without certain limitations, the plastic principle of the new style. The energy and the relief of the recently restored frescoes in Venice derive clearly from Masaccio and Donatello. The powerful figures, the symmetrical arrangement and the graduated perspective of the Trebbio frescoes reappear in the Convento degli Angeli *Crucifixion* whose composition, governed by the central theme, achieves an extraordinary *terribilità*. Andrea gave careful emphasis

13

ANDREA DEL CASTAGNO. THE LAST SUPPER. FRESCO. 1445-1450. CENACOLO DI SANT' APOLLONIA, FLORENC

to the movement of bodies and to facial expression: the tension in his scenes is always as dramatic as that of his faces. The *Famous Men and Women* is a good example of the resulting force and solidity. Castagno's art captivates the memory. His *Dante* and his *Pippo Spano* are not easily forgotten. Their type derives as much from the picture chronicle as from statuary.

This hard style prevailing in Florence in the middle of the century only appeared intermittently in Tuscany. The monumentality, the taut line and the austere chiaroscuro found an echo further afield, with Francesco del Cossa in Ferrara, with Mantegna and with Melozzo da Forli. It reappeared at the end of the century under the hard line of the Umbrian Signorelli.   A. C.

ANDREA di CIONE. *See* Orcagna.

ANDREA da FIRENZE Andrea di Bonaiuti, *called* (Florence, second half of the 14th century). The name of this

artist is closely associated with the remarkable frescoes which decorate the chapel called the Spaniard's Chapel at Santa Maria Novella in Florence. This church belonged to the Dominican Order, which wanted to make it even richer and more beautiful than the Church of St Francis at Assisi. In order to help them, a rich merchant built at his own expense, beginning in 1350, a new chapel, the decoration of which was entrusted to Andrea da Firenze, who was for a long time confused with Andrea Orcagna, until the discovery of a document in 1916 revealed that it was actually Andrea Bonaiuti, who as we know from other sources was working at Santa Maria Novella from 1337. This vast work cannot have been executed by one artist only. Andrea must have had helpers. It consists mainly of three frescoes: the *Passion,* the *Triumph of the Church Militant* and the *Triumph of St Thomas Aquinas.*

In the composition of the first fresco the influence of the Sienese artist, Pietro

Lorenzetti, is noticeable with reminiscences of Giotto. The historian, Venturi, has shown that the fresco painted on the east wall, represents not the Triumph of the Church Militant, but the Triumph of Penitence, or in a symbolic form the victory of the Preaching Friars over the heretics. The third fresco is devoted to the glory of St Thomas, who inspired Dominican doctrine. The saint is shown surrounded by the Evangelists and Prophets and trampling underfoot the false teachers. This work was undoubtedly finished about 1367. During the ten years which followed Andrea executed at the Camposanto at Pisa the fresco, which records the *Legend of St Raynerius,* a work for which he was paid 529 liras and 10 sols by a certain Ludovico Orselli. Some historians attribute two more *Crucifixions* to Andrea, one at the Camposanto at Pisa, the other in the Vatican, but these attributions are today contested. A. L.

ANDREA del SARTO Andrea d'Angio-

lo, *called* (Florence, 1486-Florence, 1531). Beside Raphael and Leonardo da Vinci, Andrea del Sarto is the most significant representative of Florentine classicism. Son of Angiolo di Francesco, a tailor, whence the name of Sarto, Andrea began as a goldsmith's apprentice and was then taught for several years by Piero di Cosimo. Like all Florentines he studied the cartoons of Leonardo and Michelangelo and learned a great deal from the soft and veiled transitions practised by the former. Andrea's earliest work is the grave and sustained *Noli me tangere* at the Uffizi. In 1509 he decorated the walls of the entrance to the Annunziata with scenes from the *Life of San Filippo Benizzi,* touching in their intimacy and executed with a knowing assurance, free of routine. But his first major commission was to decorate in terre verte the little Chiostro dello Scalzo. He began in 1511 with the *Baptism of Christ* and finished in 1526 with the *Birth of John the Baptist.* In 1517 he painted for the nuns of the Con-

ANDREA
DA FIRENZE.
YOUNG
GIRLS DANCING.
DETAIL
FROM THE FRESCO
'THE TRIUMPH
OF PENITENCE'.
SPANISH CHAPEL,
SANTA MARIA
NOVELLA,
FLORENCE.

15

ANDREA DEL SARTO. PORTRAIT OF LUCREZIA, WIFE
OF THE PAINTER. ABOUT 1520. PRADO, MADRID.

sition. In the Pitti *Assumption* Andrea begins to overdo the effects of drapery and reflected light. Finally mention should be made of his penetrating portraits (*Self-portrait,* Pitti) which reveal, in all modesty and earnestness, the personality of the artist as much as that of his sitters. He had an evident influence on numerous artists, attracted by elegance and grace, and inclined to remain within the comfortable limits of Tuscan eclecticism.   A. C.

ANGELICO Guido di Pietro, *as a friar* Fra Giovanni da Fiesole, *called* Fra (Vicchio, 1387 - Rome, 1455). When the 'Primitives' were rediscovered at the time of the Nazarenes and the Pre-Raphaelites, Fra Angelico appeared as the finest example of a pure art born of a pure heart. The suavity and the freshness of the painter friar are obvious; but today greater weight is given to two historical factors: on the one hand the efforts of the Dominicans to maintain the tradition, which had flour-

vent of San Francesco the *Madonna dell' Arpie,* now in the Uffizi, the 'noblest of all Florentine Madonnas' (Wölfflin), a masterpiece of calm and balance with a faultless rhythm, subtle and dreamy, and with a kind of reflective awareness that distinguishes it, for instance, from Raphael's Sistine Madonna. Invited to the French Court by Francis I in 1518, Andrea did a portrait of the Dauphin and painted the Louvre *Charity* which reflects again the same, slightly melancholy ease. The following year he returned to Florence to buy works of art for the French king but the money was squandered and he did not go back to France. In 1521 he attempted the grand manner and did a historical fresco, *Caesar Receiving Tribute,* for Poggio a Caiano, followed in 1524 by the *Deposition* (Pitti) and in 1525 by the *Madonna del Sacco,* an exceptionally skilful compo-

ANDREA DEL SARTO. HEAD OF A WOMAN.
DRAWING. ÉCOLE DES BEAUX-ARTS, PARIS.

RA ANGELICO. LAMENTATION OVER THE DEAD CHRIST. 1440/45. CONVENT OF SAN MARCO, FLORENCE.

ished in the painting of the Trecento, of art in the service of religious devotion, and on the other the new artistic trends that appeared in the years 1425-1430. Seen in this context the artistic personality of Angelico takes on a new aspect.

Born in the Mugello, Guido di Pietro entered in 1407 with his brother, Benedetto, the Dominican convent in Fiesole established in 1400 by Giovanni Dominici. After a year's noviciate Guido took the vows under the name of Fra Giovanni. He participated actively in the life of the convent and found himself involved in the Great Schism. He retired with his bretheren to Foligno in the cause of Gregory XII, the Florentine Republic having declared itself for the anti-pope, Alexander V. In 1418 the Dominicans returned to Fiesole. Fra Giovanni began to play a considerable part in church politics in Tuscany. In 1449 he became prior of his convent

with the full assent of Cosimo de' Medici; he held this office for three years.

The earliest record of Fra Giovanni as a painter dates only from 1432 when he executed an *Annunciation* for the Servi in Brescia (lost), and the circumstances of his training remain obscure. The following year Ghiberti was engaged in designing the marble frame for the altarpiece commissioned from Fra Giovanni by the Arte dei Linaiuoli (now at the Museo di San Marco). This imposing work shows to what an extent Angelico was alive to new ideas in Florence: the majestic and firm silhouettes of the two St Johns are no less revealing in this respect than the clear spatial articulation of the scenes in the predella. The same applies to the series of altarpieces he painted between 1435 and 1440 with their now traditional arrangement of the Virgin flanked by saints—e.g. the altarpiece for San Domenico in Cortona,

FRA ANGELICO. DESCENT FROM THE CROSS. CONVENT OF SAN MARCO, FLORENCE.

very similar to the Linaiuoli one or that for San Domenico in Perugia, dated to 1437 (now at the Galleria Nazionale, Perugia). Three works, now at the Museo di San Marco, datable to the years after the return of Cosimo de' Medici and illustrating the theme of the *sacra conversazione,* show an even more solid organisation of space: the one intended for the Convent of San Vincenzo d'Annalena (Museo di San Marco) where it was not installed until 1453; that for the high altar of San Marco—the Virgin flanked by eight angels and eight saints; and that for a Franciscan church at Bosco ai Frati (before 1445). The *Coronation of the Virgin* at the Louvre and the

Annunciation at Cortona (Museo del Gesù) with its magnificent rhythm are thought to be from the same period. Angelico's reputation was by now secure. In a letter written in 1438 to Piero de' Medici, Domenico Veneziano refers to Filippo Lippi and Fra Angelico as evidently outstanding. The large *Deposition* painted for the Santa Trinità (Museo di San Marco) with its landscape, its figures and its architectural decor shows the artist at his most ambitious about 1440.

When the Convent of San Marco was handed back to the Dominicans and restored, it fell to Fra Angelico to supervise the decoration of the convent cell by cell; he is likely to have employed

FRA ANGELICO.
SERMON OF
ST PETER. 1433.
SCENE FROM
THE PREDELLA
OF THE LINAIUOLI
ALTARPIECE.
CONVENT
OF SAN MARCO,
FLORENCE.

several assistants. Summoned to Rome in 1447 by Eugenius IV to paint the Chapel of Nicholas V in the Vatican, Fra Angelico took with him several aids, Benozzo Gozzoli among them. He also agreed to spend his summers in Orvieto to paint a *Last Judgment* in the Chapel of San Brizio. But he went only once and then returned to Florence to minister to the needs of his convent. He died in 1455 in Rome and was buried in the Dominican church of Santa Maria sopra Minerva. The humanist, Lorenzo Valla wrote the epitaph: '. . . Let me not be praised because I seemed another Apelles, but because I gave my riches, O Christ, to Thine. For some works survive on earth and others in heaven . . .'

Fra Angelico's earliest training was probably as a miniaturist and illuminator. He seems close to Lorenzo Monaco by the delicacy of his colours and a candour that does not exclude preciosity. There is even a 'gothic' aspect in works like the reliquary from Santa Maria Novella (mentioned by Vasari) with its background of gold guilloche and its elongated figures, or the Vatican *Madonna* which, in spite of recent attempts to attribute it to Zanobi Strozzi, can be safely left to Angelico. He delighted in the arabesque and the fine contour, but was no less alive to volume and amplitude. In the *Coronation of the Virgin,* for instance, the figures are arranged not vertically but in depth, along a sharp curve; the drawn out silhouettes and the stylised

FRA ANGELICO.
THE ANNUNCIATION.
FRESCO.
AFTER 1437.
CELL IN
THE CONVENT
OF SAN MARCO,
FLORENCE.

drapery seem to take on a new value. The same applies to the *Virgin Enthroned with Eight Angels and Eight Saints* seen in front of the Garden of Paradise (San Marco), in which the throne of the Virgin stands against a spacious background of greenery.

Thus from 1430 onwards Fra Angelico reacted to the challenge of the Brancacci Chapel. Though by training closer to Masolino, of whom there are echos in the layout of the San Domenico altarpiece (Fiesole), he retained something of the gravity of Masaccio in the way he set out volumes in space. In the Linaiuoli altarpiece with its Virgin, who is at once sculptural and pretty, he is close to Ghiberti. Architectural

features contribute to the firm composition of the *Annunciation* in Cortona. Here the painter created a kind of model subsequently much repeated by himself and even more by his pupils. The picture shows a loggia whose thin columns recall Michelozzo, Cosimo's architect. The perspective of the portico opens a regular succession of intervals which frame the figures and expand the space around them. The effect created by the even diffusion of light and the clear cut division of the axial column does not achieve the monumentality of Piero della Francesca. But Fra Angelico's subsequent development justifies a comparison with Domenico Veneziano, who was working at San Egidio about

1440 and whose *Madonna di Santa Lucia* dates probably from 1445. Fra Giovanni was thus not alone in his concern with the effects of light. He develops upon it in the Perugia and Annalena altarpieces, particularly the latter in which the luminous area around the throne epitomises an aesthetic based on the principle of splendour.

In the 15th century it is almost a rule for the panels of the predella to show a more spontaneous manner, sometimes even with a popular note. The greater freedom of the artist here encourages invention and Fra Angelico, like any good Tuscan story-teller, often made delightful improvisations. The tone is that of Jacopo da Voragine's *Golden Legend* which was in fact the main sources of the narratives; for example, the scenes from the *Life of St Nicholas of Bari,* the Perugia altarpiece (Galleria nazionale dell'Umbria; Vatican) and those from the *Lives of St Cosmas and St Damian* on the high altar of San Marco. These small compositions are precise and clearly organised, but with a tendency to simplification and brightness of colour, which give them sometimes a dreamlike quality.

The San Marco cycle is enough to remind us how wrong it would be to interpret Fra Angelico's art outside its Dominican context. Here he was not speaking to the world at large, but to those withdrawn from it. The themes treated in the cycle, which is largely the work of studio hands, are deliberately reduced and neutralised. Against grey backgrounds rows of saints are aligned on either side of Christ on the Cross, a conception still Trecento in spirit and expressing for the last time monastic serenity and gothic 'pathos'. The contrast is striking with the sweep, the elaborate structure and the 'Roman' properties—fluted pilasters, arches majestic and cold—of the *Life of St Stephen and St Lawrence,* painted in the Chapel of Nicholas V, in the Vatican, whose

pontificate marked the point at which the Church accepted the 'modernism' of humanistic culture. In San Marco Fra Angelico is still obviously attached, in spite of the setting, to Trecento narrative; the contrast between the externally 'modern' forms and the emotional tenderness of the figures emphasises his isolation and his originality. His greatest influence was not in Florence itself, where naturalistic tendencies grew stronger towards 1460, but in central Italy. The sweetness and grace of his style stimulated the school of Perugia. It could be suggested that Perugino's success in Florence at the time of Savonarola was a distant echo of the Angelic Brother's pious art.   A. C.

FRA ANGELICO. ST DOMINIC. DETAIL FROM THE FRESCO 'THE MOCKING OF CHRIST'. AFTER 1437. CONVENT OF SAN MARCO, FLORENCE.

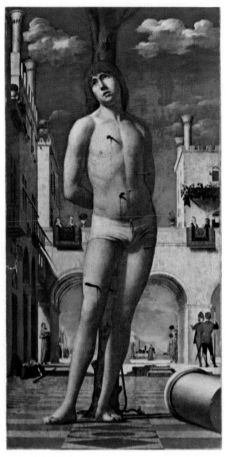

ANTONELLO DA MESSINA. ST SEBASTIAN.
ABOUT 1475. GEMÄLDEGALERIE, DRESDEN.

ANTONELLO da MESSINA (Messina, *ca* 1430 - Messina, 1479). Southern Italy, part of a Tyrrhenian community linking Valencia with Provence and Naples, made a major contribution to Italian painting in the years 1450-1460 in the person of Antonello da Messina. After training with Colantonio in Naples, Antonello was until 1456 in Milan where he may have met Petrus Christus. The *Crucifixion* now at Sibiù in Romania

dates from this time. Between 1465, the date of the *Salvator Mundi,* and 1473, the date of the *Polyptych of San Gregorio* (Messina), the only securely dated work is the *Ecce Homo* of 1470 (New York, Metropolitan Museum). It is the first of a series of pictures on this theme, one of which (1474) is in Vienna. The image of piety acquires a new intensity of suffering as a result of an increasing interest in the human face. Concurrently with this series Antonello painted a remarkable set of portraits: the *Portrait of a Man* in Cefalù, the one at the Museo Malaspina (Pavia), and that in the Altman Collection (New York). The *Portrait of a Condottiere* at the Louvre is signed and dated 1475, the *Portrait of a Man* in Turin (Trivulzio Collection) is dated 1476. In both the manly face, rendered with sovereign authority, gains relief against a dark background. Only one portrait (Berlin, 1478) has a landscape in it. The *Polyptych of San Gregorio* was painted in 1473. In the following year Antonello was commissioned to paint an *Annunciation* (now at the Museo di Palazzo Bellomo, Syracuse) for Santa Maria dell'Annunziata in the Palazzolo Acreide, the contract providing for the Madonna and the Angel to appear in an interior. Then, perhaps after a brief stay in Florence, we find the painter in Venice, where in 1475-76 he executed for the Church of San Cassiano a large altarpiece now dismembered (Vienna). He died in Messina in 1479.

Antonello trained with Colantonio, whose work revealed Flemish, Provençal, Spanish and French influences. The pupil acquired an exact knowledge of the art of Van Eyck from pictures in Neapolitan collections through his master and through Petrus Christus, whom he may have met in Milan. Nordic influence is clearly discernible in the robust naturalism, the articulation of space and the figures of the Sibiù *Crucifixion*. In the altarpiece for San Nicola, known through a copy in the Cathedral of Milazzo, in the *Three Angels* at Reggio Calabria and in the *St Jerome* (London, National Gallery) the definition of space and light comes from Petrus Christus. These elements grew weaker in the years 1465-1473 when Antonello's own style began to assert itself. He now attempted to give his compositions a more monumental harmony and to simplify his forms. In the *Salvator Mundi* he breaks with the Flemish tradition, altering the position of the hand originally held near the cheek. These changes in composition led, as in Piero della Francesca, to a new harmony which found magnificent expression in the *Madonna and Child* (London, National Gallery). Vasari mentions a trip to Rome which may account for Antonello's acquaintance with Piero. The Palermo *Annunciation* is stylistically close to the *Salvator,* especially in the perspective rendering of the hands, whence a plausible proximity in date. The light is so intense that the violent relief of the forms almost announces Caravaggio.

The force of expressionist inspiration in Antonello can be seen in his treatment of the theme of the *Ecce Homo* which had an evident fascination for him. He made of it the very image of suffering by stamping it with the unchanging features of human distress even to the smallest detail; even tears rolling down cheeks have a vivid reality. The series of masterly portraits offers a parallel illustration of Antonello's style and the growing skill of his psychological analysis. Antonello's achievement here is enhanced by his mastery of the two terms of modern representation—volume and space. In the *Polyptych of San Gregorio* the whole composition is informed by its perspective and the three main personages appear in a unified space. But the focus is not in the centre of the picture: the Virgin bends slightly to one side and the illusionist space is projected outside the picture by a circular movement rein-

forced by the oblique light. One is put in mind of a careful and intelligent study by Piero della Francesca. In the Syracuse *Annunciation* Antonello probably drew his inspiration from a picture by Van Eyck. The scene takes place in an interior lit from the side, as in the *St Jerome.* The smooth column, dividing

ANTONELLO DA MESSINA. VIRGIN AND CHILD. NATIONAL GALLERY OF ART, WASHINGTON.

the room, separates the Virgin from the Angel and her face emerges from darkness. This interest of Antonello's in Flemish motifs seems to have been constant and is still to be observed in the pictures painted after his arrival in Venice in the spring of 1475: the *Crucifixion* (Antwerp) and the *Pietà* (Venice, Museo Correr). The San Cassiano altarpiece, badly damaged, is remarkable in the way it combines light and

23

ANTONELLO DA MESSINA. THE VIRGIN OF THE
ANNUNCIATION. MUSEO NAZIONALE, PALERMO.

perspective. The architectural setting and the figures are particularly well attuned in the *St Sebastian* (Dresden) in which Venetian houses, arranged like stage flats, join in the background a terrace carried by an arcade. The monumentality of the Saint's figure is emphasised by its central position, recalling Piero and Giovanni Bellini. The oblique light lends a sort of animation to the whole picture which evokes memories even of Mantegna's *Dead Christ* with the foreshortened figure of the man lying asleep. In the London *Crucifixion* the harmony between architecture and landscape is almost perfect. The figures occupy a natural position in a circular space of which the axis is the Cross. Antonello thus demonstrates his outstanding feeling for synthesis in a less purely intellectual manner than Piero's. This lesson, so timely, was not

lost. It is difficult to exaggerate the importance of the trip to Venice in 1475. Antonello made a durable impression on the Bellini whose atelier was the seminary of all the new generation of painters.   A. C.

ANTONIO VENEZIANO Antonio Francesco da Venezia, *called* (Venice, before 1340 - Florence ?, after 1387). Antonio, after receiving some training in his native town, came to Florence in his youth and was the pupil, not of Agnolo Gaddi as Vasari has claimed, but of Taddeo. In 1370 he was paid for some paintings in the Siena Cathedral. In 1374 he is listed in the Guild of Physicians and Apothecaries of Florence. He went to Pisa in 1384 to work on the decoration of the Camposanto (south wing) and finished, from 1384 to 1386, a cycle of the *Legend of St Raynerius* begun by Andrea da Firenze and interrupted since 1377. The three scenes painted by Antonio are in the lower register; they were already damaged and altered by repainting before the war, and suffered from the incendiary raid of 1943. Without rejecting the Giotto tradition, Antonio gave it a more popular and naturalistic direction; on the other hand, probably under the influence of Sienese art, he gave more importance to landscape and architectural backgrounds. After finishing his work in Pisa, he returned to Florence. Nothing is known about him after 1387.   P.-H. M.

ARCIMBOLDO Giuseppe (Milan, 1527/1530 - Milan, 1593). A court painter to the Habsburg kings Ferdinand I, Maximilian II and Rodolf II, who worked in Vienna until about 1587, then went back to Milan where he died. We only know a few authenticated works by him, and a large number of imitations of his manner, which was very popular. The Vienna, Prague and Graz museums own most of his work. His still-lifes are visual fantasies in which the shape of a face is suggested by an extraordinary combination of fruit and vegetables, symbolising the Four Seasons, the Four Elements, etc. They were usually kept in collections of monstrosities and curios. In those extravagancies of mannerist origin, naturalism gave way to riddles, truth to invention, and everyday reality to the bizarre and the extreme. Those elaborate distortions of the still-life form, which produced strange arrangements of fruit, fish or vegetables, were hardly surprising in Prague where mannerism lingered so long at a time when, in France, the second school of Fontainebleau was at its peak.   s. b.

ASPERTINI Amico (Bologna, 1474/75 - Bologna, 1552). Formed during his youth in the milieu of Costa and Francia, Aspertini soon abandoned the elegant classical manner of these masters and revealed the moral anxiety and anticonformism of a temperament which was

GIUSEPPE ARCIMBOLDO. SUMMER. 1563.
KUNSTHISTORISCHES MUSEUM, VIENNA.

ARCIMBOLDO. THE KITCHEN. DRAWING.
ÉCOLE DES BEAUX-ARTS, PARIS.

considered excessively 'strange'. In the frescoes of the St Cecilia Oratory in San Giacomo Maggiore, Bologna (1506) there is a striking contrast between the fragile grace of Costa and Francia and the formal boldness of Aspertini. In fact he created an entirely original style in Bologna, in which, however, is discernible the memory of Filippino Lippi, whose work Aspertini studied in Florence and Rome, were he spent several years at the beginning of the century, that of certain Umbrians, and occasionally experiments similar to that of Pordenone or Lotto in Venetia, of Altobello Melone in Cremona or of Dosso Dossi in Ferrara. This style is already mannered, violently anti-classical with its strangely enlarged shapes and bright unusual colours, and it allows full expression to an imagination full of poetry, passion and even 'grotesque' fantasy. Aspertini can be judged by a series of reredoes

PIETRO LORENZETTI.
CRUCIFIXION
(DETAIL). FRESCO.
ABOUT 1330.
LOWER CHURCH,
BASILICA
OF ST FRANCIS,
ASSISI.

preserved in the Pinacoteca and in several churches in Bologna and above all by a cycle of frescoes painted in 1508-1509 in the church of San Frediano in Lucca.   M. L.

ASSISI. The Roman remains prove that Assisi was a prosperous town in ancient times, but there was little to distinguish it during the early Middle Ages. Like many other towns of the West, it did not flourish again until after 1000 A.D. One of the buildings of this first renaissance is the Cathedral of San Rufino (11th century), which was constructed by order of Bishop Ugone. As for the paintings, the little that survives belongs to the School of Spoleto (*Christ of San Damiano,* now at Santa Chiara).

The major event in the history of Assisi was the founding of the Franciscan Order. St Francis (1182-1226) lived at a period that marked in Italy the transition from romanesque to gothic. It would be an exaggeration to say that he was responsible for an artistic evolution that took shape before his time, but it is undeniable that there is a connection between the Franciscan spirit and the 'new style'. Less than two years after his death in July 1228, Francis of Assisi was canonised and, over the tomb of the saint through the initiative of Fra Elia, two basilicas rose; the Lower Church is still in the romanesque, the Upper Church is gothic, loftier and brighter. Before the end of the 13th century, when the time came to decorate the churches with paintings,

GIOTTO.
ST FRANCIS
GIVING AWAY
HIS CLOAK.
FRESCO.
ABOUT 1300.
UPPER CHURCH,
BASILICA
OF ST FRANCIS,
ASSISI.

the artists flocked to Assisi. The result of this gathering, which continued and grew in the 14th century, was an ensemble of painting that was perhaps the richest in all Italy. There the finest painters met from Rome (Cavallini, Rusuti, Torriti, whose presence in Assisi is hardly surprising because they were all devoted to the Franciscans; Torriti in fact placed St Francis and St Anthony in the Court of Heaven in the same rank and on the same scale as St Peter and St Paul); from Florence (Cimabue, then Giotto and his pupils); from Siena (Pietro and Ambrogio Lorenzetti, Simone Martini); from Pisa (Giunta Pisano); from Bologna (Andrea di Bartolo).

In this vital artistic centre, where for a century the leaders of schools of painting throughout central Italy followed each other and where their influence fermented in every way, it must be admitted that the local artists make a rather poor showing. They hardly contributed except as assistants to the outside masters; thus Pace d'Assisi, who did however decorate the cloister of San Francesco (1354) worked with Andrea di Bartolo. Although there was no school strictly speaking, the native painters of Assisi were extremely numerous in the 14th century. In that golden age of the town, all the religious institutions were covered with frescoes; the smallest confraternity had its oratory and hall decorated with paintings and a *Maestà* at the entrance. These works, generally anonymous, derived from a local art, which was strongly influenced by Sienese art and did not last for more

GIOTTO.
ST FRANCIS
PREACHING
TO THE BIRDS.
FRESCO.
ABOUT 1300.
UPPER CHURCH,
BASILICA
OF ST FRANCIS,
ASSISI.

than a century. The tradition died out before 1450.

Although, in the second half of the Quattrocento, Assisi had become an impoverished dependant of Perugia, it retained its prestige. The weakened Assisi were revived by a new influx of artists from neighbouring towns among whom were Matteo da Gualdo, Pierantonio Mezzastris from Foligno (about 1430-1506), a pupil of Gozzoli, Niccolò di Liberatore, called Alunno, who was also born at Foligno about 1430; Andrea di Aluigi, called Ingegno, who was a pupil of Perugino.

In the 16th century, the town of St Francis fell into a half-oblivion from which it did not emerge until very much later, when one of the masters of mannerism, Dono, or Adone Doni (1500-1575) was born there. The son of a patrician family, Doni was influenced in his youth by Giulio Romano and Michelangelo. He worked at Perugia, Assisi and elsewhere in Umbria. Several of his works can still be found at Assisi and its neighbourhood. The most curious is a large fresco in the refectory of the convent of Santa Maria degli Angeli: a gigantic Crucifixion, which includes no less than fifty-two figures larger than life.   P.-H. M.

B

BACHIACCA Francesco Ubertini Verdi, *called* (Florence, 1495 - Florence, 1557). Having been formed at a time when Florentine painting was succumbing to the pursuit of the singular and the rare, Bachiacca reveals himself in a strange pair of panel paintings, the *History of Joseph* (London, National Gallery), painted for a room to the decoration of which Andrea del Sarto, Granacci and Pontormo were also contributors. The overhanging rocks in relation to the architecture create a complex and uncertain space. The colour is subtle and changing. There is also a *Baptism of Christ* by him (Berlin) and other pictures, which were exported to France and England. About 1525 Bachiacca was in Rome with Giulio Romano and Benvenuto Cellini. Later he entered the service of Cosimo de' Medici and produced rather brilliant cartoons for tapestries—the *Months* and '*Grotesques*' (Uffizi). He belongs to the type of artist, half-painter, half-artisan, who carried over the Florentine naturalist tradition into mannerism.   A. C.

BACICCIA Giovanni Battista Gaulli, *called* (Genoa, 1639 - Rome, 1709). His complex early training, with Genoese models (Pierino del Vaga, Barocci and Rubens) was followed after 1657 by a study of the great Roman masters (Raphael, Cortona, who had a major influence on Gaulli, and Bernini, who gave him protection and friendship); this accounts for a style which was simultaneously loose yet refined, his rapid brushwork (there are many beautifully satisfying sketches), and his fresh colours, with harmonious pinks and blues. His inspiration is superficial, but his portraits are perceptive and sincere (*Pope Clement IX,* Rome, Accademia di San Luca),

his religious compositions have a fine moving spirit behind them (*St John the Baptist preaching,* Dijon, Musée des Beaux-Arts), and above all in the great decorative works we find some of the best expressions of baroque 'illusionism' (Sant'Agnese in Piazza Navona, about 1665, and the Gesù ceiling, 1668-1683, with the dazzling *Triumph of the Name of Jesus* in the nave; both in Rome); these qualities make him the true successor to Bernini and Cortona, and one of the forerunners of 18th century art.   J. T.

BALDOVINETTI Alesso (Florence, 1425 - . . ., 1499). Pupil of Domenico Veneziano, associate of Andrea del Cas-

BACHIACCA. BAPTISM OF ST ACACIUS.
DETAIL FROM THE PREDELLA OF 'THE LIFE OF ST ACACIUS'. ABOUT 1511. UFFIZI, FLORENCE.

tagno and Piero della Francesca at Sant' Egidio, Baldovinetti did not quite achieve the leading role that one might

ALESSO BALDOVINETTI. PORTRAIT OF A LADY.
NATIONAL GALLERY, LONDON.

have expected of him. From 1450 onwards he was occupied as a decorator and mosaicist at the Baptistery in Florence, and he remained in charge for half a century of the work on the cupola. In 1453 he was commissioned to decorate with mosaic the soffits over the north door and in 1455 those over the Gate of Paradise. His emblem carrying angels are firmly planted in the curves of the arches. Another interesting mosaic by him is the one with St John the Baptist in the tympanum over the south door of the Duomo in Pisa (1467). In 1454 Baldo-

vinetti was working in Florence with Andrea del Castagno at the Ospedale di Santa Maria Novella where he painted an *Inferno*. The spacious *Nativity* for the cloister of the Annunziata (1460-1462) is perhaps his best work together with the *Annunciation* for San Miniato (1466), where he also decorated the Chapel of the Cardinal of Portugal with large and luminous figures of Prophets, Evangelists and Doctors. The panel with SS John the Baptist, Catherine, Lawrence and Ambrose for San Ambrogio and the *Trinity with St Benedict and St Giovanni Gualberto* (Florence, Accademia) date from about 1470. The frescoes for the choir chapel in Santa Trinità (1471-1497), covered up in 1760, have been partly retrieved.

Baldovinetti became one of the leading mosaicists in Florence at a time when the city took over from Venice the primacy in that art. The favour mosaic came to enjoy was such that Lorenzo de' Medici could think of it as suitable for decorating the entire cupola of Santa Maria del Fiore. The large scale of Baldovinetti's compositions was well adapted to this medium. Finally, there is a great simplicity in his Madonnas and a remarkable sensitiveness in his calm and luminous landscapes. The Louvre *Madonna* and the *Nativity* at the Annunziata are perhaps the two best examples. A. C.

BARBARI Jacopo de', *also called* Jacob Walch (Venice, *ca* 1440 - . . ., *ca* 1516). Jacopo is one of the chief intermediaries between north Italy and the Germanic world, which was so active in his day both artistically and otherwise. He probably met Dürer in Venice in 1494-1495 before engraving for the merchant, Kolb, the admirable view of Venice (1500) which remains one of the masterpieces of the art. A little later he was in the service of the Emperor Maximilian. Then, between 1503 and 1505, he worked for the Elector of Saxony;

in 1505 he moved to Weimar and finally to the court of the Archduchess Margaret, Regent of the Netherlands. Royal and princely favour in this period went to portrait painters. Barbari's *Henry of Mecklenburg* (1507, Mauritshuis) anticipates Cranach. The celebrated *Luca Pacioli* in Naples, signed JA. BAR. is no longer attributed to Jacopo. His anatomy studies influenced Dürer. His work is difficult to establish. The Berlin *Virgin with the Child and Saints,* one of his earliest works, betrays the influence of Alvise Vivarini. But Jacopo's Venetian formation was counterbalanced by Dürer's influence, noticeable in the uneven and somewhat blurred treatment of his figures. In the Dresden *Galatea* and the Weimar *Christ* he moves away from the sustained style established by Antonello. *Still-Life with a Gauntlet* (1504, Munich), perhaps an emblematic picture, rendered with sovereign assurance, has a precise realism unique for the period. Finally, Jacopo may be credited with genre scenes in a northern manner and elaborate allegories (*Naked Couple* on the back of the *Portrait of a Man,* Berlin).   A. C.

BARBIERI Giovanni Francesco, *called* Guercino. *See* Guercino.

BARNA (Siena, second half of the 14th century). So little is known about the painter's life that his very existence has been doubted. None the less, the artist who painted the large composition decorating the Collegiata at San Gimignano (north wall of the nave) was, from the beginning, called Barna (or Berna). It is a complete cycle of the *Life of Christ,* about thirty scenes in three tiers. According to Vasari, the painting was nearly finished in 1381, when the master had a fall from the scaffolding. He died two days later and his nephew Giovanni d'Asciano completed his work. This pictorial rendering of the New Testament is still largely influenced by

Duccio's iconography (the *Flagellation,* for instance); but some of the scenes show the influence of Simone Martini, and Pietro and Ambrogio Lorenzetti. The *Annunciation* is reminiscent of that of Martini (Uffizi), and throughout his

BARNA. THE TAKING OF CHRIST (DETAIL). FRESCO. COLLEGIATA, SAN GIMIGNANO.

work we find the same dramatic feeling as in the paintings of the Lorenzetti brothers (the *Betrayal,* the *Crucifixion*). Chiaroscuro lends life and a third dimension to the figures. In the history of Sienese painting, Barna's place is between the great masters who inspired him and the coarser and more realistic painters of the end of the century, like Bartolo di Fredi and Bartolo di Andrea. The only surviving painting of Barna which can be attributed to him with any certainty is the *Crucifixion* of the

PIETRO DA CORTONA. STUDY FOR THE FRESCOES ON THE CEILING
OF THE CHIESA NUOVA, ROME. DRAWING. ALBERTINA, VIENNA.

episcopal palace at Arezzo which he painted in 1369 for Duccio di Vanni Tarlati.

Milanesi, in his edition of Vasari (1657), claims that the painter of the San Gimignano frescoes is identical with another older Sienese painter, Barna Bertini, who worked around 1340. There is also a Barna di Torino who was in Siena in 1378 and has left a few wood carvings.   P.-H. M.

BAROCCI Federico, *also called* Il Barocci (Urbino, *ca* 1535 - Urbino, 1612). One of the greatest personalities of the second half of the 16th century in Italy, and even today one of the least known. He served an apprenticeship in Rome and after returning to Urbino, completed it by a careful study of Correggio, from whom he took his rather short figures, his vague draperies, the smoothness of form and the delicate, genteel charm of his figures. Yet he experimented boldly

in his efforts to achieve unusual harmonies, and modelled his flesh with the help of pinks and blues, particularly in his magnificent studies in pastel. Rather than the small compositions, however, which reveal a slightly affected charm (the *Holy Family with Cherries,* Vatican), we should admire the great religious works which are enlivened by an amazing use of space (the *Martyrdom of St Vitalis,* 1583, Brera) and intricately devised details (the *Circumcision,* Louvre).   J. T.

BAROQUE. The word, of uncertain origin, is found at first as an adjective with the sense of bizarre or irregular. As a noun it seems to have gained currency towards the end of the 18th century through writers on classicism such as Milizia: 'The baroque, he writes, is the superlative of the bizarre, the excess of the ridiculous', and gives as an example the Italian architect Borromini.

But in the writings of German historians baroque gradually loses its pejorative connotation, even with those who, like Burckhardt, are hostile to it. From about 1887/88 onwards, the word can be said to be in common use in Germany as a term for the period following the Renaissance. France, much more reserved and attached to a specifically French nomenclature for the successive styles of her art—Louis XIV, Louis XV, Louis XVI—did not adopt the term until the very end of the 19th century, and many art historians have avoided it altogether.

The word has in fact two distinct meanings, a frequent source of confusion. One is aesthetic: baroque is defined in relation to classicism, as a reaction against it. 'Emotion and movement at all costs', says Jacob Burckhardt. Movement is indeed the distinctive characteristic of this style, and in the visual arts it manifests itself in variously transitional states, curved rather than straight lines and spiral columns. Inimical to the separation of the arts, baroque tends to develop such media of expression as will unite them, e.g. the theatre and festivals. Liable to inflation, it has affinities with rhetoric. Fond of illusion, it has frequent recourse to *trompe-l'œil*. Thus, as Wölfflin has shown, it is a permanent and recurrent type; it belongs to all periods and is the inevitable antithetical complement of classicism. Eugenio d'Ors used to amuse himself by enumerating the species of the genus baroque. Besides, classicism and baroque, especially the latter, never exist in a pure state. Every style has in it a classical and a baroque element. In different periods one or the other preponderate. Pergamum is baroque in relation to the Parthenon, German sculpture of the 15th century is baroque in relation to that of the Renaissance.

But in a narrower sense, which is the one relevant here, baroque is a chrono-logical rather than an aesthetic term. It designates a particular Baroque Age covering roughly the whole of the 17th century and the 18th until about 1750, when a classical reaction set in at Rome. Some historians, by no means unchallenged, detach from it the last period, called 'rococo' and characterised by the influence of French decorators.

As for baroque proper, it was born in Italy, more particularly in Rome, after the mannerist interlude which separates it from the Renaissance. It has been represented as the style of the Counter-Reformation, of the new phase of Catholicism after the Council of Trent which was at once more serious, more realist and more mystical. Its chief propagator was, according to this theory, the newly founded Order of Jesuits. True, the baroque coincides in time with intense architectural activity on the part of the Papacy, signalised by the erection of numerous churches and Maderno's basilical solution for St Peter's (1620). It is also a fact that commissions for religious subjects account for a large part of baroque works. But the explanation is insufficient. As for the Jesuits, recent research has shown that their influence on the style of their churches was far from decisive. The lavish decoration for which they can be held responsible is a relatively late development.

The artists who can be regarded as the originators of baroque in Rome are, in architecture, Maderno and above all Bernini, Borromini, and Pietro da Cortona; in sculpture, Bernini whose work as a sculptor is closely linked with his architectural creations. In painting the problem is more complex. Mannerism, which lasted until about 1590-1600, altrough like baroque it had its sources in Michelangelo and the followers of Raphael, is a style so essentially different that it cannot be considered as a kind of pre-baroque, as it has often been. Its origin was on the whole provincial; Mantuan at the Palazzo del Tè, where

Giulio Romano had been transplanted; Parmesan with Parmigianino, the pupil of Correggio; Florentine above all, with Pontormo, Bronzino, Salviati, Vasari; Sienese with Beccafumi; Genoese with Cambiaso. Rosso, from Florence, and Primaticcio, from Bologna, carried it to Fontainebleau, where it had a brilliant flowering. At Rome, the Zuccari were rather mediocre representatives of the style, but they were developing the décor of *grotesques* designed by Raphael. Where painting proper is concerned, at least three different currents should be distinguished, which can be illustrated by three major works at Rome: Caravaggio's painting at San Luigi dei Francesi, which represents the current of realism, with startling contrasts of light and shadow; the ceiling of the Galleria Farnese by the Carracci and Domenichino, paintings that were later described as classical, but that differ considerably less than has been said from the work of Caravaggio; the later ceiling of the salon in the Palazzo Barberini, which was only completed in 1640 by Pietro da Cortona, a continuous expanse of painting that had a decisive influence on all 17th century decoration. Artists like Guercino and Guido Reni are indebted to these various tendencies. In other centres in Italy, baroque sometimes assumes such a different character that there almost seems to be several baroque styles rather than one. At Naples, Ribera dominated painting with his Caravaggist followers; in south Italy (Lecce) and in Sicily, one type can be detected in the architecture. In the north, Venice is rather in a class on its own, but the special glory of Genoa is its magnificent palaces and Turin possesses in the Theatine monk, Guarini, one of the most original architects of the whole baroque movement.

Baroque makes a vigorous appearance in Flanders with Rubens as its very incarnation and church pulpits of extraordinary boldness as its distinctive product. In Spain it dominates in part the *Siglo d'oro:* Velasquez and especially Zurbaran owe it a great deal. Architecturally, baroque which succeeds plateresque not without borrowing a number of features from it, appears in the work of the Churrigueras, and their pupils and imitators. From Spain it spread to Central and South America. Occasionally it entered into curious combinations with indigenous art, especially in Mexico.

On the other hand, there are countries in which baroque encountered serious resistance. Although unquestionably baroque traits have been found in Rembrandt, the style made little headway in Holland and even in Rembrandt it is combined with personal features of so distinctive a character that its presence is by no means obvious. In Britain it had a cool reception: Palladio was the predominant influence here, and one can hardly call him baroque. With the Adam brothers Britain was one of the first to turn again to classical antiquity.

In France, the reputed home of classicism, matters are less simple than is usually thought. That the temptation of the baroque was, at one stage, very strong cannot be doubted. In architecture the imitation of Italian churches is obvious. Charles Le Brun, the apostle of classicism, is in fact quite often entirely baroque in his drawings of fountains, while the ornamental style of Jean Le Pautre is obviously baroque in inspiration. The decisive influence in the Gallery of the Louvre and the interiors of Versailles was Pietro da Cortona. Applied arts, particularly silver, are in no way behind the excesses of the rest of Europe. But these soon provoked a violent reaction. Bernini's departure under a cloud (he had been summoned to France in 1664-1665) was due mainly to personal jealousy, but there is no doubt that the result of it was, as it were, a refusal of baroque which found expression in the colonnade of the

Louvre and the exteriors of Versailles. As for the transformation of ornamental style that occurred about 1730, i.e. the creation of rococo, whether or not attributable to Italian influence it cannot be separated from the general development of baroque, although the rococo style is rare in Rome.　　　P. C.

BARTOLO di FREDI (Siena, *ca* 1330 - . . ., 1410). In 1353, Bartolo di Messer Fredi de' Battilori opened a *bottega* (which was at the same time a shop and a workshop) together with Andrea Vanni. Later, Luca di Tommè and Bartolo's son, Andrea, also worked there. When he worked outside Siena, he remained within the district (San Gimignano, Montecalcino). At San Gimignano, he first worked at the Collegiata (Old Testament scenes, between 1356 and 1367) and later (1390) at the church of Sant'Agostino which he decorated with a *Life of the Virgin* of which only the *Birth of the Virgin* and the *Dormition* are still extant. Other important works are the Montecalcino *Descent from the Cross* (1382), a polyptych of 1388 (partly in Montecalcino, partly in the Siena Pinacoteca) and a *Madonna* (Uffizi). In all the works of Bartolo's youth and maturity, we find reminiscences of Sienese art from the first half of the century. In his old age, he became more sensitive to the influence of French or Franco-Flemish miniatures and joined the main stream of European gothic. The principal works of his last period (about 1395-1410) are the *Adoration of the Magi* (Siena, Pinacoteca), the *Presentation in the Temple* (Louvre) and the triptych in the Perugia Museum. His manner is characterised by a somewhat rough realism and vivid, varied colours with sharp contrasts. The piquant scenes of *Married Life* decorating the Sala del Podestà in San Gimignano have been attributed to his workshop.

The work of his son, ANDREA DI BARTOLO (Siena, *ca* 1360 - . . ., 1428)

FRA BARTOLOMEO. VIRGIN AND CHILD. DRAWING. ABOUT 1500. LEHMAN COLLECTION, NEW YORK.

was less important and very little of it has survived. We know that he painted altarpieces for several chapels in the Siena cathedral, but they have been lost. Extant works are an *Annunciation* (Santi Pietro e Paolo in Buonconvento) and a signed *Assumption* painted for the Pienza cathedral, now in New York (Metropolitan Museum).　　　P.-H. M.

BARTOLOMEO Baccio della Porta, *called* Fra (Florence, 1472/75 - . . ., 1517). After an early apprenticeship together with Albertinelli in the atelier of Cosimo Rosselli, Bartolomeo became a Dominican in 1500 under the impact of Savonarola's preaching. From his very earliest works, the *Annunciation* in the Duomo at Volterra, painted jointly with Albertinelli (1497), and the portrait of *Savonarola* (Florence, Museo di San Marco) his style was restrained and severe. In 1499 he began a fresco of the *Last Judgment* in the cemetery of Santa Maria Novella. In 1504 he was com-

BARTOLOMEO VENETO. THE COURTESAN.
STÄDELSCHES KUNSTINSTITUT, FRANKFURT.

missioned to paint the *Vision of St Bernard* (Florence, Accademia) which he did not complete until 1507. The picture is all subtle effects and exquisite relationships. A short stay in Venice, important in his career on account of the date, gave him a certain taste for colour (*The Eternal Father with Mary Magdalene and St Catherine of Siena,* Lucca, Pinacoteca). Back in Florence he resumed his collaboration with Albertinelli (*see* this name) and, in the class of large compositions, fixed on the theme of the mystical dialogue. He rendered it in a calm and simple, somewhat grey manner; e.g. the *Marriage of St Catherine,* of which there are two versions, one at the Louvre and the other, painted in 1512 for the Convent of San Marco, in the Uffizi. Bartolomeo's last works are somewhat spoilt by grandiloquence; e.g. the *Madonna della Misericordia* (Lucca, Pinacoteca), or by an obvious imitation

of Raphael filtered through the veiled shadows of Andrea del Sarto; e.g. the *Salvator Mundi* (Pitti). The intervention of a collaborator, Bugiardini, becomes noticeable in these pieces, especially the Uffizi *Pietà*. In a class apart, somewhat lacking in assurance but of a fine conception, is the fresco *Noli me tangere* painted in 1517 for the chapel of the little convent of Santa Maria Maddalena near Le Caldine where he retired shortly before his death.

Fra Bartolomeo was a magnificent draughtsman. With a style softened by *sfumato* but admitting of large spatial schemes and well balanced groupings, he was one of the first to attempt a synthesis of the new trends in painting. He thus belongs to the High Renaissance of which he gave a popularised and somewhat cold version in the interest of devotional art. Under Michelangelo's influence he rendered his figures with a solemn monumentality that did not always go well with his chiaroscuro. But he dominates, from a considerable height, the artistic production centred in San Marco after Savonarola.   A. C.

BARTOLOMEO VENETO (beginning of the 16th century). The work of this painter, who can be credited with about fifty works, mainly portraits, begins with a sentimental *Madonna* against a view of Padua in the background, signed and dated 1503 (Venice, private collection). His style, recalling in the *Circumcision* (signed and dated 1506, Louvre) the tonalities of Giovanni Bellini, is comparable in its occasional hardness to that of the painters of Bergamo; e.g. the *Portrait of Alberto Pio* (Milan) or the *Lady with a Lute* (1520, Brera). Wishing to adapt himself to the taste of the day Bartolomeo seems at one point to have turned for inspiration to the Lombards and to the elegant *sfumato* of Boltraffio. In the *Portrait of Lodovico Martinengo* (1530, London, National Gallery) the manner is objective and merely descriptive. But his accomplished portraits, acute and somewhat cold, of young women with golden locks and holding flowers in their hands; e.g. the *Young Courtesan* (Frankfurt-am-Main), earned him a solid reputation in the last century.　　　　　A. C.

BASCHENIS Evaristo (Bergamo, 1617-Bergamo, 1677). There is an unbroken record of the Baschenis family from 1400. Evaristo was its most illustrious member, a man of genius. To this day the best collection of Baschenis' works is to be seen at the Accademia Carrara in Bergamo. He worked at first with his father and seems to have been well acquainted with Cremonese art. About 1647 he was ordained. He has left a battle scene in the style of Jacques Courtois and a few religious subjects, but his fame rests on his still-lifes, especially those with musical instruments. The reception accorded to these should no doubt be associated with the contemporary successes of the Cremonese lute-makers, the Amati. As for Baschenis' style, restrained, careful of outline, fond of beautiful, well rounded and simple volumes, M. Sterling thinks that he found it in Caravaggio.　　P. C.

BASSANO Family of. A famous family of painters of whom the most important were Jacopo and Francesco da Ponte, known as Bassano. A mountain village, a family of craftsmen and a genre that became a success throughout Europe —the name of Bassano stands for all these.

JACOPO (Bassano, 1510 or 1518-Bassano, 1592). Jacopo was born in Bassano about thirty miles from Venice. To think of him as a kind of peasant painter is not altogether wrong. He was influenced by the manner of Bonifacio Veronese with echoes of Paris Bordone and perhaps some of the Emilian painters. He was the son of a village artist, Francesco (the Elder), with whom his training began. He reached Venice about 1534 and established contact with Lorenzo Lotto, Palma Vecchio and especially Titian. The study of Parmigianino's etchings was the fashion of the day and mannerism was beginning to appear. Jacopo caught the trend in the *Madonna between St James and the Baptist* (Munich, Alte Pinakothek). In the *Deposition* for the church of San Luca in Crosara, he is close to Pordenone and even more so in the fresco decoration of the façade of the Casa Michieli in

EVARISTO
BASCHENIS.
MUSICAL
INSTRUMENTS.
ABOUT 1650.
ACCADEMIA
CARRARA,
BERGAMO.

37

Bassano. *Samson* (Dresden) is perhaps the most representative work of this period. The results of his study of Parmigianino, Titian and German engravers crystallised between 1540 and 1550 in the *Adoration of the Shepherds* and es-

JACOPO BASSANO. PENELOPE. MUSÉE DE RENNES.

pecially in the *Beheading of the Baptist* (Copenhagen), whose elegant profiles and refined colours reflect the new fashion. About 1560 Jacopo adopted a new manner, tensely emotional with a dark tonality and various contrivances; e.g. the *Crucifixion* for San Teonisto in Treviso (1562, now at the Museo Civico). When El Greco reached Venice, Bassano was inventing a nocturnal world, scintillating, rich and confused. The example of Tintoretto, from 1472 onwards, contributed further to this development. Fantastic light effects began to appear in Jacopo's compositions, both religious and genre. Works like *Susanna* (Nîmes) or the *St Jerome* (Venice, Accademia) preserve some solidity of form under the effect of light, but the rural strain asserts itself and converts every picture into

a deeply felt pastoral. Tintoretto's oblique perspective appears everywhere; e.g. the *Martyrdom of St Lawrence* (1571, Belluno, Duomo) or *St Paul Preaching* (1574, Marostica). A dark sky, foliage on the horizon, cattle and peasants become inevitable elements in any scene whether religious or profane. Bassano repeated himself to satisfy a demand. His last works in which he was joined by his sons, Francesco and Leandro (Bassano, 1557 - Venise, 1622), are typical products of the family atelier. Their success is another indication of the rôle of the Bassani in the diffusion of composition through light.

FRANCESCO (Bassano, 1549 - Venice, 1592), Jacopo's eldest son, trained with his father in whose workshop he remained for most of his career. The *Adoration of the Shepherds* (Dresden), modelled on a similar picture by Jacopo (Rome, Galleria Nazionale d'Arte Antiqua), is a good example of this dependence. Between 1570 and 1580, Francesco turned to Biblical and pastoral subjects with a tendency to the anecdotic. The canvas at San Giacomo dall'Orio in Venice belongs no doubt to these years. It recalls the Marostica picture of 1574, a particularly clear example of Tintoretto's influence. In 1579 Francesco settled down in Venice and devoted himself to historical painting. His success, at first throughout Italy (he found admirers in Florence, like Niccolò Gaddi), then throughout Europe, was probably due to pictures of small format like the series of *Seasons* in which he gave a watered down version of the pastoral matter learnt in the family workshop. He took part in the decoration of the Sala del Maggior Consiglio and the Sala dello Scrutinio in the Palazzo Ducale after the fire of 1577. The large canvases with scenes from Venetian history (*Pope Alexander III presenting the Blessed Sword to Doge Ziani,* etc.) lack originality and distinction. While Francesco specialised in crowded compositions and used the father's chiaroscuro, Leandro and the other brothers specialised in the genre scenes of crafts, seasons, beloved of the north.

The success of the Bassani shows the attraction that a naive image of rustic existence held for the Venetian town-dweller. Jacopo's secret was to have seized the opportunity offered by the confused need of mannerism for naturalness and singularity. His ingenuity consisted in combining rustic themes with the changing light in nature. Father and sons thus paved the way for the advent of the genre scene, thereby bringing to a close the period of greatness in Venetian painting.   A. C.

BAZZI Giovanni Antonio. *See* Sodoma.

BECCAFUMI Domenico di Pace, *called* Domenico (Arbia, near Siena, *ca* 1486 - Siena, *ca* 1551). Domenico di Pace was a peasant's son and tended his father's sheep as a child; he was adopted and educated by his father's employer, Lorenzo Beccafumi. Vasari thought highly of his painting and also of his morals, which he contrasted with those of Sodoma.   But during the following centuries, Beccafumi gradually fell into worse and worse disfavour until the end of the 19th: the Pre-Raphaelites even refused to acknowledge him as a genuine Sienese.   Later and less prejudiced critics realised that his mannerism and his unusual light effects heralded the greatest achievements of the next century.   In a way, Beccafumi is no longer part of the Sienese school, because he discarded a dying tradition and benefited instead from the teachings and discoveries of Michelangelo, Raphael, Fra Bartolomeo and even Sodoma; he was also inspired by gothic sculpture. On the other hand, his use of bright, vivid colours belongs to the best Sienese tradition. Moreover, he always remained faithful to his native town: he opened a workshop there and returned after his visits to

BECCAFUMI. THE BIRTH OF THE VIRGIN. 1543. PINACOTECA, SIENA.

Florence, Rome, Pisa and Genoa.   His main works are: *St Catherine Receiving the Stigmata* (Siena, Pinacoteca), the *Meeting at the Golden Gate* (Siena, Ospedale di Santa Maria), the 1513 *Trinity* and the *Mystic Marriage of St Catherine* (1528), both in the Siena Pinacoteca where we also find the two masterpieces of his mature period: the *Christ in Limbo* and the *Birth of the Virgin*.   P.-H. M.

BELLINI (The). A famous family of painters, which consisted of Jacopo Bellini and his two sons, Gentile and Giovanni. The course of Venetian painting was largely determined by them.

JACOPO (Venice, *ca* 1400 - Venice, 1470/71). The earliest reference to Jacopo dates from 1424. He trained with Gentile da Fabriano in whose

39

honour he christened his eldest son. He married in 1428 and with Anna's dowry bought in the following year a house in Venice. He must have achieved early fame, and not only in Venice, for in 1436 he was invited to Verona by the bishop, Guido Memmo. There he painted a *Crucifixion* for the chapel of St Nicholas in the Duomo with stuccos and gildings and over forty figures, each allegedly a portrait. In 1441 he was in Ferrara, at the court of the Este where, according to the sonnet by Ulisse Alioti, he competed with Pisanello for the best portrait of the young Lionello d'Este. He won and commissions became numerous. His sketchbooks contain projects for funeral monuments for Niccolò III and Borso d'Este. Thus in the middle of the century, Jacopo was a painter in vogue. He shared all the fashionable interests. He studied the antiquities of Padua, Monselice, Este, Montagna and Brescia. He supported Mantegna in the latter's rebellion against Squarcione, and made him accept the commission for the Eremitani chapel; in 1453 Mantegna married Jacopo's daughter. Jacopo introduced the new style in Venice. His two sons, Gentile and Giovanni, were soon helping him in his atelier. The works of this period are joint productions; e.g. the Gattamelata altarpiece at the Basilica of Sant'Antonio in Padua (lost), the large canvases executed for the Scuola di San Giovanni with the Lives of the Virgin and of Christ, and for the Scuola di San Marco with the Passion and the history of Jerusalem. But up to 1466 commissions were taken by Jacopo alone. He died between January 1470 and November 1471.

His greatest works have disappeared, so that it is difficult to form an opinion of his art. But it is clear that, though a master of the gentleness and grace of late gothic, he sought to perfect and enrich his style in every way. The signed *Christ on the Cross* (Verona, Museo Civico) is dry and hard, but of a remarkable luminosity. The same applies to the Verona *St Jerome* and the *Annunciation* of San Alessandro in Brescia, the latter attributed for a long time to Fra Angelico. Jacopo painted many Madonnas: the signed *Virgin and Child* at the Accademia in Venice remains heavy in spite of a certain popular directness; the one in Lovere, also signed, is more beautiful; the small Madonna, found in a church near Imola and now at the Brera in Milan, is dated 1448. Jacopo's originality is most strikingly revealed in the two volumes of drawings (London and Paris) compiled perhaps for his sons. They are an extraordinary assortment of documents, copies after the antique, studies in spatial composition. Fascinated by perspective, Jacopo experimented with it in unusual ways, the results often recalling stage design.

GENTILE (Venice, *ca* 1429 - Venice, 1507), the elder of the two sons, trained as an apprentice with his father. The earliest work bearing his signature, dated 1465, is the large tempera at the Accademia in Venice portraying the first patriarch of the city, Lorenzo

Giustiniani, a hieratic figure with his gaunt profile, glowing with spirituality. In 1466 Gentile was working with his father, Squarcione and Bartolomeo Vivarini on a series of canvases for the Scuola di San Marco. The fine portrait in profile of the *Doge Francesco Foscari* (Venice, Museo Correr) who died in 1457, is attributed to the son rather than to the father. Gentile was to become an official portraitist. He painted the Emperor Frederick III during the latter's visit to Venice in 1469 earning the title of knight and count palatine. In 1472 he did a portrait of Cardinal Bessarion (lost) for the Scuola della Carità. From September 1479 to November 1480, he stayed in an official capacity at the Court of Constantinople. The celebrated portrait of *Mehmet II* (London, National Gallery) remains a remarkable historical document. From Constantinople he may have gone to

GENTILE BELLINI. JANISSARY. DRAWING. BRITISH MUSEUM, LONDON.

GENTILE BELLINI. PROCESSION OF THE TRUE CROSS OVER THE PONTE SAN LORENZO. 1500.
ACCADEMIA, VENICE.

Egypt. In any case he became the great 'Orientalist' in Venice as his canvases in the Palazzo Ducale show. For the Scuola di San Giovanni he did a whole cycle: the celebrated *Procession of the Reliquary of the Cross in the Piazza San Marco* (1496), the *Procession of the True Cross over the Ponte San Lorenzo* (1500), the *Miraculous Healing of Pietro de' Ludovici* (1501)—all three now at the Accademia— in which accurate reporting and the ability to deploy crowds are equally remarkable. In 1492 Gentile had agreed to paint again the large canvases by his father and brother painted for the Scuola di San Marco and destroyed in the fire of 1485. *St Mark Preaching in Alexandria* and the *Martyrdom of the Saint,* begun about 1504 or 1506, were interrupted by illness. Gentile asked Giovanni to finish them. A vision of the East, dazzlingly white, *St Mark Preaching* is very much in the spirit of Gentile but

embellished by the hand of Giovanni (now at the Brera).

GIOVANNI (Venice, *ca* 1430 - Venice, 1516), *called* Giambellino, always considered as the younger son, must have been born about 1430. His early years are obscure. He may have been illegitimate as he is not mentioned in either of the two testaments of Jacopo's wife. In 1459 he was no longer living with his father. He had the reputation of a good and pleasant man. His name appears next to Gentile's after their father's on the altarpiece the three did for the Basilica of Sant'Antonio in Padua in 1460. But the first major commission came only ten years later, in 1470—*Noah's Ark* and the *Deluge* for the Scuola di San Marco. The pictures were probably never executed, for in 1482 exactly the same commission was given to Bartolomeo Montagna. Giovanni seems to have been content for a long time with what he had learnt in his father's atelier. A personal style gradually emerges in the Madonnas, small private commissions with charming bright colours and luminous skies. The early one, the *Correr Madonna,* the *Davis Madonna* and the *Crespi Madonna* recall, with their elongated hands, Byzantine icons. Mantegna's influence does not appear until quite late, about 1465-1470, in the Berlin *Madonna* and the *Transfiguration* at the Museo Correr with his energetically carved out landscape. The panels devoted to the theme of the Passion are no less vigorous: the *Blood of the Redeemer* (London, National Gallery), the *Pietà degli Avogadori* (Venice, Palazzo Ducale), the *Crucifixion* (Venice, Museo Correr), the *Dead Christ* (Milan, Museo Poldi-Pezzoli) and *Christ Blessing* (Louvre). Giovanni distributes his emphases in a way that suggests new and deeper insights into these themes. Take for instance the *Agony in the Garden* (London, National Gallery), similar to Mantegna's, but instinct with a new spirituality. This gift for expression achieves yet greater results in the *Pietà* at the Brera.

Giovanni now had his own workshop and the series of altarpieces commissioned from him marks the stages of his artistic development: the pala for the Carità, for Santi Giovanni e Paolo, and finally the pala for San Francesco in Pesaro in which Giovanni gives his full measure and shows all he has received from Antonello da Messina. When his brother went to Constantinople (1479) he took over the frescoes begun by Gentile in the Sala del Maggior Consiglio. The fire of 1577 has destroyed these sumptuous evocations of Venetian feasts like the *Reception of Alexander III* or dramatic scenes like the *Sea Battle of Salvore.* Having mastered the technique of oils and worked out modes of composition that ensured a harmonious structure of his pictorial space, Giovanni could devote himself to tonal effects and chromatic unity. In the pala for

GIOVANNI BELLINI. VIRGIN AND CHILD. ACCADEMIA DE' CONCORDI, ROVIGO.

San Giobbe the perspective carries unobtrusively a twoway movement of light, which is reflected by the gold mosaic of the apse. In the Naples *Transfiguration* Christ's white robe concentrates the light; the landscape vibrates and takes on a new value as in the *St Francis in Ecstasy* (New York, Frick Collection). In all these pictures Giambellino finds a relation between space and the variation of tone which becomes a serene, pure and altogether unique celebration of the real world. In 1488, at sixty, he signed two works: the triptych for the Frari, one of his finest pieces, and the *Madonna with the Doge Agostino Barbarigo* for the Convent of Santa Maria degli Angeli in Murano. From his correspondence with Isabella d'Este we know that, like Lorenzo Costa, Mantegna and Perugino, Giovanni was invited to paint mythological subjects for the princess's *studiolo* (from

GIOVANNI BELLINI. PIETÀ. ABOUT 1470. BRERA, MILAN.

1496 onwards). But the extraordinary vitality of the old painter can be seen from his reaction to the work of his pupil, Giorgione. The portrait of the *Doge Loredano* (London, National Gallery) is already in the spirit of Giorgione and Titian. About 1505 Giovanni painted the pala for San Zaccaria in which he deepened the contrasts between light and shadow, and exploited to the full the harmonies between distinct colour and diffuse tonality. His light is even richer and his accents sharper in the *Baptism of Christ* (Vicenza) and the late *Madonnas* (Rome, Galleria Borghese; Venice, Accademia). In his last work, the pala with three saints in San Giovanni Crisostomo, Bellini displays the intimate magnificence that seemed to him so important already in the paintings of the seventies.

The Bellini workshop dominated the development of Quattrocento art in Venice. They were first and foremost Venetians, devoted chroniclers of the native scene and its exquisite decor of which they captured in their images the significant detail. In the four paintings of the *Miracles of the Relic of the Cross* Gentile does not content himself with representing the progress of a majestic procession; he re-enacts one of the city's great popular feasts. The Bellini were above all alive to the problems of the day. Jacopo knew already that the traditional formulas were no longer valid and that reform would have to be radical. Giovanni reproduces the very atmosphere of the Byzantine churches of the Lagoon. His long career made him the dominant figure in the second half of the century. Open to all novelties he knew how to assimilate and 'Venetianise' them. Starting from Mantegna he

GIOVANNI BELLINI. YOUNG WOMAN AT HER TOILET. 1515.
KUNSTHISTORISCHES MUSEUM, VIENNA.

ended with Giorgione. His brother-in-law's dryness and severity grew softer under his brush and, drawing on what he had learnt from Antonello, he transformed Mantegna's grandiose vision of space into a new intuition of space-light. By concentrating his efforts on tonal unity, Giambellino brought Venetian painters, even those who did not share his predilection for serene images, to a point of maturity at which the reforms of Giorgione and Titian as well as the resistance of Lotto became possible. The fire of 1577 destroyed most of Giovanni's secular pictures hanging at the time at the Palazzo Ducale, so that he is known to us predominantly as a religious painter. However, the curious *Feast of the Gods* (about 1510, Washington) in which the landscape was completed by Titian, this mythological picture at once humorous and learned, and the no less curious *Noah's Drunkenness* (Besançon) whose attribution seems now firmly established, show a different Bellini, giving free rein to his fancy. Considering, moreover, that Gentile was a better portraitist than his brother, or at least a more attentive and productive one, it is fair to say that Jacopo's two sons between them mapped out a complete programme for the new generation of Venetian painters, defining as they did two complementary aspects in the history of Venetian paintings: Giovanni sought to deepen his vision by an effort of style; Gentile brought the atmosphere of the Orient, a vision of the exotic and a taste for the picturesque. This is what Venetian art was to thrive on for over two centuries.   A. C.

BELLOTTO Bernardo (Venice, 1720 - Warsaw, 1780). Nephew and pupil of Canaletto to whom some of his paintings have been mistakenly attri-

BENCOVICH

GIOVANNI BELLINI. ST GEORGE AND THE DRAGON. PANEL FROM THE PREDELLA OF THE 'CORONATION OF THE VIRGIN'. ABOUT 1473-1474. MUSEO CIVICO, PESARO.

rigo Bencovich, *known as* Federighetto, *also as* Il Dalmatino, was for a long time neglected by the Venetian School to which he belongs, because much of his work was done abroad. His place of birth has been variously conjectured as Venice, Ragusa (Dubrovnik) and Sebenico (Sibenik). In 1707 we find him at Froli (*Juno Ceiling* at the Palazzo Foschi), and in 1715 in Venice where he painted pictures for the Pommersfelden gallery owned by the Schoenborns, who were keen admirers of his art. He was then for many years in Vienna with short trips to Venice where, about 1725, he did an altarpiece for the church of St Sebastian (the *Blessed P. Gambacorti*). He also worked in Würzburg and his last years were spent in Gorizia. It seems that he was taught by the mannerist, Carlo Cignani, and that he was in touch with Crespi, who was so important for 18th century Venetian painting. Mariette has stressed Correggio's influence on him.   P. C.

BENOZZO di LESE. *See* Gozzoli.

buted, Bellotto was the great traveller among the Venetian *vedutisti*. He seems to have been in Rome with his uncle about 1742. His peregrinations began in 1745, at first inside Italy; then, summoned by Augustus III, King of Poland and Elector of Saxony, he went to Dresden where he was court painter from 1747 to 1759 and whither he returned after a few years first in Vienna then in Munich. Finally he settled down in Poland, at the court of Stanislas II Poniatowski and died in Warsaw. His art disproves the contention that Venetian painters cannot exist without the air of Venice. Under the more subdued skies of central and eastern Europe his painting, at times rather dark, achieves a remarkable density, an uncommon architectural solidity. He paints stone as those who strove to equal him painted water.   P. C.

BENCOVICH Federigo (... *ca* 1677 - Gorizia, 1753). The Dalmatian, Fede-

GIOVANNI BELLINI. PORTRAIT OF A MAN. ACCADEMIA CARRARA, BERGAMO.

46

BENVENUTO DI GIOVANNI. FINANCES OF THE REPUBLIC IN PEACE AND WAR.
BICCHERNA TABLET. STATE ARCHIVES, SIENA.

BENVENUTO di GIOVANNI (Siena, 1436 - Siena, *ca* 1518). Benvenuto, a pupil of Vecchietta, was not yet twenty when he painted in the Siena Baptistery frescoes with scenes from the *Life of St John the Baptist*. His first dated painting (1466) is the *Annunciation* in the Volterra Museum, which is reminiscent, by the placing of the characters and accessories, of the famous work by Simone Martini, but which also reveals other influences, including that of Liberale da Verona who was in Siena that year. While borrowing ideas here and there (we find in his works echoes of Matteo di Giovanni, Gozzoli, Pollaiuolo), Benvenuto's work remained original. His best works were painted between 1466 and 1485: the 1470 *Annunciation* (Sinalunga, Osservanza Church); the 1475 triptych (signed and dated) and a 1483 altarpiece (Siena, Pinacoteca). Two fragments from the same predella (about 1485) are now in France: the *Massacre of the Innocents* (Aix-en-Provence) and the *Martyrdom of a Holy*

Bishop (Louvre). In the end, Benvenuto's art declined. His colour became drier and more opaque, his compositions closer to the old Sienese models. His last works are difficult to differentiate from the paintings of his son, Girolamo (1470-1524). P.-H. M.

BERETTINI Pietro. *See* Pietro da Cortona.

BERGOGNONE Ambrogio da Fossano, *called* (Fossano, *ca* 1455 - . . ., 1523). His name is mentioned for the first time in 1481, among Milanese painters, and the nickname which sometimes follows his signature: 'Il Bergognone', only appeared in 1495, when the artist was already famous. It may have been an allusion to his origins, which would account for the obvious influence of Flemish art on his style; but on the other hand that art was well known in Milan at the time. He must have been trained between 1470 and 1480, under Foppa's influence, and he probably had

47

BERGOGNONE. DESCENT FROM THE CROSS.
ABOUT 1485. FONDAZZIO CAGNOLA, GAZZADA.

towards the Renaissance style, perhaps under the influence of Leonardo da Vinci. Back in Pavia in 1512, he again worked at the Certosa, with assistants, in 1514. His last works show the continued influence of the Lombard tradition and the survival of an outdated art which could neither renew itself, nor fully assimilate Renaissance ideas. S. B.

BERLINGHIERI (The) (13th century). Berlinghiero Berlinghieri, a painter of Milanese origin, settled in Lucca at the beginning of the 13th century, became the father of an artistic family and opened a workshop which became the most flourishing school of painting of the Italian Duecento. A document of 1228 mentions his name and those of his three sons: Marco, Barone and Bonaventura. Berlinghiero is otherwise unknown, but several art historians attribute to him the painted Cross of the monastery of Santa Maria degli Angeli in Lucca (now in the Lucca Pinacoteca) and several other crosses and Madonnas, including that of the Accademia in Florence. The Cross of Santa Maria degli Angeli, which is one of the most beautiful examples of the Byzantine manner in Italy, is adorned with paintings on all four limbs and bears the inscription *Berlingeri me pinxit,* without any Christian name. We only know that one of the members of the family painted it.

But we do know that Bonaventura, the most gifted of Berlinghiero's sons, born in Lucca about 1205-1210, painted the signed and dated Pala, in the church of San Francesco of Pescia (1235). In the centre, St Francis is standing, extraordinarily thin, with sparkling eyes; on each side, three scenes from the saint's life. This work, still Byzantine in technique, but none the less original, has often been quoted as one of the first pictorial renderings of a Franciscan outlook. Among other paintings attributed with some likelihood to Bonaventura, we must mention the

contacts with the art of the Ligurian coast. He worked from about 1488 to 1494 at the Certosa di Pavia where, with the help of his brother Bernardino and of his assistants, he painted the frescoes in the transept and the nave. He then painted many pictures and polyptychs in which the influence of the new artistic movement is obvious in the composition, the architecture and the perspective, while the inspiration remains personal, sometimes archaic. The colour is subtle, with harmonies in delicate shades of grey, and there is a remarkable feeling for intimate landscape. We find the same qualities in the Incoronata cycle in Lodo, where he painted frescoes in the apse, the presbytery, and a series of four compositions (1498). Those works seem to show an evolution

BONAVENTURA
BERLINGHIERI.
ST FRANCIS
PREACHING TO
THE BIRDS. PANEL
FROM THE 'LIFE
OF ST FRANCIS'.
1235. CHURCH
OF SAN FRANCESCO,
PESCIA.

Scenes from the Life of St Francis (Florence, Santa Croce) and *St Francis receiving the Stigmata* (Florence, Accademia). P.-H. M.

BICCHERNE (Tablets of the Biccherna). The *Biccherna* was originally a building in the parish of San Pellegrino, in which, from the 12th century onward, the town of Siena had lodged various administrative offices, including the tax collector's. These offices were gradually·transferred to the Palazzo Pubblico. From 1275 to the beginning of the 14th century, only the tax collector's office remained at the Biccherna and, when it was moved in its turn, people went on calling it by the name of its old building. The so-called 'Biccherna' registers in which collected taxes were listed, were kept between two small wooden boards held together by a strap: the *tavolette*. For a long time, the *tavolette* remained unadorned, but around the middle of the 13th century, the administrators, who only remained six months in office, started having their arms or their portraits painted on them to leave some token of their time of office behind them. The first painted *tavoletta* is a portrait of the friar, Ugo di San Galgano (1258). In the 14th century, the *tavolette* art blossomed out into a variety of subjects; for instance, the allegory of the *Good Government of Siena* by Ambrogio Lorenzetti (1344). About the middle of the 15th century, these small commemorative pictures were no longer used as a cover for the registers: they were hung on the walls. After 1460, they were all framed. The Biccherna officials commissioned them from the masters of

49

SANO DI PIETRO. 'LIBER ANDATURUM'.
BICCHERNA TABLET. STATE ARCHIVES, SIENA.

the time: Giovanni di Paolo, Sano di Pietro, Francesco di Giorgio Martini, Benvenuto di Giovanni, Neroccio de' Landi (from 1460 to 1500); later, Beccafumi, Giorgio di Giovanni, Salimbeni. The custom was kept up until 1682; the last *biccherne* are no longer on wood, but on canvas. With a few rare exceptions, all these paintings are kept in the Siena State Archives. They constitute a unique group of paintings, of great interest to the art historian since they are all dated and show clearly the evolution of styles.   P.-H. M.

BICCI Neri de (Florence, 1419 - Florence, *ca* 1490). The way in which he treats the hair and clothes of his figures suggests that Neri de Bicci worked at first in a

goldsmith's workshop. His works also reveal the influence of Fra Angelico and Domenico Veneziano. In his turn he had a studio where a great variety of work was undertaken and where many artists, such as Cosimo Rosselli and Francesco Botticini, were trained. Amongst the numerous paintings by him which still exist many were painted on a gold background. An *Annunciation* (1458) in the Uffizi should be mentioned. Two other *Annunciations* are preserved in the Accademia, Florence, as well as a *Madonna surrounded by four Saints* at the Convent of San Marco. Other paintings by this artist can be seen in the Cologne Museum and galleries in Great Britain and the United States.   A. L.

BOCCACCINO Boccaccio (Ferrara, *ca* 1465 - Cremona, 1525). Trained in the Ferrarese workshops and especially influenced by Ercole de' Roberti and Costa, he was later very strongly influenced by the art of Venice, where he stayed on several occasions, and that of Lombardy. From the mixture of these different schools of painting he created a style that was refined and slightly old-fashioned, coming half-way between Raphael's classicism and Giorgione's romanticism. We see its freest and most original expression in a cycle of frescoes in Cremona Cathedral (1515-1518).   M. L.

BOCCATI Giovanni di Piermatteo, *called* Giovanni (born in Camerino, active in Perugia between 1445 and 1480). Boccati settled down in Perugia in 1445. In 1447 he painted the large *Madonna del Pergolata* (Perugia, Galleria Nazionale dell'Umbria). The Virgin appears sitting under a decoration of flowers and foliage in the midst of a group of saints and little curly headed angels, singing in their marble stalls. This was the painter's favourite theme in his early period (Ajaccio Museum, etc.). Mannered, with a delicate feeling for colour, he is obviously influenced by Domenico Veneziano and Filippo Lippi and there is reason to suppose that he stayed in Padua and Florence. Later he worked in Urbino decorating the Sala della Jole at the Palazzo Ducale with a series of large murals representing warriors (about 1455). He was fond of pretty effects, as can be seen from the vast polyptych in Belforte del Chienti (1468), a remarkable attempt at a unified composition, and from the *Madonna dell' Orchestra* (Perugia), all grace and suavity with its tabernacle encasing the Virgin, its brocades and its angelic faces. Boccati is a second rate painter, but representative of a provincial style that prevailed between Perugia and the Adriatic coast. His work has recently been differentiated from that of a compatriot of his, Giovanni Angelo da Camerino, the author of the celebrated Barberini panels (Boston and New York).   A. C.

BOLOGNA. The Felsina of the Etruscans and the Bononia of the Romans, the illustrious university city of the Middle Ages has remained to this day one of the most important centres of Italy, with its reputation for intellectual activity and elegance. Although little remains of the two hundred or so towers, which bore witness to the internal strife of the medieval city and lent fame to its skyline, the Middle Ages have nevertheless bequeathed to the city some impressive buildings such as San Stefano (5th-13th centuries) and some spacious gothic churches (Basilica of San Francesco, 13th, San Petronio, 14th-15th centuries). The Renaissance provided some splendid civic edifices (Loggia dei Mercati, Palazzo Bevilacqua). From the 16th to the 18th centuries Bologna, which formed part of the Papal States, was enriched by convents and churches (San Salvatore, 1605-1623), palaces (Albergati, Poggi, Davia-Bargellini, Bentivoglio and the Archiginnasio) many of them decorated with fine frescoes. The arcaded streets,

GIOVANNI BOCCATI. VIRGIN AND ANGEL MUSICIANS. MUSÉE D'AJACCIO.

the many churches richly furnished with pictures, the impressive ensemble of the Piazza Maggiore dominated by the unfinished façade of San Petronio, the Palazzo Comunale and the Palazzo del Podestà lend the city a strongly individual aspect, at once genial and severe.

A series of frescoes preserved in the churches (San Stefano, San Martino) show that painting was early practised in Bologna, but it was only much later that it reached its full glory. Recent scholarship has granted a due measure of importance to artists such as Vitale or Jacopo da Bologna, Simone de' Crocefissi or Lippo Dalmasio. Marco Zoppi stood out amongst the painters influenced by Mantegna, but it was not until the Ferrarese, Costa, decorated the Palazzo Bentivoglio (about 1483) that the real awakening took place. Francia,

51

with his delicate art, which was imitated by a whole group of second class painters, furnished Bologna with its first individual expression. Mannerism developed, not only with the brilliant decorations of Tibaldi and Niccolò dell'Abbate, but also with the work of a whole group of painters, still little known such as Prospero Fontana (1512-1597), Sammachini (1532-1577), Passarotti (1529-1592) or, a little later, the Fleming, Denys Calvaert (1553-1619). It is however the personalities of the three Carracci with their swift and brilliant careers, which enabled Bologna to rank with the greatest centres of art and to furnish a model even to Rome (Galleria Farnese) and to the rest of Europe. In their wake emerged a whole group of powerful and individual geniuses: Domenichino, Guido Reni, Francesco Albani and Guercino, who divided their time between Bologna and Rome and won an international reputation. Less brilliant than these, painters such as Lionello Spada (1576-1622), Cavedoni (1577-1660), the delicate Schedoni (1578-1615) or the

romantic Alessandro Tiarini (1577-1668) combined to lend the art of Bologna its surprising diversity.

This flowering continued during the 17th century with less original painters such as Simone Cantarini (1612-1648) or Elisabetta Sirani (1638-1665), faithful disciples of Guido Reni, such as Cignani (1628-1719), Franceschini (1648-1729), or Gioseffo dal Sole (1654-1719), more or less held in thrall by the over illustrious examples of their predecessors. But in the painting of Guido Cagnacci (1601-1681) or Giuseppe Maria Crespi (1665-1747) their style, a little lacking in inspiration, nevertheless showed an intense and individual lyricism. Increasingly isolated examples such as excellent decorators like the Gandolfi at the end of the 18th century, and the astonishing development of scenic painting with the Bibiena, Stefano Orlandi (1681-1760) or Vittorio Bigari (1692-1776) who covered the ceilings of churches and palaces with illusionistic paintings, do not compensate for the absence of great creative artists. In the 19th

NICCOLÒ DELL'ABBATE. GROUP OF YOUNG GIRLS. DRAWING. LOUVRE, PARIS.

NICCOLÒ
DELL'ABBATE.
THE CONCERT.
PALAZZO POGGI,
BOLOGNA.

century, the School of Bologna from the Carracci to Crespi fell into even deeper disrepute. It is only now, with the biennial exhibitions at the Archiginnasio of Bologna, that the school, with all its wealth of diversity, has found once more its real title to fame: to have allied the most noble pictorial language with the analysis of human passions.   J. T.

BOLTRAFFIO Giovanni Antonio (Milan, 1467 - Milan, 1516). He belonged to a noble family and took part in contemporary political life, but none the less dedicated himsel to art while still very young. Trained in the Bergognone tradition, influenced by Foppa and Zenale, he was soon attracted by Leonardo and became one of his most devoted disciples. When Leonardo had to leave Milan, he left Boltraffio in charge of his workshop. In 1515, in the church of Sant'Onofrio in Rome, he painted frescoes in which the Leonardesque elements are more in evidence than the Lombard tradition. He is mainly famous for his excellent portraits: for instance the *Portrait of a Woman* (Chatsworth, Collection of the

Duke of Devonshire). The *Two Kneeling Worshippers* in the Brera are in fact the lower part of a large altarpiece in which Christ or the Virgin was adored by two worshippers whose faces are among the artist's most beautiful portraits. In that work, the painter used the same device as in his masterpiece, the *Casio Family Virgin,* now at the Louvre, originally commissioned in 1500 for a Bologna church, and in which we see Girolamo Casio and his father being presented to the Virgin by their patron saints. Among his famous paintings, we must also mention the *Loeser Madonna* and the *Narcissus* in the Uffizi. Boltraffio, with his elegant, aristocratic style, is among the best Lombard painters of the Renaissance. His smooth finish gives greater fulness to his figures and his rich colours sometimes suggest northern influences. He was one of the best pupils of Leonardo, whose themes he interpreted with a very individual talent.   S. B.

BONFIGLI Benedetto (Perugia, *ca* 1420 - Perugia, 1496). In the middle of the century the combined influence of the clear style of certain Florentines like

BOLTRAFFIO. HEAD OF BACCHUS. DRAWING.
ACCADEMIA, VENICE.

with Titian for a time and practised in the manner of Palma Vecchio several of whose pictures he completed. He owes his importance to the virtuosity of his colour whose elements he played upon with a truly mannerist freedom. A good example of this is the *Rich Man's Feast* (Venice, Accademia) and the *Finding of Moses* (Brera), a Biblical scene translated into an episode at court. He also produced some over ambitious canvases like the *Adoration of the Magi* (Venice, Accademia) or *Jesus among the Doctors* (Pitti), a large number of narrative pieces full of richly dressed people and well appointed equipages, and several *sacre conversazioni* in a landscape. By his full bodied and lively colours Bonifacio contributed to the final development of Venetian design by light and set the stage for Jacopo Bassano who was probably his pupil.   A. C.

Gozzoli and of Sienese preciosity roused the artists of Perugia. Bonfigli was among the most active. He was working at the Vatican in 1450, when Fra Angelico was there. In Perugia he collaborated in the frescoes of the Cappella dei Priori which owe a great deal to Gozzoli. The colours of his altarpieces have the brightness of enamel, the figures are carefully delineated and smiling. In the Perugia *Annunciation,* refinement is pushed to the point of preciosity. The angels, with their tunics falling in folds, and their carefully set hair crowned with chaplets of roses are frivolous rather than graceful. The coloured revetments of the architectural decor add a note of festive brilliance to the composition.   A. C.

BONIFACIO VERONESE Bonifacio de' Pitati, *called* (Verona, *ca* 1487 - Venice, 1553). Bonifacio was almost certainly

BORDONE Paris (Treviso, 1500 - Venice, 1570/71). Bordone's was mainly a provincial career, directly influenced by Titian whose pupil he seems to have been. His themes are those of Giorgione and Titian: *sacre conversazioni* in early evening landscapes (Glasgow), anecdotic and mythological scenes (*Bathsheba,* Cologne; *Diana as Huntress,* Dresden, destroyed in 1945) and portraits *(Cardinal Granvelle).* In 1535 he painted for the Scuola di San Marco the *Consigning of the Ring to the Doge* (Venice, Accademia). His works are to be found all over Venezia, in Lombardy and even in Augsburg where he went about 1540 at the invitation of the Fuggers. The pictures in the Cathedral of Treviso, after 1550, sum up his art with its lack of rigour and predilection for reflected light. He settled down into convention rapidly, smooth surfaces, lively colours and a somewhat facile sentimentality.   A. C.

BORGHESE (The). Marcantonio Borghese (1504-1574), who came from a family of lawyers and magistrates well known in Siena since the 13th century, settled in Rome where, in less than a century, his family rose to equal the greatest Roman houses. His son, Camillo, became Pope under the name of Paul V (1605-1621). Paùl's nephew, Marcantonio II, became one of the richest landowners in Latium. Cardinal Scipione Borghese, another of the Pope's nephews, was called 'Delizia di Roma' because of his kindness and generosity: he was a patron of the arts and built on the Pincio the family museum which soon began to fill with art treasures. Generation after generation went on enriching the Villa Borghese until the end of the 18th century, when Marcantonio IV (1730-1800) had it rebuilt in the style of the time. His son, Camillo, married Pauline Bonaparte in 1803. His brother-in-law, Napoleon I, then chose the most valuable pieces from the collection and had them taken away to France. In the 19th century, the Borghese partly reconstituted their collection. It has belonged to the Italian state since 1902. A fair number of the paintings, which were collected together again in the *casino*, can now be seen at the Galleria Borghese. Among these are the *Hunt of Diana* by Domenichino, the *Last Supper* by Bassano, Caravaggio's *David* and the famous painting by Titian, traditionally known since the 18th century as *Sacred and Profane Love,* which has been identified as the illustration to a passage from Ariosto. P.-H. M.

BORGIA (The). The Borja family was of Spanish origin and became famous in Italy in the 15th and 16th century. Calixtus III, during his short pontificate (1455-1458), raised the fortunes of the family. His nephew Rodrigo Borgia, born at Jativa, near Valencia, about 1431, and made a cardinal in 1456, soon became notorious through his dissolute

and ostentatious way of life. He had a palace built near the Campo dei Fiori, in Rome, now the Palazzo Sforza Cesarini. Elected Pope in 1492 under the name of Alexander VI, he started building, welcomed scholars (Pomponio Leto, Jean Lascaris), entrusted Sangallo with the transformation of the Castel Sant'Angelo and asked Pinturicchio to decorate his private apartments, both at the Castel Sant'Angelo and at the Vatican (1492-1496). He died in 1503, leaving a number of illegitimate children. His favourite son, Cesare (1475 - 1507), had in his service Pinturicchio and Leonardo da Vinci, whom he employed as an architect and a military engineer. He encouraged the development of industry in Romagna and built, among other things, the Palazzo della Rota at Cesena. A figure in one of the frescoes in the Borgia Apartments in the Vatican, the *Disputation of St Catherine,* is believed to be a likeness of his sister, Lucrezia. P.-H. M.

BOTTICELLI Alessandro di Mariano Filipepi, *called* Sandro (Florence, 1444/45-Florence 1512). Walter Pater notes with disappointment that Botticelli's life does not in the least correspond to the image of the artist, subtle, daring and slightly neurotic, derived from a decadent view of his work. Sandro was the son of a tanner from Borgo d'Ognissanti. He was born at the end of 1444 or the beginning of 1445. He had three brothers, lived with all three and owed something to each: his surname to the eldest, Giovanni, called Botticello ('little barrel'); the second, Simone, was a goldsmith's apprentice and Sandro joined him probably about 1460; the third, also Simone, was an ardent follower of Savonarola when the Medici were overthrown (1494-1498) and, though Sandro did not become a militant *piagnone* like his brother, he was profoundly affected by the moral crisis in Florence at the end of the century.

SANDRO BOTTICELLI. PRIMAVERA. ABOUT 1478. UFFIZI, FLORENCE.

His career was rapid and brilliant. It seems to have begun in a goldsmith's workshop, an illustration of Vasari's comment concerning the 'very close connection between the goldsmiths and the painters at the time [about 1460]'. His training as a painter was probably with Filippo Lippi, which would explain his predilection for portrayals of the Madonna. By 1470 Sandro had already his own atelier and in 1472 Fra Filippo's son, that is Filippino Lippi, was working in it as an aid. One of Botticelli's earliest pieces is the allegory of *Fortitude* for the Hall of the Arte di Mercanzia. In 1475 Giuliano de' Medici commissioned from him, for a *giostra,* a banner with the image of Pallas. By now Sandro had made his mark in official circles and in 1476/77 Cosimo and his family appeared as the Magi in the *Adoration* he executed for the altar of Guaspare del Lama in Santa Maria Novella. In July 1478 came a distinctly political commission to paint the *damnatio* of the Pazzi and their accomplices; he represented them hanging over the Porta della Dogana. From the same period come several portraits incomparable in the precision of their outline, among them the posthumous effigy of Giuliano de' Medici (Washington, National Gallery).

However, to gain a full view of Botticelli's unique position in the Florentine milieu we must go to the allegorical representations he was commissioned to paint for the various Medici villas: the *Primavera* (Uffizi), commonly dated to about 1478; the *Birth of Venus* (Uffizi), of a later date, in which the symbolism belongs to humanistic ideals, under the protection of Venus-Humanistas, in honour of Lorenzo di Pierfrancesco, Lorenzo's cousin; or the panel with *Mars and Venus* (London,

SANDRO BOTTICELLI. THE BIRTH OF VENUS. ABOUT 1486. UFFIZI, FLORENCE.

National Gallery) commemorating a marriage. These compositions illustrate the doctrines of the Florentine Academy in a manner acceptable to its protectors and its followers.

So far Botticelli had not been honoured by a commission for mural painting. In 1474 an attempt in Pisa, by the side of Benozzo Gozzoli, was unsuccessful. But in 1480 Botticelli proved himself in the superb representation at the Ognissanti of *St Augustine in his Cell*. In 1481 he was one of a large team of Umbrian and Tuscan artists to be invited to decorate the walls of the Sistine Chapel. His part was important: scenes from the *Life of Christ* on the right, from the *Life of Moses* on the left, painted with a sustained rhythm and several brilliant compositions like Jethro's daughter, much admired by Swann, and, a little further on, the tragic scene of the punishment of Korah, Dathan and

Abiram for their rebellion against Moses and Aaron, with a Roman triumphal arch in the background. Back in Tuscany Sandro contributed to another decorative ensemble, Lorenzo di Medici's Villa della Spedaletto near Volterra (frescoes ruined). Finally, there are the two celebrated marriage allegories from the Villa in Chiasso Macerelli (later Villa Lemmi) near Florence (now at the Louvre; the identification of the bride and bridegroom as Giovanna degli Albizzi and Lorenzo Tornabuoni, and the dating by the marriage, are not certain). The curious *Calumny of Apelles,* based on Lucian's description (about 1494, Uffizi), is another witness to Sandro's and his patrons' learned propensities.

In the period after the return from Rome, Botticelli was in frequent demand for religious pictures, many of them sizeable ones, like the *St Barnabas* altar-

SANDRO BOTTICELLI. HEAD OF FLORA. DETAIL
FROM THE 'PRIMAVERA'. ABOUT 1478.
UFFIZI, FLORENCE.

piece (Uffizi) for the church of the Saint or the *Coronation of the Virgin* for a chapel in San Marco. His workshop specialised in the Madonna and Child, and the innumerable variations on the theme have a delicacy of feeling and invention that is nearly always original and winning: *Madonna of the Magnificat* (Uffizi), *Madonna of the Pomegranate* (Uffizi), *Madonna with Child and Angels* (Ambrosiana). Towards the end of the century Pietà and scenes of martyrdom become numerous: the *Entombment* (Milan, Museo Poldi-Pezzoli; Munich, Alte Pinakothek), episodes from the Life of St Zenobius (Dresden, London, New York), etc. And it is, no doubt, the religious crisis of his last years that inspired the paintings charged with

allusions to contemporary afflictions, like the *Mystic Crucifixion* (Cambridge, Mass., Fogg Art Museum) and the *Mystic Nativity* (London, National Gallery). But Botticelli's most personal work after 1490 was without doubt the series of illustrations on parchment for Dante's *Divine Comedy*. The undertaking was financed by Lorenzo di Pierfrancesco who seems to have supported Sandro in this period. In fact the artist's last years were unhappy. Commissions fell off; his intense style had ceased to be fashionable. Vasari cites him as a warning example of an improvident artist and a 'sophisticated' mind.

Yet neither this failure at the end nor the fact that he was ignored outside Florence even at the time of his success detract from Botticelli's stature, fortified as this is by the profound affinities of his art with the philosophical and poetic aspirations of humanism. Nor should one forget the craftsman in him, his early connection with goldsmiths (a number of Baccio Baldini's engravings are from drawings by Botticelli) and marquetry workers (he supplied cartoons for the decoration of the Sala dei Gigli in the Palazzo Vecchio). He retained their arabesques, the precision of their contour and the constant inflexion of their line. It has been well said that Botticelli dressed his figures with skill and invention. But the little world of dancing silhouettes in their gauze apparel, of mounted knights and equipages out of courtly romances also betrays its artisan origins. Scenes like that were very frequent in contemporary decoration, especially on Florentine *cassoni* (ornamental chests). What remained was to transmute these themes into great art and to exploit at a conscious level the instinctive feeling for line and pattern shown by Tuscan workshops about 1460. Botticelli did precisely this.

There is reason to suppose that Botticelli combined what he learnt from Filippo Lippi, regarding the intensity of colour, with the influence of Pollaiuolo and Verrocchio. His early work shows him concerned with fullness of form and richness of tone, which he intensifies to the point of saturation in small panels, like the *Judith and Holophernes* (Uffizi). His predilection for free arabesque and sharp contours led him sometimes to subdue his colour, reduce his figures to the rhythm of an outline and treat space like a tapestry background. The *Primavera*, the *Birth of Venus* and the frescoes from the Villa Lemmi exemplify this tendency. In the middle period, from 1480 to 1490-1495, Botticelli was still given to using perspective effects, as in the *Annunciation* from San Martino della Scala, articulated by the long and beautiful flagstones, or in the architectural setting of the *Calumny* ; but at the same time, to banish all inertness from his compositions, he filled tiles and decorative panels with ornamental motifs or figures in bas-relief. This is perhaps the essential principle of Sandro's art: his purpose is to endow with a 'physiognomic' intensity each being, each object as it achieves integration in his crystalline, elegant, tense and somewhat withdrawn universe. There is here a kind of neo-gothic, a return to the unreality of the 14th century. But these lilies, these bronze foliages, these gold fillets in the hair, these pure profiles that he produces with such assurance are, as it were, personal treasures: they obviate the need to explore nature further (whence the conflict with Leonardo who could not understand Botticelli's lack of regard for landscape). The same festive note and preciousness occur in his altarpieces and his mythological allegories. And when in the end his art closes on itself, becomes a private system of arabesques and nervous silhouettes, given at times a monumental stature (the *Pietà*) or an architectural setting (*Story of Virginia Romana, Death of Lucrece,* etc.), this is not to be taken as a sign of regret or remorse. Rather, at a point when decidedly other

SANDRO BOTTICELLI. VENUS. DETAIL FROM 'THE BIRTH OF VENUS'. ABOUT 1486. UFFIZI, FLORENCE.

orientations were emerging—the 'tonal' unity of the Venetians and Leonardo's *sfumato*—it is the withdrawal of a pure and meditative artist who preferred to go on refining, as the drawings for the *Divine Comedy* clearly indicate, the moving figures of the closed world that was his beyond the shadow of a doubt.   A. C.

BRAMANTE Donato di Angelo (Monte Asdrualdo, near Urbino, 1444 - Rome, 1514). He was probably trained between 1470 and 1475 at the palace of Urbino where the Duke of Montefeltro employed numerous artists. He was, in fact, a painter before he became an architect, and even an 'excellent' painter; his Milanese disciple Cesariano claimed in 1521. It is now believed that he worked on the portraits in Federico da Montefeltro's Studiolo at the Urbino palace. His art is closely connected with that of Melozzo da Forli. Around 1475, Bramante left Urbino; in 1477, he was in Bergamo and painted the impressive representations of *Philosophers* on the façade of the Palazzo del Podestà. Between 1480 and 1485, he painted the *Men at Arms* frescoes, which were meant as decoration for the fencing room in the Casa Panigarola in Milan (now at the Brera). About 1490, he probably painted the *Christ at the Column* formerly in the abbey of Chiaravalle, now also at the Brera. He then turned to architecture and worked in Milan and in Rome where he died in 1514. Between 1480 and 1500, Bramante exerted an undeniable influence on Milanese painting; his interest in *trompe-l'œil* and perspective renovated the complicated gothic architecture of Lombard polyptychs by adding a feeling for space in keeping with the discoveries of the Renaissance and reminiscent of Melozzo da Forli and of the artists who worked in Urbino between 1465 and 1475: Laurana, Piero della Francesca, Paolo Uccello. s. b.

BRAMANTINO Bartolomeo Suardi, *called* (Milan, *ca* 1465 - Milan, *ca* 1530). Apart from a short stay in Rome, in 1508, where, according to Vasari, he met Perugino, Pinturicchio and Sansovino and worked at the Stanze in the Vatican, Bramantino lived in Milan and made his career there, both as an architect and as a painter. He worked in this double capacity for the Trivulzio family for whom he drew the plans of the Gian Giacomo Trivulzio chapel in the church of San Nazaro Maggiore and designed a series of tapestries which are mentioned in the account book of Magno Trivulzio. In Milan, he painted in 1513 a *Deposition* for the Carthusian monks of Chiaravalle. In 1519, he worked for Milan Cathedral. He had to leave the town for political reasons, but in 1530, through his fame and the help of Morone,

SANDRO BOTTICELLI. ENTOMBMENT. 1500. ALTE PINAKOTHEK, MUNICH.

he was allowed to return and was appointed by Francis II Sforza as architect and painter to the court.

It is generally believed that he had been trained by Butinone and had assimilated his master's knowledge of the art of Padua and Ferrara. He was influenced by Foppa in his use of colour and even more by Bramante who gave his style its grandeur. The works he painted between 1485 and 1505 show the evolution of his style towards that final artistic freedom: for instance the Boston *Madonna,* the Sansepolcro *Nativity* and *Pietà* (Ambrosiana) and the *Adoration of the Magi* (London, National Gallery) in which we notice distant reminiscences of Leonardo. S. B.

BRONZINO Agnolo Torri, *called* (Florence, 1503 - Florence, 1572). With the official portraitist of the Grand Duchy we come to the second generation of Tuscan mannerist—cold, refined, impeccably cultured and with an almost unlimited capacity for decoration. Apprenticed to Raffaellino del Garbo, Bronzino learnt from him the firm Tuscan technique of drawing. But he owes his real training to Pontormo whom he helped in the Certosa di Val d'Ema at Galluzzo (1522-1525) and whose clear colours and supple forms have left their mark in the two *tondi* of the *Evangelists* in the Capponi Chapel at Santa Felicità attributed to Bronzino. The artist was expelled from Florence in 1530 by the bishop and took service with Guidobaldo II of Urbino. He painted a portrait of the Duke (Pitti) and decorated the Villa Imperiale at Pesaro. He was able to return to Florence in 1532 and again helped Pontormo, then working at Poggio a Caiano. He also did decorations for other Medici villas which have not survived. In 1539 he was commissioned to decorate the chapel of Eleonora of Toledo, the Duke's wife, at the Palazzo Vecchio, and thereafter rose rapidly to

BRONZINO. PORTRAIT OF ELEONORA DA TOLEDO AND HER SON, DON GARCIA. ABOUT 1545. UFFIZI, FLORENCE.

the position of court painter. He painted a large number of portraits which set the tone at court and gave him an immense reputation—*Cosimo I de' Medici in Armour, Eleonora da Toledo with her Son, Garcia ; Bartolomeo Panciatichi* and *Lucrezia Panciatichi* (all at the Uffizi). In 1546-1547 he was invited to Rome and painted several eminent persons there, among others *Giannettino Doria.*

Eleonora's chapel, completed only in 1564, included a very affected *Pietà* and scenes, somewhat confused, from the *Life of Moses.* Compositional sophistication is here as exaggerated as in the allegory of *Venus, Cupid, Folly and Time* (London, National Gallery). Bronzino's production included tapestry cartoons and he continued with his official portraits. He took over the work of Pontormo (died 1558) at San Lorenzo, completing the *Martyrdom of St Lorenzo* in 1569. His last piece, the *Trinity* for the Capella

BRONZINO PORTRAIT OF A YOUNG MAN.
FRICK COLLECTION, NEW YORK.

dei Pittori at the Annunziata, dates from 1571.

Throughout his career Bronzino remained close to Pontormo. The older painter's tormented motifs reappear in his work, more intense and almost stifling. Like Pontormo, he fixed his attention too exclusively on Michelangelo's example, as in the *Christ in Limbo* (1552) which he painted for the chapel of Giovanni Zanchini in Santa Croce. But what interests us above all in his work is the conception and the brilliant brushwork of his portraits. They are his title to glory and deserve attention. Accomplished and full of artifice, crystalline and icy, they analyse human character with unusual power. Their firmness comes from a balanced construc-

tion in which direct light has a precise value. In the portrait of *Guidobaldo* the form is admirably compact. That of *Ugolino Martelli* has a concentration that recalls Pontormo. The play of cold tones, greens and violets, is as deliberate as in Lotto, but here it is combined with a vigorous contour. In the portrait of *Eleonora da Toledo with her Son* the brocades and the silks dominate the composition and govern the pose. The personage becomes a splendid mannikin, an unforgettable dress. No other painter took up the Flemish preoccupation with texture so thoroughly and so successfully. In the courtly art of portrait painting, Bronzino towers over his period and has been closely studied by stylists in portraiture, particularly Ingres, who greatly admired him.   A. C.

BUTINONE Bernardo (active between 1484 and 1507). His date of birth is unknown and usually placed around the middle of the 15th century. He is first mentioned in a document of 1484: the artist then lived in Milan and already had a famous workshop. The Brera Triptych which originally came, it is believed, from Santa Maria del Carmine, may date from that year. In 1485, he was commissioned to paint, together with Zenale, the large polyptych in the church of Treviglio. About that time, he was painting the frescoes on the pilasters of the main nave of Santa Maria delle Grazie, in Milan. Shortly after 1490, he was asked by Duke Gian Galeazzo Visconti to decorate, with Zenale, the ballroom of Castello Sforzesco. Also with Zenale, he worked on the frescoes of the Grifi chapel in San Pietro in Gessate, which they signed with both their names. Trained in Foppa's workshop, influenced by Mantegna and the Ferrari school, he evolved an expressionistic art, with hard, brittle outlines and strange, metallic colours, which has its own grandeur.   S. B.

C

CAMBIASO Luca (Moneglia, near Genoa, 1527 - Madrid, 1585). He was the son of a painter who was his first master and probably taught him a mixture of mannerism, Venetian and Lombard art. At the age of 15, Luca painted with his father the *Roman Stories* in the Palazzo Saluzzo, via Lomellini in Genoa. Two years later, with Lazzaro Calvi, he decorated the Palazzo Doria (now Spinola). He probably went to Rome before 1547, which would explain the mannerist foreshortenings, reminiscent of Michelangelo, of some of the figures of the Palazzo Doria. In February 1547, with his father and Francesco Brea, he worked on the Taggia *Resurrection* and on the frescoes of Santa Maria del Canneto. His close friendship with the architect Alessi probably dated from that period; he worked with him at San Matteo during the following years and their collaboration went on at the Palazzo Imperiale in the Piazza Campetto and, till 1567, in the Lercari chapel, Genoa Cathedral. A journey in Emilia around 1560 accounts for the influence of Correggio and Parmigianino, which is found in many of his works, for instance the Palazzo Bianco *Madonna* and the altarpiece in Santa Maria della Cella in Genoa. In 1562, in the Spinola chapel in the church of Santa Caterina, he painted the figures of *St Benedict, St John the Baptist* and *St Luke,* which are now in the church of San Lorenzo. After a second journey to Rome and Florence, he painted, in 1580, *St Augustine surrounded by Saints* at San Bartolomeo di Vallecalda. He was then at the height of his powers, which had developed between 1568 and 1580. He had assimilated mannerist tendencies from Tuscany, Rome, Venice and Emilia. In 1583, after hesitating for a long time, he decided to leave Italy with Lazzaro Tavarone, who' had been called to Spain by Philip II to decorate the main vault of the Escorial. He remained at the Spanish Court till his death.

Cambiaso's paintings are numerous, but we lack landmarks which would allow us to understand the development and variety of his gifts. He sometimes painted strange nocturnal scenes (*Madonna with a Candle, Christ before Pilate,* Genoa, Palazzo Bianco). He was a spirited draughtsman with a rapid line. He tended towards geometric forms, using sketches by Bramante or even by Dürer, and giving his figures a cubist look. These various aspects of his talent probably stem from his deepest tendency, which is mannerist, for he was always attracted by the bizarre and the unexpected; it is a mistake to interpret these unusual sides of his art as an anticipation of Caravaggio or of 17th century chiaroscuro.   S. B.

CANALETTO Antonio Canale, *called* (Venice, 1697 - Venice 1768). Canaletto's father was a painter of theatre sets and his son began by working for him. In 1719 Antonio is found in Rome and it is there, it seems, that he rapidly acquired the special skill that was to make him celebrated: he became a painter of *vedute,* of townscapes. This was a remunerative pursuit at a time when travellers were numerous in Italy and expected to take back with them souvenirs of the places they had visited. The Dutchman, Van Wittel, called by the Italians Vanvitelli, was still alive and active as a delicate practitioner of this art. Was Canaletto influenced by him or, in Venice, by Carlevaris, also a *vedustista,* though a rather dry and mediocre one ? By 1720 Antonio was

CANALETTO. THE DOGE ON THE BUCENTAUR ON HIS WAY TO THE 'WEDDING WITH THE SEA'
CRESPI COLLECTION, MILAN.

a member of the painters' guild in Venice and he found effective patrons and protectors especially among Englishmen staying in the city. Owen McSwiney, impresario and agent for collecting works of art, recommended him to the Duke of Richmond, and from 1736 onwards, he was assiduously patronised by Joseph Smith, English consul in Venice, a keen admirer and collector of his works. Smith is probably responsible for the painter's visits to England, from 1746 to 1750, from 1751 to 1753, and finally in 1754-1755. He may have returned to Rome in 1740, though the five Roman *vedute,* executed for Smith and dated 1742, were probably painted in Venice. In 1763 he became president of the Academy of painting and sculpture of his native city. Inundated by commis-

sions, he began to make increasing use of studio assistants; he also had many imitators, some of them very skilful, such as Marieschi or Antonio Visentini who worked for Smith.

Canaletto's *vedute* are precise without ever being dry; they show an exceptional sense of harmony which nothing is allowed to impair. By comparison, Panini, his Roman opposite number, sometimes strikes a false note. Canaletto's Venetian skies are generally cloudy, sometimes almost leaden, as one would expect in this waterlogged city with its relatively frequent storms. Sometimes the sky and the water have the same tonality of slate, but if there is a wind blowing, white circumflexes appear above the lagoon. Architecture is always scrupulously rendered, almost with a ruler. For a first rapid outline of his compositions, the artist used no doubt a *camera lucida,* noted on the leaves of his sketchbooks indications of colour and put in lighting by broadly treated hatchings. He obviously did more work on drawings commissioned by patrons like Smith, who had accumulated 142 drawings and 54 paintings (4 lost since) when George III bought his library in 1763.

The little figures that appear in these *vedute*—they are obviously more numerous when the subject is a feast, like Ascension Day—are drawn with great vivacity. To please patrons, who appreciated such *capricci,* Canaletto would not hesitate to put the Colleoni Monument on a high socle *all'antica* and give it a setting of ruins, or to mount the Horses of St Mark's on pedestals and transport them in front of the Doge's Palace—all this with astonishing plausibility.

The numerous English *vedute* show that he was not at all a slave of the Venetian atmosphere. His renderings of Whitehall or the grass-land of Bad-minton are just as good, without the slightest crudity in rendering the greens. As a special offering to Smith he executed a series of thirty-one engravings (1741) in which the features of the city are distinct up to the horizon.   P. C.

CARAVAGGIO Michelangelo Merisi or Amerighi, *called* (Caravaggio, 1573 - Port' Ercole, 1610). Caravaggio's father was employed as administrator by the Marchese di Caravaggio, a small town near Milan. Caravaggio himself is known to have been apprenticed for four years to a somewhat obscure painter, Simone Peterzano. He has also been connected with the Crespi, a Lombard family of painters, and, less directly, with artists like Lotto and Romanino. Federico Zuccaro, a contemporary of his, detected Giorgione's influence in his art, but in fact what he may have inherited from these various sources seems secondary. He reached Rome when he was about sixteen and, considered a child prodigy, was immediately taken up by powerful patrons like Cardinal del Monte

CANALETTO. THE GRAND CANAL AND SAN SIMEONE PICCOLO. NATIONAL GALLERY, LONDON.

CARAVAGGIO.
THE FORTUNE-
TELLER.
ABOUT 1590.
LOUVRE, PARIS.

and the Marchese Giustiniani, who remained faithful in spite of his misdemeanours.

His first major commission, which brought him immediate fame, was for the Contarelli chapel in San Luigi dei Francesi in 1590; he shared it with the Cavaliere d'Arpino and it took a long time to complete. The first picture done by Caravaggio, *St Matthew and the Angel,* caused a scandal and was rejected. Subsequently acquired by the Kaiser Friedrich Museum in Berlin, it was destroyed in the Second World War. The artist replaced it by another version and proceeded to paint the *Calling of St Matthew* and the *Martyrdom of St Matthew.* The ensemble was not on display until 1600; it seems that its execution took a comparatively long time.

Earlier than this spectacular exploit or contemporary with it are the fat and fleshy *Bacchus* at the Uffizi, the one at the Galleria Borghese and the *Medusa,* also at the Uffizi. The Uffizi *Bacchus* has in front of him a basket with fruit; a similar basket, rich and resplendent, appears by itself in a picture at the Ambrosiana in Milan. Caravaggio did not return to these still-life themes. The *Rest on the Flight to Egypt,* the *Repentant Magdalene* (Rome, Galleria Doria-Pamphili), *The Fortune-Teller,* at the Louvre, the *Amore Vincitore,* in Berlin, show the artist, if not amiable, at least at peace with himself, and hardly the man to cause a revolution in painting. The revolution occurred suddenly with the work for San Luigi dei Francesi. Its success in artistic circles was complete; the public was partly won over, partly scandalised. The reasons for this can be summed up in two words: light and realism. Almost black, opaque shadows are contrasted without transition, by means of a boldly drawn line, with equally stark lights. There is no modulation in outline or detail. The light is not natural light and seems to anticipate modern electrical projectors. The background is almost always black throwing the representation into striking relief. There is nothing to distract attention: neither landscape nor ornament. It has been observed that this almost theoretical light is exactly what is used in studios to teach young artists how to place their

CARAVAGGIO.
THE LUTE-PLAYER.
ABOUT 1595.
HERMITAGE,
LENINGRAD.

shadows. Realism: Caravaggio obviously made a point of introducing common people into his religious scenes, popular types or worse. At least three of his works were refused by those who had commissioned them: the *St Matthew* of the Contarelli altar, with his legs crossed and the sole of his left foot turned outwards in the foreground; the *Conversion of St Paul,* and the *Death of the Virgin.* There is not only realism here, but bravado as well. Berenson's description of Caravaggio as anti-baroque and incongruous does not take sufficiently into account the artist's genuinely lyrical vision of the 'scum of the earth'. The subject of the *Calling of St Matthew* is ruffians, insolently plumed, playing cards; Christ is relegated to the background. The principal figures in the *Martyrdom of St Matthew* are first the fierce looking naked executioner, then the child running away with its mouth open to cry, unforgettable types which both recur in a series of pictures inspired by the Contarelli ensemble, particularly in scenes of martyrdom for which the Contarelli paintings served as a kind of model.

Close in date (1600-1601) and manner are the vast canvases in the Cerasi chapel at Santa Maria del Popolo: the *Crucifixion of St Peter* and the *Conversion of St Paul.* It is difficult not to see a deliberate challenge in the enormous rump of St Paul's horse, which obstructs the picture while the rider lies on the ground in a somewhat grotesque posture, legs apart and arms in the air. Contemporaries were shocked by the dirty feet of the executioner attaching St Peter to the cross; but the composition of this picture, set out along two intersecting diagonals, has a magnificent sweep.

Caravaggio's life was no less scandalous. From 1600 to 1607 he engaged the constant attention of the police and the law courts: brawls, sword fights, ill-treatment of loose women whose interested protector he may or may not have been, outrageous behaviour towards some of his fellow-painters, suspect friendships with others or with the architect, Onorio Longhi. All this ended with a murder in 1606.

What is remarkable is the admiration he inspired. There was always somebody to get him out of difficulties:

Cardinal del Monte, Cardinal Scipione Borghese, the French ambassador, the Modenese ambassador, the Marchese Giustiniani. Even when he found it safer to leave Rome, negotiations were in progress to drop the proceedings against him.

And all this time he went on painting without interruption; the pictures dating from these years are among the most calm and peaceful of his whole career. In 1604 he completed for the Chiesa Nuova (Santa Maria in Vallicella) the most moving of his religious paintings, the *Entombment,* now at the Vatican: taut, compact, inscribed in a triangle, without trace, this time, of bravado.

Conceived in the same spirit are the two Virgins, roughly contemporary: the *Madonna di Loreto* (Rome, Sant'Agostino), in which the Virgin turns sideways, with her Son in her arms, towards the kneeling peasants, and the Virgin with the Child Jesus and St Anne, called the *Madonna dei Palafrenieri* (Rome, Galleria Borghese) because it was done for their altar at St Peter's; here the Child, one of the most delightful nudes of Caravaggio, places his foot on his mother's to help her crush the serpent.

Probably also from this period is the *David* holding the truncated head of Goliath (Rome, Galleria Borghese). It is thought, not without likelihood, to be a self-portrait; the lurid sense of humour would suit Caravaggio rather well. Another work that can be assigned to the years in Rome is the *Death of the Virgin,* now at the Louvre, one of the most remarkable among Caravaggio's paintings for its effects of colour, with the cinnabar red of the Virgin's dress harmonising with the rusty hue of the crying woman. Painted for the Santa Maria della Scala in Trastevere, the work was removed on account of its excessive realism. It was bought by the Duke of Mantua on the advice of Rubens but, before being sent off, it was publicly exhibited for a week, an indication of how celebrated the painter had become; probably by then he had already reached Naples in his flight for safety.

He must have found there quite a number of bad characters like himself, with Ribera as the chief and fiercest among them. He painted several pictures, like the *Flagellation,* now at San Domenico Maggiore, Naples, and, above all, the *Seven Works of Mercy* (Naples, Monte della Misericordia), combined on one canvas and on which the light from a torch creates deep contrasts. But he did not stay in Naples long. Soon we find him in Malta where he had perhaps already arrived in 1607. On 14th July 1608, he received from the Grand Master, Alof de Wignacourt, the Cross of the Knight of Grace, which, however, did not make him a member of the Order. He proceeded to paint Wignacourt's celebrated portrait now at the Louvre, a consummate study

CARAVAGGIO. MARY MAGDALEN. ABOUT 1590. GALLERIA DORIA-PAMPHILI, ROME.

CARAVAGGIO. THE CALLING OF ST MATTHEW (DETAIL). ABOUT 1597.
CHURCH OF SAN LUIGI DEI FRANCESI, ROME.

of the reflection of light on armour with the livid page helmeted and wearing a coat with a red facing. The masterpiece of the Maltese period is no doubt the *Beheading of John the Baptist* at the Cathedral in Valetta. Caravaggio avoids here, as in all his late works, violent oppositions; the figures stand out not against a uniform and abstract background, but against the grey of a prison building. The scene is no less grue-some for that and the executioner is about to behead the Saint with some kind of razor. In the foreground Salome, the only note of almost bright colour, holds a charger.

Restless as ever, Caravaggio did not stay in Malta for long. Quarrelsome and violent, he fell foul of a Cavalier di Giustizia, was imprisoned, escaped and appeared at the end of 1608 in Syracuse, where he painted for the

69

CARAVAGGIO.
CONVERSION
OF ST PAUL.
ABOUT 1600.
CHURCH
OF SANTA MARIA
DEL POPOLO, ROME.

Church of Santa Lucia the *Burial of St Lucy,* now in a ruinous condition. He went on to Messina where the Museo Nazionale has an *Adoration of the Shepherds* and a *Resurrection of Lazarus,* large pictures, with stronger contrasts, it seems, than the *St Lucy ;* they have suffered a great deal from early restorations. Caravaggio's last canvas is another *Adoration of the Shepherds,* executed in Palermo, and also sadly damaged, especially the area of the Virgin's face.

Caravaggio's end is rather obscure. He returned to Naples, was violently set upon and left for dead. In Rome, where he had not lost his protectors, efforts were being made to obtain his pardon. He set out in a felucca and, for reasons that are not clear, put in at Port'Ercole, near Orbetello which was a Spanish *presidio.* He was arrested, then released only to find the felucca gone. He developed malaria and died on the 18th July, 1610. On the 31st it was officially announced that he had obtained the Pope's pardon. 'He died badly as he had lived badly'—such was the merciless funeral oration of his enemy, Baglione, who was taking vengeance for the contempt shown him by Caravaggio.

But his friends, Marini in particular, knew what a painter had died, when he was not yet thirty-seven, after a dazzling career, and destined to be of quite extraordinary importance for the history of painting. Even apart from his influence, the stature and the temperament of the artist, who used to attack his canvases directly—there are practically no sketches by him—were to dominate the beginning of the century.   P. C.

CAROTO Giovanni Francesco (Verona, *ca* 1480 - Verona, *ca* 1555). Giovanni Francesco Caroto was very susceptible to influence and followed many exemples one after the other: for instance Mantegna, whose pupil he was, Liberale da Verona, the Lombard artists (he worked for a long time in Lombardy), and finally Correggio. These tendencies, more or less assimilated and mixed with the Veronese traditions of colour, result in a skilful, though at times rather affected, eclecticism. In addition he often reveals distinct qualities as a landscape painter (*Landscapes* at Santa Maria in Organo). There are a great many of his works in the churches and in the museum at Verona. His brother Giovanni (*ca* 1488 - *ca* 1566) a subtle and highly individual colourist, is traditionally believed to be Veronese's first master.   M. L.

CARPACCIO Vittore (Venice, *ca* 1455 - Venice, 1525). Carpaccio is certainly one of those painter-chroniclers of Venice who have contributed most to the legend and the prestige of the city. His name occurs regularly in documents from 1486 onwards and his career is easy to follow thanks to his habit of inserting into his compositions little pieces of paper with his signature and the date. One of these *cartellini* appears in the *Arrival of St Ursula in Cologne* (1490), the first of a big series of paintings for the Scuola di Santa Ursula completed in 1500. From then on commissions

GIOVANNI FRANCESCO CAROTO. CHILD HOLDING A DRAWING OF A PUPPET. CASTELVECCHIO, VERONA.

became regular: from 1502 to 1510 for the Scuola di San Giorgio degli Schiavoni, founded by Cardinal Bessarion, a series of panels illustrating the *Lives of SS George, Jerome and Tryphonius*; a cycle for the Scuola dei Albanesi (now dispersed in Milan, Venice and Bergamo); for the Doges' Palace in 1500 and in 1507 large compositions like *Pope Alexander III at San Marco* and the *Meeting between the Pope and the Doge in Ancona* (all destroyed in the fire of 1577). Carpaccio's output was very considerable and based on clearly defined workshop formulas: the St Thomas altarpiece for San Pietro in Murano; in 1510 the *Presentation in the Temple,* very Belliniesque in its layout inside an apse (Venice, Accademia); in 1514 the great pala, somewhat rigid, for San Vitale. The allegory of the *Dead Christ with*

CARPACCIO. LEGEND OF ST URSULA: PRINCE ETHERIUS TAKING LEAVE OF HIS FATHER.
DETAIL FROM THE 'DEPARTURE OF THE BETROTHED'. ABOUT 1495. ACCADEMIA, VENICE.

St Jerome and St Onophrius (New York) and the *Burial of Christ* (Berlin) belong, no doubt, to this period. Nature appears in them parched, stony and macabre, with an extraordinary gold light.

Carpaccio grew older and times changed but he did not change with them. He kept at his work systematically in the Scuola di Santo Stefano and elsewhere (the pictures are dispersed in Berlin, Milan, Stuttgart and Paris). He painted several variants of the story of *St Stephen among the Orientals* (Paris, Berlin), the Bergamo *St Roch and Worshipper,* a polyptych for the church of Santa Fosca, the *Martyrdom of the Ten Thousand,* much restored (Venice, Accademia). He also did work for provincial centres: an altarpiece with St Francis—in fact the Madonna enthroned with six saints in echelon on steps—for Pirano (1518), a *St Paul* for Chioggia

(1520), organ shutters for the Duomo at Capodistria. A document concerning his son, Pietro, and dated 26th June 1526, refers to Vittore as dead.

Carpaccio's starting point was without doubt the precise manner and the panoramic deployments of that ancestor of the *vedutisti,* Gentile Bellini. But to these he brought a new sense of narrative and atmosphere. Before Tintoretto there is no other Venetian story-teller of comparable calibre and Carpaccio contributes something unique—northern tapestry ensembles are perhaps a parallel —with his cycles for the Venetian scuole, confraternities or beneficent societies, which were both numerous and well endowed. The subject of the earliest of these cycles, the *Legend of St Ursula,* was popular both in southern and northern Europe. Carpaccio keeps close to the text of the *Golden Legend* by

Jacques de Voragine available in an Italian translation since 1475. The individual scenes are 'cut' as in a film, so that each has a colourful and picturesque setting, which is that of Venetian festivals. The Breton court in the *Arrival of the Ambassadors* has gondolas and coloured façades taken from Coducci's buildings. Elsewhere, as in the *Dismissal of the Ambassadors,* the Palazzo Ducale appears with its austere marble walls. The *Departure of the Betrothed* presents a review of Mediterranean architecture with the towers of Rhodes and Candia, known from the engravings of Breydenbach's *Peregrinatio* (1486), and,

on the right, a sort of Ca' d'Oro. The *Dream of st Ursula* is in a class apart with its breadth and realism, an indoor scene with a superb rhythm sustained by light, a demonstration of the painter's versatility. Carpaccio was also concerned with portraiture. Several contemporary faces appear in the procession of the *Martyrdom* and in the groups of the *Meeting of St Ursula and the Pope in Rome.* The same interest is observable in the panel (cut on the left) known by a misnomer as the *Courtesans* and representing Venetian ladies on a terrace in the midst of a colourful *far niente.* The sense of tonal colour, of colour relationships that

VITTORE CARPACCIO. A YOUNG WARRIOR
THYSSEN COLLECTION, LUGANO

as *St Jerome in His Study*—the subject in fact is St Augustine receiving the vision of St Jerome—is strikingly original in its precision and the entirely Flemish intimacy of its 'humanist' interior, a beautiful Venetian *studiolo*. The buildings in *St Jerome bringing the Lion to the Monastery* have been identified: they are those of the Scuola itself. As for the *Burial of St Jerome,* it is impregnated with an oriental atmosphere dear to Carpaccio, who created at the Schiavoni an exotic style, varied and penetrating.

As has been said, in the last fifteen years of his life Carpaccio held aloof from the new departures initiated by his contemporaries. He could not or would not, like Mantegna and Giovanni Bellini, adapt his style to the times. Somewhat unexpected pictures like the *Knight* (Schloss Rohoncz) with the extraordinary vegetation as its principal poetic theme, a composition that recalls Dürer, or the admirable genre scene in the so-called *Two Courtesans* (Venice, Museo Correr) show his particular sense of rich forms and warm but restrained tonalities. This amber coloured world has something bizarre and grave about it that possesses a winning charm, as in the *Presentation in the Temple* (1510) or in the panels with the *Legend of St Stephen* with their strange buildings and an atmosphere of silent torpor.

There is in Carpaccio a naive love of forms, which is characteristic of the Quattrocento, combined with a Venetian love of appearance. The picturesque —windows, carpets, silhouettes, dress, turbans and gowns—is always with him. Everything becomes a feast and a pageant. Nor is the setting neglected: whether landscape *(Meditation on the Passion)* indoors *(St Ursula's Dream)* or architecture *(Legend of St Stephen* and *Legend of St Ursula)*, it is handled with great skill. Hence the curious force of these images in which simple, straightforward narrative seems shot through with the strangeness of dreams. The

unify the composition, was clearly a lesson learnt from Antonello da Messina and Giovanni Bellini. These influences are obvious in pictures with traditional themes like the *Blood of the Redeemer* in Udine (1496), the *Dead Christ* in New York and the *Sacra Conversazione* in Caen. In these strange works Carpaccio is concerned to elicit a symbolic significance from mineral and arid landscapes far removed from the narrative freshness of the *Legend of St Ursula*.

The cycle in the Scuola di San Giorgio degli Schiavoni consists of nine canvases illustrating the lives of the Dalmatian protector saints, George, Tryphonius and Jerome. Here too the story is taken from the *Golden Legend* but with an unexpected attention to detail: the celebrated scene known until recently architectural settings of his pictures make up an incomparable album of Venetian life. What with Gentile Bellini is a formula becomes in Carpaccio an original invention, as enlargements infallibly show. His space, minutely articulated and filled in, constructed from careful preparatory studies (large wash drawing for the *Presentation in the Temple,* Windsor) is the space of the 15th century. The success of masters like Giorgione and Titian was bound to condemn it to obsolescence. But at the turn of the century Carpaccio achieved a poetic image of the city that was to remain the most complete until the romantic and moving evocations of Francesco Guardi.   A. C.

CARRACCI Agostino (Bologna, 1557 - Parma, 1602). Three years older than his brother, Annibale, Agostino Carracci at first collaborated in the former's painting (friezes at the Palazzo Fava and the Palazzo Magnani, at Bologna) and shared his interests (journey to Parma with Annibale, about 1585). It was Agostino Carracci who provided, with his *Communion of St Jerome* (about 1593/94, Bologna, Pinacoteca) the most complete and the most generally admired illustration of the ideals of the Accademia degli Incamminati. Summoned to Rome when Annibale undertook the decoration of the Galleria Farnese, he was unable to work in harmony with his brother, but he nevertheless gained from his stay in Rome (1597-1599) a more forceful style in which the Roman vigour of his figures is allied with a daring modelling (portrait of *Johanna Parolini Guicciardini,* 1598, Berlin, Dahlem). The Farnese family attracted him to Parma where he began a career (frescoes in the Palazzo del Giardino) which was prematurely interrupted by his death. Between that of his brother, Annibale, and his cousin, Lodovico, the more cerebral figure of Agostino appears a little indefinite, but his reputa-

VITTORE CARPACCIO. TWO COURTESANS.
ABOUT 1510. MUSEO CORRER. VENICE.

tion, so long upheld by the immense fame of his *Communion of St Jerome,* together with a very important collection of prints, has benefited by the reappraisal which has now taken place.   J. T.

CARRACCI Annibale (Bologne, 1560 - Rome, 1609). Together with his cousin, Lodovico, and his brother, Agostino, Annibale Carracci served his apprenticeship in Bologna. The prevalence there of late mannerism, exemplified by Prospero Fontana and Tibaldi, explains Annibale's enthusiasm on discovering the work of Correggio at Parma (about 1585), the influence of which permeates his *Baptism of Christ* (Bologna, San Gregorio) painted in the same year and his *Pietà* (Parma, Pinacoteca). During

ANNIBALE CARRACCI. SELF-PORTRAIT.
DRAWING. LOUVRE, PARIS.

in the history of European painting. The decorative solutions, both complex and logical, the mythological scheme with its subtle allusions, the lyricism, a trifle ponderous but relieved by a powerful vitality and a robust sensuality, which appears to ignore the reservations of the Counter-Reformation, the clear colours allied to sculptural forms, make of it a model which was studied by painters for two centuries. Shortly after the completion of the ceiling, Annibale suffered the first attacks of the disease which was to carry him off prematurely. His last works, the athletic *Vénus aux Amours* (Chantilly, Musée Condé), the grandiose *Pietà with St Mary Magdalene and St Francis* (Louvre) emphasise the urge towards monumental power which informed all his work without, however, excluding the frankest of realism (*The Bean Eater,* Rome, Galleria Colonna), nor the subtle analysis of landscape (*Sacrifice of Isaac,* Louvre; *The Flight into Egypt,* Rome, Galleria Doria-Pamphili). Admirable drawings (Louvre; Windsor) show with what ease Annibale had discovered the balance achieved by the great masters of the Renaissance between creative freedom and the observation of nature. Thanks to him, mannerist theories were invigorated by a firm and vigorous naturalism, during those years when Caravaggio for his part was turning to nature in order to reject them and to create a fresh idiom. This return to the great tradition allowed the classicists of the 18th century to recognise in the Carracci their progenitors and masters. This resulted in considerable renown, succeeded in the 19th century by a long period of discredit which has just ended in a complete and well-deserved rehabilitation (Exhibition at Bologna, 1956). J. T.

his stay in Venice (1585-1586) he was impressed by the marvels of Venetian painting. The Carracci then inaugurated the famous Accademia degli Incamminati and sought both by their teaching and their works (frescoes at the Palazzo Magnani, Bologna, 1588-1591) to impose a new standard of taste in Bologna. The important *Charity of St Roch* (1595, Dresden) with its vigorous structure and narrative eloquence, proves fully the mastery already attained by Annibale at the time of his arrival in Rome (1595). Cardinal Odoardo Farnese commissioned him to paint the Camerino (1595-1597, *Story of Hercules and Ulysses*) in his palace (the present French Embassy) and then entrusted him with the decoration of the gallery which was to become the famous Galleria Farnese. This immense ensemble which required the collaboration of various assistants (Agostino Carracci, then Domenichino, Albani, etc.) became a work of supreme importance

CARRACCI Lodovico (Bologna, 1555 - Bologna, 1619). First cousin of Annibale Carracci and five years his senior, Lodovico grew to maturity in the late

ANNIBALE CARRACCI.
ADONIS
DISCOVERING VENUS.
ABOUT 1594-1595.
KUNSTHISTORISCHES
MUSEUM, VIENNA.

mannerist atmosphere then prevailing in Bologna. At first, perhaps, he tended to play the part of leader in the joint undertakings and studies of the family, such as the frescoes in the Palazzo Fava (1584) and the foundation of the Accademia degli Incamminati (1585-1586). But his *Conversion of St Paul* (1587-1589, Bologna, Pinacoteca) with its dramatic violence and its investigation into the problems of light, his *Virgin Enthroned with Saints* (1588, Bologna, Pinacoteca) recalling both Tintoretto and Veronese, his *Preaching of the Baptist* (1592, Bologna, Pinacoteca), with its rich colour contrasts, all show a definite leaning towards the Venetian painters with their brilliant palette and animated composition. This orientation was not affected even by a stay in Rome (1602) and the example set by the frescoes of the Galleria Farnese. His important later works (frescoes in San Michele in Bosco, Bologna; works in the cathedral at Piacenza; numerous altarpieces) are of uneven merit but rich to the last in audacious innovations *(Martyrdom of St Margaret,* 1616, Mantua, San Maurizio) and develop in the direction of a romantic use of colour *(Adoration of the Magi,* 1616, Brera). They testify to a sensitive and restless personality entirely unlike that of his cousin, Annibale.   J. T.

CASTAGNO Andrea del. *See* Andrea del Castagno.

CASTIGLIONE Giovanni Benedetto (Genoa, 1610 - Mantua, 1665). His name is mentioned in contemporary sources as a pupil of Paggi's, then of Giovanni Andrea Ferrari's. According to one of his biographers, he was deeply influenced by Van Dyck, but it is obvious that Strozzi's work also made an impact on him. He travelled widely to Florence, Rome, Naples, Bologna, Parma, Venice, but we know nothing about his activities as a painter during his journeys. From 1639 to 1661, he was in the service of Charles II of Nevers, Duke of Mantua. The chronology of his works cannot be based on any known date and has to be worked out from a stylistic study. But his masterpiece, the *Crib* in the church of San Luca in Genoa, bears the date 1645. It is a typically baroque composition in which still-life elements are less important than in his other works where they are usually treated with more emphasis than the subject itself, as for instance in *Christ driving the money-lenders from the Temple,* one of his most famous pictures (Louvre). Castiglione presented all his subjects in the same way, whether they were religious, like *Abraham's Journey* (Genoa, Palazzo Rosso), mythological, like the *Faun* (Rome, Galleria Nazionale d'Arte Antica), or pastoral. His manner is not unlike genre painting, and realistic details are allied to a brilliant interpretation of the subject, which remind us of the Bassano family. In his own day, Castiglione was probably more famous as a draughtsman and an engraver than as a painter: with light strokes, which can render the most subtle changes of light and shade, he drew varied scenes, usually with a pastoral background, showing an inexhaustible imagination. Castiglione has often been confused with Antonio Maria Vassallo, who is another example of the importance of Flemish influence on Genoese art. s. b.

CATENA Vincenzo Biagio (Venice *ca* 1470 - Venice, 1531). Catena's art was firmly rooted in the 15th century. His vision, somewhat over emphatic and dry, deriving from Lazzaro Bastiani and the Vivarini, could not easily adapt itself to the innovations of the new colourists. Thus the *Madonna with the Baptist and Jerome* (Venice, Accademia) and the *Madonna with the Baptist and Mark presenting Doge Loredan* (1501-1521), the latter an ex-voto for the little church in the Palazzo Ducale, are still hard and rigidly schematic. But the influence of Giovanni Bellini loosens the composition of the *Sacre Conversazioni* in Glasgow, Budapest, Berlin and Modena. On the other hand the *Martyrdom of St Catherine* (1520, Venice) and the *Noli me tangere* (Milan, Brera), the latter sufficiently close to the former to justify the attribution, show Giorgione's influence, though there is not sufficient ground for connecting Catena with works of the Giorgione circle like the *Woman Taken in Adultery* (Glasgow). If the *Adoration of the Shepherds* in the Allendale Collection should turn out to be by him, he would qualify as a master of mellow colourism. In fact, the certain attributions, *Christ giving the Keys to St Peter* (Prado), a little theatrical, and the beautiful *Judith* (Venice, Querini Stampalia) mark the climax of an artistic evolution that reflects the authority of the prevailing styles. The originality it achieves consists sometimes in little more than the faithful practice of a certain harmony of colours. A. C.

CAVALIERE d'ARPINO Giuseppe Cesari, *called* (Arpino, 1568 - Rome, 1640). Son of a painter of ex-votos, he migrated to Rome and came under the influence of Roncalli. His rise to fame was rapid. From 1588 to 1591 he was in Naples where he decorated the cupola of the sacristy at San Martino. Back in Rome he won favour with the leading aristocracy by his seemingly delicate and accomplished style, and it is, no doubt, his success that induced the young Caravaggio, freshly arrived from Milan, to work with him for a while. In 1596 the Senate commissioned him to decorate the great hall in the Palazzo dei Conservatori; this he did not finish. Among his other Roman works the best known are the *Scenes from the life of John the Baptist* in the Lateran Baptistery, and the somewhat dull fresco in the Cappella Paolina at Santa Maria Maggiore. The Cavaliere's style is not the product of a deliberate and successful eclecticism, but derives from the decorative mannerism of the Zuccari, of Pulzone and others. However, in the frescoes at the Palazzo dei Conservatori he reverts occasionally to a fairly pure Raphaelism.   A. C.

CAVALLINI Pietro (13th-14th century). Vasari calls him 'a Roman painter', but we have no proof that he was born in Rome. The dates of his birth and death are also uncertain. We only know that he died very old, about the middle of the 14th century. His first documented work, a mosaic in Santa Maria in Trastevere, dated 1291, shows the masterful touch of a mature artist. He must have been at least 15 years older than Giotto and not his pupil as Vasari claims, with his usual Florentine bias. Cavallini is closer to Cimabue, Duccio and the other masters of the end of the Duecento, who were still influenced by the Byzantine style, but ready to interpret it more freely.

About 1293, Cavallini decorated the church of Santa Cecilia in Trastevere with frescoes of which only a fragment of the *Last Judgment* is still extant. These paintings, without backgrounds but with large, empty surfaces that convey a sense of space have, like the mosaics of Santa Maria in Trastevere, a classical majesty. The colours are remarkable: bright, with a wide range of tones and a use of shading which gives modelling to the faces. In 1308, Charles of Anjou called Cavallini to Naples. Back in Rome, he worked at San Paolo fuori le Mura (about 1315) where he made the mosaics on the façade (now replaced). Many of his works, authenticated by Ghiberti, have now disappeared. Works attributed to him, or to his school, are the fresco on the tomb of Cardinal Matteo d'Acquasparta, who died in 1302, in Santa Maria in Aracoeli, in Rome, and the frescoes in Santa Maria di Donna Regina, in Naples.   P.-H. M.

PIETRO CAVALLINI. ST JOHN THE BAPTIST. DETAIL FROM THE 'LAST JUDGMENT'. SANTA CECILIA IN TRASTEVERE, ROME.

CAVALLINO Bernardo (Naples, 1622 - Naples, 1654). The decisive years in the career of Cavallino coincide more or less with the death in 1637 of Caracciolo, called Batistello, who had dominated the artistic life of Naples. The young artist came under the influence of Massimo Stanzioni and Artemisia Gentileschi. Timid yet independent, somewhat romantic in temperament, he had a melancholic and feminine streak, a rather vaporous morbidity not without a certain charm but also slightly insipid, as in the *St Cecilia* in the Museo Nazionale, Naples, or in the *Departure of Tobias* at the Galleria Nazionale d'Arte Antica in Rome. The *St Cecilia* is his only dated picture (1645). Very little is known about Cavallino. He died in

Naples of an illness which, according to legend, he considered too shameful to disclose. P. C.

CAVAZZOLA Paolo Morando, *called* (Verona, 1486 - Verona, 1522). A pupil of the Morone, Cavazzola owes to them his feeling for calm, monumental plastic constructions. Yet, receptive to more recent ideas, he gave to his mature compositions a nobility and a dramatic unity derived from Roman examples, and bathed them in a richly coloured chiaroscuro, learned from the Lombards and the Venetians. His most accomplished works, the *Pietà* in the Verona Museum (1517) or the portrait of *Giovanni Emilio de' Meglio* (Dresden), for example, reveal an intense, disciplined style both sober and penetratingly naturalistic, which in the final analysis is not without resemblance to Ortolano of Ferrara. M. L.

CENNINI Cennino d'Andrea (Collo di Valdelza, *ca* 1350/60 - Florence, . . .). Cennini was a Florentine painter and a pupil of Agnolo Gaddi. All his works have disappeared, but we still have a treatise, which is our principal source of information on the techniques of the Italian Primitives. *Il Libro dell'Arte* is not a theoretical writing, but a handbook of practical advice for apprentice painters and craftsmen. In nearly two hundred chapters, he discusses the grinding and mixing of colours, the preparation of grounds and plaster coating, oil painting, pens and brushes, the methods of painting faces, clothes, trees, etc. P.-H. M.

CERQUOZZI Michelangelo (Rome, 1602 - Rome, 1660). According to Passeri, Michelangelo Cerquozzi was apprenticed to the Cavaliere d'Arpino and was taught by a Fleming, Jacob de Hase. Hase specialised in battle scenes and imparted this skill to his pupil, who became known as the Michelangelo of Battles.

From 1626 onwards Cerquozzi was closely connected with Pieter van Laar, called Il Bamboccio. The two became the leading representatives of a new manner, the *bambocciata,* a kind of Caravaggism applied to popular and burlesque scenes treated in pictures of small format. The manner was practised mainly by Dutch painters living, somewhat dissolutely, in Rome at the time. From 1647 onwards Cerquozzi collaborated frequently with the Neapolitan, Codazzi, called Codagora. He died in easy circumstances, the fruit of his success and, Passeri adds, of his avarice. P. C.

CERUTI Giacomo (active between 1724 and 1738). Probably born at the end of the 17th century, perhaps in Brescia where he seems to have spent most of his life, he travelled as far as Venice and Padua. His biography is difficult to establish because of the scarcity of documents about him and the unevenness of his work. As well as portraits and genre scenes where he was at his best, Ceruti has also painted mediocre religious compositions. His nickname, 'Il Pitocchetto', probably refers to his painting scenes of low life, only one of which is dated: the portrait of *Giovanni Maria Fenaroli* (1724); in 1728, he painted fifteen symbolic portraits for the Broletto, commissioned by the Podestà and vice-captain of Brescia. In 1734, he signed and dated the *Beggar* in the Bassi-Rattgeb Collection in Bergamo. The family of the Counts Fenaroli in Corneto, for whom the artist worked, must have valued his paintings, for they originally owned a whole cycle of popular scenes (now in the collections of Count Salvagedo and Count Padernello at Brescia). The usual subjects of genre painting (Card players) alternate with Beggars, Artisans, and the accurate and magnificent representation of the worst physical deformities *(The Dwarf).* These paintings of low life contrast with the brilliant gallery of portraits by Ghislandi (Fra Galgario), and seem strangely modern by their restrained and straightforward treatment. Ceruti's work shows various influences from Venice and Genoa. His rustic subjects, which look like a new version of some of Caravaggio's themes, and revive the great European current of realism in art, have rightly been rescued from oblivion. s. b.

CESARI Giuseppe. *See* Cavaliere d'Arpino.

CIMABUE Cenni di Pepi, *called* (Florence, *ca* 1240/50 - Pisa?, 1302?). Cimabue has always been famous because he is mentioned, along with Giotto, in Dante's *Purgatorio*. Dante records that Cimabue thought himself to be the greatest living artist until Giotto's fame eclipsed his (*Purgatorio*, XI, 94-96). The early Dante commentators added to this, saying that Cimabue was extremely vain and arrogant, and they also mention some pictures by him. In spite of his great fame, it is extremely difficult to gain a clear picture of his style since so many of his works have perished or been almost irretrievably damaged. The only certain documented work by him is the mosaic in the apse of Pisa Cathedral, and, in particular, the figure of St John for which there are documents of 1301 and 1302. The last is of the 4th July, 1302; and as nothing more is heard of Cimabue after that date, it is presumed that he died shortly afterwards. Unfortunately, the mosaic has been remade and is a rather uncertain guide to Cimabue's last style.

The earliest record of him occurs in the archives of Santa Maria Maggiore in Rome, where, on the 8th June, 1272 'Cimabove pictore de Florentia' witnessed a document. From this we are entitled to assume that Cimabue must have been born before 1251 since he is already recorded as a painter and

GIACOMO CERUTI. IL PORTAROLO.
PRIVATE COLLECTION, PADERNO FRANCIO CORTE (BRESCIA).

since a man of less than 21 would not normally witness a document: Vasari gives 1240 as the date of his birth. All the paintings attributed to Cimabue lack documentary support and the attributions are for the most part of the late 15th or early 16th centuries. It has been suggested that two documents of 1301, referring to a large *Maestà* painted for a hospital in Pisa, relate to the large painting in the Louvre, but this hypothesis is not generally accepted.

Strangely enough, there is no record of Cimabue's work in the *Commentaries* of Ghiberti in spite of the fact that Cimabue was a famous Florentine. Ghiberti mentions him as Giotto's master and dismisses him as 'remaining faithful to the Greek manner'. Practically every deduction made about Cimabue is based on the attribution to him of the very large *Maestà* from Santa Trinità in Florence, now in the Uffizi.

CIMABUE. VIRGIN AND CHILD SURROUNDED BY ANGELS. LOUVRE, PARIS.

Trinità *Madonna* represents Cimabue's style, it can be seen that he derives from earlier Florentine painters such as Coppo di Marcovaldo (the Siena *Madonna* of 1261) and that he continues the use of a network of gold lines to act both as highlights and as a decorative linear rhythm. It is usually thought that the Santa Trinità *Madonna* must date from about 1285 since it is held to be roughly contemporary with the *Rucellai Madonna* of that year, but many writers put it in the 70's, or 90's. The large altarpiece in the Louvre is rejected by a number of authorities, but those who accept it as by Cimabue's own hand tend to date it rather later. Some of the mosaics in the Baptistery at Florence are also attributed to him, but the only other works generally accepted as his are two large crucifixes and a number of frescoes in the Upper and Lower Churches at Assisi. The Assisi frescoes seem to be by him but they are almost entirely ruined. The *Madonna of St Francis* in the Lower Church has obviously been repainted many times. In the Upper Church there are numerous frescoes in the transept and choir including two *Crucifixions* and a series of scenes from the *Life of the Virgin*. The vault of the Upper Church also contains a number of frescoes attributed to him, including one of the Evangelist St Mark, which has a view of Rome in the background. On a building identifiable as the Capitol there is a shield bearing the arms of the Orsini. Two members of this family were Senators in 1288 and we know also that Pope Nicholas IV issued a Bull in 1288 authorising the decoration of the Basilica at Assisi. From this we may conclude that the frescoes in the Upper Church date from 1288 or somewhat later.

The two large crucifixes are those in Arezzo and formerly in Santa Croce in Florence. The Arezzo crucifix is probably an early work (i.e. before 1285 and perhaps even as early as 1260/65) since it relates to similar works

So far as we know, this Madonna was first attributed to Cimabue in the *Libro di Antonio Billi,* a compilation of the late 15th or early 16th century. It is, however, known that the *Madonna* was removed from the high altar of the church in 1471, which may explain the silence of early writers. A much earlier source, the Anonymous Florentine Dante Commentator, who wrote about 1395-1400, mentions a picture by Cimabue in Santa Maria Nuova in Florence, and he also claimed that Cimabue's descendants were still alive. There is no reason whatever to identify this picture with the *Rucellai Madonna* in Santa Maria Novella, which is attributed to Duccio, and it would seem that the Santa Maria Nuova picture is now lost. Assuming that the Santa by Coppo di Marcovaldo. The Santa Croce crucifix (now in the Uffizi), on the other hand, is far more advanced both in the modelling of the body and in the rendering of a pathetic effect through the somewhat exaggerated curve given to the body of Christ. This would seem to provide an essential link between the earlier types of crucifix and the one in Santa Maria Novella, which is often held to be a work by the young Giotto. In that case, the traditional master-pupil relationship between Cimabue and Giotto explains itself, and, if the Giotto crucifix is of 1295 or later, Cimabue's must be later than 1285 but earlier than 1295.

In general, Cimabue represents a dramatic and linear tendency in opposition to the more classic art of Cavallini and the influence of both men can be discerned in the decoration of the Basilica at Assisi and in the formation of the style of Giotto. Cimabue 'held to the Greek manner' (Ghiberti), but his passionate intensity of feeling, expressed by means of outline and facial expression, determined one of the leading characteristics of Florentine art and must be seen as an indispensable preliminary stage in the dramatic and realistic art of Giotto.   P. M.

CIMA da CONEGLIANO Giovanni Battista (Conegliano, *ca* 1459 - Conegliano, 1517 or 1518). In the midst of the extraordinary effervescence in Venice at the end of the 15th century, there were a few placid painters like Cima da Conegliano. Their peasant core resisted the excitement of Giorgionesque romanticism, though the old Bellini might succumb to it, but they took up and developed the grand vision of space of the new style. This is apparent already in the calm rhythm and simple articulation of the *Madonna of the Pergola* painted in 1489 for San Bartolomeo in Vicenza (now at the Museo Civico), with the satisfying contrast between the penum-

CIMA DA CONEGLIANO. DANIEL IN THE LIONS DEN. AMBROSIANA, MILAN.

bra in the foreground and the luminous zone around the Madonna. In 1493 Cima painted the great pala for the Duomo in Conegliano, a *sacra conversazione* under an open cupola as was the current fashion, and moved to Venice. He began to supply Venetian churches with carefully dated and signed altarpieces which enable one to plot the development of his style: the *Baptism of Christ* for San Giovanni in Bragora (1494), the *Annunciation* for the Capella Zeno in Santa Maria de' Crocicchieri (Hermitage), the large pala for the Carità (1496-1499, Venice, Accademia), the pala of *St Peter Martyr* with its architectural setting opening out into landscape in the background, painted for the church of

Corpus Domini (1509, Brera). Having earlier worked in his native Conegliano, Cima decorated other parishes outside Venice. The *Incredulity of Thomas,* spacious and simple like a painting of Perugino's, was painted in 1502 for the Duomo of Portogruaro (London, National Gallery), the *St Catherine* for San Rocco in Mestre (London, Wallace Collection), a polyptych for Sant'Anna in Capodistria, in 1513.

Cima's manner changed little. He retained throughout an astonishing calm with interesting undertones of rusticity and a certain tendency to be solemn. His brushwork combines the firmness of Montagna from whom he borrows the full backgrounds—an entire rock, an entire mountain—of his groups of sacred personages (*Pietà,* Modena, Galleria Estense), with the gentle scansion of Giovanni Bellini whom at times he follows very closely: the Conegliano pala resembles that of Santi Giovanni e Paolo, the onè from the Carità that of San Giobbe.

The *Madonna of the Pergola* with its pendent foliage is a pretty variation within a type elaborated already by Antonello and Bellini. In his little anecdotic scenes Cima combines exotic colour with Carpacciesque costumes (*Mark healing Ananias,* Berlin). He is at his best in clear and gentle landscapes with distant views suffused by a calm light: the *Madonna dell'Arancio* (Venice, Accademia), the *Adoration of the Shepherds* at the Carmini in Venice and the *Madonna Enthroned between the Baptist and the Magdalen* at the Louvre. The forms are accomplished, the tones saturated and the space ample. Where Mantegna is hard, Cima is suave. The *Baptism of Christ* has become a pastoral with accents of light. In this Cima is a little isolated, while his growing interest in monumental types prepares the way for the solid and, at times, heavy classicism of the 16th century. A. C.

CLEMENT VII Giulio de' Medici, Pope (Florence, 1478 - Rome, 1534). Posthumous son of Giuliano de' Medici and nephew of Lorenzo il Magnifico, Giulio de' Medici was made a cardinal in 1513 and elected Pope in 1523. The return of a Medici to the Holy See was greeted with enthusiasm by the scholars and artists who remembered Leo X. Their expectations were soon disappointed. Clement VII, absorbed by politics and pursued by disasters (sack of Rome in 1527) was rather parsimonious as a patron of the arts. Thanks to him, however, the building of St Peter was continued. As for painting, he handed over the unfinished decoration of the Stanze and of the Sala di Constantino at the Vatican to two pupils of Raphael: Giulio Romano and Francesco Penni; he commissioned several portraits from Sebastiano del Piombo, one of which is in the Museo Nazionale at Naples; in 1533, he decided to complete the decoration of the Sistine Chapel, called on Michelangelo and approved a first project. P.-H. M.

COLANTONIO (active from 1440 to 1470). Colantonio was a Neapolitan painter. His extant works are the *St Vincent,* painted about 1456 for San Pietro Martire, in which he shows himself closely dependent on Flemish art, and the *St Jerome,* the only surviving part of an altarpiece for the Franciscan church of San Lorenzo (Naples, Museo Nazionale). The spatial articulation of the latter, at once firm and impregnated with light, and its sense of structure suggested at one time the Master of the Annunciation of Aix as the possible author. The polyptych for San Severino has not survived. Though what is known about Colantonio is not enough to reconstitute his career, it signalises the conjunction in southern Italy of Italian and Flemish elements whence originated the elevated style of Antonello da Messina, a pupil of Colantonio's. A. C.

COPPO di MARCOVALDO (Florence, *ca* 1225 - Siena, after 1274). Coppo di Marcovaldo was a soldier in the Florentine army; he fought the Sienese at Monteaperti, was taken prisoner and settled in Siena. One year later, he painted, for Santa Maria dei Servi, the Virgin known as the *Madonna del Bordone* (1261). In 1265 he went to Pistoia where, with his son Salerno, he worked on the decoration of the cathedral (frescoes in the St James chapel); of these various paintings (he was in Pistoia again in 1269) nothing is left except one painted cross, his only authenticated work apart from the *Madonna del Bordone*.   P.-H. M.

CORREGGIO Antonio Allegri, *called* (Correggio, *ca* 1489 - Parma, 1534). Unforeseen, scintillating, scarcely longer than that of Raphael, less varied but as daring as that of Michelangelo, Correggio's career was set almost entirely in a small provincial town and its details are little known. The man eludes us: the artist is hardly more than the sum of his works. The date of his birth, between 1489 and 1494, and the situation of his parents, modest, according to Vasari, distinguished and even noble according to certain modern experts, are still under discussion. A group of works, attributed to Correggio's early years, including a *Holy Family* and a *Deposition* at Sant'Andrea, Mantua, appear to suggest a thorough artistic education at Mantua itself in surroundings furnished with examples of Mantegna's painting. But the vehemence and the rough hewn masses of the latter's work are softened by a delicate *sfumato* and betray the direct influence of painters such as Costa, and no doubt an echo of the experiments of Leonardo da Vinci. The first altarpiece of which the authenticity is established, the *Madonna of St Francis* (1514/15, Dresden) embodies a series of motifs which, though derived from the 15th century, possess a gentle-

CORREGGIO. JUPITER AND IO. ABOUT 1530. KUNSTHISTORISCHES MUSEUM, VIENNA.

ness in their curving lines and above all an animation and a facility of composition, which is perhaps due to the

CORREGGIO. DANAË. ABOUT 1530-1532. GALLERIA BORGHESE, ROME.

influence of Raphael's *Madonna of San Sisto* (hung in Piacenza, now in Dresden, about 1513). A series of half-length figures of Virgins (Orléans; Hampton Court; Milan, Castello Sforzesco) attributed to years 1514-1517 and the large *Madonna of Albina* (1517, the original lost, but copies exist) show the same care in imparting rhythmic movement to rounded, tenderly modelled forms.

The rapid way in which Correggio's style advances to maturity leads to the supposition that about 1517/19 he must have travelled to Rome where he contemplated the paintings of Raphael (Villa Farnesina) and Michelangelo. From this time onwards his greatest works succeed one another. At the convent of San Paolo a *Camera* (abbess's parlour, about 1519) with its ceiling divided into compartments by a delicate

trellis of leaves and fruit, betrays the influence of Mantegna. However, the pairs of children at play, which fill the oval gaps in the trellis, show a new manner. The classical figures in the lunettes (*Adonis*, the *Three Graces*, *Juno Chastised*) represent beautiful nudes of somewhat shortened proportions whose seductive forms with their sensual appeal, were to invade irresistibly even the altarpieces of churches. Started in 1520, the cupola of San Giovanni Evangelista, Parma, with the *Vision of St John at Patmos*, generally known as the *Ascension of Christ*, dispenses with accessory decorations and creates with nudes, clouds and a few draperies a controlled and luminous composition in which the religious theme appears to join with Michelangelo in a passionate hymn in praise of the human body.

The cupola of the cathedral, dedicated in this case to the *Assumption of the Virgin* (1524-1530) adopts and amplifies the same theme. In spite of its considerable dimensions, no architectonic subdivisions have been employed. The cupola is conceived as a funnel of clouds open to a distant sky. The Virgin and her entourage disappear in a whirl of long legged angels, contemptuously alluded to at the time as a 'hash of frogs', which show a skilful and daring foreshortening. The balance between figures and decorative details is definitely upset in favour of illusion created by mass and the play of light and movement.

Correggio's pictures show evidence of equally promising experiments. His compositions frequently depend on sweeping diagonals (the *Madonna della Scodella,* Parma, Pinacoteca) or affect floating rhythms (the *Deposition,* Parma, Pinacoteca), accentuated by insubstantial draperies, volatile poses and skilful foreshortening. He experimented in spatial compositions with increasing complexities and refinements (*Vice* and *Virtue,* Louvre). A chiaroscuro pursued at times almost to the point of pure research into values, blurs both forms and colours (the *Nativity* known as *Night,* Dresden). At times, grace of expression verges towards a worldly suavity (the *Madonna of St Jerome,* known as *Day,* Parma, Pinacoteca; the *Mystic Marriage of St Catherine,* Louvre) and even an affected rhetoric (the famous *Madonna of St George,* Dresden). In the case of the mythological subjects this is redeemed by an avowed sensuality ranging from the false innocence of adolescence (*Leda,* Berlin) to languid opulence (*Io,* Vienna). The great masterpieces, *Danaë* in the Borghese Gallery, Rome, the *Antiope* of the Louvre, are the cry of desire itself, naked and urgent. In Correggio's art there is neither grandeur, tragedy, nor a lofty intellectual quest. It is an art which seems to renounce the great experiences of the

COSSA. APRIL. DETAIL OF THE REPRESENTATION FROM THE FIRST DECADE. 1470. PALAZZO SCHIFANOIA, FERRARA.

geniuses of the Renaissance and their inner insistence on clarity and style, but reflects each seductive nuance of feeling from coquetry to voluptuousness. This very renunciation entailed the discovery of a new world and a new language, the repercussions of which were immense. In the case of Parmigianino, Barocci, Lodovico Carracci or Lanfranco its influence was direct. At the beginning of the 19th century it was pushed to the point of plagiarism by Prud'hon. The baroque artists of the 17th and 18th centuries acknowledged Correggio as their real master.   J. T.

COSIMO THE ELDER *See* Medici, Cosimo de'.

COSSA Francesco del (Ferrara, *ca* 1435 - Bologna, *ca* 1478). Formed in the same artistic milieu as Tura, who was

COSSA. APRIL: GROUP OF LOVERS AND THE
THREE GRACES (DETAIL). 1470. PALAZZO
SCHIFANOIA, FERRARA.

among whom were Cicognara and
Baldassare Estense. To depict the
months of *March, April* and *May,* Cossa
has represented in three tiers contemporary scenes attesting the glory of Duke
Borso, the signs of the Zodiac (the
Ram, the *Bull* and the *Twins*), and the
triumph of *Minerva, Venus* and *Apollo.*
This capital work is one of the most
successful of all the secular cycles of the
period. Cossa here shows himself to
be the equal of Tura in his plastic force,
the implacable energy of the figures
and contours and the enamellike
brilliance of his colours, coupled with
the expression of a certain courtly good
humour, a more relaxed prosaic note,
which are individual qualities. He also
reveals a sense of light and space and
movement (in the hunting scene in
April, for example) which are completely
personal. Disappointed by the meagre
salary he received for this work, Cossa
went shortly afterwards to Bologna
where he found new clients. There he
made stained glass windows (one of
them is in the Musée Jacquemart-André
in Paris), frescoes which have since
disappeared, and altarpieces of which
three survive: the *Annunciation* (Dresden),
in which he shows admirable facility for
creating architectural perspective, a
Madonna with St Petronius and St John
(1474), in the Bologna Museum and
above all a huge polyptych now split up,
painted for the Griffoni Chapel in San
Petronio (1473). This is a complex
work but is logically composed, crowded
with familiar details and unusual inventions, but expressive of a luxurious
solemnity. In the centre, placed in
front of imaginary, brightly lit landscapes are *St Vincent Ferrer* (London),
surrounded by *St Peter* and *St John the
Baptist* (Brera) and on an upper level a
harsh and terrible *Calvary* between
St Florian and *St Lucy* (Washington).
The predella and pilasters were the
work of Ercole de' Roberti who at this
period was collaborating with Cossa.

slightly older, Cossa benefited from the
latter's experience and the example of
Borso d'Este's miniaturists. However,
his style is completely original in the
major works of his Ferrarese period: the
frescoes painted for Borso d'Este in the
Hall of the Months in the Palazzo
Schifanoia (1470). Cossa was largely
responsible for three of the twelve
frescoes of this cycle. What remains
of the others was the work of Ercole
de' Roberti and more secondary artists

LORENZO COSTA.
THE ARGONAUTS.
MUSEO CIVICO,
PADUA.

With the Roverella Polyptych painted by Tura at the same period, the Griffoni polyptych constitutes one of the summits of the poetic and plastic genius of Ferrara. M. L.

COSTA Lorenzo (Ferrara, 1460 - Mantua, 1535). Costa did not reside for long in his native city; he worked in Bologna from 1483 to 1506; then, till his death, at the Court of Mantua where he succeeded Mantegna. He is none the less the heir of the great Ferrarese style and especially of Ercole de' Roberti and he produced a modified version of it during his most original period which extends from about 1485 to the closing years of the century. The mural paintings in the Bentivoglio Chapel in San Giacomo Maggiore in Bologna (1488-90) and the big altarpieces in San Petronio (1492) and San Giovanni in Monte (1497) which date from this period, reveal a stately classicism, delicate and at the same time solid, and remarkable qualities as a

portraitist and landscape artist. Costa was not insensitive to the example of Venice, but it should be noted on the other hand that his style is also to be counted among the sources of Giorgione's style. Later, Costa did not always completely avoid a certain lifelessness when he too closely followed Francia and the Umbrians, but he is often redeemed by a real narrative gracefulness (*Allegories* for the Studiolo of Isabella d'Este, in the Louvre), a tender melancholy in facial expressions and sometimes elegance of line, perhaps due to the influence of Filippino Lippi and the younger Aspertini. M. L.

CRESPI Giuseppe Maria, *called* Lo Spagnuolo (Bologna, 1665 - Bologna, 1747). He started his apprenticeship very young, studying the works of Ludovico Carracci and Guercino in front of him in the Bolognese workshops (Canuti, Cignani, Burrini) and continued it at Venice, Modena, Parma

CARLO CRIVELLI. VIRGIN AND CHILD.
METROPOLITAN MUSEUM, NEW YORK

Florence, Private Collection), but more often remains welded to the solid and popular Carracci tradition (the *Hovel*, Bologna, Pinacoteca). It is true to say that this realism is blended with a strange inspiration, and the effects of strong light and shade often invest the most inoffensive subject with a faintly morbid mysteriousness (*Portrait of Fulvio Grati*, Bologna, Private Collection) which is the secret of Crespi's art.   J. T.

CRIVELLI Carlo (Venice, between 1430 and 1435 - . . ., 1493 or 1495). Crivelli's career can only be understood in terms of the distinctive artistic culture that developed in the townships of the Marches between Venezia and Umbria. His success in that region is due partly to an accident. Expelled from Venice after an elopement in 1457, he took refuge in Dalmatia (he was still at Zara in 1465), then returned to Italy. In 1468, at Massa Fermana, he completed the polyptych with the *Madonna between four Saints*, separated by colonnettes, which was followed by many others: a vast ensemble with two tiers and a predella for the Duomo of Ascoli Piceno (1473), two others for San Domenico in the same town—its thirteen parts have been reassembled under the name of the Demidoff Altarpiece (1476, London, National Gallery); the *Annunciation with St Emidius* of 1486, also in London, with the saint holding a model of Ascoli. The admirable *Coronation of the Virgin* for San Francesco in Fabriano, dated 1493 (Brera) marks the conclusion of a career punctuated by a series of great *montages* of panels fashionable in Italy at the time. Quite a number of them have been dispersed and are known only as fragments, like the *Panciatichi Pietà* in Boston (1485). Crivelli painted also small devotional panels for private chapels, curious ones like the *Madonna with the Instruments of the Passion* (Verona, Museo di Castelvecchio), or exquisite like the minute

and Urbino; this training caused Crespi to cultivate the chiaroscuro technique where now again a few splashes of brilliant colour shine out from dark and tawny shadows. During his long and laborious career at Bologna he was engaged on large-scale decorative works (the *Gods and the Seasons*, 1691, Bologna, Palazzo Pepoli) and altarpieces (the *Communion of St Stanislaus*, Ferrara, Chiesa del Gesù), but a large proportion of his work was devoted to genre scenes (the *Flea-catcher*, Uffizi). His style shows an attempt to abandon Guercino's type of lyricism for an almost photographic reality, which at times seems to foreshadow the lesser painters of the 19th century (the *Dish Washer*,

Madonna and Child (Ancona, Pinacoteca).
Crivelli's work offers the clearest
evidence for the decorative and plastic
tendencies in the last third of the 15th
century, all the more so as it is in fact
a series of variations on a very limited
stock of elements and compositional
patterns. He starts from the crystalline
and mineral art of the Vivarini but with
a strong admixture of Paduan elements
which gave him a predilection for arabesques, precious stones, and rich
garlands of fruit which he treated with a
lively, even acid, colour and sharp
inflexions. The *Madonna against a
Mandorla of Cherubs* at Corridonia
(about 1472) and the Ascoli polyptych
of 1473 have already this precise and
elegant repertory in which exquisite
effects are obtained from a parchment,
a head of hair, a profile or a raised
finger. The elegance and distinction
are enhanced by a rhetorically amplified
use of gothic formulas, then enjoying
their last vogue. Crivelli's originality
is to associate the gofferings and the
jewellery with delicate emotions the
expression of which can be studied in
the figures of young female saints and
in the small panels. The highlights
and the gold backgrounds do not
exclude elaborate effects of perspective.
The Byzantinism of the ornaments
goes together, paradoxically, with mo-
dernity, decorative richness with mimetic
expression. This may account for the
poignancy and spiritual elevation of a
panel like the lunette with the *Pietà*
above the Brera *Coronation* (1493). The
emphasis on luxurious forms and
materials does not derive solely from
the school of Murano and, through it,
from the Byzantine tradition. The
compact and tense style cannot be entirely separated from the evolution of the
Paduan school, or the example of the
Ferrarese. It had no future. With
Pietro Alemanno and Vittore Crivelli,
Carlo's brother, the manner sank to the
level of a provincial convention. A. C.

CARLO CRIVELLI. MARY MAGDALEN.
RIJKSMUSEUM, AMSTERDAM.

D

DADDI Bernardo (Florence ?, *ca* 1290 - Florence ?, after 1355). Although slightly younger, Bernardo Daddi may be considered as a contemporary of Giotto. The first signed work we possess of his dates from 1328. It is the *Madonna surrounded by the Saints,* now in the Uffizi, formerly in the church of the Ognissanti. His admiration for Giotto appears here and is also revealed in the two frescoes in the Pulci-Beraldi Chapel in Santa Croce, Florence. We also find Giotto's restraint in the three triptychs which have been preserved, one in the Bargello in Florence, the other at the Fogg Art Museum, Harvard (1334) and the third in the Pinacoteca, Siena (1336). From about 1338 the influence of the Sienese school is felt in Bernardo Daddi's work, particularly in the *Annunciation* in the Louvre and in certain paintings which were for a long time attributed to the school of Ambrogio Lorenzetti: such as the panels which composed the predella of Santa Maria Novella which are now scattered. One must also mention Bernardo Daddi's *Crucifixion,* in the Louvre and the *Coronation of the Virgin,* surrounded by angel musicians, in Berlin.   A. L.

DALMASIO Lippo di. *See* Scannabecchi.

DA PONTE Jacopo and Francesco. *See* Bassano.

DOMENICHINO Domenico Zampieri, *called* (Bologna, 1581 - Naples, 1641). Trained first in the workshop of the Flemish painter, Calvaert, and then under Ludovico Carracci, Domenichino became one of the team led by Annibale in the Palazzo Farnese at Rome. It is here that we see the earliest examples of his style (the *Woman with a Unicorn,* fresco). His carefully contrived construction and concern with expression made the *Communion of St Jerome* very famous (1614, Vatican), but these qualities do not preclude his search for gracefulness, reflected in the round faces of his young girls (the *Diana and her Nymphs,* about 1617, Rome, Galleria Borghese), and powerful movement, seen in the great altarpieces (the *Martyrdom of St Sebastian,* about 1630, Rome, Santa Maria degli Angeli), nor his use of innumerable people in the frescoes which mark the chief phases of his career: San Gregorio Magno, Rome (1608), abbey of Grottaferrata (1608-1610), San Luigi dei Francesi, Rome (about 1611-1614), Sant'Andrea della Valle, Rome (1624-1628), Naples Cathedral (1630-1641). His is an artificial style where Carracci's outbursts of lyricism have been abandoned in favour of a studied, intellectual approach, but because of the generally 'classical' fashion in that century his refinement was appreciated; hence Poussin's praises and Domenichino's reputation for a long time as one of the greatest painters to follow .Raphael.   J. T.

DOMENICO di BARTOLO (Asciano, *ca* 1400 - Siena, 1447). A pupil and nephew of Taddeo di Bartolo, according to Vasari, Domenico was on the roll of Sienese painters in 1428. His first

DOMENICO VENEZIANO. ALTARPIECE FOR SANTA LUCIA DE' MAGNOLI. ABOUT 1445.
UFFIZI, FLORENCE.

dated work, the very beautiful *Virgin and Child surrounded by Angels* in the Siena Pinacoteca (1433) shows a remarkable assimilation of the new Florentine art, at a time when the Sienese remained mostly attached to their own local tradition. In 1438 Domenico seemed to take a step backward and return, with the Perugia polyptych (Church of Santa Giuliana, now in the Pinacoteca), to a more gothic outlook. Finally, between 1440 and 1444, he contributed to the decoration of the *Pellegrinaio* (Siena, Ospedale di Santa Maria della Scala) painting two large scenes with several episodes where, as Vasari wrote, 'perspective and decoration are ingeniously composed'. P.-H. M.

DOMENICO VENEZIANO (Venice, *ca* 1400 - Florence, 1461). Domenico's career is illuminated by two important documents: the much quoted letter to Piero di Cosimo de' Medici, dated 1 April 1438 from Perugia, in which the artist asks to be recommended to Piero's father, and compares himself to Fra Angelico and Filippo Lippi; and a record of payment, dated 7 September 1439, in respect of fees owing from the Ospedale di Santa Maria Novella for frescoes painted in the choir of San

DOMENICO VENEZIANO. PORTRAIT OF
A YOUNG WOMAN. ABOUT 1460.
KAISER FRIEDRICH MUSEUM, BERLIN.

Palazzo Comunale in Perugia. On 10 July 1457 he and Filippo Lippi assessed Pesellino's painting for the Compagnia della Trinità in Pistoia. About 1460, shortly before his death, he painted at Santa Croce scenes from the lives of St Francis and St John the Baptist; one fresco survives, with superbly expressive figures of the two saints, formerly attributed to Andrea del Castagno. Domenico's work is thus imperfectly known, and a number of doubtful attributions have been made, as for the little panels known as the *Franciscan Flagellants* (Munich; Chantilly).

One wishes one knew, but one does not, whether Domenico came to Florence before 1439 and whether his influence there can be similarly dated; for his light and clear colour was a contribution to Florentine painting that matched and modified the monumental style of Masaccio. The picture for Santa Lucia reveals the strong personality of the mature artist. The central piece with its figures in an architectural setting is both luminous and enlivened by a firm rhythm. Here, we see at once, is the starting point of Piero della Francesca. The *Carnesecchi Tabernacle,* a fresco painted about 1440 on a street tabernacle in the via de' Cerretani in Florence and transferred to canvas in 1851 (now at the National Gallery, London), shows other qualities and other influences. The standing *putto* recalls Gentile da Fabriano. As for the Madonna, massive and rigid in her abrupt perfection, and the plunging view of God the Father, they both suggest interests and preoccupations that would not have been foreign to Uccello. Perhaps this should be taken as evidence of fairly close contacts between the two painters in the years 1430-1440. It is also usual to attribute to Domenico the superb *tondo* with the *Adoration of the Magi* (Berlin) in which tonal richness and the articulation of space are gothic in inspiration.

Egidio by Domenico and his assistants (Piero della Francesca is mentioned among them). These frescoes, which included the *Betrothal of the Virgin* and the *Meeting of Joachim and Anna,* have unfortunately disappeared. The *Madonna* from Santa Lucia de' Magnoli, signed, now at the Uffizi, is generally thought to be later, about 1445; its predellas are dispersed: the *Annunciation* and the *Martyrdom of St Zenobius* in Cambridge, *St Francis Receiving the Stigmata* and *St John in the Desert* in Washington and the *Martyrdom of St Lucy* in Berlin. In 1454 Domenico was invited, together with Fra Angelico and Fra Filippo, to give an opinion on the frescoes commissioned for the Capella dei Priori at the

DOMENICHINO.
THE WOMAN
WITH A UNICORN.
ABOUT 1602.
PALAZZO FARNESE,
ROME.

The exploration of Domenico's work begins and ends with the Santa Lucia altarpiece. About this complete masterpiece, our only fixed point, scholars have tried to regroup a number of portraits which could suggest Uccello: *Matteo Olivieri* (Washington, National Gallery), *Michele Olivieri* (New York, Private Collection), *Profile of a Noblewoman,* elegant and clear (Boston, Gardner Museum), and, more hypothetically, a number of decorative panels. The importance of Domenico Veneziano can hardly be exaggerated. Vasari gave him pride of place as the one responsible for introducing oil painting in Tuscany. This is factually wrong but is a way of stressing a new departure in colour and texture. The bright tones make one forget the occasionally incomplete modelling. Domenico opened new possibilities by integrating gothic gracility and singing colours into a more vigorous order of perspective and light. This predilection for concentrated effects created perhaps a new receptivity to Flemish painting. And a symbol of

Tuscan resistance may be found in the legend, recorded by Vasari, of Andrea del Castagno, jealous of his fellow artist, assassinating him on a street-corner after eliciting from him the secret of 'oils'. Castagno died in 1457, Domenico Veneziano in 1461 but the great divide in Tuscan painting occurs about 1460.   A. C.

DONO Paolo di. *See* Uccello.

DOSSO DOSSI Giovanni Luteri, *called* (Ferrara, *ca* 1490 - Ferrara, 1542). Dosso Dossi spent the major part of his fertile career in Ferrara, working in particular for Alfonso I d'Este, but he is known to have been also in Mantua, Trento and Pesaro. Of much greater importance for his art were his visits to Rome, where he probably met Raphael, and especially to Venice. Influenced in his early days in Ferrara by Garofalo, he was still more so by Venetian painting and above all by Giorgione and Titian. The latter, moreover, worked in Ferrara where

Dosso must have seen him painting. Shortly after Garofalo, Dosso thus acclimatised Giorgionesque romanticism in Ferrara, though in a less classical manner than the elder artist, and with a pictorial freedom and energy learned from Titian. Excelling in the use of colour, he bathed his *Sacre Conversazioni* in a bright atmosphere, rich in warm contrasts and shimmering effects. Imaginary or familiar landscapes, forming a poetic framework for these compositions, are among the most intensely lyrical of the period. They give the allegorical or mythological scenes, which the artist made his speciality, a great deal of their charm. Those *Witches* (Rome, Galleria Borghese; Washington), those *Rustic Idylls* (New York, Metropolitan Museum), those *Argonauts* (Washington), those *Apollos with Musical Instruments* (Rome, Galleria Borghese), those symbolic but passionate nudes, whilst they recall the vivid imagination of Ariosto, bring to life again in some way the unexpected fantasy and magic of the great Ferrarese painters of the 15th century. Like the latter, Dosso Dossi has also left portraits of vital intensity.

At the end of his life, after working in collaboration with his younger brother, Battista Dossi, his manner became somewhat stiff under the growing influence of Raphael's classicism. M. L.

DUCCIO di BUONINSEGNA (Siena, *ca* 1255 - Sienna, *ca* 1318). Although this painter worked in various Tuscan towns and was highly thought of during his life, we know very little about him. His name appears in the records for the first time in 1278. He was then decorating manuscript binding. In 1285, he was given his first important commission in Florence. He cannot have been under thirty then, and therefore must have been born around 1255 or slightly earlier. The generally accepted date for his death is 1318/19, shortly after completing his masterpiece, the Siena *Maestà*. His works can be divided into three main periods: 1278-1290, 1290-1308, and after 1308.

On April 15th, 1285, the Florentine Brotherhood of the Virgin Mary, the Compagnia dei Laudesi, commissioned from him a large altarpiece for the Rucellai chapel in the Church of Santa

Maria Novella, now in the Uffizi, which is usually called the *Rucellai Madonna*. The attribution of this work raises a problem. If, as Vasari claims, it is by Cimabue, we must suppose that the painting commissioned from Duccio has been lost. Father Vincenzio Fineschi was the first, in his *Memorie Istoriche* (Historical memoirs of famous men from the convent of Santa Maria Novella, Florence, 1790), to disagree with Vasari and recognise Duccio's hand in the *Rucellai Madonna*. Fineschi's opinion was contested for a long time, and even today some art historians only accept it with reservations. However, the attribution to Duccio of the *Madonna* in Santa Maria Novella seems likely and is widely accepted. But we notice that, in that youthful work, Duccio is still very near Cimabue, which is probably due both to direct influence, considering the fame of the Florentine master, and to common sources (Byzantine tradition and Franciscan inspiration). On the other hand, marked differences in the style of the two painters already appear: the Sienese painter shows a more sensitive approach, particularly noticeable in the suppler movements of the characters, the elegant folds in the materials, the bright ornaments and subtle colour effects. The *Virgin surrounded by three Franciscans* (Siena, Pinacoteca, about 1290) also belongs to that youthful period of the painter's career.

During the second period (1290-1308), Duccio's personality asserted itself and his fame spread. Siena remained the centre of his activities and we find frequent references to his presence in that town, but he also travelled to accept commissions in various towns of Tuscany. Numerous works came out of his workshop. Several polyptychs are by his own hand, and among them the *Virgin surrounded by St Peter, St Paul, St Augustine and St Dominic* (Siena, Pinacoteca).

Several outstanding pictures painted either by Duccio himself or under his supervision belong to his last period: the London triptych (Buckingham Palace) with the *Crucifixion* in the centre, the *Annunciation* and the *Virgin Enthroned* on the left, the *Coronation of the Virgin* and *St Francis Receiving the Stigmata* on the right. But none of these works equals the large Siena *Maestà* which is not only the painter's masterpiece, but one of the masterpieces of Italian art in the 14th century. In 1302, the town of Siena had already commissioned from Duccio a *Virgin Enthroned* for the chapel in the Palazzo Pubblico; unfortunately, this work is now lost. The painting we know, which is in a perfect state of preservation, was commissioned in 1308 for the cathedral. It was completed in 1311 and taken with pomp and circumstance to its appointed place, one June 9th. According to the contemporary chroniclers, there was general rejoicing. One of them writes: 'Many prayers were offered and many alms were distributed.' A large wooden panel, painted on both sides, originally showed on the side turned towards the west the *Madonna surrounded by Saints,* and on the other side a number of individual scenes from the *Life of Christ*. The panel was later sawn through and its two sides are now juxtaposed, in the Opera del Duomo. It has been preserved almost intact: only a few fragments from the predella are missing and scattered through various collections in Europe and America (in London: the *Annunciation, Christ healing the Blind* and the *Transfiguration ;* in Berlin: the *Nativity ;* in New York: the *Temptation of Christ* and the *Resurrection of Lazarus ;* in Washington: the *Nativity* and the *Calling of St Peter and St Andrew*). The *Rucellai Madonna* already prepared the transition from Byzantine to gothic; in the *Maestà,* Duccio developed a new style which was to dominate Sienese art through-

DUCCIO.
THE ANNUNCIATION.
PANEL FROM
THE PREDELLA
OF THE 'MAESTÀ'.
1308-1311.
NATIONAL GALLERY,
LONDON.

DUCCIO.
THE CALLING
OF THE APOSTLES
PETER AND ANDREW.
PANEL FROM
THE PREDELLA
OF THE 'MAESTÀ'.
1308-1311.
NATIONAL GALLERY
OF ART,
WASHINGTON.

DUCCIO.
THE TEMPTATION
OF CHRIST
ON THE MOUNTAIN.
PANEL FROM
THE 'MAESTÀ'.
1308-1311.
FRICK COLLECTION,
NEW YORK.

DUCCIO.
THE HOLY WOMEN
AT THE TOMB.
PANEL FROM
THE 'MAESTÀ'.
1308-1311.
MUSEO DELL'OPERA,
SIENA.

99

out the 14th century. In the general organisation of the panel and in the use of gold for the background, something of the 'Greek manner' is left, but the flatness is replaced by receding planes and depth is suggested by chiaroscuro; the colour range is richer and allows new combinations and unexpected contrasts: a variety of accents with clear tones is particularly noticeable; the forms are more supple, the sinuous outlines more elegant; the iconography is new as well as the style and the austere hieratic approach of the old masters has been softened and no longer hinders the expression of tender emotion. These changes can be found in each part of the *Maestà,* in each one of the sections which make up the back and the predella. The episode of the *Women at the Sepulchre* is one representative example among others. The eastern iconography, according to a text by St Matthew, only mentioned two holy women; Duccio, following the Gospel of St Mark, has represented three: Mary Magdalen, Mary the mother of James, and Salome; the painter has chosen the moment when, not 'in the sepulchre' as it is written, but on the tomb, they see the Angel: 'They saw a young man sitting on the right side, clothed in a long white garment.' Their well balanced group occupies the left of the picture; on their faces we can read astonishment and fear tempered by a pathetic hope. The various colours of their veils, the pink stone of the tomb, the red shoes of the angel contrast with the greyish rocky background and make up a strange ensemble; but the eye is soothed, almost reassured, by the serene and noble attitudes of the characters.

If we are to believe Vasari, Duccio worked, apart from Siena and Florence, in Pisa, Pistoia and Lucca. One of his pupils, Meo da Siena, spread his influence as far as Umbria. It is not easy to establish a list of the works by his hand: the size of his workshop and the numerous imitations of his manner make attributions particularly difficult in his case.   P.-H. M.

DUECENTO. The Byzantine influence which had been felt in Italy from the early Middle Ages onwards was stronger than ever during the 13th century, partly for historical reasons (conquest of Constantinople by the Crusaders in 1204), but mainly because of the prosperity of the large coast towns, Venice, Genoa, Pisa, who traded with the East. That is why the history of Italian painting during the Duecento used to be considered, and not without some justification, as the history of the influence of Byzantine art and of the gradual throwing off of that influence with Giotto at the beginning of the 14th century. The influence of the countries west of the Alps was still too weak to counteract that of Byzantine art, but in Italy itself Niccolò Pisano initiated a return to antiquity which heralded the triumph of humanism. Regional artistic traditions survived everywhere in Italy, especially in Rome and in Latium. Moreover, the spreading of Franciscan ideas, together with the *Golden Legend,* introduced a feeling for nature, for the human and the divine, which later found expression in a new style, and which already in the Duecento suddenly enriched artistic iconography.

In Rome and Latium an uninterrupted tradition going back to the beginning of the Christian era and revived in the 11th and 12th centuries allowed more freedom to the Duecento painters in the interpretation of their Greek models. Roman paintings of the 13th century stem from the cycles of San Clemente (Rome) and Castel Sant'Elia, near Nepi; for instance, in Tuscania (apse of San Pietro) where, in an *Ascension,* painted according to Byzantine iconography, we find a typically Roman motif: Christ holding in his

GALEN AND HIPPOCRATES. FRESCO. ABOUT 1231-1255.
CRYPT OF THE CATHEDRAL OF ANAGNI.

upraised hands the globe and the book of the Law; at Subiaco (chapel of St Gregory at the Convento di San Benedetto); and particularly at Anagni. The frescoes of Anagni Cathedral (decoration of the crypt, painted between 1231 and 1255) are the most important example of Roman painting of that time. It is a narrative cycle stretching from the Old Testament to more recent hagiography and its central theme is the creation of man and of the world: Hippocrates and Galen, who are shown having a learned conversation, explain its genesis and continued existence by the combination of the four elements. About the end of the century, a few first rate artists, whose works stand out because of their use of bright colours, benefited from the experience of both Roman painting and

the Byzantine style, which was still dominant, but not for long: Cavallini (mosaics of Santa Maria in Trastevere, 1291 and frescoes at Santa Cecilia, 1293); Torriti at Assisi (about 1280) and in Rome (Santa Maria Maggiore, 1295). Rusuti came later, and takes us into the next century (Santa Maria Maggiore, mosaic on the façade, 1308).

In Tuscany, a similar evolution took place, but it is more difficult to follow than in Latium because there were so many artistic centres. In Florence, various tendencies were combined or were in conflict. The mosaic on the façade of San Miniato (first years of the 13th century), is purely Byzantine, by its subject at least: the *Deesis,* but the style is difficult to assess as the work has been very much restored. The mosaic in the choir of the Baptistery of San Giovanni is in a better state of preservation and shows Venetian influence; the Florentine painted crosses of the second half of the century (Florence, Accademia; San Gimignano Museum) do not differ from those painted in Pisa or Lucca; and finally, Coppo di Marcovaldo, a Florentine who settled in Siena, is one of the precursors of Cimabue. From the beginning, Sienese painting stood out because of its more marked character: the first master of the century was Guido da Siena and the last Duccio, who held a place similar to that of Cimabue in Florence or Cavallini in Rome. Arezzo and Pistoia had no real artistic school, but gave birth to two remarkable artists: Margaritone d'Arezzo and Manfredino da Pistoia; the latter painted the frescoes of San Michele di Fassolo in Genoa (1292).

Pisa and Luca were, in the 13th century, the most active artistic centres not only in Tuscany, but in the whole of Italy, judging by the number of extant works from that region. Painting on wood is characteristic of that school and there are three favourite themes: the Virgin enthroned or the *Maestà ;* the painted Cross on a rectangular or cross-shaped panel, decorated with narrative scenes; and the *paliotto* or altar-frontal dedicated to one saint whose full-length portrait occupies the central part while his life or legend is told in the side panels. The two first mentioned themes are directly inspired by Greek models; the last, in which more variations could be introduced, enriched religious iconography with new elements. All three were modified in the course of the Duecento. Christ as the Berlinghieri represented him—full face, impassive, with open eyes—was replaced by a dying Christ distorted by suffering. The latter interpretation of the crucifix was introduced by Giunta and persisted till Cimabue. In the same way, the earliest Madonnas are represented entirely frontally—the

position of the *Maestà* in the proper sense of the word—with the Child full face, but that rigid attitude was soon replaced by a more graceful bearing: the Virgin in a three-quarter view, her head bent, and the Child placed sideways, begins to move and smile. In spite of this evolution of the iconography and, up to a point, of the style, the technique remained the same: clearly divided surfaces, flat colours, perspective ignored or greatly simplified. The third theme is characteristic of Italian art of the Duecento; the central character varies from one *paliotto* to the next; St Francis is depicted most frequently, but we also find representations of St Magdalen and St Michael.

The situation was slightly different in northern Italy. When the Crusaders conquered Constantinople (1204), a large amount of booty was sent to the West, first to Venice which remained in the 13th century the largest market for Byzantine art. But, being an ever open refuge for Greek artists, Venice was at the same time a living centre where new works were composed. The decoration of San Marco was continued, in particular in the atrium, with the *Creation* mosaics whose iconography is entirely Greek: Adam's soul is represented by a butterfly (psyche); a growing number of angels are shown in constant attendance on the Lord, etc. From Venice, Byzantine art spread to all northern Italy: in the Veneto (Treviso, chapter house of the Convent of San Niccolò, end of 13th century), in Lombardy, in Liguria, in Piedmont and in Emilia where the finest example is to be found in Parma (paintings of the Baptistery cupola, about 1270).

In southern Italy, from the 11th century onwards, a so-called 'Benedictine' art developed; its first patron was Abbot Desiderius (1057-1087) who asked Greek artists to decorate Monte Cassino. Most of the paintings from that time have been destroyed with the

ST SYLVESTER OFFERS CONSTANTINE A MIRACULOUS ICON TO HEAL HIM. FRESCO.
ABOUT 1246. CHAPEL OF ST SYLVESTER, CHURCH OF THE QUATTRO CORONATI, ROME.

buildings they decorated; but there remain the large frescoes of Sant'Angelo in Formis (11th-12th centuries) where the traditional regional style asserts itself strongly, in spite of obvious borrowings from Greek models. From the Duecento we can only find, apart from a few small painted churches in the Abruzzi, the frescoes in Santa Maria del Casale, near Brindisi, painted by Reinaldo da Tarento (about 1200-1210). Neapolitan art did not renew itself until the beginning of the 14th century, mainly through the efforts of Robert of Anjou who invited to Naples the best of the Roman and Tuscan artists: Cavallini, Montano d'Arezzo, Simone Martini, etc.

The Duecento is not one of the great centuries of Italian painting, but it represents a turning point in its history. Vasari, through an over simplification, only saw the dominance of the *maniera greca* until Cimabue, and its final discarding with Giotto. But things are really more complex. There is not *one* 'Greek manner'; Byzantium and its empire offered western artists many models which differed from each other not only by their worth, but by their inspiration and their aims: visions of the immutable celestial world as well as lively, dramatic scenes whose characters were human enough to appeal to the Italy of St Francis. As for the great innovators of the end of the century, they could not have started from nothing. Far from denying the past, they made it their mission to interpret its teachings. P.-H. M.

E - F

ESTE (The). The history of the Renaissance in Ferrara is closely linked with the history of the House of Este from the beginning of the 15th century to the death of Alfonso I (1534). Under the reign of Nicolò III (1384-1441), Ferrara was already becoming a cultural centre. Brunelleschi stayed there in 1432, Antonio Alberti in 1438, and Pisanello several times between 1430 and 1440. One of the numerous sons of

Nicolò III, Lionello, succeeded him (1407-1450). The young prince, a pupil of the great humanist, Guarino da Verona, was cultured and a poet himself; he collected manuscripts and attracted to his court several famous painters. He commissioned his portrait from Jacopo Bellini, Pisanello and Mantegna. Rogier van der Weyden decorated the cabinet in the castle of Belfiore, and Angelo da Siena executed decorations which were to be finished later by Cosimo Tura. Borso d'Este (1413-1471), Lionello's brother and successor, increased the family prestige still more: in 1452, he received from the Emperor Frederick III the titles of Duke of Modena and Reggio, and Count of Rovigo, then, in 1471, from Pope Paul III that of Duke of Ferrara; but above all, he happened to reign during a period which was vital for art history: strongly marked by the teaching of Piero della Francesca (whose Ferrara works are lost, but whose influence is obvious), the Ferrara school was developing, with Galasso, Stefano da Ferrara, Baldassare Estense, Cosimo Tura, Francesco Cossa. Borso commissioned the decoration of the Palazzo Schifanoia, which was begun in 1391 and finally completed in 1469 (in the Sala Maggiore there are frescoes, illustrating allegories of the months and scenes from the life of Borso). At his death, his brother, Ercole (1431-1505), succeeded to the dukedom. The last quarter of the century was the most glorious period for Ferrarese painters. To the previous names can be added those of Ercole de' Roberti, Michele Ongaro and Domenico Panetti. Ercole was not content with encouraging local workshops, he also enriched his collections with works by masters from further afield (Mantegna, Giovanni Bellini, Leonardo da Vinci, Francesco Francia). Through her marriage with Francesco Gonzaga, his daughter, Isabella, was to become Marchesa of Mantua and his son, Alfonso I (1476 - 1534), was to continue for nearly thirty years the family tradition of patronage. But Ferrarese art was on the wane and the painters at Alfonso's court came mainly from outside. In 1514, in Ferrara, Giovanni Bellini began the *Feast of the Gods* later finished by Titian, which Vasari greatly praised. One of Bellini's pupils, Pellegrino d'Udine, settled in Ferrara for ten years (1502-1513).

The patronage of the princes of Este is an acknowledged fact, but their motives have been criticised. Some historians have stressed their cruelty, their indifference to public welfare, while others have pointed out that they merely behaved like everybody else in their day. We must admit they lacked the warm generosity of the Gonzaga. At the death of Raphael (1520), Alfonso d'Este did not utter a single word of regret: his one and only worry was to get back from the master's estate the fifty pieces of gold he had paid when commissioning a picture from him.   P.-H. M.

FERRARA. The work produced by the Ferrarese painters in the 14th century seems to have been limited in scope. The surviving examples show close imitation of the Emilian and Paduan styles, which was introduced by Serafini da Modena. At the beginning of the 15th century the Ferrarese continued to follow the example of neighbouring cities. Hence Antonio Alberti, who, however, worked mainly in the Marches, adopted the 'international gothic style'. Ferrara at last became an artistic capital toward 1440. The sovereigns of the House of Este, who had been ruling

Ferrara since 1208, then transformed Ferrara into a city of luxury open to the new Renaissance spirit. In the surrounding district, palaces and villas, 'delizie estensi', show the extent of this refinement. Pisanello, Jacopo Bellini (1441), Piero della Francesca, Rogier van der Weyden (1449), the young

BALDASSARE ESTENSE. PORTRAIT OF DUKE BORSO D'ESTE. CASTELLO SFORZESCO, MILAN.

Mantegna (1449), as well as French and Flemish artists worked for the court. At the same time, there arose a local school of great originality. The evidence of this stimulating exchange of ideas has mostly disappeared, especially the secular decorations of the castle of Belfiore, begun under the supervision of Maccagnino (1449-1456) and continued by Cosimo Tura (1459-1463). Certain *Allegories* attributed to the

BALDASSARE ESTENSE (?). FAMILY PORTRAIT.
ALTE PINAKOTHEK, MUNICH.

Ercole I having succeeded Borso) and in turn he imposed on the local studios his strong personality.

The incisiveness, the plastic vitality and the feverish lyricism of the Ferrarese manner is well exemplified in the work of three men: Tura, Cossa and Ercole de' Roberti. None of the other artists in this city attained the level of these men. Brief mention must be made of the delicate miniaturist, Giraldi, and a painter whom R. Longhi nicknamed 'Vicino da Ferrara', who should perhaps be identified with a certain Baldassare Estense, who is known for his skill as a portraitist. At the end of the century, the influence of the great Ferrarese style extended over the whole region: Lorenzo Costa, who, like Cossa and Ercole, also went to Bologna, extended it to this city, as also, on a smaller scale, did Bianchi-Ferrari to Modena or Marmitta to Parma. But in Ferrara itself the local artists exhausted the possibilities of this style and fell into a rather tiresome preciosity (Gian-Francesco Maineri, Grimaldi) or an often pious affectation (Coltellini, Panetti).

About 1510-1520, encouraged by the patronage of Duke Alfonso I, who also called upon Giovanni Bellini and Titian, Ferrarese painting acquired new vigour and became acquainted with 'modern' tendencies. Two currents which are often confused can be detected during this period: the first, dominated by Dosso Dossi and enriched by contact with Venetian innovations, links up with the tradition of picturesque fantasy and formal originality of the Ferrarese Quattrocento. So the curious Lodovico Mazzolino (active from 1504 to 1527), whose inventions are reminiscent of Aspertini of Bologna, renewed the unrealistic stylisations of Ercole. A second group of painters, also sensitive to the warm poetry of Giorgione, tended towards a more solemn classicism inherited from Costa. Such is the

former (Berlin, Florence, Budapest) or the work of Pannonio (Budapest) and Tura (London) give some idea at any rate of the spirit of this capital collection and reveal the charming complexity of an incisive style, ornate to the extent of seeming mannered, still bearing the imprint of the elegant gothic style, and at the same time showing the luminous discipline of Piero della Francesca. The miniatures of the rich Bible illuminated for Borso (1455, Modena) constitute another example of that brilliant culture. Cosimo Tura soon dominated this team of artists and continued to do so up to about 1485. Francesco del Cossa, having completed the frescoes of the Palazzo di Schifanoia (1470), left Ferrara for Bologna and was soon followed by Ercole de' Roberti, but their brilliant style lost nothing of its originality. Ercole returned to Ferrara in 1486, to take over the work of Tura (Duke work of Boccaccio Boccaccino during his youth in Ferrara, of Niccolò Pisano, and especially of Garofalo and Ortolano who were also influenced by Raphael. Ortolano, born before 1487 and active from 1512 to 1524, is an artist of the first order. Similar at the outset to Garofalo, he elaborated a noble, sculptural style, showing the characteristics of a true naturalism and a rustic simplicity. After 1540 and the death of Dosso Dossi, the Ferrarese school soon lost its autonomy and its own particular characteristics. They may still be discerned, often combined with details borrowed from Roman classicism or Emilian mannerism in the work of excellent painters like Girolamo da Carpi and Bastianino, and the example of Ferrara was the deciding factor in the formation of Niccolò dell'Abbate. However, the delicate style of Scarsellino (about 1551-1620), is linked mainly to the trends of Venetian and Bolognese painting, as in the work of Carlo Bonone (1569-1632), even if there is still descernible in these artists a faint echo of that passionate fantasy and lyricism which is the special characteristic of the Ferrarese genius.   M. L.

FERRARI Gaudenzio (Valduggia, Piedmont, *ca* 1470 - Milan, 1546). His art owes much to the great Lombard tradition of Bergognone, Foppa, Solario, Boltraffio. He may also have been Perugino's pupil in Rome and have admired the work of decorative painters belonging to Raphael's school; those two influences can be seen in many of his works. He soon became a lively, imaginative decorative painter himself. His first important work was in the church of Santa Maria delle Grazie in Varallo where he painted, during the first years of the 16th century, scenes from the *Life of Christ* in a style imbued with characteristics of the Quattrocento and reminiscences of Perugino. At the Sacro Monte in

Varallo, where forty-five chapels are grouped on a hill, he painted, according to an old tradition, an important cycle of pictures and sculptures treated with a remarkable verve and freedom of handling; they are a striking expression of popular faith; for instance, the large *Crucifixion* fresco (1520-1523) in which Ferrari renewed an old theme, while at the same time following the line of the great gothic fresco painters.

Several documents mention his working on the church of the Assumption and San Lorenzo at Morbegno in the Valtellina, between 1520 and 1526; the style of those paintings is so personal that it has allowed art historians to attribute similar works to Ferrari; for instance,

GAUDENZIO FERRARI. ANGEL OF THE
ANNUNCIATION. DRAWING. UFFIZI, FLORENCE.

the San Albondio altarpiece in Como Cathedral. These compositions show that the artist already knew Dürer's engravings, particularly those of the *Little Passion*. After working in Novara and Vercelli, Gaudenzio Ferrari settled in Milan in 1539 and worked on the frescoes of the Santa Corona Chapel in Santa Maria delle Grazie, in which the forms and attitudes are exaggerated, a defect common to many of his contemporaries. In the late frescoes of Santa Maria della Pace in Milan, we find again the beauty and freedom of handling of his mature works, whose rich manner, full of drama and movement, anticipated the baroque period.   S. B.

FETI Domenico (Rome, *ca* 1589 - Venice, 1624). Pupil of Lodovico Cigoli, Domenico Feti or Fetti underwent very complex influences. That of Borgiani drew him towards the milieu of Caravag-

gio, but that of Elsheimer made him paint little genre scenes, in particular a series of parables, now dispersed all over Europe: the *Multiplication of Loaves* is at the cathedral in Mantua, the *Lost Sheep* at Dresden. Supported by Cardinal Federigo Gonzaga, he became court painter in Mantua in 1613, and did a number of frescoes for the Cathedral. In 1621 he moved to Venice and remained there to his death. He seems to have greatly admired the Venetian School and the German, Liss. The opulent and majestic *Melancholia* at the Louvre, one of his masterpieces, shows to what an extent he continues the Venetian tradition. The Vienna Museum has a considerable number of pictures by him. His background landscapes have an intrinsic value and show a lively sensibility.   P. C.

FILIPEPI Sandro. *See* Botticelli.

DOMENICO FETI.
THE LOST
PIECE OF SILVER.
PALAZZO PITTI,
FLORENCE.

FLORENTINE SCHOOL OF THE 14TH CENTURY. THE VISITATION.
DRAWING. UFFIZI, FLORENCE.

FIORENZO di LORENZO (Perugia, *ca*
1440 - Perugia, 1522/25). There is an
exquisite moment in Umbrian painting
about 1460, though not without a certain
lack of substance, and Fiorenzo di
Lorenzo is fairly representative of it.
He signed two works: the *Madonna della
Misericordia* (Perugia, Galleria Nazionale), dated 1476, for the hospital of
Sant'Egidio, and an altarpiece of 1487
(same museum). For Santa Maria
Novella in Florence he painted a polyptych (commissioned in 1472, executed
between 1487 and 1493), and for the
monastery of Monteluce a fresco with
the *Crucifixion* (1491). Like Niccolò da
Foligno, Caporali and Bonfigli, Fiorenzo
was influenced by Gozzoli, though he
combined this influence with an interest
for the richer and more angular manner
of the Paduans and of B. Vivarini.
When Perugino and Pinturicchio rose
on the Perugian horizon, Fiorenzo
entered their orbit, as can be seen from

the beautiful *Madonna* (Paris, Musée
Jacquemart-André), which is sometimes
attributed to the early Perugino.   A. C.

FLORENCE. In the middle of the
13th century, when all Italy was dreaming of a return to the 'Latin' style, the
decoration of the Baptistery of Florence
awoke the Florentines to their vocation:
Cimabue and Giotto were given the
opportunity to re-invent painting. The
churches of the great orders were built
with new styles. The Dominicans
began, in 1246, to raise the Convent of
Santa Maria Novella. In 1250 the
Servi erected the Annunziata, the
Humiliati the church of Ognissanti,
and the Augustinians Santo Spirito. A
little later the Franciscans began Santa
Croce, the monks of Vallombrosa
Santa Trinità and the Carmelites the
Carmine. But the most ambitious and
the most extraordinary building was
going to be the new cathedral. Its

FLORENTINE SCHOOL. PORTRAIT OF A LADY.
ATTRIBUTED TO UCCELLO (SOMETIMES TO
DOMENICO VENEZIANO). BACHE COLLECTION,
METROPOLITAN MUSEUM, NEW YORK.

middle of the 14th. From 1330 onwards all official building was supervised by the commission in charge of the Cathedral. The architectural style is characterised by a firm rhythm and neatly defined forms. In painting everything can be summed up in the name of Giotto whose work on the Baptistery may be considered as his apprenticeship. His genius had flowered at Assisi, then Padua before he returned a little later to Florence. His fame spread outside Tuscany, but he remained an isolated figure. He changed everything and there was nobody to continue the changes, though a large number of painters drew their inspiration from him. They were the *giotteschi* who gave a watered down, milder version of the master's art. The art of Andrea Pisano, who came to Florence to cast in bronze the Baptistery doors (completed in 1336), went well with elegant *giottismo* in a minor key. From this time onwards there existed in Florence a sensitive, cultivated circle interested in art and ever ready to encourage innovators.

1350 to 1375 was a period of general crisis in Tuscany and it affected Florentine painting as well. The province was ravaged by pestilence and the misery of the times is reflected in the increased activity of preachers calling to penitence, the austerity of commissioned work and a certain weakness in art. The programme of the Spanish Chapel (1365) testifies to a revived didacticism, and there is a hieratic emphasis in the great Strozzi polyptych by Orcagna (1354-1357). About 1385 Agnolo Gaddi decorated Santa Croce with frescoes from the *Legend of the Cross,* a theme Piero della Francesca was to handle again in Arezzo. But the last *giotteschi* came under Sienese influence which established itself in Florence with Lorenzo Monaco. Finally in 1401 took place the great competition for the second door of the Baptistery. All the leading Tuscan sculptors participated:

'chief master of works', Arnolfo di Cambio, was already in Rome at the end of the 13th century. The cupola as planned was to be something unique. It was the time of Dante. In 1300, the year of the Jubilee, he was *priore delle arti.* The *Signoria* was in its heyday. Thus in every sphere, appeared the master figures: they were to give Florence a unique prestige and their action was to have echoes throughout the Peninsula. Secular architecture was developing: the Palazzo Vecchio, the seat of the *Signoria,* is in this domain as characteristic as the Cathedral in that of religious building. The palace of the *Podestà,* or the Bargello, begun in the 13th century, was completed in the

Jacopo della Quercia, Francesco de Valdambrino, Brunelleschi and Ghiberti. This confrontation was the opening signal for a period of intense activity during which the Florentines, completing their achievement as a communal polity, were, in fact, to bring about the revolutionary birth of modern times. The Cathedral workshop was the centre of this activity. In direct competition with Milan which was disputing her claim to hegemony, the city on the Arno was bent on developing her own style and asserting her peculiar intellectual genius. Brunelleschi solved the problem of the dome of the cathedral left in abeyance by the gothic masters; he gave an original outline to this structure with the octagonal drum. He innovated in everything: the Palazzo di Parte Guelfa (1418) and the old sacristy of San Lorenzo. His plans show an astonishing assurance, the result of their subjection to the mathematical rigour of the laws of perspective. These fertile ideas were applied by Michelozzo in the Convent of San Marco and in the Palazzo Medici. They were codified in a treatise by Leone Battista Alberti (1404-1472) to whom architecture was an integral part of the larger context of humanist culture. Thus in the middle of the Quattrocento, rules and models were elaborated that henceforth no artist could afford to ignore.

Meanwhile the Medici had secured their hold on political power. Back from his exile, Cosimo dominated the old Signoria in 1434. Donatello was his favourite sculptor, a dominating personality that impressed his mark on every domain of art, challenging painters, decorators and architects as well as sculptors. *St George* (1416), *St John the Baptist* (1415) and *David* (1440) are the astonishing masterpieces of his bold and forceful style. Suavity, on the other hand, was the characteristic of Luca della Robbia (1400-1482). His *Cantoria,* executed as a companion piece to that of Donatello, is restrained and almost

FLORENTINE SCHOOL. STUDIO OF BOTTICELLI. PORTRAIT OF A WOMAN. PALAZZO PITTI, FLORENCE.

reticent. The public responded to all these initiatives. The cultural climate of Florence was more stimulating than ever. In painting, the rapid rise of Masaccio (1401-1428), a pupil of Masolino, brought with it the rejection of the sweetness and softness of Lorenzo Monaco and Gentile da Fabriano. Severity has always been the dominant trait of the Tuscan genius. Working in the Brancacci Chapel at the Carmine, Masaccio showed the same intransigence as Donatello, concentrating almost exclusively on modelling and tonality.

The years 1430 to 1440 were relatively barren: Masolino had gone and Masaccio was dead. Only with the arrival of

FLORENTINE SCHOOL. LORENZO DI CREDI AND LEONARDO DA VINCI (?).
ANNUNCIATION. LOUVRE, PARIS.

Domenico Veneziano in 1438 was Masaccio's imposing heritage taken up again. Several currents sprang from it. The reformed or Observant Dominicans had for their prior a painter called Fra Angelico who decorated the Convent of San Marco for them. His modelling is clear and he has a refined feeling for space which he articulates with light architectural decor in the manner of Michelozzo. The Carmelite Filippo Lippi went further in the emphasis on rich colour. On the other hand the draughtsmen, fascinated by perspective, Paolo Uccello and Andrea del Castagno, developed within short time an astonishing degree of abstraction. The formal repertory of Tuscan painting had never been so varied. Its diffusion was rapid and decisive; the activity of Donatello and Uccello in Padua and of Castagno in Venice is an indication of this. Michelozzo and Filarete disseminated the new architectural types in the north. A common spirit and parallel formal inventions bound closely together architecture, sculpture and painting.

The advent of Lorenzo de' Medici in 1469 marked a turning point in Florentine culture. The old civic and moral ideal gave way to a more ambitious vision: the infinite potentialities of man, the humanistic role of Florence, the cultivation and enjoyment of beauty. The growing conflict between the deep rooted naturalism of the Florentines and a nascent aestheticism caused artists to become more refined and less productive. Sculpture was now in the ascendant, subordinating the other arts to itself. Verrocchio's workshop, in competition with Pollaiuolo's, enhanced yet more the feeling for plastic values. When he had finished his training, Leonardo da Vinci left Florence in 1482. His art, which responded to all current problems, was to mark the following generation. With his subtle precision Botticelli was the greatest painter of the end of the century, but his reputation did not spread beyond Tuscany. He began in the footsteps of Pollaiuolo and Verrocchio, but his keen graphic sense kept him clear of the contorted forms of the former and the emphasis on relief of the latter. From 1480 onwards Florentine taste, as established by the bankers and the humanists of the Medici circle found satisfying the abstractions of this master, the bourgeois epic of Ghirlandaio and the airs and graces of Filippino Lippi. But at the end of the century the Florentines, quick as always in their response to stylistic change, turned to the facile suavity of Perugino and the mellowness of Leonardo.

After Lorenzo's death Florence, invaded by the French (1494), underwent a major political and religious crisis. To Savonarola the crisis appeared meaningful and universally valid as the edification through suffering of Florence as a 'Christian Republic'. A devotional style came for a time into vogue and Fra Bartolomeo employed himself in distilling the principles of a new religious art from the examples first of Perugino and then of Raphael. It took a Michelangelo to see the real possibilities inherent in the terrible lesson of the 'Piagnone'. By 1500 Florence was again the centre of initiatives and tensions. In the vast Sala del Consiglio of the Palazzo Vecchio, Michelangelo back from Rome found himself pitted against Leonardo back from Milan. This encounter between the demiurge of solid form and the subtlest intellect in Florence led nowhere. However, absent again, they both continued to weigh on the artistic destiny of their city. Andrea del Sarto was to begin with a carefully dosed combination of Leonardo's delicacy and Raphael's form. Pontormo, then Rosso, were to draw their inspiration from the career of Michelangelo. Florence became quite naturally the city of mannerism with the cold and elegant Bronzino, the brilliant Ammanati and the great history of Vasari who was the first to conceive the universal history of art in terms of modern Tuscan art.   A. C.

FOPPA Vincenzio (Brescia, *ca* 1427 - Brescia, 1515). He is generally considered as the founder of the Milanese school of painting and, according to Vasari, was trained in Padua: it is believed nowadays that he developed in Bembo's circle his gift for the rendering of colour and light, by contacts with the works of Stefano da Verona and Jacopo Bellini. His activity was centred in Genoa, Pavia, Milan and Brescia. In 1462, in Pavia, he signed a painting—now lost—for the Carmine church; in 1468, he was made a citizen of the town, thanks to the patronage of Duke Galeazzo Maria. The same year, he went to Milan and painted in Sant'Eustorgio the frescoes of the Portinari chapel dedicated to St Peter Martyr, a most important cycle of paintings showing a turning point in Lombard art because of its tight composition and of its experimenting with perspective. After 1470, or so, his

FLORENTINE SCHOOL. STUDIO OF LEONARDO DA VINCI. LA BELLE FERRONNIÈRE. LOUVRE, PARIS.

FRANCESCO DI GIORGIO

VINCENZO FOPPA. THE MADONNA WITH A BOOK.
CASTELLO SFORZESCO, MILAN.

for other cities. During that period, he seems to have been attracted by the new stylistic discoveries of the Renaissance to which he added his own melancholy strain, as for instance in the *Epiphany* (London, National Gallery) and the *Annunciation* (Milan, Borromeo Collection). His last dated work is the *Orzinuovi Standard* (1514). This great painter has been called the creator of the Lombard style: he deeply influenced the whole district as far as Piedmont and Liguria, and created traditions which dominated Lombard painting till Leonardo da Vinci. His restrained and austere art, with its gift for colour and effects of light, may also be at the origin of some artistic trends in Brescia, from Moretto to Savoldo. With his numerous pupils, he played the same part in Milan, Pavia and Brescia, as Tura in Ferrara. S. B.

FRANCESCO di GIORGIO MARTINI (Siena, 1439 - Siena, 1502). A pupil of Vecchietta and, like his master, a versatile artist, Francesco di Giorgio is one of the most powerful personalities of the Sienese Renaissance. He painted mainly during his youth, until about 1480, and, without losing that feeling for decoration which is the hallmark of Sienese art, he was influenced by the latest stylistic developments from Florence (Botticelli, Pollaiuolo, Filippino Lippi). Later, he devoted himself almost exclusively to architecture and sculpture and his work in these fields was so brilliant that his paintings were almost forgotten for a long time. Nowadays they are appreciated again and we find the poetic realism of a picture like his *St Dorothy and the Infant Christ* (London, National Gallery) very moving. Other paintings worthy of mention are the *Coronation of the Virgin* (1472), the *Annunciation,* slightly later, in the Siena Pinacoteca and the *Virgin and Child* of the Campana Collection (about 1475). P.-H. M.

visits to Genoa became frequent, and allowed him to have numerous contacts with Flemish and Provençal art. Between 1474 and 1476, for instance, he worked with Zanetto Bugatto on the Spinola altarpiece for the church of San Domenico in Genoa. After 1480, his style matured and opened up to Renaissance art under the influence of Leonardo, and particularly Bramante, as we can see from the fragments of frescoes from Santa Maria of Brera, painted in 1485. Between 1488 and 1490, he became more active in Liguria; in 1488, he painted the Fornari picture and the large polyptych commissioned by Cardinal Giuliano della Rovere, later finished by Ludovico Brea, for Savona Cathedral (1490). In December 1489, the town of Brescia gave him a pension and entrusted him with the teaching of young artists; he therefore came back to his native town where he stayed to the end of his life, while still working

FRANCIA Francesco Raibolini, *called* (Bologna, *ca* 1450 - Bologna, 1517). At first his style bore traces of Ferrarese influence, especially Ercole de' Roberti (the *Crucifixion,* Bologna, Museo Civico). He was, however, aware of the 'looser' style current, which at about the same time characterises the art of Perugino or of Lorenzo Costa, also at Bologna, and Francia soon adopted a style which was elegant and delicate in spite of being monotonous. The peaceful lines of his landscapes, the pale colours and the simple rather stolid shapes, bathed in an even light, create an atmosphere of great gentleness and poetry, and make a very fitting background for traditional religious scenes (*Madonna and Saints,* Bologna, Pinacoteca) which he depicted with figures in graceful, serene poses, bereft of any of their tragic depth (*Deposition,* Parma, Pinacoteca). A good many of his altarpieces or frescoes (*Scenes from the Life of St Cecilia,* Bologna, San Giacomo Maggiore, Oratorio di Santa Cecilia) are still preserved in the churches of Bologna and Emilia and these testify to his tremendous success in that district.   J. T.

FRANCIABIGIO Francesco di Cristofano Bigi, *called* (Florence, *ca* 1482 - Florence, 1525). Franciabigio is one of a group of Florentines who composed variations, with a certain aptness, on the achievements of early classicism. Pupil of Albertinelli and Piero di Cosimo who had already assimilated the harmonious style and composition of Leonardo, he was the companion and collaborator of Andrea del Sarto in the cloister of the Annunziata, in particular for the *Marriage of the Virgin.* In the Chiostro dello Scalzo he painted the *Last Supper.* Finally, he was asked to contribute to the vast and pompous programme of decoration of the Salone at Poggio a Caiano with a *Triumph of Cicero* in which he somewhat forced his talent. Less sharp than Andrea del Sarto, more

FRANCESCO DI GIORGIO. THE ANNUNCIATION. PINACOTECA, SIENA.

delicate than Bugiardini or Ridolfo Ghirlandaio, Franciabigio was obviously dominated by the two masters of gracefulness and subtle expression: the *Triumph of Hercules* (Uffizi) and the *Job* (Uffizi) show Leonardo's influence; the basic elements of the *Young Man* (Louvre) and the *Holy Family* (Vienna) derive from Raphael. The chief merits of Franciabigio's not vey considerable output are the grace of his figures, a certain freshness of colour and airy landscapes. Finally his refinement has a veil of melancholy, is restrained and serious—the marks of a minor but authentic classicism.   A. C.

G

GADDI Agnolo di Taddeo (Florence, *ca* 1345/1350-Florence, 1396). According to Vasari, Agnolo Gaddi died aged sixty-three; his birth date would then be 1333. But on the other hand, we know that Taddeo, at his death (1366), entrusted him to the care and teaching of Jacopo da Casentino: he cannot have been over twenty then. He is mentioned for the first time in 1369, among the painters working at the Vatican for Urban V. In 1380, in Florence, he decorated the Loggia de' Lanzi (the frescoes are lost); then, between 1380 and 1390, the choir of Santa Croce *(Legend of the True Cross)* and finally, in Prato Cathedral, the Cappella della Cintola, 1394-1396. Agnolo was brought up in the Giotto tradition and went on painting in the narrative manner of the Florentine Trecento, but by temperament he had more affinities with Siena and his style, which has sometimes been called 'retarded gothic', is nearer to Simone Martini than to Giotto. Lorenzo Monaco was his pupil. Among the painters he influenced, directly or indirectly, were Starnina and Stefano Zevio. P.-H. M.

GADDI Taddeo (Florence, beginning of 14th century - Florence, 1366). Taddeo was the son of Gaddo Gaddi, a painter, mosaicist and monumental mason, whose works have been lost, and owed most of his training to Giotto who, according to Vasari, had held him at his baptism, and under whom, according to Cennino Cennini, he worked for 24 years. His first dated work is the Berlin Triptych (1334), but already in 1332 he had started working on the decoration of the Baroncelli Chapel in the Santa Croce, Florence, which he continued under the direction of Giotto, until the death of his master (1337), and only finished in 1338. In those *Scenes from the Life of the Virgin* we do not find the width and the feeling for space of Giotto's composition. But although he is more concerned with picturesque and narrative details, Taddeo is none the less the most faithful disciple of Giotto and the best representative of a tradition of narrative painting which lasted till the end of the century. His attempts at light effects are striking *(Annunciation to the Shepherds)*. After completing the Santa Croce frescoes, Taddeo worked at San Miniato al Monte, then in Pisa (church of San Francesco, 1341-1342). Later, he painted an altarpiece for the church of San Giovanni Fuoricivitas in Pistoia (1353) and a *Madonna,* signed and dated 1355 (Uffizi). His native town honoured him and he was, at the end of his life, a member of the commission for the building of the Duomo (1359-1366).   P.-H. M.

GALGARIO Giuseppe Ghislandi, *as a friar* Fra (Borgo di San Leonardo, near Bergamo, 1655 - Bergamo, 1743). The son of a portrait and perspective painter, who joined the workshop of the Bergamo painter, Cotta, then that of the Florentine, Bartolomeo Bianchini, in Bergamo. In 1675, he became a lay brother of the Order of Minims in Venice, where he lived for twenty-five years, studying the great masters of Venetian painting and working with Sebastiano Bompelli, a portrait painter from Friuli. Back in Bergamo, he only stayed there a short time before going to Milan to train under the German painter, Solomon Adler, who was then famous in that town. After that long training, Fra Galgario started his real career as a painter when he was nearly fifty. He specialised in portraits and soon became famous for them. His dated and signed works were painted between 1711 and 1738. His activity is marked by short journeys to Bologna in 1717 and Milan where he went several times in 1718 to paint the portrait of *Prince Lievestein,* the Governor of the city. Already in his very first works, the portraits of the *Marquis Giuseppe Maria Rota* and of *Captain Antonio Brinzago,* painted during the first years of the 18th century, we find his characteristic qualities: a

brilliant finish, which stresses the beauty of the costume, and a detailed study of the face, showing psychological insight. Other well known portraits are those of the Roncalli family, of the *Count Gian Battista Vailetti* (Venice, Accademia), of *Doctor Bernardi,* a Bolognese (1717), of the Domenican father *Giovanni Battista*

FRA GALGARIO. PORTRAIT OF ISABELLA CAMOZZI. COLLECTION OF COUNT CAMOZZI VERTOVA, COSTA DI MAZZATE (BERGAMO).

Pecorari degli Ambiveri (1738); the latter is the last dated work of the artist.   S. B.

GAROFALO Benvenuto Tisi, *called* (Ferrara, *ca* 1481 - Ferrara, 1519). The numerous works of Garofalo preserved in Ferrara and elsewhere (Madonnas with Saints, religious or mythological scenes) show obvious technical qualities, a placid, limited inspiration and a temperament which welcomed the example of his contemporaries. Garofalo first followed the local tradition of Boccaccio Boccaccino and Costa, then he sought inspiration in Venice, afterwards from Raphael in Rome (1515-1516) and later showed himself sensitive to the influence of his compatriots, Ortolano and Dosso Dossi, as well as sometimes to certain echoes of Emilian mannerism. Thus he finally arrived at a classical art which avoids academic formalism in the elegance of its colours and above all in the delicate romanticism of the backgrounds of his landscapes. The fact is that even before 1510, Garofalo knew Giorgione in Venice (according to Vasari he was even a friend of his) and he revealed and transmitted to Ferrara, even before Dosso, the luminous poetry of this artist.   M. L.

GENOA. Built in a amphitheatre on the side of a hill, facing the sea, Genoa the 'Proud' was always a maritime power and, in the beginning, a warlike republic, heaped behind a mole in the shelter of a narrow wall, bristling with towers of which the Torre degli Embriaci still remains. The Cistercian monk, Fra Olivieri, after consolidating the old mole, built the Palazzo San Giorgio in 1270, which was restored and enlarged in 1535 and 1571. The little church of San Matteo, built in 1125 by Martino Doria, then reconstructed in 1278, survives as a typical example of those medieval churches that were often designed as fortresses. From the same period, there remain a few pieces of sculpture, notably fragments from the tomb of the Empress Marguerite of Luxembourg by Giovanni Pisano (Palazzo Bianco). Like the sculpture, the painting of the time was considerably influenced by Siena and Florence. The names of Manfredino da Pistoia, Taddeo di Bartolo, Barnaba da Modena, Niccolò da Voltri and Turino Vanni all of whom worked in Genoa, are a reminder of this.

A humbler, local school flowered with Pellerano da Camogli, Giovanni Re and Francesco d'Oberto. But soon the attraction of Siena and Florence gave way before other influences from the Rhine and Flanders: a number of pictures could then be seen in Italy by Van Eyck, Rogier van der Weyden or Gerard David and it became customary to attribute them indiscriminately to 'Justo d'Allamagna', Justus of Ravensburg, who painted the fresco of the *Annunciation* on the walls of Santa Maria di Castello. The contributions from the Piedmontese and particularly the Lombards finally gave a distinctive character to so many varying tendencies: a Nice-Ligurian school grew up in which the best known names are Giovanni Massone, P. F. Sacchi, Lodovico Brea, Fra Simone de Carnoli, Manfredino da Castelnuovo and Niccolò Barbagelata, who are all less impressive than the attractive and still mysterious personality of Carlo Braccesco, who probably painted the *Annunciation* (about 1480) in the Louvre.

Until the end of the 16th century, Genoa remained faithful to this precious, but backward, art. However, when Andrea Doria had given peace and security to the Republic and built his palace of Fassolo, the whole town was opened to the Renaissance. While Galeazzo Alessi was bringing new life to architecture and changing the face of the town, Girolamo Pennachi from Treviso, then above all Pierino del Vaga, a pupil of Raphael, left admirable frescoes in the Palazzo Doria, which inspired the work of Calvi, Cambiaso, Castello, Paggi, and Tavarone. Genoa then lived through a period of glory and wealth: her artistic life flourished and, at the beginning of the 17th century, encouraged the arrival of the great Flemish artists, Rubens and Van Dyck, the Wael brothers and the German, Peter Roos. The palaces, where G. B. Castello and Rocco Lurago displayed a less pure taste than Alessi, were covered with frescoes:

GENTILE DA FABRIANO. ADORATION OF THE MAGI. 1423. UFFIZI, FLORENCE.

the artists were legion and the School of Genoa showed its originality in a racy, fierce art where influences from Lombardy, Tuscany, Bologna and Flanders mixed. Among its best representatives were Bernardo Strozzi, called Il Cappucino, Pellegrino and Domenico Piola, Domenico Fiasella and Giovanni Castiglione. Alessandro Magnasco, a native of Genoa, spread his strangely coloured manner through Lombardy.   S. B.

GENTILE da FABRIANO Gentile di Niccolò di Giovanni di Massio, *called* (Fabriano, *ca* 1360 - Rome, 1427). Born in a small town of the Marches—Fabriano had its great moment in the history of painting at the end of the 14th century—and formed in the local tradition, reaching Venice in 1408 where he decorated the Palazzo Ducale (frescoes, lost), in Florence from 1423 to 1425, then in Siena, arriving in Rome in 1427 to decorate San Giovanni in

Laterano (frescoes, destroyed in the 17th century) Gentile is, with Piero della Francesca, one of the rare artists to have linked in his person the main Italian centres and to have reflected, at a certain juncture, their common culture. But his importance can only be guessed because of the loss of the major part of his work.

The Roman frescoes were continued by Pisanello, which is a useful indication, and Gentile can be imagined to have treated mural decoration as a kind of tapestry which he filled with animal motifs, flowers and silhouettes borrowed from manuscript illumination. In Venice Gentile had among his pupils Jacopo Bellini, Jacobello and Giambono, each of whom probably developed a different aspect of the master's art: the agility of his line, his refined exiguity, the sumptuousness of his flutings and arabesques. What can be inferred from this as to the authority of Gentile's

GENTILE
DA FABRIANO.
PRESENTATION
IN THE TEMPLE
(DETAIL).
PANEL FROM
THE PREDELLA OF
THE 'ADORATION
OF THE MAGI'.
1423.
LOUVRE, PARIS.

example is confirmed by the few surviving portraits, like those in the *Madonna* triptych in Berlin. Gentile was thus one of the chief exponents of the gothic revival in the early 15th century. He was one of those who, for a short while restored to full vigour the traditional procedures by fortifying them with 'naturalist' inventions. Thus treated, the refinements of courtly poetry and of the knightly romance, in a word the best the 'international style' had to offer, shone with a final splendour even in monumental art. The most characteristic instance of Gentile's winning manner is the *Adoration of the Magi* painted for the Santa Trinità in Florence: with its aristocratic silhouettes, gold and silver highlights, elaborate detail, the magic of pageantry, a fine indifference to realism and many other features, some of them new, we are at the summit of an art condemned to total rejection. In Florence itself a reaction was imminent but the charm of Gentile and of what he stood for was to survive for a long time, especially in Siena where his brief stay and his prestige could only fortify against Masaccio's reform an old inclination to the luxurious and the refined.   A. C.

GENTILESCHI Artemisia (Rome, 1597 - Naples, after 1651). Artemisia Gentileschi, Orazio's daughter, was taught by her father and by Agostino Tassi. One of her earliest works, *Susanna and the Elders* at the Castle of Pommersfelden, bears the date 1610 (unless it should be read 1619) but her artistic personality is indistinguishable at this stage from that of Orazio. In her *Daughters of Lot* this dominant influence is still present. She left Rome with her father in 1621 and settled down in Florence. Here she painted a *Judith and Holophernes* (Uffizi) which exceeds in ferocity anything the Caravaggisti had done so far in what was for them a favourite subject. The heroine is engaged in sawing through the victim's neck and blood is spurting in every direction. This gruesome note is exceptional with Artemisia. After visits to Rome and Naples, she joined her father in London (1638/39) where she outshone Orazio. The *Portrait of a Woman* at Althorp House, Northamptonshire, belongs to the school of Van Dyck and is not by Artemisia, in spite of the long standing attribution. In 1640 she returned to Naples and seems to have been not without influence among the Caravaggisti. She was commissioned to paint three pictures of the choir of the cathedral at Pozzuoli. Her *Judith and the Servant* in Naples shows her exploring the night effects of the *tenebrosi*. She executed a few portraits, which are inferior to her other works.   P. C.

GENTILESCHI Orazio Lomi, *called* Orazio (Pisa, *ca* 1565 - London, 1647 ?). Third son of Giovanni Battista Lomi, Orazio is known under the name of his mother, Maria Gentileschi. By the time he reached Rome in 1585 he had been trained by his brother, Aurelio Lomi, in the tradition of painters like Bronzino and Pontormo. He was one of the first to understand the importance of Caravaggio whom, however, he interpreted with a great deal of freedom. He was in Genoa from 1621 to 1623, then in France. From 1626 onwards he lived in England as court painter.

During his long career, Gentileschi never treated lighting with the brutality of Caravaggio's most characteristic masterpieces. He does not allow his contrasts to harden and the lines separating his lights from his shadows are not nearly as incisive. The transitions, particularly in the lights, appear subdued, giving the forms a gentle roundness. His colour range with its mauves and greens is less clear than Caravaggio's.

The chronology of his works is uncertain. *David and Goliath* (Dublin Gallery) and *St Cecilia* (Rome, Galleria Nazionale d'Arte Antiqua), still predominantly Caravaggist, are tentatively dated about 1610. The years 1623 to 1626 were a particularly happy period in his career. In 1623, at Genoa, he painted the *Annunciation,* now at Turin, a replica of the one executed for San Siro. The modesty and grace in the attitude of the Virgin, standing in front of the angel on his knees, marks this picture as, perhaps, Gentileschi's masterpiece. The *Rest on the Flight into Egypt,* known in two, more or less equal versions at the Louvre and in Vienna, and a third one at the Birmingham City Museum, seems datable to about 1626. The artist must have been attached to this composition with its obtuse angle pointing downwards and its somewhat wan light.   P. C.

GHIRLANDAIO Domenico Bigordi, *called* (Florence, 1449 - Florence, 1494). Domenico was the eldest of three brothers. The two younger ones distinguished themselves, one in painting, the other in mosaic. The three together set up a *bottega*, which became very active under the patronage of a restricted middle class clientèle. Its output was considerable and there is practically no church in Florence without a Ghirlandaio altarpiece. The brothers' manner was solid,

a skilful popularisation of the art of Baldovinetti and Filippo Lippi from which it derived. After the decoration of the chapel of St Fina in the Collegiata at San Gimignano (1475), still somewhat immature, came a series of commissions for the cathedrals of Pisa (*Coronation of the Virgin,* now lost), and Lucca, and for the Ognissanti in Florence where Domenico's *St Jerome* is a somewhat feeble partner for Botticelli's brilliant *St Augustine,* but his *Last Supper* in the refectory is a success. In 1481-1482 Domenico belonged to the team of painters commissioned to decorate the Sistine Chapel. He contributed the *Resurrection* (lost) and *Christ calling St Peter and St Andrew.*

Back in Florence he worked on the decoration of the Medici villa at Vol-terra (damaged fresco) and of the Sala dei Gigli in the Palazzo Vecchio. His habit of introducing portraits of contemporary personages into religious scenes was much appreciated. Francesco Sassetti engaged Domenico to paint frescoes of the *Life of St Francis* for the family chapel at Santa Trinità and an altarpiece with the *Adoration of the Shepherds* (1485), while Giovanni Tornabuoni commissioned the artist to decorate the choir of Santa Maria Novella with frescoes of the *Life of the Virgin* and the *Life of John the Baptist.* Domenico, at his most characteristic here, produced an ingenious contemporary setting combining interiors with street perspectives.

The output of the Ghirlandaio *bottega* was uneven: as against the very conventional *Coronation of the Virgin* (1486, Narni), the tondo of the *Adoration of the Magi* (1487, Uffizi) is a good picture, as is the grave and amiable *Visitation* of 1491 (Louvre). The *Adoration of the Magi* for the Ospedale degli Innocenti (1488) betrays the hand of assistants, while the seriousness and the well defined gifts of Domenico are clearly present in the portrait of *Giovanna Tornabuoni* (New York) and in the *Old Man and his Grandson* (Louvre). As Davide was a mosaicist, the workshop entered the competition for the mosaics intended for the chapel of St Zenobius in the cathedral and produced the *Annunciation* mosaic over the Porta della Mandorla of the cathedral (1490). There survive several panels by him; among others a *Madonna enthroned with Angels* (Paris, Musée Cluny) commissioned by Jean de Ganay, interesting for its texture—large cubes of colour—rather than for its composition.

Ghirlandaio was a populariser and an eclectic. He was resolved to follow the fashion of the day. Thus he obviously took account of the Flemish influence, in particular the Portinari Triptych of Hugo van der Goes. The extreme realism of the *Old Man and his Grandson* and the minute detail of the *St Jerome* at the Ognissanti are, in fact, northern in spirit. The St Francis cycle at Santa Trinità and the John the Baptist cycle at Santa Maria Novella offered exceptional opportunies for anecdote, which Ghirlandaio exploited with great success by placing contemporary personages, undisguised, in the midst of sacred happenings. The composition is almost always ingenious and details like the servant carrying a tray with fruit on her head in the *Birth of John the Baptist* stand in their own right. Domenico's calm line had a great capacity for assimilation. Without lapsing into pedantic archaeology he was able to integrate into his decorative backgrounds reliefs and other motifs

DOMENICO GHIRLANDAIO. PORTRAITS OF FRANCESCO SASSETTI AND HIS SON, TEODORO. METROPOLITAN MUSEUM, NEW YORK.

from the antique. The *Adoration of the Shepherds* at Santa Trinità with its sarcophagus carrying the text of an augur's prophecy is a piece of learned epigraphy. Domenico remained foreign to the anxieties exercising his contemporaries like Filippino Lippi. His compositions are well balanced and serene, and the generous sweep of the Louvre *Visitation* anticipates the 16th century. Yet the ultimately justifying unity and convincing poetic invention are lacking. And one can only register surprise, not at the success of Ghirlandaio with art lovers and historians of the last century, but at the consistently high valuation he has enjoyed.   A. C.

GIAMBONO Michele (Venice, active be-

DOMENICO GHIRLANDAIO. GIOVANNA TORNABUONI AND HER SUITE. DETAIL FROM
'THE NATIVITY OF THE VIRGIN'. FRESCO. 1485-1490.
SANTA MARIA NOVELLA, FLORENCE.

tween 1420 and 1462). Venetian painter and mosaicist. He was recorded as a married man in 1420 and was still alive in 1462. He was the son and grandson of painters, but he may have been influenced by Jacobello del Fiore and was certainly influenced by the international gothic style as practised by Gentile da Fabriano and Pisanello. Giambono's principal signed works are a *Madonna* in the Galleria Nazionale, Rome, and a large polyptych in Venice (Accademia), together with the mosaics in the Mascoli Chapel, San Marco, begun in 1444. The *Coronation of the Virgin* (Venice, Accademia) is almost certainly his copy of the painting of the same subject in

San Pantaleone, Venice, by Giovanni d'Alemagna and Antonio Vivarini: this copy was ordered for the church of Sant'Agnese in 1447.   P. M.

GIORDANO Luca (Naples, 1632 - Naples, 1705). Luca Giordano was called *Luca fa presto* in admiration as much as in contempt. His father, who was a copy painter, no doubt taught him the rudiments. He is thought to have had Ribera as his master but the influences he underwent were so complex and his visual memory so retentive that it is difficult to distinguish the various strands in his artistic make-up. One finds in his works reminiscences of Pietro da

Cortona, Veronese, Titian, Tintoretto, the Bassani, Lanfranco, the Carracci, not to mention Dürer, Rembrandt, Rubens or even Van Dyck. Barely thirteen, he left his native city for Rome where, after having executed many copies and perhaps even fakes, he was engaged as assistant by Pietro da Cortona who initiated him into the grand style of decoration. Giordano's own career began about 1650. Back in Naples he was immediately given important commissions both for easel paintings and frescoes, as he was skilled in both techniques. His *Virgin under a Canopy* (Naples, Museo Nazionale) is considered by some to be an early work. In 1665 Giordano became master in the painters' guild. About 1677 he was at Monte Cassino decorating a vault which is now destroyed. His presence in Venice is attested, at a date difficult to determine, by his paintings at Santa Maria della Salute. Cosimo III de' Medici summoned him to Florence where between 1684 and 1686 he painted the vast ceiling of the gallery of the Palazzo Medici-Riccardi *(Apotheosis of the Medici)*. Then, at the invitation of the King of Spain, Charles II, he went to Madrid, arriving in 1692 to execute gigantic paintings in Buen Retiro, then in San Lorenzo at the Escorial, and in the sacristy of the Cathedral of Toledo. The Prado possesses a good fifty of his works. The advent of Philip V brought him back to Naples (1702). Here he achieved the climax of his fame with the *Story of Judith* painted on the ceiling of the Certosa di San Martino (1704). According to contemporary estimates his oil paintings totalled five thousand. His importance in the history of Italian decoration is considerable. Though a Neapolitan, Giordano took up the great Venetian tradition and paved the way for Solimena.   P. C.

GIORGIONE Giorgio Barbarelli, *called* (Castelfranco, 1477/78 - Venice, 1510).

Giorgione stands for all that is most subtle, most captivating and most 'musical' in Venetian painting about 1500. From him derives its constant preoccupation with atmosphere and tonality. Factual knowledge about his career is scant and uncertain, the catalogue of his works incomplete and conjectural. Eminent art lovers, like Walter Pater whose memorable essay of 1873, have felt this ambiguity or, perhaps, this mystery to be appropriate to Giorgione's singular art. His name appears in a document of 1508: Lazzaro Bastiani, Vittore Carpaccio and Vittore Veneziano intervene as arbitrators in one of those arguments, frequent during the Renaissance, between artist and client concerning the amount of the fee. The work in question was the fresco cycle on the façade of the Fondaco dei Tedeschi (there survives a fragment, badly damaged). In 1510 Isabella d'Este was inquiring after a 'nocturne' left behind by the painter recently deceased; this is our evidence for the date of his death (between September and November). But the most important information is supplied by the art lover and collector Marcantonio Michiel who, fifteen years later, toured the collections of Venice and Padua, and counted thirteen pictures by Giorgio del Castelfranco indicating that some of them had been completed by the master's pupils, Titian and Sebastiano del Piombo. Vasari in the second edition of his *Lives,* which appeared in 1568, included information which he may have obtained from Titian in Venice. He describes the rapid evolution of Giorgione: a period of solitary formation, followed by an apprenticeship with Giovanni Bellini, then the discovery of Leonardo and of *sfumato* out of which Giorgione, towards the end of his career, was to make something entirely his own. This is about all we know for certain concerning this young painter who, like Raphael, died young.

The catalogue of his works runs to no more than about twenty items. First comes the *Trial of Moses* (Uffizi), the attribution of which is more certain than that of the *Judgment of Solomon* (Uffizi). The Allendale *Nativity* (Washington, National Gallery), a capital work but difficult to date is perhaps one of the 'nocturnes' so much admired in Giorgione's day. Another group is made of the *Bust of a Shepherd with a Pipe* (Hampton Court), the *Bust of a Youth as Sebastian* (Vienna), the Benson *Holy Family* (Washington) and the *Epiphany* (London), the last mentioned finished, no doubt, by another hand. From about 1500 dates the Leningrad *Judith* transferred from wood to canvas in 1838 and attributed until the end of the last century to Raphael. The altarpiece of 1504, *Madonna with St Francis and St Liberale,* intended for a chapel in the Duomo of Castelfranco, concludes the early phase of Giorgione's development in the course of which he achieved an incomparable mastery in the treatment of graduated colour and atmosphere. To the following years are dated the *Laura* in Vienna, the *Terris Portrait* (San Diego, California), the *Tempest* (Venice, Accademia) and the *Three Philosophers* (Vienna), the last two seen by Michiel in the houses respectively of Gabriel Vendramin and Taddeo Contarini, the *Madonna Reading,* set against a green cloth embroidered with gold, somewhat listless and not quite certainly by Giorgione (Oxford), the *Portrait of a Man* in a bright tunic with the initials V. V. (Berlin), the *Sleeping Venus* in Dresden, and the *Concert Champêtre* at the Louvre. In 1508 the frescoes on the façade of the Fondaco dei Tedeschi, known through the engravings made by Zanetti in 1760-1771 before their almost total disappearance, mark, it seems, the beginning of a new, more monumental phase. To the last years are held to belong the *Self-Portrait* (Brunswick), a fragment of a larger picture known

through an engraving by Hollar (1650), perhaps the two *Singers* at the Galleria Borghese, Rome (there seems to have been a third one at some stage), the *Portrait of an Old Woman* holding a streamer with the words 'Col tempo' (Venice, Accademia), and *Christ Carrying the Cross and Other Figures* (Venice, Scuola di San Rocco).

When Giorgione joined Bellini's workshop, the Venetian artistic milieu was in effervescence. The shift from Mantegna's plasticity to a vision dominated by colour was a recent event and there was still room for innovation. Some historians, like R. Longhi, have discerned an Emilian influence in Giorgione's early works. Their sweetness and formal equilibrium derive, it would seem, from central Italy. In the *Trial of Moses* the landscape is more sensitive and more supple than the figures. This is observable in other paintings as well, until a softened contour and a refined tonality bring about an effortless fusion of figure and landscape, the latter becoming pure vibration. Thus Giorgione developed the manner of Bellini, restraining and intensifying its effects. This may have made Leonardo relevant for him. Though a direct influence, suggested by a picture like the Hermitage *Judith*, need not be pressed, Leonardo's *sfumato* offers a useful analogy for explaining the decisive change brought about by the young Venetian. In the Castelfranco altarpiece the vibration of the atmosphere, which suggests third dimension without perspective devices, can be read as a transposition of Leonardo's *sfumato* into a peculiarly Venetian luminosity of colour. The vertical structure of the painting, at first sight not without awkwardness, enables the artist to relate the landscape modelled by light to the holy personages in the foreground who are illuminated obliquely from the right. The composition is rigorously balanced. The plane of both fore-

GIORGIONE. SLEEPING VENUS. ABOUT 1509. GEMÄLDEGALERIE, DRESDEN.

ground and background is parallel to that of the picture. This is brought out by the distribution of light which governs the whole and establishes its unity. Giorgione's light is not merely the endless play of lights and darks, of veiled appearances and bold forms; it is generated by the vibration of colour which it incorporates in its chiaroscuro, as in the admirable Allendale *Nativity* (Washington, National Gallery). Hence his fondness for those rare moments when twilight, the fires of the evening or the sky overcast with a storm disclose an unknown world in the midst of the familiar one.

These remarkable insights were paralleled by a new technique. According to a tradition recorded by Vasari, Giorgione used brushes and colour straightaway, without any preparatory drawings. This was a departure with important consequences. His palette includes dark reds, golden yellows, browns and,

above all, dazzling whites like vibrations of light, which convey the quality of a sheet of water, of a piece of cloth or of a crystal. This audacity pointed the way for the whole of Venetian painting. Oppositions between cold and warm tones persist throughout Giorgione's work, but in the late paintings the colour becomes considerably darker.

The themes of Giorgione's paintings were varied and the meanings he charged them with were apparently new and personal, which distinguished his work from the uncomplicated *sacre conversazioni* of Bellini. The subjects were, no doubt, suggested by the clients but the artist proceeded to give them his own interpretation in his own style, the content of what he had to contribute being conditioned by a sensibility whose operation was such as to touch the very definition of style. In the *Tempest* the painter develops a narrative theme taken from a story which remains

GIORGIONE.
THE TEMPEST.
ABOUT 1505.
ACCADEMIA,
VENICE.

enigmatic. He is interested in the transient moment and shows nature subject to atmospheric change. The stroke of lightning has, for an instant, robbed things of their usual colour. The two broken columns acquire an eerie aspect which adds to the isolation of the mother lost in the midst of a strange and poignant coming together of the four elements.

X-ray examination of the *Three Philosophers* has revealed underneath figures of the Magi engaged in astrological calculations at the corner of a dark rock; but this does not invalidate the view that Giorgione's purpose was to depict the masters of human knowledge, representing perhaps the three philosophies of antiquity, of the more recent past and of his own day. The philosophers stand each on a different level of a natural platform. The old man has the nobility of knowledge securely acquired; the man in his prime, an Oriental, symbolises certitude; while the adolescent looks at the world with anxious attention. Here too an instantaneous image is sublimated into a universal idea. As is well known, the frescoes on the façade of the Fondaco dei Tedeschi were supposed to be hermetic. There is an esoteric streak in Giorgione deriving no doubt from his humanist contacts.

Giorgione's vision can be both realist to the point of verism, as in the two *Singers* or the *Portrait of an Old Woman* which recalls northern masters, and dreamlike. The two tendencies come together in the *Concert Champêtre* in which everything conspires to sustain a melancholy reverie: the close relations between the female nudes and nature, the harmonious continuity between the curve of a hip and the slope of a hill, the music, the twilight, the pastoral.

The artist's early death combined with the habit prevalent in Renaissance ateliers of completing work left unfinished has made the problem of attributions in many instances well nigh insoluble. There is no doubt that Sebastiano del Piombo, Titian and Palma Vecchio, mentioned by the early chroniclers, set their hands to Giorgione's last canvases, but categorical attributions of the *Three Philosophers* to Sebastiano or the *Concert* to Titian have obviously overshot the mark. The difficulty is in itself a reflection of the decisive turn taken by Venetian painting about 1510. Its classical period begins with Giorgione whose period of activity is contemporary both with the beginnings of Titian's career and the new departures, ventured on by the old Bellini under his pupil's influence. Giorgione put an end to the excesses of narrative and imposed a greater concentration on the painterliness of painting. Statements of his ideas are few but definitive. He consorted with humanists, joining Bembo and his friends in the park at Asolo to discuss music, philosophy and love. But, in contrast to the intellectual painters of Florence, the absolute in man lay for him in the fugitive instant, at the point of change. It is he, no doubt, who invented and associated the two great themes of modern painting, the female nude and landscape. What Giorgione began was not to end until Manet. A. C.

GIORGIONE. JUDITH. HERMITAGE, LENINGRAD.

GIOTTO di BONDONE (Colle di Vespignano, 1266 ? - Florence, 1337). Giotto has always enjoyed great fame as the founder of modern painting. This is partly due to the fact that Dante mentions him in the *Purgatorio* as the most famous painter of the day, who had eclipsed the renown even of Cimabue; and the innumerable commentators on

Dante kept his fame green down to the time of Vasari, who definitely asserted that Giotto was the founder of the modern style. He, and not Cimabue or Cavallini, 'although born among inept craftsmen, by the gift of God revived that art, which had fallen into decay, and he brought it into a state that could be called good'. Giotto was traditionally a pupil of Cimabue, and it is likely that he was also much influenced by the Roman Cavallini (he certainly knew the great Roman works of the late 13th century), so that he did not start without the benefit of the great advances made by these two; and perhaps even more important was the great impetus to naturalism given by the sculptors Niccolò Pisano and his son, Giovanni, Giotto's contemporary. The Arena Chapel, Padua, contains a *Madonna* carved by Giovanni Pisano which shows that Giotto's revolution in painting was paralleled by the works of Giovanni and his father. Indeed, much of the impact of the new art, whether of the Pisani or of Giotto, was due to the activity of St Francis (died 1226, canonised 1228)

GIOTTO. THE DREAM OF JOACHIM (DETAIL).
FRESCO 1303-1305. SCROVEGNI CHAPEL,
PADUA.

and to the *humanitas* in religious matters spread all over Europe by his Order. In the art of Giotto, for the first time, human beings are made the sole means of expression of deep emotions which are Christian in content. The Fall and Redemption of mankind are seen as dramatic events and Giotto's large and simple figures are set in a space which is realised sufficiently to add the force of naturalism to the Christian message they are made to express by gesture and facial expression. No greater contrast with the set types of Byzantine iconography can be imagined, and it may be that the reversion to more hieratic forms which took place after his death was partly due to inability on the part of his successors to create figures capable of bearing such a charge of emotion.

Giotto was born at Vespignano, in Florentine territory, either in 1266/67 or 1276/77; the date being of crucial importance for the understanding of his earliest works. His death is recorded in the contemporary Villani Chronicle, on 8 January, 1336 (= 1337 by our reckoning) and later in the 14th century he is stated to have been 70 when he died. He would thus have been born in 1266/67, but a later tradition, followed by Vasari, gives the date 1276 for his birth. This is the less worthy of credence in that it cannot be traced back to a date prior to the end of the 15th century at the earliest (in one of the two known versions of the *Libro di Antonio Billi*).

The importance attached to establishing the correct date of Giotto's birth is justified by the contribution it would make, if fixed beyond dispute, in solving the ' Assisi Problem', which is perhaps the most debated question in the study of early Italian art. The chronicler Riccobaldo Ferrarese, before 1319 (i.e. in Giotto's lifetime and at the height of his fame) states explicitly that Giotto painted at Assisi, in the Franciscan church. It must therefore be accepted

GIOTTO.
THE MEETING
OF JOACHIM
AND ANNA.
FRESCO. 1303-1305.
SCROVEGNI CHAPEL,
PADUA.

that Giotto painted in Assisi, but the question is, what did he paint and does it still exist ? Until the 19th century it was universally believed that he was responsible for the great narrative cycle of scenes from the *Life of St Francis* in the Basilica di San Francesco, a series of 28 large frescoes forming the official painted biography of the saint in the vast church dedicated to him and in which he is buried. Several art historians, mostly German, have maintained that this cycle is not by Giotto—to whom it has erroneously been attributed since the mid-15th century at least— but by some other, unknown artist. No other works by this painter are known and he appears to have been given this very important commission, which involved the invention of a pictorial equivalent to the official biography recently compiled by

St Bonaventura, without having given any previous proof of his powers in work that has come down to us. This view, which is less popular now than it was, is based on the alleged impossibility of reconciling the style of the St Francis scenes with the fresco cycle, certainly by Giotto, in the Arena Chapel at Padua. This, which is also recorded by Riccobaldo Ferrarese as well as by other writers, is datable with reasonable certainty *ca* 1305-1310. Those who refuse to attribute the Assisi frescoes to Giotto argue that they must have been painted about 1300 and are totally different in style from the Paduan cycle of a few years later. The dates are, however, not conclusive: first, the Assisi frescoes cannot be dated with certainty, and the date 1300 is based on hypotheses about the patron at Assisi which cannot be sub-

GIOTTO. NATIVITY (DETAIL). FRESCO. 1303-1305.
SCROVEGNI CHAPEL, PADUA.

all'Arena was clearly built as a frame for a great fresco cycle and was consecrated on the Feast of the Annunciation (25 March), 1305. In all probability, the frescoes were begun soon after that date and were certainly finished by about 1309/10. The whole of the west wall is occupied by a huge *Last Judgement,* including a portrait of the donor accompanied by angels and holding a model of the church. The rest of the nave, but not the choir, is covered with four tiers of frescoes. The top tier contains scenes from the lives of SS Joachim and Anna, after which the Incarnation is symbolised on the chancel arch by an *Annunciation* and from then on the next two tiers are taken up with scenes from the Life and Passion of Christ. The main cycle ends with *Pentecost,* and the fourth and lowest tier is devoted to grisaille allegorical figures of the Virtues and Vices.

Analysis of almost any one of these frescoes will make clear the power and range of Giotto's conception of the drama of Redemption, and, at the same time, the qualities which put him apart from his contemporaries and were scarcely understood by his successors. The *Suitors waiting for the Miracle of the Rods* has an air of hushed expectancy and nervous tension which it would be difficult to parallel around 1300; it is obtained by the simple compositional device of dividing the field horizontally and vertically. The *Meeting of Joachim and Anna at the Golden Gate* shows Giotto's mastery of simple architectural forms as compositional elements: in this case the gate is an essential part of the story, so it is made to provide two major vertical elements—the towers—and a great arch which swoops down on to the two important figures. They stand framed by the left-hand tower, and the line of the rusticated base of the tower runs into the arch at the point where the two heads meet and the two bodies unite into a single monumental form. At the

stantiated. If Giotto were born in 1276, it is clear that he could not have worked at Assisi much before 1300, and even then would have been rather young for so important a commission: those who accept his authorship of the St Francis cycle naturally maintain the earlier birth-date as the more probable.

Whatever views may be held on the Assisi problem it is universally admitted that the Arena Chapel, built by a member of the Scrovegni family, contains the works which are the touchstone for all questions of Giotto's style as well as for the understanding of his dramatic sympathy and an unprecedented power of narrative, both in concentration on essentials and in the faculty for discerning the one telling detail which will strike home to the beholder, that make Giotto stand apart from all other painters of his time and for centuries before. The chapel of Santa Maria Annunziata extreme left is a blank space, separating the leading figures from the servant who enters from behind the frame: this gap, or caesura, is the most important dramatic element of Giotto's compositional repertory, and powerfully reinforces the effect produced by his expressive faces (the servant girls at the right). In these ways our attention is focussed on the point which has the concentrated attention of the actors themselves.

Apart from the Assisi frescoes there are several other works which can claim to be by Giotto and to date from a period before the Arena Chapel or even before 1300. It is likely that Giotto studied in Rome and he probably returned there at about the time of the great Jubilee of 1300. He is known to have worked for Cardinal Stefaneschi and in Old St Peter's, but there are now only three surviving works from these important commissions. The first, and far the most important, is the huge mosaic of the Ship of the Church *(La Navicella)*, which was transferred from Old St Peter's to the present Basilica: this, though certainly Giotto's, was almost entirely remade in the 17th century and is thus useless as a guide to style. However, two fragments, in the Grotte Vaticane, and in San Pietro Ispano at Boville Ernica, near Rome, seem to show the original style. A fresco fragment of *Boniface VIII proclaiming the Jubilee,* in San Giovanni in Laterano, Rome, has been attributed to Giotto and recent cleaning shows that it has affinities with the Assisi frescoes. The third and most problematic work is the polyptych in the Vatican, which seems to be, beyond doubt, the Stefaneschi Altarpiece from Old St Peter's. It is a very poor work indeed and raises in the most acute form the problem of authenticity, since it has every claim to be regarded as a documented work. At least three other works are signed: the altarpieces in the Louvre, in Bologna, and Santa Croce in Florence, but they

are also of very much lower quality than the Padua frescoes; on the other hand, the *Ognissanti Madonna* (Uffizi) is neither signed nor well documented, yet it is universally accepted as an authentic work. The *Dormition of the Virgin* (Berlin) has also been held, on style alone, to be by Giotto himself. Clearly, the answer is partly to be found in the practice, common in the Middle Ages and long after, of putting the master's name on works that merely came out of his workshop—the modern conception of artistic originality did not exist in the 14th century.

Two other controversial works must be mentioned: the Crucifix in Santa Maria Novella and the *Madonna* in San Giorgio

GIOTTO. NOLI ME TANGERE (DETAIL). FRESCO. 1303-1305. SCROVEGNI CHAPEL, PADUA.

GIOTTO. APPARITION OF ST FRANCIS
(DETAIL). FRESCO. BETWEEN 1317 AND 1323.
SANTA CROCE, FLORENCE.

alla Costa, both in Florence. The Crucifix is perhaps the finest of all these attributed works, but it is not very similar in style either to the Assisi frescoes or the Stefaneschi Altarpiece. Those who accept that the Santa Maria Novella Crucifix is identical with one mentioned, as by Giotto, in a document of 1312 usually date it about 1295.

Giotto's later style is generally agreed to be found in two sets of frescoes in Santa Croce, Florence. He is thought to have decorated four chapels in this, the main Franciscan church in Florence. The Bardi Chapel contains a series of scenes from the *Life of St Francis;* according to the views of the spectator they are like or unlike the Assisi scenes. They are certainly superior and this may be held to prove that they are therefore later. The other chapel, of the Peruzzi family, contains scenes from the *Lives of St John Baptist* and *St John the Evangelist.* Both cycles may be expected to shed new light on Giotto's style in the near future, for the Bardi frescoes were cleaned, with astonishing results, in the late 1950's, and the Peruzzi frescoes are now (1961) being worked on. No dates can be assigned with any confidence to these works. Giotto is known to have been in Naples in the early 1330's: he is referred to as a member of the royal household on 20 January, 1330, and he was probably there until 1332/33, but no work by him survives and his late style is only fitfully reflected in the works of local artists.

In 1334 Giotto's fame was such that his fellow-townsmen made him overseer of the cathedral works, on account of his fame as a painter and not because he was an architect. However, he began to build the Campanile, but it was changed after his death in 1337. The history of Florentine painting from then until the 15th century is the history of Giotto's influence and the way in which it was largely misunderstood by his followers, known collectively as the *Giotteschi,* especially Daddi, the Gaddi, Maso, Orcagna and his brothers.   P. M.

GIOVANNI da MILANO Giovanni da Caverrago, *called* (active between 1346 and 1369). Originally from Como, he was trained in Lombardy, probably by Stefano and Giusto di Menabuoi, who taught him the principles of Giotto's art, and he was also influenced by Vitale da Bologna and Tommaso da Modena. He settled in Florence, obtained citizenship there in 1366, and already by 1365 was well enough known to get a commission from the 'capitani' of Or San Michele for frescoes in the Rinuccini Chapel in Santa Croce. Those frescoes, representing the lives of the Virgin and of Mary Magdalen, the *Pietà* (Florence, Accademia) and the polyptych from the church of the Ognissanti (Uffizi), give us an idea of the art of Giovanni da Milano. His lyricism and sensitivity already anticipate Sassetta, with whom he has been confused, and the Tuscan masters of international gothic. The beautiful colour range, the homely poetic inspiration and the feeling for space of his compositions, in which Lombard influences are mixed with Sienese charm, make him the greatest painter in Lombardy, in the 14th century.　　　s. B.

GIOVANNI da MODENA (Bologna, active during the first half of the 15th century). We can learn very little from documents concerning Giovanni da Modena, but a series of frescoes is attributed to him in the churches of Bologna (particularly one *Last Judgment* painted in San Petronio about 1410); also some panels, amongst which is a large *Crucifix* in the Pinacoteca at Bologna. These works full of power and pathos, mark him out as the most original of the Bolognese painters of the early Quattrocento. An artist of violence and extremes, he emerges as one of the last Italians to use a gothic manner of expression.　　　M. L.

GIOVANNI di PAOLO (Siena, *ca* 1400 - Siena, *ca* 1482). He never left the town where he was born and where his name is mentioned for the first time in 1423. The influences on his formative years were those of Paolo di Giovanni Fei, Taddeo di Bartolo, then Gentile da Fabriano (at Siena in 1426) and later on Sassetta, but in the course of his long life his artistic personality became increasingly more individual. For a long time he was neglected and regarded as an inferior painter, but he is now considered one of the great Sienese masters of the 15th century. Berenson called him 'the El Greco of the Quattrocento', referring probably to the extremely elongated forms he sometimes gave his figures, in his *Heaven,* for example. His nervous draughtsmanship, violent colours, vigorous and imaginative interpretation of reality have caused the terms expressionism and even surrealism to be used in connection with him. It is a fact that his works are imbued with a dreamlike atmosphere, intensified the further he moved away from his models. His principal works are: the *Madonna* of 1426 (Castelnovo Berardenga); the polyptych of 1442 (Uffizi); *The Presentation of Christ at the*

GIOVANNI DA MILANO. MARTYRDOM OF
ST CATHERINE. PANEL FROM THE PREDELLA OF
THE POLYPTYCH OF PRATO. MUSEO CIVICO, PRATO.

Temple of 1447-1449 (Siena, Pinacoteca); the extraordinary *St Nicholas of Tolentino saving a sinking Ship* (small picture from a predella, Philadelphia, Johnson Collection, about 1455); *The Last Judgment, Heaven and Hell* (Siena, Pinacoteca, about 1460-1465); the cycle of John the Baptist (Chicago, Art Institute).   P.-H. M.

GIOVANNI da UDINE Giovanni di Francesco Ricamador, *called* (Udino, 1487 - Rome, 1564). Trained in Friuli by a local painter, then soon leaving for Venice where he may have known Giorgione, Giovanni was captivated by the gracious and appealing style of Raphael and became his regular assistant. According to Vasari, Raphael entrusted Giovanni with the painting of the organ in *St Cecilia*. Giovanni's great opportunity came in the Vatican Loggie where he was allowed to develop his *grotteschi*

GIOVANNI DI PAOLO. ST NICHOLAS OF TOLENTINO
SAVING A SINKING SHIP.
JOHNSON COLLECTION, PHILADELPHIA.

(1517-1519). He created a bizarre and fantastic world of great ornamental force by covering his stucco surfaces with a mass of motifs taken from the Golden House of Nero. Leo X was delighted. The ornament became fashionable and Giovanni worked it at the Villa Madama (1520), at the Farnesina and at the Palazzo Vecchio in Florence. He carried the formulas of Raphael's workshop to the palaces of Udine, Venice (Palazzo Grimani) and Genoa where he went with Pierino del Vaga. In this way Giovanni, as Vasari realised, was one of the great renovators of the language of decoration in the west.   A. C.

GIULIO ROMANO Giulio Pippi, *called* (Rome, 1492 or 1499 - Mantua, 1546). Of the generation known as that of the 'heirs' the most powerful personality was, without doubt, Giulio Pippi. The acquired name indicates sufficiently his importance in Roman circles and the authority he enjoyed as the leading representative of the style in vogue. His career falls into two distinct parts: continuation of Raphael's work at the Vatican, then, from about 1527 onwards, service with the Gonzaga in Mantua where Giulio's creativity was given quite exceptional scope. His forceful temperament had already singled him out in the team working on the Stanze under Raphael's direction. In 1515-1516 he was made responsible for translating into paint the master's cartoons for the Stanza dell'Incendio; the *Battle of Ostia* is in his own hand. Then, in the Loggie, he co-ordinated the team work on the 'Bible of Raphael' which was set out in the midst of a new decor consisting of medallions and *grotteschi*. At least six scenes in the Loggia di Psiche at the Farnesina are by Giulio. He is also partly responsible for pictures like the *Holy Family of Francis I* (Louvre) and the *Transfiguration* (Vatican). Among religious paintings the *Holy*

GIULIO ROMANO.
THE MARRIAGE OF
PSYCHE AND CUPID.
FRESCO. 1527-1531.
PALAZZO DEL TÈ,
MANTUA.

Family known as '*La Perla*' (Prado) and the *Madonna della Gatta* (Naples) are two masterpieces of Giulio's sprung from Raphael's teaching. After the latter's death (1520) Giulio continued to work on the Stanze, the commission being eventually confirmed by Clement VII. His great achievement is the Sala di Costantino (1517-1525) with its grandiloquent battle scene, which left a lasting imprint on artistic taste in Rome. Giulio also worked at the villa of Cardinal Giulio de' Medici on Monte Mario (Villa Madama) where one finds the prototype of large loggie decorated in the classical manner.

In Mantua Giulio was welcomed by Federigo Gonzaga to whom he had been introduced by Baldassare Castiglione. His great opportunity was the Palazzo del Tè erected in the fields to the south of the city. He was made both its architect and its decorator and could thus give free rein to his vitality and his invention. All kinds of unusual departures in the arches or in the use of the orders attest his striving for originality. In the decoration of the interior this shows itself in the contrast betwen the cycle fraught with terror and seething with movement in the Sala dei Giganti and the voluptuous images of the Sala di Psiche (1527-1531). When Charles V visited the Palace in 1530, it was inaugurated as the seat of court festivals for which it was intended to provide the

GIUSTO DE' MENABUOI. NATIVITY. ABOUT 1376.
BAPTISTERY, PADUA.

perfect setting. This boldness and these contrasts are a constant feature of Giulio's undertakings: drawings for the decoration of the choir of Verona Cathedral, tapestry cartoons on the theme of Scipio Africanus, a mythological cycle (six pictures in Great Britain), *Nativity with St Longinus and John the Baptist* (Louvre).

Giulio Romano both carried further the late manner of Raphael, with its reddish browns and its harder forms, and developed the principles of classical composition. His rich temperament captured something of the power and the animation of Michelangelo. Finally, his fertile imagination led him to create, beyond classical dignity and grace, a new type of decoration peculiarly suited, with its emphasis on illusionism and theatrical

splendour, to life at court. From this point of view the Palazzo del Tè is the well-spring of mannerism.   A. C.

GIUNTA PISANO Giunta Capitini, *called* (Pisa, beginning of 13th century, active until 1254). In 1236, Fra Elia, the first General of the Franciscan Order, called Giunta to Assisi to work on the decoration of the new basilica of St Francis. Nothing remains of his work there, except the record of a painted cross which bore the inscription: *Frater Elias fieri fecit ... Giunta Pisanus me pinxit ... A.D. 1236.* Other painted crosses are attributed to him (Pisa, San Paolo a Ripa d'Arno; Turin, Gualino Collection). He is usually considered as the originator of the type of painted cross which Cimabue was to raise to its highest expression at the end of the century. Christ is no longer represented as an impassive image with wide open eyes, but as dying or dead, his face and body distorted with pain. These two very different renderings of the same subject are both Byzantine, but the second, which is so often found in the Balkan countries, is more 'provincial'. Its use in Italy during the Duecento coincided with the spread of Franciscan ideas and revealed an evolution of religious feeling.   P.-H. M.

GIUSTO de' MENABUOI (Padua, active from 1363 to 1391). Born and trained in Florence, he worked for fifteen years in Lombardy, Viboldone in particular, and at Padua after 1370. It is here that he left behind his chief works, some frescoes at the Santo, the Eremitani and, above all, the Baptistery. The latter cycle, which he completed in about 1376, is one of the most complex of his time. Although he portrays the world according to Christian doctrine, his work does reveal a certain gravity, subtly archaic, which brings to mind the solemnity of Rome. However, the grandeur of his forms does not preclude a lyrical feeling, nor a delicate touch in their execution which he probably learnt from Stefano Fiorentino, the most original of Giotto's pupils.   M. L.

GONZAGA (The). For two centuries, from the rise of the great Lodovico, second Marchese of Mantua (1414-1478), to the death of Ferdinando I, sixth Duke (1587-1626), the Gonzaga never ceased to encourage the arts by their lavish patronage and expensive tastes that contributed to their final ruin. Under the reign of Lodovico II and his wife, Barbara of Brandenburg, Mantua became one of the most splendid courts in Italy. It was frequented by many scholars and artists, including the sculptor, Luca Fancelli, Leone Battista Alberti and Andrea Mantegna. This cultural tradition was maintained by the sons of Lodovico, Cardinal Francesco Gonzaga (1444-1483) and Federigo I (1442-1484), then by his grandson, Francesco II (1466-1519), admirably helped by his wife, Isabella d'Este, thanks to whom the reputation of Mantua was at its highest at the beginning of the 16th century. To Federigo II, first Duke of Mantua (1500-1540), we owe the building and decoration by Giulio Romano of the celebrated Palazzo del Tè. He was followed by Francesco III, Guglielmo, Vicenzo I and his sons, Francesco IV and Ferdinando. The generosity of this dynasty of patrons was uninterrupted. Under Vicenzo I (1587-1610), their patronage reached its peak. Day after day, celebrations and performances succeeded each other. The most famous foreign painters (Rubens, Van Dyck) visited Mantua and the private museum of the dukes, the Galleria del Palazzo, acquired masterpieces which made it into a veritable school of art. Ferdinando I still kept up, or tried to keep up, this standard of living, in spite of a treasury run down by his father's lavish bounties and by the expenses of the Montferrat

ANDREA MANTEGNA. PORTRAIT OF THE FUTURE CARDINAL FRANCESCO GONZAGA. 1461. MUSEO NAZIONALE, NAPLES.

var. But ruin was near; the most precious pieces from the Galleria were sold and scattered for ever during the short reign of Vicenzo II, Ferdinando's brother and successor.

A catalogue of Gonzaga portraiture would surprise us by its length, which is the best proof of the family's sincere interest for the arts. Busts and medals are innumerable. As for paintings, we shall mention only, among the most remarkable, the frescoes in the Camera degli Sposi (Mantua, Reggia dei Gonzaga), the portraits of *Cardinal Francesco* by Mantegna (Naples, Museo Nazionale) and of *Lodovico the Protonotario,* son of Lodovico II, also by Mantegna (Uffizi); *Isabella d'Este* by Titian (Vienna, Kunsthistorisches Museum) and by Pordenone (Milan, Castello

BENOZZO GOZZOLI. PROCESSION OF THE MAGI.
DETAIL FROM THE PROCESSION OF THE
MOORISH KING. PALAZZO MEDICI, FLORENCE.
ACCORDING TO TRADITION, THE THREE PAGES
ARE DAUGHTERS OF PIERO IL GUTTOSO: BIANCA,
MARIA, NANNINA.

holm (Royal Museum), a sketch by
Rubens.   P.-H. M.

GOZZOLI Benozzo di Lese, *called* (Florence, 1420 - Pistoia, 1497). Gozzoli's
agreeable and precious genius reflects his
training. He began as a goldsmith's
apprentice, then worked with Ghiberti
on the Baptistery doors (1441). Later
he assisted Fra Angelico whom he
followed to Rome and Orvieto. He
spent some time in central Italy. He
painted a cycle for the Franciscans of
Montefalco (Convent of San Fortunato),
and another for the nuns of Santa Rosa
in Viterbo (lost). His reputation as a
decorator was sufficiently established by
1459 for the Medici to engage him to
paint the chapel in their new palace in
Florence. Benozzo gave the best of his
verve and fantasy on this occasion. He
was less original in his altarpieces like the
*Virgin and Child enthroned among Angels
and Saints* (London, National Gallery),
painted for the Compagnia di San Marco
in Florence (1461). His reputation as
a fresco painter earned him commissions
in San Gimignano at the church of
Sant'Agostino (1463-1465), then at the
Palazzo del Popolo; also two altarpieces,
one of which for Sant'Andrea (*Madonna
and Child,* 1466). From San Gimignano
he went to Pisa where he covered an
entire wall of the Camposanto with Old
Testament subjects. This kind of provincial exile—he stayed for seventeen
years—seems to have suited Gozzoli.
His flowery style was beginning to date
and, in fact, went quite well with the
large compositions executed by Traini a
century earlier.

Beside the great fresco cycles and some
altarpieces, Benozzo's workshop produced a large number of banners and
devotional paintings on wood and
canvas. It contributed to the dissemina-
tion in Umbria and Tuscany of a bright,
smiling, pretty type of painting that
sums up the dominant taste of the
'sixties. Gozzoli's art is that of the

Sforzesco), not forgetting the sketch by
Leonardo in the Uffizi; *Federigo II* by
Titian (Prado), *Eleanora,* wife of Duke
Guglielmo, by Titian (Kassel, Gemälde-
galerie); the *Family of Vicenzo I* by
Rubens (Mantua, Palazzo Comunale);
the portraits of *Vicenzo I* and his second
wife *Eleanora de' Medici* by Porbus and
of *Ferdinando* by Domenichino. In
Mantua, there is a full-length portrait of
Vicenzo II by Susterman, and in Stock-

BENOZZO GOZZOLI.
THE PROCESSION
OF THE MAGI.
FRESCO. DETAIL.
1459.
PALAZZO MEDICI,
FLORENCE.

story-teller, graceful and witty rather than stylistically inventive. In the Medici Chapel the procession of the Magi making its way through a dream-like Tuscany is composed, in accordance with tradition, of people of all ages in festive headgear and exotic clothes—a recollection, perhaps, of the Greeks and Orientals present at the Council of Florence in 1439, and in any case an echo of the pageants organised periodically by the Confraternity of the Magi at San Marco. A sky punctuated by cypress trees and a landscape articulated by stone terraces envelop a gay and elegant humanity. We find it again in the Augustine cycle at San Gimignano and in the Biblical scenes at Pisa, where, for instance, the vine-growers of the Arno valley and Tuscan burghers watch from an arbour the adventures of Noah and his sons. Disarmingly voluble and naive, Gozzoli made use of the inventions of contemporary art. At the end of the 15th century he was already viewed with indulgence as a master of the old generation.   A. C.

GUARDI Francesco (Venice, 1712 - Venice, 1793) *and* Giannantonio (Venice, 1699 - Venice, 1760). The Guardi are a good example of a *bottega* (half studio

FRANCESCO GUARDI. VISIT OF THE DOGE TO SANTA MARIA DELLA SALUTE. LOUVRE, PARIS.

half shop) in the Venetian tradition. The family came from the Trentino and had been ennobled in the 17th century. Giacomo, the father (1678-1716), was the founder of the painting concern. The elder son, Giannantonio, was born in Vienna in 1699. It was he, no doubt, who trained his brother Francesco, the *vedutista,* and the two worked together until Giannantonio's death in 1760. Their sister, Cecilia, married Tiepolo, which is not sufficient for assuming that this painter worked with either of her brothers. In 1756 Giannantonio, one of the founders of the Venetian Academy, joined it as a figure painter; Francesco, born in 1712, did not become a member until 1784 as a painter of views. In fact it is almost impossible to tell what in the work of the two brothers belongs to each. The major influence that appears in their work seems to have been that of Sebastiano Ricci, although borrowings can be discerned from Tintoretto and Veronese.

The two artists seem to have worked jointly on scenes from *Gerusalemme Liberata* and in particular on the canvases decorating the organ loft of the church of Angelo Raffaelle, delicate and free, relating through a luminous haze the *Story of Tobias* (1750). The *Ridotto* and the *Parlatorio delle monache,* delightful genre pictures, are more commonly attributed to Francesco. With great colouristic charm, they are a valuable document for the festive aspect of Venetian life in the permanent carnival of the 18th century. They seem to date from 1745-1750 and are rather close to Longhi, though free of that artist's naive clumsiness.

Roughly from the middle of the century onwards, Francesco seems to have devoted himself primarily to the painting of *vedute.* He was not nearly as successful as Canaletto, a fact that gave rise to the legend that he imitated that artist. In propounding this theory his contemporaries thought they were doing him honour, and indeed the *Venetian Festivals,* of which Brustolon made engravings, seem to derive from Canaletto; expert opinion here is not unanimous.

But in general Guardi differs profoundly from his senior and rival. He has been well described as almost an impressionist. His lines instead of being dry and, in buildings, as straight as though traced with a ruler, seem to vibrate in a diffuse atmosphere. He plants his figures in a spirit that is quite foreign to Canaletto. One simple stroke, unerringly placed, is enough for him to indicate a silhouette or a movement. These diminutive beings are alive with their characteristic attitudes and professional or class gestures.

His sepia wash drawings render with an incredible weightlessness the slightly shimmering light of the city. Among these masterpieces of painting, as sought after today as they were neglected during the painter's lifetime, particular mention may be made of the series of four pictures from the Gulbenkian Foundation, now in Lisbon.   P. C.

GUARIENTO di ARPO (active in Padua from 1338 to 1368/70). A painter who was probably a native of Padua, he is considered as a master of his art. His importance would have remained local, had he not been summoned in 1365 to Venice to decorate the Sala del Maggior Consiglio of the Palazzo Ducale. All past historians mention the two frescoes which he executed there: *Paradise* and the *Coronation of the Virgin,* works which were partly destroyed and of which only fragments have been preserved. Everyone agrees in attributing to him the frescoes which decorate the choir of the Church of the Eremitani at Padua and the Chapel at Carrara. The Museo Civico, Padua, owns several pictures by Guariento and his only signed work, a *Crucifix,* is in the Pinacoteca, Bassano.   A. L.

FRANCESCO GUARDI. THE RIO DEI MENDICANTI. ACCADEMIA CARRARA, BERGAMO.

GUERCINO Giovanni Francesco Barbieri, *called* (Cento, near Bologna, 1591 - Bologna, 1666). A pupil of Ludovico Carracci, he retained from his master what he had learnt of the effect of light, consolidating it by a period in Venice (1618), but to this he added a robust naturalism which supplied a truly Bolognese answer to Caravaggio's Roman school. When he actually went to Rome (1621), Guercino established his reputation there by a series of huge works (the *Aurora* in the Casino of the Villa Ludovisi, 1621; the vast *Burial of St Petronilla* painted for St Peter's, 1622-1623, now in the Museo Capitolino). Little by little, however, the powerful drama of his compositions, with their massive, restless figures and their dark, stormy colouring broken by violent flashes of light, gives way under the influence of Guido Reni and the 'classicist' circles in Rome to a calmer style, where his forms are more stable, and where he no longer scorns to make gracefulness his aim. This refined style belongs to the painter's latter decades when he had finally returned to set up his workshop at Bologna (1642). Throughout the whole of his work, however, we do find an almost romantic inspiration which fires not only his grandiose decorations with a great sense of poetry, from the most unpromising religious subjects (*St Gregory the Great with St Ignatius and St Francis Xavier* about 1625/26, London, Denis Mahon Collection) to the stirring episodes from the Bible (*Jacob Blessing the Sons of Joseph,* 1620; the *Angel Appearing to Hagar,* 1652-1653, ibid.), but also the pagan works (the *Death of Dido,* about 1630, Rome, Galleria Spada) —not to mention his magnificent pen drawings where the firm, thick strokes show up his skill and confidence in dealing with tone values.   J. T.

GUIDO da SIENA (Siena, 13th century). The famous *Virgin and Child* in the Palazzo Pubblico, Siena, which is one of the first examples of Sienese painting, shows how the artist, while still following the traditional iconography, tried to free himself from the strict rules of Byzantine art. The Virgin is seated and the Child has his legs crossed; both look majestic without stiffness. The work is signed and dated at the bottom of the picture: *Me Guido de Senis . . . depinxit . . . A.D. MCCXXI.* For stylistic reasons, the date 1221 is not usually accepted by modern critics and the painting is believed to be at least 40 years later. But the inscription is clearly legible and, according to the experts, reveals no alterations or corrections. We must either suppose that the artist was very much in advance of his time, or account for his style by the obvious repainting done about the end of the 13th or beginning of the 14th century. A number of Madonnas and small panels with scenes from the Life of Christ (Museums in Siena, Arezzo, San Gimignano, Utrecht, etc.) are attributed to Guido and his school.   P.-H. M.

GUERCINO. VENUS AND ADONIS. DRAWING. MUSÉE DE BAYONNE.

J - L

JACOBELLO del FIORE (active from 1394 - Venice, 1439). He is documented from 1394, and his style shows him to have been the most important Venetian artist of the transition from the 14th century, semi-Byzantine style to the international gothic style practised in Venice by Gentile da Fabriano, who influenced Jacobello's later works. The earliest surviving signed and dated work by him is a triptych of the *Madonna della Misericordia,* of 1407, formerly in a private collection in New York. Most of his documented works are in Venice, the earliest being the *Lion of St Mark* in the Palazzo Ducale (1415) and the latest the *Coronation of the Virgin* (1438, Accademia). This is a copy of the famous picture in the Palazzo Ducale by Guariento: Jacobello's painting was formerly signed and dated, but the inscriptions are now lost.   P. M.

JULIUS II Giuliano della Rovere, Pope (Albissola, near Savona, 1443 - Rome, 1513). Julius II, the nephew of Sixtus IV, became a cardinal at twenty-eight (1471) and was elected Pope in 1503. From the beginning, he was a patron of the arts. Far from detracting from his political and religious activities, this patronage was for him closely associated with them. His aim was the renewed supremacy of Rome, over Florence in particular, which he wanted to ensure in the arts as in everything else. The building of St Peter's was begun in his pontificate and entrusted to Bramante with important work at the Vatican also, where he started a collection of antique sculpture. As early as 1505, he commissioned his own tomb, but Michelangelo had hardly started on that gigantic undertaking when he commissioned him to do the ceiling of the Sistine Chapel (1508-1512). At the same time, he asked Raphael, then only 25 whose genius he discerned and preferred to better known masters of the time, to decorate rooms in his new suite. The *Stanza della Segnatura* (1509-1511) was the only one to be completed in his lifetime.   P.-H. M.

LÉON X Giovanni de' Medici, Pope (Florence, 1475 - Rome, 1521). He was the son of Lorenzo il Magnifico and Clarissa Orsini and was introduced by his tutor, Angelo Poliziano, to the splendid culture of the golden age of Florence. He was elected Pope at the age of 38 on 11th March, 1513. He died in December 1521, after a short reign which was brilliant enough to justify the flattering title of the 'Age of Leo X'. His reputation as a patron of the arts rests on a not always judicious generosity and has been criticised. Leo X partly abandoned the great undertakings of the previous Pope and he was not so good a patron either to Michelangelo, or to Leonardo, who stayed in Rome from 1513 to 1515, before settling in France, as Julius II or Francis I. On the other hand, during his papacy, Raphael finished the *Stanza d'Eliodoro* at the Vatican, painted the *Fire in the Borgo,* designed and executed, with the help of the decorator, Giovanni da Udine, the *Loggie,* and painted the portrait of the Pope attended by the cardinals,

LEONARDO DA VINCI. THE VIRGIN OF THE ROCKS.
ABOUT 1483-1487. LOUVRE, PARIS.

Lodovico de Rossi and Giulio de'
Medici. For the art historian, the
name of Leo X is inseparable from
that of Raphael.   P.-H. M.

LEONARDO da VINCI (Vinci, 1452 - Le
Clos-Lucé, near Amboise, 1519). Heir
to all the ideals of the Quattrocento,
Leonardo also marks the beginning of
the High Renaissance. A pure Florentine, his most lasting influence was in
northern Italy and Tuscany. Although
an accomplished artist, it is as a man of
science and an inventor that he has
become one of the most famous figures
of the Renaissance. Son of Ser Piero,
notary to the Medici family, he was born
in the small village of Vinci, near

Pistoia. About 1469, he was admitted
to Verrocchio's studio, where he was
trained in all the various techniques and
distinguished himself by painting the
angels on the left side of the *Baptism of
Christ* (Uffizi) and the small *Annunciation* (Louvre), a fragment which may
have belonged to the predella of the
Pistoia Altarpiece. From 1478 onwards,
he began to get important official orders,
such as an altarpiece for the St Bernardo
chapel in the Palazzo Vecchio, an order
which he handed over to Filippino Lippi,
then in 1481 the *Adoration of the Magi*
for the monks of San Donato which he
left unfinished (Uffizi). In addition to
several Madonnas (Munich, Leningrad),
this early period includes the *St Jerome*
in the Vatican and the *Ginevra de' Benci*
(Vaduz, Liechtenstein Collection). In
1481-1482, he left for Milan; in a famous
letter offering his services, Leonardo
sets out his universal qualifications as
a technician and artist. The real reasons for his leaving are not clear; Leonardo could have been given a commission by Ludovico il Moro, but
Leonardo may also have been the
cause of it himself, perhaps wanting to
try his luck in the service of a patron
who was both amenable and generous.
    Leonardo first of all made studies for
the statue of Francesco Sforza on horseback for Ludovico, but ten years later
it was still unfinished. On april 25th,
1483, the Confraternity of the Immaculate Conception commissioned a painting with side panels for the church of
San Francesco. This is the *Virgin of the
Rocks* (Louvre). In 1506 this painting
was copied (the *Virgin of the Rocks*,
London, National Gallery) and two
panels with angels were added by a
pupil, Ambrogio da Predis.
    The *Lady with an Ermine* (Cracow,
Czartoryski Collection), the portrait of
Cecilia Gallerani and the *Portrait of a
Musician* (unfinished, Ambrosiana) date
from this period. At this time Leonardo
was concerned with problems of archi-

146

tecture; he took part in the discussions on
the Milan cathedral spire (1487) and
later on the cathedral at Pavia. He was
engaged on the *Last Supper* for the
refectory of Santa Maria delle Grazie
from 1495 to 1497 at the same time as he
was decorating the Sala delle Asse for
the duke's castle. These varied activities were combined with personal
studies with which he was chiefly
occupied from 1490 onwards; he started
to develop his *Treatise on Painting* and
numerous theoretical studies.

In February, 1500, he was at Mantua
at the court of Isabella d'Este, whose
portrait he probably drew (cartoon in
the Louvre), but in April he was at
Venice and planning the defence against
the Turks. On April 24th, he arrived
at Florence, where his activities attracted
everyone's attention and where he stayed
until 1506. In October 1503, he
received the commission for the *Battle
of Anghiari,* a fresco intended to decorate
the Palazzo Vecchio. Several months
later, Michelangelo was invited to
paint the opposite wall. It was during
this year that Leonardo must have
started the Mona Lisa portrait, the
Gioconda (Louvre) which was finished in
1507 and which he took to France.
The *St Anne* cartoon (Louvre) belongs
to the same period. Raphael was
deeply impressed by Leonardo's works
when he arrived in Florence in 1504.
In 1506, however, abandoning the
Palazzo Vecchio fresco unfinished, Leonardo responded to Charles d'Amboise's
insistent offers and returned to Milan,
where he found fresh scope in sculpture
with the monument to Trivulzio, a
condottiere under Louis XII of France.
In 1512, however, after the French were
driven out, Leonardo was obliged to
leave the city. He entered the service
of Giuliano de' Medici whom he followed to Rome after his brother Giovanni's
election as Pope Leo X in 1513. Leonardo was then accompanied by Melzi
and Salai, his faithful pupils. Giuliano,

LEONARDO DA VINCI. THE VIRGIN OF THE ROCKS.
ABOUT 1506-1508. NATIONAL GALLERY, LONDON.

however, died in 1515. Leonardo
decided to accept the invitation of the
new French king, Francis I. He left
for Amboise where he settled on Ascension Day in 1517. As engineer to the
king, he drew up plans for the castle of
Romorantin and organised several court
masques. He died at Clos-Lucé on
2nd May, 1519.

We can understand Leonardo only
by starting with Verrocchio; it was
under his influence that Leonardo began
to develop his encyclopaedic investiga-
tions. As painter and sculptor, he owes
his gentle technique and finish to this
studio. His early works are clearly
inspired by the desire to surprise by
horror or fascinate by a suave and mysterious expression. But Leonardo's role

LEONARDO DA VINCI. VIRGIN AND CHILD
WITH ST ANNE. ABOUT 1506-1510.
LOUVRE, PARIS.

was to perfect the studio's formulas; he must have carried out many of these youthful works in the style of his master, who, in return, made very skilful use of Leonardo's discoveries; for example, in the composition of the Pistoia Altarpiece. The unfinished *Adoration of the Magi* already reveals how complex his researches were.

When Leonardo settled in Milan, this arrival in a new surrounding marked his emergence as an artist and virtuoso; possibly he never realised all his capabilities in the city of his youth. In the *Virgin of the Rocks* the traditional subject of the Madonna is given a personal interpretation; the meeting of the two children anticipates the Passion and

troubles Mary, a theme taken up later in the *Madonna with the Scales* (lost, but known from copies) and the *St Anne* (Louvre). Here Leonardo also develops the *sfumato* technique, which merges contour and volume in a new, more suggestive realism where his newly discovered means of expression have full play; colour becomes less independent in these subtle gradations of light and shade, which in turn accentuate and echo the sea-green light of the grotto. The composition is also carefully arranged and the central group fits into a triangle. All this work bears witness to methodical reflection, the intensity, variety and extent of which are shown in the increasingly numerous writings. The *Last Supper* and the *Battle of Anghiari*—the former in a calm setting, the latter in a confusion of movement— were an original solution to problems of the moment; some painters concentrated on precision and the multiplicity of detail, while an artist like Perugino, for example, simplified single elements and the composition as a whole. Leonardo concentrated the effect; he tried to relate the pyramid formation, dominating space, with the expressive power of the gestures, but by adding the dim atmosphere of chiaroscuro and the singularity of the twisted figure, he goes beyond the conflict of linear elegance and mass; this is seen in the *Leda* (lost, known only from sketches and copies), and later in the *St Anne*.

Leonardo also gave fresh life to the two most attractive aspects of painting: portraiture and landscape. He created a new development in portraiture, especially portraits of women, at the same time showing his taste for the bizarre and search for type in his 'caricatures' or studies of physiognomy. There are very few portraits in profile (the *Belle Ferronnière,* the attribution of which is contested, and the portrait of *Isabella d'Este* of which only the cartoon remains) but many full face portraits: that

LEONARDO DA VINCI. ADORATION OF THE MAGI. 1481. UFFIZI, FLORENCE.

of *Ginevra de' Benci* remarkable for depth, relief and modelling of form, the *Musician,* and the *Lady with an Ermine.* In all these portraits we see an exceptional search for physiological reality and modelling of form, together with a subtle use of significant surroundings which add a symbolic note; for example, the juniper in the *Ginevra de' Benci.*

Leonardo arrived at some extraordinary results through meditating on landscape and its problems. His first landscape, dated 1473, is a drawing, a view of the Val d'Arno. In order to integrate the landscape with the picture successfully, he has tackled the problem by means of infinitely small things, in

other words, the detail of foliage and plants, which appear in the *Annunciation* in the Uffizi, in copies of the *Leda,* in the foreground of *St Anne ;* but also in an infinitely large way, in other words, the global effect, sometimes by a shadowy vault with glimpses of the far distance as in the *Virgin of the Rocks,* and sometimes just with broad expanses of distance, as in the *St Anne* and the *Gioconda.* The cold, sea-green atmosphere, which dominates all his works, harmonises with the *sfumato* technique; it has the effect of an envelope that creates a gradual transition to the blue distance in the Flemish manner, and these find their justification in the cosmogonic theory

LEONARDO DA VINCI. PORTRAIT OF GINEVRA
DE' BENCI. ABOUT 1478. LIECHTENSTEIN
COLLECTION, VADUZ.

and the absorbing study of water which
engrossed Leonardo after 1500.

His works are strangely limited in
number and punctuated with false
starts he abandoned or rejected, but his
significance as an artist and even as a
man is tremendous. Leonardo's pictorial output is accompanied by a
quantity of notes and expositions of
problems which indicate a most open
mind to every conceivable curiosity.
There is nearly always a rare and strange
slant to the artistic discoveries, a curiosity especially connected with the phe-
nomenon of life accepted in its totality,
both in its marvellous and monstrous
aspects; there is a frequent similarity
between the battles of living creatures
and battles of the elements, a tendency
expressed by the portrayal of inextric-
ably interlaced shapes, and which ends
after 1500 in the *non finito,* the rough
sketch being for Leonardo more important than the painting. These three
aspects, pictorial, graphic and specul-
ative, do not overlap, but centre in the
same preoccupations which always lead
him back to painting. For example, the
philosophical notes on the mystery of
conception, the series of drawings
concerning the organs of a woman, the
studies of hair and drawings of flowers
are all united in the *Leda.*

Immediately after the Florentine period, even before it spread into Europe
and predetermined certain mannerist
characteristics, Leonardo's influence
shows itself at work, in Lorenzo di
Credi and Piero di Cosimo. After the
Milanese period the growing part played
by assistants makes attribution difficult.
Besides, many of Leonardo's 'ideas'
were not developed by him: the *Gioconda*
has inspired a whole series of nude
Giocondas. The spell of his genius
and the originality of his suggestions,

LEONARDO DA VINCI. ISABELLA D'ESTE,
WIFE OF FRANCESCO II GONZAGA.
ABOUT 1500. DRAWING. LOUVRE, PARIS.

as it were, froze the talents of young painters; his style is so firmly imprinted on them that if their Leonardesque qualities were removed, little would remain. Boltraffio, for example, stayed with the master all through the Milanese period: Ambrogio da Predis, Marco d'Oggiono, Luini and Salai remained in his orbit. Cesare da Cesto has to his credit the copies he made of the vanished *Leda*. Without Leonardo's precision Raphael, Fra Bartolomeo and Andrea del Sarto would not have achieved their noble, gentle and disciplined art.

Leonardo has presented himself as a technician, not a philosopher or humanist. Yet he brought a new dignity to his work as an artist and an engineer. People were fascinated by his brilliant conversation, his original conclusions, and the special charm that accompanies elegance, independent ways and manners, a great moral sense and self-observation. To some extent he was the incarnation of a new type, the Wise Man traditionally described by humanists under the name of Hermes or Pythagoras. Leonardo's fame was something of a legend, and this was further underlined by the fact that his written works were scattered,

leaving us ignorant of his doctrine and the rather literary cult of which he was the object, during the long period when his speculations were not supported by attention to graphic design, and draughtsmanship failed to rise to the dual realm of its fulfilment: the art of an engineer who understands the marvels of mechanics, and the art of a painter who expresses the highest aspirations of the mind.   A. C.

LIBERALE da VERONA (Verona, *ca* 1445 - *ca* 1529). Probably trained in Verona, Liberale worked, from 1466 to 1476 at least, in Tuscany. He was then painting for Monte Oliveto Maggiore and the Cathedral of Siena a series of miniatures which count among the most original of the 15th century. Their expressionism and preciosity were inspired by the old gothic traditions of Verona, renewed by contact with modern trends from Padua and Ferrara. Even some of the Sienese themselves experienced the influence of his graphic dexterity and interpreted his original ideas. Such is also the case of Girolamo da Cremona, his collaborator in Siena; the latter was formerly credited

LIBERALE
DA VERONA.
THE RAPE
OF EUROPA.
DETAIL OF
A 'CASSONE'
PANEL FORMERLY
ATTRIBUTED
TO FRANCESCO
DI GIORGIO.
LOUVRE, PARIS.

FILIPPINO LIPPI. SELF-PORTRAIT. DETAIL
FROM A FRESCO. SANTA MARIA DEL
CARMINE, BRANCACCI CHAPEL, FLORENCE.

with several pictures which indubitably belong to Liberale's Sienese period. Returning to Verona towards 1488, he became the most important artist in the city, taking on pupils and receiving numerous commissions. Whilst showing his knowledge of the recent inventions of Mantegna, the Ferrarese and certain Venetians (he is known to have been in Venice in 1487), he recaptured in the best paintings of his fertile Veronese period the linear and poetic fantasy and even the passionate lyricism which make his Sienese miniatures so admired. Mention must be made, at least, among his paintings preserved in Verona, of the *Adoration of the Magi* in the cathedral in which the sinuous rhythms and the fabulous unreality of the Verona of Pisanello seem to be recaptured. M. L.

LIPPI Filippino (Prato, 1457 - Florence,

1504). He was the son of the Carmelite brother, Fra Filippo Lippi, and of Lucrezia Buti, a nun at the Convent of Santa Margherita in Prato, where Filippo Lippi was chaplain in 1456. He was the spoilt child of the Florentine school. Trained by his father, he then worked, as early as 1472, in Botticelli's workshop. His panels for *cassoni* and his charming devotional pictures soon seem to have made him popular. In 1482, he was asked to paint a fresco for the Sala dell'Udienza in the Palazzo della Signoria in Florence (the decoration was never done), and the following year, two Annunciation *tondi* for the Palazzo Comunale in San Gimignano. He must already have won Lorenzo's approval, for he was invited to decorate the Villa Spedaletto, near Volterra, in collaboration with his friends Botticelli, Ghirlandaio and Perugino on their return to Rome (which allows us to date the work 1482-1483). About ten years later, he decorated another Medici villa, the one at Poggio a Caiano (unfinished *Laocoon* fresco). He was not considered unworthy of completing the frescoes in the Brancacci Chapel in the Carmine; under Masaccio's fresco, he painted a scene representing the fight between St Peter and Simon Magus. About 1485-1486, he painted for Piero del Pugliese, at the Campora cloister, the *Vision of St Bernard* (Badia), a powerful and sensitive masterpiece.

In 1485, Filippo Strozzi, who had returned from exile under Piero de' Medici, became Prior at Santa Maria Novella. He made a contract with Filippino to decorate the family chapel in the church of the Dominicans. The work (the *Story of St Philip and St John*) was only completed in 1502, for Filippo Strozzi the Younger. It is the most important decorative scheme painted in Filippino's 'last manner'.

In 1488, he had been called to Rome, through the patronage of Lorenzo de' Medici who described him as 'better than Apelles'; on his way, he stopped in Spoleto to design his father's funeral monument. In Rome, he decorated with Dominican allegories, including the *Triumph of St Thomas Aquinas,* the chapel founded by Cardinal Caraffa in Santa Maria sopra Minerva. He was then enjoying considerable popularity. His commissions were numerous and he painted many humanistic allegories (*Music,* Munich) as well as traditional religious paintings. He was asked to replace the *Adoration of the Magi,* commissioned from Leonardo in 1481 by the monks of San Donato in Scopeto and left unfinished. Filippino delivered the picture in 1496. It is a complex composition filled by a restless crowd of strangely dressed characters; Filippino was more and more attracted by the picturesque: weapons, costumes, archaeological decors copied out of his notebooks. In the Strozzi Chapel, his style is lively, almost frenzied; we find the same characteristics in the *Meeting of St Anne and Joachim* (Copenhagen), signed and dated 1497, in the *Marriage of St Catherine* (1501) for the church of San Domenico in Bologna, a crowded, complex panel with seven figures; in the large *St Sebastian* for the church of San Teodoro in Genoa (Palazzo Bianco). In 1503, he completed for Prato the *Madonna between St Stephen and St John,* now in a bad state of preservation, and the Servites in Florence commissioned from him a *Deposition* which Perugino was to finish (Florence, Accademia).

A whole series of colourful, delicate panels—for instance Esther's *cassone* in Chantilly—which were once attributed by Berenson to the anonymous 'Amico di Sandro' are now believed to be youthful works of Filippino. He understood better than anybody the subtle grace of Botticelli. But he gradually moved away from those beginnings under the combined influence of Flemish 'naturalism' and archaeological interest.

When he arrived in Rome in 1488, he was delighted by the poetic costumes and the archaeological details in his master's frescoes in the Sistine Chapel, and he made full use of them. In the Caraffa Chapel, he revealed a strange aspect of his genius: a taste for whimsical virtuosity which can occasionally lapse into a heavy and didactic style in his less inspired moments. The decoration of the Strozzi Chapel in Florence suited the Florentine liking for the religious oddities of paganism. Stormy scenes filled with strange architectural backgrounds, such as the altar of Mars in the Miracle of *St Philip casting out the Dragon,* are lit from behind or touched with golden glints. We find the same type of inspiration in the two panels of

FILIPPINO LIPPI. RAISING FROM THE DEAD OF THE SON OF THEOPHILUS (DETAIL). FRESCO. SANTA MARIA DEL CARMINE, FLORENCE.

FRA FILIPPO LIPPI. SALOME. DETAIL FROM
THE 'BANQUET OF HEROD'. FRESCO. 1452-1465.
CATHEDRAL OF PRATO.

Moses striking Water from the Rock and
the *Adoration of the Golden Calf* (London,
National Gallery).

Filippino's models changed frequently: the St Bernard Virgin was inspired by
Flemish artists, or at least by their frag-
mentary changing view of nature; but
he was less successful than Piero di
Cosimo and his landscapes lacked vitality
and sunshine. At the Carmine, he imitated the solemn approach of Masaccio,
and the lively characters of the *Adoration
of the Magi* are reminiscent of Leonardo.
Filippino was so versatile that he even
returned to the Trecento use of a gold
ground for his *Crucifixion between the*

Madonna and St Francis, painted for a
'piagnone' (1496). His prolific work
finished on a violent climax which was
an eloquent testimony to the crisis of
artistic styles; Filippino's final 'romanticism' was a reaction against the new
classicism, against the orderly, supple
style of Umbrian artists. It already
announced mannerism.   A. C.

LIPPI Fra Filippo (Florence, *ca* 1406-
Spoleto, 1469). Fra Filippo joined the
Carmelites in Florence at the age of
eight, took orders in 1421, and is
first recorded as a painter in 1431;
he knew Masolino and Masaccio, who
both influenced him decisively. In
1434, he was in Padua and painted the
Trivulzio Pala on a blue ground (Milan,
Castello Sforzesco). Back in Florence
in 1437, he painted the pretty *Madonna* on
wood now at the Galleria Nazionale
d'Arte Antiqua, Rome, and the *Madonna
surrounded by Angels and Saints* for Or
San Michele (now at the Louvre). A
letter from Domenico Veneziano to
Piero de' Medici, dated 1438, shows that
the Carmelite brother was already then
considered as a master. In 1442, a
papal Bull from Eugenius IV appointed
him rector and abbot of the parish of
San Quirico at Legnaia, on the road to
Pisa, near Florence. His activities are
well documented: the large San Lorenzo
Annuciation with large angels looking
like inquisitive Levites turning round, the
Coronation of the Virgin (Uffizi) begun
before 1442 and finished, or at least
paid for, in 1447. The splendid Bartolini tondo with a Madonna and scenes
from the life of the Virgin (1452, Pitti)
shows great mastery in the organisation
of space. Fra Filippo was by then the
favourite painter of Cosimo de' Medici
who probably excused his irregular life
with his usual saying: one does not
treat divine spirits as one treats pack
mules.

About 1452, Filippo Lippi settled in
Prato to work on the San Stefano fres-

FRA FILIPPO LIPPI. MADONNA AND CHILD, SCENES FROM THE LIFE OF THE VIRGIN. ABOUT 1452. PALAZZO PITTI, FLORENCE.

coes which were only completed twelve years later; it is a large, complex series of paintings, probably the largest he ever painted apart from the one in the Brancacci Chapel and the one (now destroyed) in Sant'Egidio. His assistant was Fra Diamante; several other works are attributed to their collaboration including the *Madonna* in the Ospedale del Ceppo (1453, Prato, Galleria Comunale). In 1456, he was chaplain in the Convent of Santa Marguerita and painted a large altarpiece (Prato, ibid.) for the chapel. There, he met the nun Lucrezia Buti, who became the mother of his son Filippino. In 1457, the Medici, still his faithful patrons, commissioned from him an altarpiece for the King of Naples. As well as his usual Madonnas, for instance the 1455 Madonna with a small angel, now in the Uffizi, he painted several *Nativities* against beautiful brown and gold landscapes: one in the Convent at Annalena, another for the Calmaldolesians (both at the Uffizi) and one for the chapel of the Medici Palace (Berlin). His last commission was in Spoleto where he was in 1466 with his young son, to decorate the apse of the cathedral with frescoes including a grandiose *Coronation of the Virgin*. He died in 1469 and, later, Lorenzo de' Medici had a tomb built for him, with an epitaph from Politian (1488).

Filippo is the only Florentine artist

PIETRO LONGHI. THE DANCING LESSON.
ACCADEMIA, VENICE.

PIETRO LONGHI. THE TOILET.
CA' REZZONICO, VENICE.

of the middle of the century who was interested in subtle colour combinations, even at the expense of draughtsmanship. That tendency was shared by Fra Angelico, and the *Adoration of the Magi* tondo (Washington, National Gallery) has been attributed to both. Filippo does not sacrifice everything else to the rendering of space and plastic values. Rather, he considers the picture as a container for lively and decorative figures and objects; the Bartolini tondo, for example, is charming without excessive naïveté. In the Prato frescoes, Filippo showed that he was well aware of the responsibilities of a modern decorator, with elaborate perspective effects and a strong organisation of the composition, though in the latter he sometimes fails. The inner depth of his temperament is perhaps revealed in Spoleto, where his enthusiastic approach almost announces the sensuous lavishness of Correggio.   A. C.

LONGHI Pietro Falca, *called* Pietro (Venice, 1702 - Venice, 1785). 18th century Venice is for us the Venice of Goldoni and Pietro Longhi. The connection between the painter and the playwright seemed so obvious even to contemporaries that Goldoni wrote a sonnet to celebrate their two muses as sisters. The painter's father, Alessandro Falca, was a silversmith. Pietro, after a period in the atelier of Balestra, went to Bologna to be taught by G. M. Crespi, who numbered Piazzetta among his pupils. Back in Venice shortly after 1730, Longhi tried his hand unsuccessfully at decoration in the grand manner (Bologna, Palazzo Sagredo) and then turned to chronicling the life of his city in cabinet pictures. He prospered on this line and was one of the first academicians in 1756. A few good portraits disappear, so to speak, in a mass of genre scenes taken both from Venetian low life: mountebanks, street dentists, pastry cooks, even a 'true portrait of

AMBROGIO LORENZETTI. PEACE AND FORTITUDE. DETAIL FROM 'GOOD GOVERNMENT'.
FRESCO. 1338-1339. PALAZZO PUBBLICO, SIENA.

a rhinoceros' (Venice, Ca' Rezzonico), dated 1751; and from fashionable society: ladies dressing, paying a visit, sitting for their portrait in the painter's studio, or seeing the nurse who looks after their child. The colour is pleasant, very subdued, a little ashen with its mauves and muffled blues. Longhi has none of the dazzling virtuosity that one associates with the Venetians. If anything, he is slightly clumsy; his personages pose with a certain affectation, their faces usually turned towards the spectator. Longhi's is a naïve vision; the upper classes of his Venice, however decadent they may be, retain a natural manner that endeared them to Stendhal, while the populace amuses itself without any restraint. Longhi's clumsiness may have been intentional. He seems able to shed it in his improvised sketches for which he generally used charcoal, heightened with white chalk and which suggest an acquaintance with French drawings.   P. C.

LORENZETTI Ambrogio (Siena, *ca* 1290- Siena, 1348). Younger than Pietro, Ambrogio was born at the end of the 13th century, about 1290. His first documented work is a picture dated 1319 (*Madonna of Sant'Angelo,* Vico l'Abbate, near Florence); he is last mentioned in the archives in 1347. During his youth, Ambrogio came under the same influences as his brother, who was probably his teacher. He sometimes worked with him: the frescoes in the Ospedale di Santa Maria della Scala in Siena, now destroyed, were signed with both

AMBROGIO LORENZETTI. FRESCO OF 'GOOD
GOVERNMENT' (DETAIL). 1338-1339.
PALAZZO PUBBLICO, SIENA.

their names; in other cases, as with the
Christ on the Cross in the church of
San Marco in Cortona, it is difficult to
attribute some unsigned paintings to
one or the other of the two brothers.
But Ambrogio's personality soon asserted itself. He was perhaps less powerful
and less dramatic than Pietro, but his
style had more elegance. Vasari claimed
that his painting was the work 'of a
gentleman and a philosopher, rather
than a craftsman'.

His numerous works are now
scattered, but most of them are still in
Siena. We must mention first the two
frescoes in the church of San Francesco:
the *Martyrdom of the Franciscans at Ceuta*

and *St Louis of Toulouse pronouncing his
Vows in front of Bonifacio VIII.* Originally, they decorated the chapter-house,
but when it was made into a refectory
in 1857, they were moved to the church.
They are large compositions in which
the scenes take place against an architectural background which stresses
successive picture planes and still shows
the influence of Pietro. They probably
date from about 1330. The *Virgin
nursing the Child* (Siena, Seminary chapel)
belongs to the same period; it is akin to
other Madonnas by Ambrogio and to the
Nuns' Heads (fragment at the National
Gallery, London) and bears the mark of
the master's originality: it would be
difficult to attribute these Madonnas to
any other hand. The Virgin's features
have a surprisingly eastern flavour which
could be a reminiscence, or perhaps it
indicates a mysterious affinity.

The *Presentation in the Temple,* signed
and dated 1342 (Uffizi) and the *Annunciation,* signed and dated 1344 (Siena,
Pinacoteca), belong to Ambrogio's
mature period. The *Annunciation* is
divided in two panels: on one side, the
angel Gabriel kneeling, on the other,
the Virgin sitting, a familiar theme of
gothic iconography which Ambrogio
adopted, like his brother Pietro, like
Simone Martini and most Sienese
painters. To the same period belong
the two surprising landscapes, 'without
a sky', the *Town on the Sea* and the *Castle by
a Lake* (Siena, Pinacoteca).

The two frescoes in the Sala di Nove
in the Palazzo Pubblico, Siena, *Good
Government* and *Bad Government,* were
rightly famous from the time they were
painted. We can make out the master's
signature: *Ambrosius Laurentii de Senis
hic pinxit utrinque,* but the work was
completed with the help of a workshop,
which is obvious from the uneven
quality of the various parts. The date is
unknown; it varies between the outside
dates of 1338 and 1348. However, evidence of payments from the town in 1338

and 1339 give some indication. One of the two compositions, the *Good Government,* is in a good state of preservation, but the other has deteriorated and some details are hardly decipherable: Vasari interpreted them as Peace and War. In fact, the subjects are more complex and the charming ideas are expressed both through symbols and allegories and through charming realistic scenes. As is usual, the symbolic figures show the causes and the 'narratives' the effects; Virtue inspires Good Government, whose work insures the happiness of the people in the cities and in the country, while the Spirit of Evil is the cause of unhappiness. The commission was probably meant to be purely political, but Ambrogio added moral and even religious implications: earthly happiness and unhappiness symbolise heaven and hell, and the traditional theme of the fight between good and evil is thus renewed and modernised.   P.-H. M.

LORENZETTI Pietro (Siena, *ca* 1280 - Siena, 1348). Vasari, who had misread a signature of Pietro Laurentii (Pietro, son of Lorenzo), changed his name to Laurati; he then mentioned Ambrogio Lorenzetti without noticing that the two painters were brothers. His praise of Pietro was influenced both by his Florentine prejudice and by his theory about the progress of the arts; according to him, Pietro was a follower of Giotto, but imitated his manner so well that he became 'a better master than Giotto, Cimabue, and all the others before him'.

We know that in 1306 a panel intended for the Palazzo Pubblico in Siena was bought for 110 lire from a Petruccio di Lorenzo. It may in fact have been Pietro Lorenzetti, and in that case, 1306 would be the first documented date in his career. We know little about his life between 1306 and 1320: at that time, Pietro kept within the Sienese tradition, that is to say, the Byzantine tradition

PIETRO LORENZETTI. A PANEL FROM THE ALTARPIECE OF THE 'BEATA UMILTÀ'. 1341. UFFIZI, FLORENCE.

interpreted and modified by Duccio. The first preserved work which we can attribute to him is the *Virgin* in the Collegiata at Casole d'Elsa.

After 1320, traces of his activity are more numerous and his evolution is easier to follow. The polyptych in Santa Maria della Pieve at Arezzo bears his signature. It is not dated but was commissioned in 1320 and must have been painted then. It shows the combined influences of gothic miniatures and Giovanni Pisano's sculptures, but reveals above all Pietro's personal temperament and his sense of drama, already apparent in the two panels of the Virgin, with the Child and the angel Gabriel. The central part of the poly-

PIETRO LORENZETTI. DESCENT FROM THE CROSS. ABOUT 1330.
LOWER CHURCH, BASILICA OF ST FRANCIS, ASSISI.

ptych (dated 1329) painted for the church of Santa Maria del Carmine in Siena is now in Dofana (church of Sant'Ansano) and the predella in the Siena Pinacoteca. The wings have been lost. The Dofana panel shows the *Virgin and Child* with St Nicholas of Bari on their right, St Anthony Abbot on their left and, in the background, four angels. Unlike most of Lorenzetti's Madonnas, where the Virgin usually bends her head towards the Child, supported on her left arm (Arezzo polyptych, Empoli Collegiata, Musée de Dijon, Museo Poldi-Pezzoli in Milan, etc.), the Dofana Virgin is represented full face, crowned, looking into the distance as if alien to this world. The predella in the Siena Pinacoteca is divided into four parts, two of which show the confirmation of the Carmelite rule by Honorius IV,

while the other two represent familiar scenes: a friar drawing water, another dreaming, asleep in his cell.

The frescoes of the Orsini Chapel (Lower Church at Assisi) attributed by Vasari to Cavallini and Giotto are now generally believed to be by Lorenzetti and his pupils. But if modern art historians all agree on the attribution, they disagree on the date; however, the obvious resemblances between the Assisi *Crucifixion* and that in the church of San Francesco in Siena (about 1331) would suggest a date around 1330, between the two outside dates of 1320 and 1340 which have been put forward. The paintings are on three tiers; on the lower tier: various scenes and figures of saints; above, filling the upper part of the wall and the arch: a *Passion* cycle composed of 11 scenes, with the last 5 (from the Crucifixion to the Descent into Limbo) by Lorenzetti's own hand.

The Uffizi *Virgin* (dated 1340) marks the beginning of a last period; to that period belongs the *Beata Umiltà* polyptych (1341) whose central part shows the saint standing, and towering very tall above a praying nun; on the wings and the predella: thirteen small, very lively scenes (in the Uffizi, except for two panels from the predella in Berlin). The masterpiece of this last period is the *Birth of the Virgin,* dated 1342 (Siena, Opera del Duomo), in which the violent drama of the Assisi paintings is replaced by a serene and spiritual atmosphere. Very little is known about the master's last years. According to a generally accepted, but unverifiable, tradition, he died of the plague in 1348, together with his brother Ambrogio.   P.-H. M.

LORENZO di CREDI (Florence, *ca* 1456 - Florence, 1537).   Lorenzo was the son of a goldsmith.   He joined Verrocchio's workshop and by 1480 he practically supervised all the painting work: most of the Pistoia 'pala', left unfinished in 1485, is his work, and, in his will, the master (who went to Venice in 1483 and died in 1488) put him in charge of all commissions.   It is therefore difficult to sort out Lorenzo's youthful work. The difficulty is increased by the fact that his carefully accurate manner does not show much development although his works are spread over a long period: the *Madonna between St Julian and St Nicholas* (Louvre), dated 1493 and not, as it was wrongly believed, 1503, provides us with a good landmark.   The *St Bartholomew* was mentioned by Albertini in 1510 in Or San Michele.   The *St Michael* for the vestry of Florence Cathedral was painted in 1523.   It is not always easy to place between those known dates the various altarpieces which their lacquered contours, their clear colours and the careful modelling in half-tones allow us to attribute to Lorenzo.   It is interesting to know that he left a *Self-Portrait,* signed and dated 1488 (Philadelphia, Widener Collection) and that, influenced by Savonarola's preachings, he burnt in 1497 all those of his pictures which had profane subjects; only the Uffizi *Venus* and a few portraits were preserved.

LORENZO DI CREDI.
ADAM AND EVE
DRIVEN
FROM PARADISE.
PANEL FROM THE
PREDELLA OF THE
'ANNUNCIATION'.
UFFIZI, FLORENCE.

LORENZO DI CREDI. VENUS. UFFIZI, FLORENCE

scrupulous organisation. He studied the modelling of figures on salmon pink or grey sheets of paper *(carta tinta)*, many of which are still extant. His architectural backgrounds are usually carefully worked out; for instance the one in the *Annunciation* panel (Uffizi). Lorenzo stands for the quiet and painstaking side of the discoveries of Verrocchio's workshop. In the *Virgin and Child* tondo (Rome, Galleria Borghese), where he used the pyramidal composition of Leonardo, he added an indefinable, craftsman's integrity to the classical assurance.   A. C.

LORENZO the **MAGNIFICENT** *See* Medici, Lorenzo de'.

LORENZO MONACO Piero di Giovanni, *called* (Siena, *ca* 1370 -Florence, after 1422). This artist was first formed by the great Sienese masters of the 14th century, but his mature period was influenced by the Florentines, particularly by Orcagna. He was in Florence in 1390, entered the Camaldolesian order in 1391, and from then on, never left the monastery of Santa Maria degli Angeli which was then a flourishing school of miniaturists. Fra Lorenzo spent part of his time illuminating manuscripts, especially between 1409 and 1413. It has been said that in his paintings he used the vivid, clear tones of manuscript illumination; but his light effects and his attempt at depth reveal a far wider range. Apart from the badly preserved frescoes in the Convent of the Oblates and in the Santa Maria Nuova hospital, Florence, Lorenzo left mainly altar paintings, now scattered between many Italian and foreign museums. The most famous are in Florence: the *Annunciation* (1408/09) at the Accademia, the *Adoration of the Magi* (1410) and the *Coronation of the Virgin* (1413) both at the Uffizi. Lorenzo Monaco is mentioned for the last time in a document of 1422. Fra Angelico was his pupil.   P.-H. M.

Lorenzo's manner, Vasari tells us, was so close to Leonardo's that their works could be mixed up: some gouache sketches of draperies on a tinted ground are difficult to attribute to one or to the other. Lorenzo particularly admired Leonardo's 'clarity and finish'. His well dusted studio was a model of

LORENZO VENEZIANO (Venice, active from 1356 to 1372). Lorenzo Veneziano is undoubtedly the most remarkable of the Venetian primitives. Under the influence of Byzantine art he executed altar pictures, painted on wood, where the figures stand out from a gold background. This method adds a special glow, reminiscent of mosaics, to work that possesses an undeniable elegance. At the Castello Sforzesco, Milan, there is a *Resurrection* by him. His most important work, signed and dated 1357, done for the church of Sant'Antonio Abate, is now in the Accademia, Venice, are known to us by one work only. His fame is based almost entirely on the *Life of the Virgin* frescoes in the Mazzatosta Chapel of Santa Maria della Verità in Viterbo. They were completed in 1469. Their lofty style and the predominance of sculptural elements show clearly the influence of Piero della Francesca, but with a more marked alinement of the figures. In the *Annunciation,* the artist, trying to break away from the austere symmetry of his master, grew nearer to Melozzo's style. The last and most beautiful of the frescoes, the *Marriage of the Virgin* (which was

LORENZO VENEZIANO. CONVERSION OF ST PAUL. PANEL FROM THE PREDELLA OF THE 'POLYPTYCH OF ST PETER'. DAHLEM MUSEUM, BERLIN.

which also possesses the *Mystic Marriage of St Catherine,* signed and dated 1359. His works can also be seen in Vicenza, the Museo Civico, Padua, and in the Louvre which has the *Virgin with a Rose* (1372).   A. L.

LORENZO da VITERBO (Viterbo, *ca* 1437 - Viterbo, *ca* 1469). Lorenzo is one of the few 15th century painters who

badly damaged in 1943 and has been restored since) is more naturalistic: in his solemn, but lively representation of a procession, Piero's disciple reveals a youthful and enthusiastic personality. A *Crucifixion with the Virgin and St John* (Budapest) is also attributed to him and—with less certainty—frescoes on the vault of Santa Maria Maggiore in Rome: a visit of the painter to Rome

LORENZO LOTTO. PORTRAIT OF A YOUNG MAN.
ABOUT 1506-1510. KUNSTHISTORISCHES MUSEUM,
VIENNA.

would, of course, account for a meeting
with Melozzo.   A. C.

LOTTO Lorenzo (Venice, *ca* 1480 - Loretto, 1556). Constitutionally moody,
unconventional and restless, this painter
was, because of his very shortcomings,
one of the great portraitists of the
Renaissance or, as Berenson called him,
'a psychological painter'. The *St Jerome*
in the Louvre, with an unusual importance given to the landscape, was not the
artist's first work, since we must read
the date as 1506 and not 1500. It came
after the monumental and Bramantesque
Two Warriors on each side of the tomb
of Agostino Onigo in San Niccolò in
Treviso, the strange portrait of *Bishop
Bernardo de' Rossi,* pink and red on a
green background (1505, Naples) and the
uneven and somewhat confused *Assumption* for the baptistery in Asolo. Lotto's
gifts and limitations were already obvious
then, and the large Recanati polyptych

(1508) allows us to see how he stood
next to the masters of Venetian art,
particularly Bellini.

His reputation was high enough for
him to be invited to Rome, among the
first group of artists commissioned to
decorate the Stanze at the Vatican. He
was sent away with the others, when
Julius II entrusted Raphael with the
direction of the works. But Lotto
showed an eager and misguided zeal
in imitating the modelling and the
flowing grace of the young master: the
Glory of St Vincent Ferrer in Recanati is
lively enough, but the *Transfiguration* in
Recanati and the *Deposition* in Iesi (1512)
are merely bad imitations.

Back in Venice in 1513, Lotto could
no longer find a place there. He
settled for a while in Bergamo where
he painted a large, grandiose altarpiece
for San Bartolomeo (1516); the *Virgin
with Four Saints,* a fresh, lively picture,
for San Spirito (1521); and another
composition, also with four saints for
San Bernardino. His *Marriage of St Catherine* dated 1523 (Bergamo, Accademia
Carrara) is an unusual painting: painstaking, sensitive and somewhat strange,
with leaning figures arranged on receding planes and along oblique lines.
The designs provided by Lotto for the
marquetry in the choir stalls of Santa
Maria Maggiore in Bergamo are imaginative, rather pedestrian, and naïvely
complicated; in the frescoes of the
Oratorio Suardi in Trescore (1524), we
find the same taste for popular illustration which was to become more and
more marked in the artist's work.

Venice rejected him. The accepted
supremacy of Titian left no place for an
artist who went on painting rather
heavily in cold colours, according to
the fashion of the old generation, and
who at the same time had a predilection
for bizarre, muddled compositions in
the Germanic manner. His first altarpiece in a true Venetian style was the
Glorification of St Nicholas of Tolentino for

the Carmelites (1529); but a long time elapsed before he was commissioned for another one, and he found more clients in the Marches: his *St Lucy* (1531) was for Iesi; and the *Crucifixion,* which he painted the same year, a grandiose, tormented work with expressionistic features reminiscent of German art, was for Monte San Giusto, near Macerata. Lotto gradually stopped trying to paint in the grand style, and became more direct and more moving, as for instance in the Cingoli Pala with the *Madonna of the Rosary* (1539), in the *St Bernardino of Siena* (1542) meant for the church of Santi Giovanni e Paolo in Venice, or in the *Madonna with Saints* (1546, Ancona). Already old and overcome by religious preoccupations, he retired to Loretto where he painted an enormous *Ascension* (1550, Ancona), now completely repainted. His career ended in silence and poverty, as a lay brother. The accounts book, begun in 1538 in Ancona, which he left, shows in detail his struggles and his disappointments.

LORENZO LOTTO. PORTRAIT OF A YOUNG MAN. ABOUT 1525. KAISER FRIEDRICH MUSEUM, BERLIN.

Lotto never stopped painting portraits; they are less uneven than his religious compositions and reveal more clearly his main characteristics and his leanings: they have the smooth technique, the straightforward lighting, the large cold composition of Bellini and Alvise Vivarini, with an unusual presentation, velvety accents in greys and browns and a sort of melancholy undertone which became more and more noticeable on the dreamy, worried faces of his models: the *Young Man with a Beret* (1526, Milan, Castello Sforzesco), the remarkable study of *Andrea Odoni* (1527, Hampton Court), the *Young Man with a Book* (Venice, Accademia), the stern *Old Man with a red beard* (1542, Milan, Brera). Lotto refused the fashionable drapery, the heroic style, and never adopted the warm, even colour of Titian.

His landscapes are original and strangely frightening. In *Susanna* (Florence, Private Collection), for instance,

the crowded, asymmetrical effect is particularly marked. Lotto had seen Dürer engravings: he introduced moving, grimacing figures, teeming groups with entangled oblique lines cut across by large shafts of light, as in the immense *Crucifixion* of Monte San Giusto and the altarpiece in San Bernardino in Bergamo, in which the small angels remind us of the slightly confused figures of Grünewald. Burlesque or trivial details, like the cat frightened by the angel in the Recanati *Annunciation,* complete the affinity with Grünewald. As Lotto lived more and more among poor people, his feeling for crowds was unusually strong: for instance in the *Alms of St Anthony* (Santi Giovanni e Paolo in Venice). Lotto was not skilled enough for classical simplicity and he never adopted the grand heroic style: he remained apart from the main artistic stream, in opposition to it, and in his work we find features which were to triumph later, in landscape painting or in the visual experiments of the Seicento.   A. C.

LUCA di TOMMÈ (Siena, *ca* 1330 - Siena, *ca* 1389). Inscribed on the roll of Sienese painters as early as 1355, Luca di Tommè, who worked with Niccolò Tegliacci in 1362, is, with Taddeo di Bartolo, one of the most productive artists of the second half of the Trecento. Nowadays, his works are scattered and only three are signed and dated: the *Crucifixion* in the Museo Nazionale, Pisa (1366) and two polyptychs both depicting the *Virgin and Child* surrounded by saints, one in the Siena Pinacoteca (1367) and the other in the Palazzo Comunale, Rieti (1370). Several other polyptychs with the same subject and style have been attributed to him. The attribution of the Trevisa *Coronation of the Virgin* is less certain. But in spite of Vasari, the frescoes of the Dragondelli altar, at San Domenico in Arezzo, painted in the manner of Barna, are attributed by modern critics either to Andrea Vanni, or to Barna himself.   P.-H. M.

LUCIANI Sebastiano. *See* Sebastiano del Piombo.

LUINI Bernardino (. . ., *ca* 1490 - Milan, 1532). Little is known about the life of Bernardino Luini whose first authenticated work is a fresco painted in 1512 for Chiaravalle Abbey, representing the Virgin with angels against a landscape background. We know that he married and had several sons, one of whom became a painter. In 1515, he signed and dated the *Madonna enthroned with Saints,* now at the Brera, originally in the Busti Chapel in Santa Maria di Brera. In 1516, he decorated the Corpus Domini Chapel in San Giorgio al Palazzo in Milan. In 1521, he painted more frescoes in the Busti Chapel of Santa Maria di Brera; at the end of that year and in 1522, he decorated with frescoes the Pio Luogo Oratory in Santa Corona, and, in 1523, painted an altarpiece for the parish church of San Magno in Legnano. In 1525, he started work in the Santuario della Madonna dei Miracoli, Saronno, which occupied him till 1531. It is then (from 1522) that he began his series of large decorative schemes, sacred or profane, at the Casa Rabia (now scattered between Berlin and Washington), at the Villa Pelucca (Brera), at the Greco Milanese Oratory (now at the Louvre), at the Casa Atellani (Milan, Castello Sforzesco), and the first part of the San Maurizio cycles in Milan where he entirely decorated the Besozzi Chapel. Beside this considerable amount of work as a fresco painter, he has left many carefully finished easel paintings, mostly religious. The development of his style through his authenticated works that he was first influenced by Andrea Solario, then by Bramantino and also by Bergognone whose spontaneous feeling we find in Luini's naïve figures and pleasant landscapes. In his frescoes, he would cleverly present familiar scenes (Villa Pelucca), biblical or mythological tales. Aware of Leonardo's technique, he knew how to make subtle use, in his paintings, of a soft chiaroscuro which gives the colours a shimmering effect. He is the most famous Renaissance artist in Lombardy.   S. B.

LUTERI Giovanni. *See* Dosso Dossi.

ALESSANDRO MAGNASCO. A GARDEN PARTY AT ALBARO. AFTER 1735.
PALAZZO BIANCO, GENOA.

M

MAFFEI Francesco (Vicenza, *ca* 1620 - Padua, 1660). Probably a pupil of Santo Feranda, he was trained in the complex and, artistically at least, somewhat confused atmosphere of 17th century Venice, then returned to Vicenza in 1647 and produced many original works. Interesting compositions reminiscent of Greco and Callot alternate with allegorical paintings of local officials, derived from the Bassano brothers: *Gaspare Ziani* (1643-1645), *Gerolamo Priuli and his son* (1649), *Gian Tomaso Pisani* (1656). Shimmering colours with moiré effects give a very personal tone to his paintings, enhanced by an unusual presentation and dramatic contrasts of light and shade: for instance in San Stefano, in Santa Corona, at Santa Maria dei Servi *(The Trinity)*, in San Nicola *(Paradise,* 1657) all in Vicenza. Maffei owes much to Tintoretto and, although we find his *Martyrdom of the Franciscans in Nagasaki* (Schio, San Francesco) somewhat contrived, his colourful, lively panels, for instance, the *Angel and Tobias* (Venice, Santi Apostoli) or the *Adoration of the Magi* (Padua, San Tommaso) have an atmosphere of poetic mystery. Maffei's personality, which is perhaps more brilliant than sound, is typical of the 18th century in Venice. A. C.

MAGNASCO Alessandro (Genoa, 1667 - Genoa, 1749). A Genoese by birth, Magnasco settled in Milan. His father, Stefano, was a painter and taught him the rudiments of his art; he died around 1680-1682. Alessandro then went to Milan and may have frequented the workshop of Filippo Abbiati, a Venetian artist who was famous at that time. There, he acquired a brilliant, quick technique which he used for the rest

MASTER OF THE MAGDALEN. ALTARPIECE OF
ST MAGDALEN. ACCADEMIA, FLORENCE.

of his life. During that period, he painted numerous portraits about which we know nothing; later, he changed over to painting pictures with small figures. In Milan, he met Sebastiano Ricci and they became close friends. Magnasco stayed in Milan till 1703, then returned to Genoa. In Florence, he became court painter to the Grand Duke of Tuscany and travelled throughout Tuscany and Emilia, with occasional visits to Lombardy; but between 1711 and 1735, he lived mainly in Milan. In 1735, he retired to Genoa where he died. He had no pupils, but imitators like Ciccio Napoletano and Coppa Milanese. His art is reminiscent of Salvator Rosa, Callot, Cerquozzi, Van Laar. With a brilliant, fiery technique, he usually depicts a fantastic world, bathed in a strange light. As only a few of his works are dated, the phases of his development are not easy to work out.

His first signed work, dated 1691 (Milan, Gallarati Scotti Collection) already represented an extraordinary architectural background and ruins with very original small figures. Between 1703 and 1711, he painted *Il Corvo Ammaestrato (The Raven's Lesson)* and the *Old Woman and the Gipsies,* now at the Uffizi, the *Hunting Scene* commissioned by the Duke of Tuscany, freer in style, with brown tones and already that bizarre poetic feeling which marks his best compositions. Between 1711 and 1735, he painted the series of pictures for Seitenstetten Abbey, in Austria, for Count Collorado, Governor of Lombardy. The *Macabre Scene* in Campomorto, near Pavia, was painted in 1731: the style reminds us of Tintoretto, with a chromatic scale reduced to essentials and a quick draughtsmanship. Between 1735 and 1740, he painted the *Garden Party at Albaro* (Genoa) and probably *Christ at Emmaus,* his most purely lyrical work. The strange, disturbed and sometimes caricature-like world which he chose to describe (monks, soldiers, nuns, gipsies) is peculiar to him, but his inspiration belongs to Lombard mannerism. His feeling for movement and light anticipate Guardi.   S. B.

MANFREDI Bartolomeo (Ustiano near Mantua, *ca* 1580 - Rome, 1620). Manfredi was first apprenticed to Pomarancio. Shortly after 1600 he settled in Rome.

He fell under the spell of Caravaggio whom he learned to imitate with such virtuosity that his works have frequently been confused with those of his master. His paintings were much sought after by contemporary patrons, among others the Marchese Giustiniani, one of Caravaggio's protectors. According to Sandrart, Manfredi exercised a major influence on the Dutch painters in Rome at the time. He was also reputed, as Baglioni relates, to be in possession of secrets which accounted for the particular freshness of his painting. Of his life little is known. His pictures, never signed, have subjects analogous to those of Caravaggio. A *Concert* of his is in Florence, a *Bacchus* at the Galleria Nazionale d'Arte Antiqua and an *Arrest of Christ,* in chiaroscuro, at the Galleria Borghese, both in Rome. His *Fortune-Teller* at the Pitti is worthy of Caravaggio's painting on the same subject.　　　　　P. C.

MANNERISM. This term, which has only recently gained acceptance in art history (Exhibitions, *Fontainebleau e la Maniera Italiana,* Naples, 1952; *The Triumph of Mannerism,* Amsterdam, 1955) is basically ambiguous. On the one hand the word *maniera* or 'manner' denotes those characteristics which typify the style of an artist—'a picture in the manner of Titian'. On the other hand, from the 15th century onwards it has been used to suggest a consciously elegant and more or less affected, 'mannered' style. This ambiguity recurs when the word mannerism is used in connexion with art history, whether with the derogatory inflexion which originally attached to the expressions 'gothic' and 'baroque' or in a frankly laudatory sense.

Mannerism has acquired several meanings: *1.* It may describe the style of an artist who, instead of seeking fresh means of expression chooses a certain 'manner', be it of his own creation or

MASTER OF THE OSSERVANZA. NATIVITY OF THE VIRGIN (DETAIL). MUSEO CIVICO, ASCIANO.

imitated from the work of a master, and continues, mechanically, to employ it. This is the sense in which the word is used by Vasari in the 16th century and by Bellori and Félibien in the 17th. *2.* Thenceforth mannerism could also be considered as an unavoidable stage in the development of a style, at which

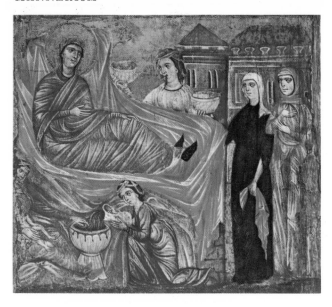

MASTER
OF SAN MARTINO.
NATIVITY
OF THE VIRGIN.
ALTARPIECE
OF SAN MARTINO.
ABOUT 1270.
MUSEO NAZIONALE,
PISA.

the creative faculty, divorced from its source of inspiration, is replaced by formulas which gradually become devoid of meaning (cf. Weisbach, Hörner). Both in the career of an artist and in the evolution of a movement, this stage may represent a final withering, or it may precede an outburst of baroque. *3*. The term may also be applied to a precise period in the history of art, at which the imitation of the great masters was especially popular, or, on the other hand an artificial elegance, characteristic of the School of Parma from the time of Parmigianino (cf. Fröhlich-Bum in his *Parmigianino und der Manierismus,* Vienna, 1921). *4*. 'Mannerism' may also refer to the whole period which followed the great creations of the Renaissance proper and which preceded the blossoming of baroque. The example of Raphael, Michelangelo, Titian and Correggio weighed heavily on their successors, but the pursuit of wordly elegance with its contorted poses and subtle

effects was carried by them to extremes. The necessity to classify a period of such original pictorial expression has gradually led to the acceptance of this meaning which applies to a particular period of art history (the works of Friedlaender, Dvořak, Weise and Chastel) and in spite of some hesitation and a number of conclusions reached on insufficient evidence (Salis, Curtius), it is now becoming generally accepted.

In the case of Italian art, the period of mannerism begins a little before the death of Raphael (1520) and extends to the time of the great works of the Carracci and of Caravaggio at Rome (1600-1610). These eighty or ninety years are, in fact, too rich and in view of the diversity of regions and the length of time concerned, too varied to be considered as a single stream of art. One is obliged to distinguish between various trends amongst which a vigorous lyricism frequently tinged with romanticism or mysticism, a worldly grace allied to sensuality, forms of a slender and almost abstract nature and subtle, varying colours. Parmigianino and the School of Parma are most representative of mannerism, although Tintoretto in Venice provides one of its finest expressions. Through Primaticcio and Niccolò dell'Abbate mannerism was established at Fontainebleau and thereafter in French art. Owing to the Italian apprenticeship served by El Greco, it is crowned in Spain with unforeseen glory. Another group of painters derives its principal lessons from Michelangelo and, remaining true to Roman and Florentine draughtsmanship with its enthusiastic study of the nude, leading to a concentration on multiplicity of form rather than delicacy of atmosphere (Giulio Romano, Daniele da Volterra, Tibaldi), precise volumes (Bronzino), somewhat massive proportions (Vasari) frequently arrives at an entirely opposite style. The often strange art of Pontormo and Beccafumi, the angular graphic style of Rosso with its hint of late gothic, which is certainly derived from the Germanic countries, frequently enrich mannerism with an intense lyricism.

With time, other differences emerge. From 1515 to 1535-1540 classicism is flouted with a freedom varying from the uneasy fantasy of Pontormo and Rosso to the startling effects achieved by Giulio Romano at the Palazzo del Tè and the intense lyricism of Parmigianino. Between 1540 and 1570 a reaction occurs. Painting tends to become a court art (Bronzino, Vasari), seeks for discipline and guiding principles (the writings of Vasari, Pino, Dolce, etc.), prefers a lyricism of a more relaxed nature (Salviati, Veronese) and more massive forms. From 1570 to 1600-1610, there are signs of a new spirit of enquiry, less hampered by famous models and searching far more deeply into the problems of plastic expression. Tintoretto at the Scuola di San Rocco experiments with space and light; Jacopo

Bassano creates realistic evocations of nature, while a great creative artist like Barocci carries out experiments which lead directly to baroque. The naturalist reaction at the end of the century, either rejecting entirely mannerist lyricism (the compact forms of Pulzone and the revolution introduced by Caravaggio) or taking place within the mannerist movement itself (Carracci at the Galleria Farnese) ousts mannerism without destroying it. The movement continues in Rome itself (the Cavaliere d'Arpino) and attains a late climax in other countries (Goltzius, Spranger, Dietterlin, Bellange). Mannerism embraces intellectuality and sensuality, delicacy and violence, surfeit and restraint. The more light is thrown by recent study on the different phases of this movement the clearer it becomes that it is not so much a question of a style as of the frequently contradictory quests of an epoch which,

BRONZINO. VENUS, CUPID, FOLLY AND TIME. NATIONAL GALLERY, LONDON.

PONTORMO. DESCENT FROM THE CROSS. 1526.
CHURCH OF SANTA FELICITA, FLORENCE.

lacking the equilibrium of the Renaissance, was eager to explore every possibility with complete confidence in its means, but a profound unease of spirit. J. T.

MANTEGNA Andrea (Isola di Cartura, near Vicenza, 1431 - Mantua, 1506). The two principal preoccupations of the Renaissance were to give order to nature through perspective and to give historical form to culture. As these two processes were taking place, a group of artists found it necessary to treat space with greater precision and to stress archaeological accuracy in modern compositions. The most representative of that group is Mantegna.

His name appears on the Padua registers as early as 1441. He is mentioned as the apprentice and adopted son of Squarcione, with whom he remained for six years. He left him at seventeen, on fairly bad terms, and immediately achieved success. Already in 1448, he was one of a team commissioned to decorate the Ovetari Chapel in the church of the Eremitani in Padua; he worked there until 1456, as the death or departure of several of his colleagues gradually increased his share in the scheme: the success of the work made him famous. In 1453, he painted an altarpiece for St Luke's Chapel in Santa Giustina (now at the Brera), composed of twelve panels according to the Vivarini formula; in 1454, a *St Euphemia* bearing a 'cartellino' with the date and his signature (Naples, Museo Nazionale). By marrying Nicolosia Bellini, daughter of Jacopo and sister of Gentile and Giovanni, he joined the most renowned family of Venetian painters. On a request from Gregorio Correr, abbot of San Zeno in Verona, he painted an altarpiece for that church (1459) on which, under a complex open loggia, eight saints surround an enthroned Madonna; the picture was brought to France in 1797 and the predella panels are still there: the *Crucifixion* (Louvre), the *Agony in the Garden* and the *Resurrection* (Tours). They are the painter's main works. About the same time, he painted an ambitious representation of *St Sebastian* (Vienna), signed in Greek, and probably a few Madonnas (Berlin, Bergamo).

Called to Mantua by Ludovico Gonzaga, Mantegna became court painter in 1459; he worked on the decoration of the palace chapel (destroyed), which may be represented in three extant prints: *Crucifixion, Entombment* and *Descent into Limbo*. We know very little about the decorating work directed by the artist at that time at the castle of Goito, and at Cavriana (1464) where a

ANDREA MANTEGNA. THE CRUCIFIXION. 1459. LOUVRE, PARIS.

man called Samuele worked under his orders. It is his most active period, and the least known. In 1464, he went with the scholar Felice Feliciano, the architect Giovanni Antenoreo and Samuel de Tradate, on a famous archaeological tour on the shores of Lake Garda, which culminated in a curious liturgical scene *all'antica*. Mantegna established his workshop near Porta Pusteria; he then had numerous commissions from the Gonzaga family: tapestry cartoons which were renowned and of which the Chicago *Annunciation* may be a remnant; the decoration of the *Camera degli Sposi* (the Bridal Chamber) in Mantua castle in 1472-1474, which is a hymn of praise to the reigning family; and finally the nine large paintings of the *Triumph of Caesar,* which were set between imitation pilasters as decoration for a room in the Mantua palace (sold to Charles I in the 17th century; they are now, in a poor state of

preservation, in Hampton Court). They were unfinished in 1492.

Meanwhile, Mantegna had produced important works: the foreshortened *Dead Christ,* a bravura piece worthy of the Florentine school, painted in 1465-1466; the *St Sebastian* (Louvre), given to Aigueperse church on the occasion of a wedding in the Bourbon family (1481) and the small *Madonna of the Quarries* (Uffizi), which Vasari dated from the artist's stay in Rome. Mantegna had been invited to Rome in 1488 by Pope Innocent VIII; he entirely decorated the little Belvedere Chapel (now destroyed). Back in Mantua, he was still occupied with official commissions, notable among which is the 1495 *Madonna della Vittoria,* where to commemorate his 'victory' over the French at Fornova, the duke is kneeling in front of the Madonna who is seated inside a strange pergola, together with protecting warrior saints. In the same vein, he painted a large altarpiece

173

ANDREA MANTEGNA. ST SEBASTIAN. ABOUT 1455/59.
LOUVRE, PARIS.

in Venice (Ca' d'Oro) is usually ascribed to the painter's last years.

Trained by Squarcione, Mantegna was influenced very early by the Paduan taste for antiquities, but he must have gone to Venice already in 1447 and seen the work of Antonio Vivarini and Giovanni d'Alemagna, the frescoes of Andrea del Castagno in San Zaccaria, finished in 1442, and met for the first time Jacopo Bellini and his sons. The frescoes in the Ovetari Chapel (ruined in 1944, now partly restored) are the triumph of a sort of severe, heavy archaeological humanism. The work had been shared out between Antonio Vivarini and Giovanni d'Alemagna on one side with the *Life of St Christopher* and on the other side Pizzolo and Mantegna with the *Life of St James*. Pizzolo died in 1453 and Mantegna probably painted most of the *Life of St James,* particularly the powerful Judgment and Torture scenes whose hard, strong, graphic style was alien to Tuscany and Umbria. The landscapes are mere reconstructions of classical architecture; the human figures, in Roman dress, move through a scenery made of rocks, blocks of masonry and stone flags. The draughtsmanship gives them hard, almost metallic outlines; perspective is used to give impressive views from unusual angles. The St Luke polyptych with its clear colours suggests some knowledge of the art of Piero della Francesca whom Mantegna may have met in Ferrara in 1449. But his main source is Donatello; the San Zeno altarpiece imitates the composition and spirit of the altarpiece in Sant'Antonio, Padua, with its statues inside a sort of pilastered loggia. The interest in antiquity and in modelling predominates. Mantegna was also influenced by the 'harsh' style of Andrea del Castagno, particularly when he painted his dramatically foreshortened *Dead Christ* (Brera), and he may have remembered the Gozzoli frescoes in the Palazzo Medici when he

for the monks of Santa Maria in Organo in Verona, signed and dated 1497 (Milan, Castello Sforzesco). Mantegna then worked for Isabella d'Este in Ferrara and his last period is dominated by the decoration of the princess's studiolo, which Richelieu acquired for the Louvre in 1652. It includes the *Parnassus* which, according to a letter, was already painted in 1497. The *Triumph of Virtue* was delivered at the end of 1502. *Comus,* the weakest of all, was completed by Costa. The *St Sebastian* decorated the *Camera degli Sposi* in Mantua.

Mantegna was responsible for the planning of that room, which remains his masterpiece. The rectangular room became a gallery, closed at both ends with heavy draperies, with in the middle an illusionistic dome in which he silhoutted against the sky laughing servant girls, a peacock and putti. A solid framework of ornamental bands and pilasters connects these scenes with the vault, decorated with medallions of mythological and antique subjects. This type of trompe-l'œil perspective went further than the Tuscan interest in the rendering of space, pointed the way to Bramante and Correggio and, through Veronese, to Tiepolo. The studiolo of Isabella d'Este was also conceived as a unified decoration in which the pictures were framed in *intarsie*. But the subjects of the allegorical paintings had been chosen by the Duchess herself; Mantegna painted *Parnassus* with gusto, but was less inspired by the *Triumph of Virtue,* and his successors Costa and Perugino, who lacked Mantegna's vitality, produced even more laborious compositions. Mantegna's talent for archaeological recontructions was inimitable; the cartoons of the *Triumph of Caesar* depict an extraordinary frieze made up of reminiscences of the artist's visit to Rome, particularly in the second series which is filled with pieces of armour, military equipment and antique vases. It is designed as a long procession from right to left, which satisfies the decorative scheme. The artist abandoned his usual cold tones to use camaieu effects which are stressed by the draughtsmanship.

In his smaller compositions and in his predella panels, Mantegna is equally powerful: the three lower scenes in the San Zeno altarpiece, *Agony in the Garden, Crucifixion* and *Resurrection,* are set in an acid, granite landscape with red rocks, inhabited by Roman warriors; such an

ANDREA MANTEGNA. JUDITH. NATIONAL GALLERY OF ART, WASHINGTON.

obsession with antiquity gives a new historic slant to the theme. Mantegna's manner was in opposition to Bellini as well as to the Umbrian school. The Louvre *St Sebastian* is the antithesis of the sweet, supple nudes of Perugino; the saint's body has the metallic grey colour of a statue. Mantegna did not always scorn fresh lively tones: we find them in the *Madonna della Vittoria*, a complex, elaborate composition in which the same background of foliage surrounds both the human and divine figures. The painting is more harmonious than the artist's other compositions, but still tense and intellectual; the Madonna's

175

ANDREA MANTEGNA. ALLEGORY (PRESUMED) OF FORTUNE AND VIRTUE.
BRITISH MUSEUM, LONDON.

gesture reminds us of that of Leonardo's *Virgin of the Rocks* which Mantegna may have seen in Milan. The Madonna painted in 1497 for the monks of Santa Maria in Organo, in Verona, shows a similar inspiration; instead of resting on a throne, she is floating in a mandorla, surrounded with cherubs' heads. The composition is organised according to an upward perspective effect which is reinforced by the placing of the saints' figures and the curtain of foliage in each angle: Mantegna's command of composition had never been more masterly.

Mantegna frequented scholars like Felice Feliciano; he was the 'antiquarian' of the Quattrocento, and enjoyed to the full the heritage of northern Italian culture. He set religious themes and the lives of the saints against the background of Roman history. He was probably the only artist of his time to be directly and permanently inspired by the antique fragments found in Italy or brought back from Greece, a taste which had been awakened by his adoptive father Squarcione. He transfigured all his subjects through his harsh treatment and produced lean, hard human figures moving through empty rocky backgrounds where all natural forms, including the human body, are enclosed in metallic or stony contours and heightened by a blue-grey light. Mantegna worked out an enormous repertory of antique medallions, military processions, monsters and tritons; he developed a whole system of ornaments directly inspired by Greek and Roman reliefs and medals. He stimulated the imagination of his contemporaries with them and, through engravings of which he was one of the first great masters, they reappear in all the arts.

His influence spread throughout

northern Italy. His manner was a sort of summing up of the knowledge, research, tendencies and tastes of the second half of the 15th century. We find echoes of it in the work of Domenico Morone, in Padua (where the strange B. Parenzo is his direct heir) and even in Venice. Bartolomeo Vivarini had a Mantegnesque period and so had Giovanni Bellini, for instance, in his *Christ in the Garden of Olives*. Without Mantegna, Ferrara would not have developed its grandiose style. Through him, Germany —particularly Dürer—discovered Italy, antiquity and the Renaissance.   A. C.

MARTINI Francesco di Giorgio. *See* Francesco di Giorgio Martini.

MARTINI Simone di Martino, *called* Simone (Siena, 1284 - Avignon, 1344). Born in 1284, according to Vasari, a doubtful but likely date since his first known work dates from 1315, Simone Martini married, in 1324, Giovanna, daughter of the painter, Memmo di Filippuccio. At that time, according to Ghiberti, he began to work with his brother-in-law, Lippo Memmi. Vasari believes that Simone was a pupil of Giotto's, followed his master to Rome about 1298 and imitated his manner. That account has no foundation. In fact, Simone was trained in his native town and was first influenced by Duccio, like all Sienese artists of his generation. We know nothing about his early works, but the *Maestà* fresco (signed and dated 1315) in the Palazzo Pubblico in Siena suggests earlier works: such an important commission could not have been given to a beginner. In it the artist shows his mastery; he finds inspiration in the Duccio *Maestà,* finished four years earlier, but he is more than Duccio influenced by gothic. The solemn style of the old master is replaced by a refined elegance and a subtle decorative sense. The characters, instead of standing out against a gold background,

ANDREA MANTEGNA. JUDITH. DRAWING. UFFIZI, FLORENCE.

occupy space which is made plausible by the use of perspective. The Virgin, enthroned on a high seat surmounted by a rich baldachin, is clearly separated from the angels and saints who surround her.

In 1317, Simone Martini was in Naples. His presence at the court of Robert of Anjou, which was once considered doubtful in spite of his obvious influence on Neapolitan painting, is now accepted as a historical fact. In Naples, he painted the portrait of King Robert kneeling to receive his crown from the hands of his brother, St Louis of Toulouse (who died in 1298 and was canonised in 1317 by Pope John XXII). Sitting erect, his face strangely pale, his eyes lost in a contemplative gaze which isolates him from the world and makes him appear indifferent to what he is doing, Louis of Toulouse is wearing a rich cloak over the Franciscan habit. The saint is shown frontally, the king in profile, a subtle way of contrasting two kinds of greatness, one from the world and one from heaven.

The equestrian figure of the *Condottiere, Guidoriccio da Fogliano,* in the Palazzo Pubblico in Siena (1328) is one of the most surprising examples of Sienese painting. The hero of Montemassi is represented in profile in a markedly realistic manner; he stands out against a dark sky, in the foreground of a barren landscape from which emerge to the right and to the left the walls and towers of a fortified town.

None of the works Simone painted between 1328 and 1333 have survived. In 1333, he painted the *Annunciation* altarpiece formerly in the Sant'Ansano chapel, in the Siena Cathedral (now in the Uffizi). This painting is one of the highest achievements of Sienese gothic. The setting is simplified to the utmost: a gold background, a bunch of lilies in a vase. The soft folds of the clothes follow the harmonious gestures of the characters. The Virgin, holding

in her hand a half closed book, turns away with a frightened movement. She is sitting and the angel kneeling, an iconographic innovation which shows the advance of the cult of the Virgin. The two side panels with saints are by Lippo Memmi.

The attribution to Simone Martini of the frescoes in the chapel of Cardinal Gentile da Montefiore, in the Lower Church at Assisi, is no longer doubtful, but their date is uncertain. Various art historians date the frescoes between 1317 and 1339, that is, between the end of his stay in Naples and his leaving for Avignon. The painting seems to be earlier than the Uffizi *Annunciation* which shows a greater mastery and a more complete assimilation of the gothic style. It represents, against a midnight blue background, episodes from the life of St Martin: the saint gives half his cloak to a beggar; Christ, wearing the half cloak, appears to him in a dream; he is knighted by the Emperor; he renounces the profession of arms. The four half-length portraits of saints in the right hand transept of the Lower Church

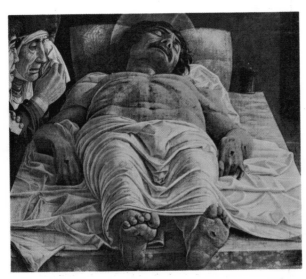

ANDREA MANTEGNA.
THE DEAD CHRIST.
ABOUT 1501.
BRERA, MILAN.

SIMONE MARTINI. GUIDORICCIO DA FOGLIANO. FRESCO. 1328. PALAZZO PUBBLICO, SIENA.

at Assisi (St Louis of Toulouse, St Francis, St Clare and St Elizabeth of Hungary) are also attributed to Simone Martini.

In Avignon, he met Petrarch and painted for him a portrait of *Laura,* now lost. All that is left of his last works (1339-1344) are parts of frescoes in the porch of Avignon Cathedral, and a polyptych (an intensely dramatic cycle of the *Life of Christ*) whose panels are divided between Paris, Antwerp and Berlin.   P.-H. M.

MASACCIO Tommaso (San Giovanni Val d'Arno, 1401 - Rome, 1428). Masaccio was, with Donatello and Brunelleschi, the founder of the heroic style in 15th century Florence which flourished at the same time as the international gothic represented principally by Ghiberti and Gentile da Fabriano. Masaccio inherited the tradition of Giotto and was the true ancestor of Michelangelo: his influence was felt by most Florentine artists of the 15th century, even though many of them reacted against it, and it was felt chiefly through the frescoes in the Brancacci Chapel in Santa Maria del Carmine, Florence. A late 15th century life of him, which is our chief source of information, describes him thus: 'He was about 27 when he died (*in the margin is added:* 15 September 1472. His brother Lo Scheggia told me that he was born in 1401, on the day of St Thomas the Apostle, 21 December)... In the Brancacci Chapel he painted several scenes, the best ones there, since the chapel was painted by three masters, all of them good, but he was marvellous... He also worked elsewhere in Florence, for churches and private people, and in Pisa and Rome and elsewhere; up to the time when he lived he is reckoned to be the greatest master.' The reference to the three masters in the Brancacci Chapel is to the fact that the fresco cycle was begun by Masolino and Masaccio, in the mid 1420's, and completed by Filippino Lippi much later in the century—so much later that it is quite easy to distinguish his style from that of the two earlier masters. The problem of deciding on the relative shares of Masolino and Masaccio must therefore be a matter of distinguishing two separate styles and allocating each to the right author. This is now very largely agreed on, mainly by comparison with the work in Pisa mentioned above. Documents exist for an altarpiece in the Carmelite church in Pisa, painted by Masaccio in 1426, which was described by Vasari, but was later dismembered and lost. The main panel, a *Madonna*, was identified, on the grounds of stylistic likeness to some of the frescoes in the Brancacci Chapel and correspondence with Vasari's description, with a panel in the National Gallery, London. A few more panels, in Pisa, Berlin, Naples, and Vienna have been identified as coming from the Pisa Polyptych, but much of it is still lost. The polyptych thus recreated can now be used as an authenticated example of Masaccio's mature style and can be used to check the style of the Brancacci frescoes. General agreement on the division of these between Masaccio and Masolino has been reached, Masaccio's chief works being the *Tribute Money*, the *Expulsion from Paradise*, *St Peter Enthroned*, *St Peter Healing the Sick by his Shadow*, and *St Peter giving Alms*, together with part of the *Raising of the Praetor's Son* (much of which is by Filippino). On the basis of the frescoes it is also possible to attribute to him the fresco of the *Trinity* in Santa Maria Novella, Florence. All these works must date from after 1422, when he entered the Florentine Guild, and before 1428. The problem of his

SIMONE MARTINI.
THE ANNUNCIATION.
1333.
CENTRAL PANEL
OF THE
ALTARPIECE.
UFFIZI, FLORENCE.

MASACCIO. THE TRIBUTE MONEY. FRESCO. 1426-1428. SANTA MARIA DEL CARMINE,
BRANCACCI CHAPEL, FLORENCE.

relationship to Masolino is complicated by the fact that, in the Brancacci Chapel, they were obviously working together and in some other works attributed to Masolino a very strong influence from Masaccio is unmistakable. Vasari interpreted this as evidence that Masaccio, the younger man, was the pupil of the more old-fashioned Masolino; an interpretation that would be tenable but for the fact that Masolino did not enter the Florentine Guild until the year after Masaccio, and no one might take pupils until he had matriculated in the Guild and paid his dues. The two works in which this extreme similarity of style is most clearly seen are the fresco of the *Baptism of the Neophytes,* in the Brancacci Chapel, and the two panels, now in the National Gallery, London, which come from a large altarpiece, the major parts of which are in Naples. All of this altarpiece appears to be by Masolino, but one panel of *St Jerome and St John Baptist* (London, National Gallery), is very close to Masaccio's style and is attributed to him by many authorities (though not by the Gallery). It is, however, very difficult to see how he could have painted only this one panel of an altarpiece and the problems of dating are also rather complex.

The quality for which Masaccio was esteemed by contemporary and later artists was not one which would ensure popular success, for he was rigidly grand and uncompromisingly austere in the pursuit of those quasi-scientific aims which distinguish the early, humanist art of 15th century Florence. His frescoes represent the figures of the Acts of the Apostles as heroic, rather rugged personages arranged in a strictly controlled space and lit by a consistent fall of light, achieving realism by means of the mathematical system of perspective developed during the preceding years by Brunelleschi and Donatello.

MASACCIO. ST PETER HEALING THE SICK BY HIS
SHADOW. FRESCO. 1426-1428. SANTA MARIA DEL
CARMINE, BRANCACCI CHAPEL, FLORENCE.

The aesthetic purpose of this severity
of form and subordination of all the
elements of the composition—figures
and landscape alike—to an over-riding
and consistent geometry and illumination was simply that of realism. By
imagining the picture plane to be no
more than a sheet of glass, behind which
a continuation of the real world was to
be found, subject to the same laws of
foreshortening and even to the same
fall of light as that which obtained on the
spectator's side, it was possible to break
decisively with the Byzantine conception
of a picture as a different world, subject
to different laws. Giotto began this

rapprochement with the visible world, but
Masaccio carried it to a logical conclusion. This heroic style, praised by
Alberti in his *Della Pittura* of 1436—
dedicated to Masaccio, Brunelleschi,
Donatello, Ghiberti and Luca della
Robbia—was the creation of Brunelleschi, Donatello and Masaccio, who was
by far the youngest of the group. Because he died so young his influence was
comparatively small, but his austere
rejection of the delights of bright
colour, gold, and charming detail did
even more to cause the younger generation to pay him little more than lip-
service. The contemporary international gothic style, the principal exponents
of which, in Florence, were Gentile da
Fabriano and Ghiberti, offered more
obvious charms both to patrons and
artists. Most of the rest of the century
saw a Masacciesque under-current, but
the increasing Florentine cult of the
outline also ran counter to the simple
masses and strong chiaroscuro of Masaccio's frescoes. Michelangelo, who
made drawings after his frescoes, was
probably the first truly to understand
his art, as he himself had been the first
for nearly a century to penetrate the
spirit of Giotto's.

Apart from the works mentioned
above there are other paintings attributed to Masaccio in Altenburg, Berlin,
Boston, Chambéry, Florence (Uffizi and
Museo Horne), Montemarciano, Rome
(San Clemente), Strasbourg and Washington.   P. M.

MASO di BANCO (Florence, second
quarter of the 14th century). Maso di
Banco, with Stefano Fiorentino and
Taddeo Gaddi, is considered one the
best of Giotto's disciples. It is important to distinguish him from Giottino,
another of Giotto's pupils, with whom
he has certain affinities. His most
important work is the decoration of the
Bardi Chapel at Santa Croce (Florence),
illustrating the legend of St Sylvester.

In the same chapel, Maso painted a *Last Judgment* which is dated about 1343. Maso di Banco's art is characterised by the excellence of his draperies, the beauty and expressivness of the faces and the attitudes of the figures that recall the dignity that Giotto conferred on his. A. L.

MASOLINO da PANICALE Tommaso di Cristoforo Fini, *called* (Panicale 1383 - 1447). Born in Panicale, not the village in the Val d'Elsa as Vasari states, but the small suburb of San Giovanni Val d'Arno, the birthplace also of Masaccio (1401), Masolino is not heard of until 1423. In that year we find him in Florence, enrolled according to custom in the guild of painters, physicians and apothecaries. He may have worked under Ghiberti on the Baptistery doors at the beginning of the century. For four years, from 1423 to 1427, he occupied a crucial position at the confluence of two styles, similar to that of Pisanello in the north.

At Empoli he decorated the Chapel of St Helena in San Stefano and painted the imposing *Pietà* for the Baptistery of the Collegiate Church. The Uffizi *Madonna* raises the question of his collaboration with Masaccio. The firm style of the young disciple had perhaps already influenced the older artist. About 1425 Masolino began the decoration of a chapel in Santa Maria del Carmine in Florence for Felice Brancacci (the *Story of St Peter*). He was joined in this commission by Masaccio and the respective attribution of the frescoes seems to be more or less established; thus, the *Healing of the Cripple* is by Masolino. However, he left Masaccio to continue alone and followed Pippo Spano, the Florentine condottiere in the service of King Sigismund, to Hungary. He was back before long, bound no doubt for Rome where he must be supposed as present about 1430 on account of the frescoes in San Clemente

MASACCIO. ST PETER GIVING ALMS. FRESCO. 1426-1428. SANTA MARIA DEL CARMINE, BRANCACCI CHAPEL, FLORENCE.

(the *Story of St Ambrose, Story of St Catherine,* and in particular the large *Crucifixion*) in which Masaccio's hand has also been discerned. Two diptychs with saints (London, National Gallery), which must have belonged to the triptych of the *Miracle of the Snow* (Naples) painted for Santa Maria Maggiore in Rome, have recently caused renewed discussion concerning the work of the two friends in Rome. After a brief stay at Todi, where he painted a *Madonna and Child* for the Church of San Fortunato (1432), Masolino moved to north Italy with Cardinal Branda Castiglione, to execute a remarkable series of frescoes for the Baptistery,

183

MASO DI BANCO. MIRACLES OF ST SYLVESTER. SANTA CROCE, FLORENCE.

the Collegiata, and the Cardinal's Palace at Castiglione d'Olona. He died in 1447.

Masolino's varied career reflects an active and unstable personality. As a pupil of Starnina, his manner remained international gothic, that colourful and precious style which, through the work of Gentile da Fabriano, was still in vogue about 1425. Masolino shows a predilection for fashionable silhouettes, for elegance of dress and for graceful demeanour. But he is interested in other things as well. His bright colours do not exclude a precise application of the modelling qualities of light, and he uses perspective to give rhythmic emphasis to space. During his successive stays in the north he must have played a decisive role in spreading, even in Venice, the novelties of Masaccio soon after their appearance. He obviously benefited from Masaccio's teaching himself, though the younger artist's vigour and solemn gravity remained

foreign to him. One sees this in Castiglione d'Olona where his imagination gets the better of his judgment. Freed from the commanding presence of his compatriot, Masolino associates here landscape with architecture and the personage in the centre in a way that has little in common with the Brancacci Chapel. This mutability enabled him, at a crucial time, to hold together two mutually opposed approaches to his art, the approach in terms of colour and the approach in terms of space. Without either of these neither the limpid world of Domenico Veneziano nor the equilibrium at a higher level of Piero della Francesca could have come about.   A. C.

MASTER of the MAGDALEN (*ca* 1250). This name is given to the unknown painter of a picture in the Accademia at Florence which follows the same pattern as the St Francis representations of the school of Pisa and Lucca: a full-length portrait of the saint and, at the sides, scenes from his life; but here, St Francis is replaced by Magdalen, clothed with her long hair. Apart from the influence of Pisan and, through it, of Byzantine art, we find in this picture echoes of Florence and Siena; it has been claimed that the Master of the Magdalen was a pupil of Migliore di Jacopo, from Pistoia. Many of the paintings attributed to him are not by the same hand, but from the same school, and probably from the same workshop. For instance; the altarpieces in the Jarvis Collection (New Haven) and in the Musée des Arts Décoratifs (Paris) where the Virgin and Child between two saints occupy the central part, and the altarpiece in the church of Vico l'Abbate, near Florence, whose iconography is particularly interesting, with St Michael enthroned in the centre and on both sides scenes from his legendary life, directly inspired by the *Golden Legend* by Jacopo da Voragine.   P.-H. M.

MASTER of the OSSERVANZA (first half of the 15th century). Sienese School. In the Osservanza Church, near Siena, there is a triptych dated 1436: the *Virgin between St Ambrose and St Jerome*. This highly individual work is unsigned and cannot easily be attributed to any known artist; several other paintings once attributed to Sassetta are now believed to be by the same hand. They are the remarkable *Scenes from the Life of St Anthony* (scattered among several American collections) and the *Asciano Polyptych* whose central panel (Asciano Museum) depicts the *Coronation of the Virgin* (upper part) and the *Birth of the Virgin* (lower part); two pieces from the predella are still extant: *Mary taking leave of the Apostles* (Settignano, Berenson Collection), and *Christ in the Tomb* (Dijon). Obvious affinities account for the earlier attribution of these pictures to Sassetta, but the Master

of the Osservanza remains closer to the Sienese 14th century tradition.   P.-H. M.

MASTER of SAN MARTINO Rainieri d'Ugolino, *called* the (active in Pisa, about 1260/70). The unsigned and undated *San Martino Madonna* (Pisa, Museo Nazionale) has been attributed to the artist who painted the *Christ on the*

MASOLINO. ADAM AND EVE. FRESCO. 1425. SANTA MARIA DEL CARMINE, BRANCACCI CHAPEL, FLORENCE.

MATTEO DI GIOVANNI. ST SEBASTIAN.
NATIONAL GALLERY, LONDON.

over the whole of Italian painting in the Duecento had two different aspects: a provincial Byzantinism like that of Anagni and the more severe Byzantinism of the metropolis. The Master of San Martino was influenced by both. But he adapted the lessons of Byzantine art to the local traditions and to his own personal tendencies.　　　P.-H. M.

MATTEO di GIOVANNI (Borgo San Sepolcro, *ca* 1430/35 - Siena, 1495). Born in Umbria, Matteo di Giovanni was probably the most popular of the Sienese masters of the second half of the 15th century. He must have been very young when he settled in Siena. He was there in 1452, 'eager to educate himself', he tells us. His first signed work, dated 1460, is a *Virgin and Child* with St Antony of Padua, St Bernardino and eight angels (Siena, Opera del Duomo). Matteo's prolific output consists mainly of Madonnas, usually on a gold background, whose gentle elegance and technical skill have brought him an uninterrupted celebrity. He also painted various other subjects. Obsessed by the theme of the *Murder of the Innocents*, he painted it three times, not counting the drawing of 1481 for the cathedral pavement: in 1482 (Siena, Sant'Agostino), 1488 (Naples) and 1491 (Siena, Santa Maria dei Servi). These compositions are intensely dramatic, and may have been suggested by a recent event: the slaughter of the inhabitants of Otranto by the Turks in 1480.　P.-H. M.

Cross (Pisa, Museo Nazionale) bearing the inscription *Rainierius quondam Ugolini Pisani me pinxit.* A date around 1270 has been suggested by comparison with Cimabue's *Santa Trinita Madonna* (about 1275, Uffizi) which is probably slightly later. The Master of San Martino recalls the Master of Anagni by his pathos, but the composition is more regular and more solemn. The Byzantine influence which made itself felt

MAZZOLA Francesco. *See* Parmigianino.

MEDICI (The). The origins of the family are obscure. The Medici took part in public life in Florence from the 13th century, but only began to play a part in art history from the 15th. Their family was then divided in two branches which soon became rivals: two dynasties founded by Cosimo and Lorenzo, sons of Giovanni di Bicci.

The chief members of the elder branch were Cosimo the Elder, his grandson, Lorenzo il Magnifico, and his great grandsons, Giovanni, who became Pope Leo X, and Giulio, who was elected Pope Clement VII (*see* the entries under these names). Other names to be remembered are Piero il Guttoso (1416-1469), son of Cosimo the Elder; Giuliano, Duc de Nemours (1479-1516), youngest son of Lorenzo il Magnifico, and his son, Ippolito, who was born in 1511, became a cardinal at eighteen (1529) and died in 1535. Piero was patron to the young Botticelli and considerably enriched the Medici collections. Many of the pictures mentioned in the 1492 inventory were probably his acquisitions. About 1515, Raphael painted a portrait of the *Duc de Nemours ;* in 1533, Titian painted *Cardinal Ippolito* (Pitti). It was Giulio de' Medici, the future Clement VII, who began negociations in 1520 with Michelangelo for the sepulchral chapel in San Lorenzo.

During the last years of the Quattrocentro, after the riots of 1494 and the exile of the elder branch of the family, the tradition was carried on by the heirs of Lorenzo di Giovanni: his son, Pierfrancesco, and his grandson, Lorenzo the Younger, cousin of Il Magnifico. Artists now turned to them, and when Filippino Lippi painted his *Adoration of the Magi* (finished in 1496) the figures are their portraits; Lorenzo the Younger, for whom Botticelli had already painted his *Primavera* and *The Birth of Venus,* commissioned from him in 1495 the illustration of the *Divine Comedy.*

The Grand Dukes of Tuscany belonged to the same junior branch. Cosimo I, whose title was confirmed by Charles V in 1537, built the Palazzo degli Uffizi, where one can still see his portrait painted by Bronzino (1545). His descendants, Ferdinand I, Cosimo II, Ferdinand II and Cosimo III, maintained till the end of the 17th century the tradition of patronage.   P.-H. M.

RAPHAEL. GIULIANO DE' MEDICI, DUC DE NEMOURS. METROPOLITAN MUSEUM, NEW YORK.

MEDICI Cosimo de' (Florence, 1389 - Florence, 1464). Son of Giovanni di Bicci de' Medici, born on September 27th, 1389, on St Cosimo's day, hence his christian name which was new in the family, Cosimo wanted to remain until his death a mere citizen of the Republic. Such moderation served his purpose: it allowed him, on occasions, to reject proposals from foreign heads of state by saying that he was only *privatus homo et mediocritate contentus*. His power was none the less very real. A great statesman and rich patron, he protected literature and scholars (Alberti, Landino, Argyropoulos, then Marsilio Ficino whom he sent for in 1459). He commissioned the erection or restoring of several buildings, among them the Palazzo, via Larga (now the Palazzo Medici or Riccardi) for which he preferred Michelozzo's designs to Brunelleschi's. Its

SANDRO BOTTICELLI. GIULIANO DE' MEDICI.
NATIONAL GALLERY OF ART, WASHINGTON.

Vecchio, where Vasari at the request of Cosimo I, the Duke of Tuscany, painted scenes from the history of Florence (1555 - 1562), Cosimo the Elder, as the 'Father of his Country', appears several times. His life is represented by four scenes; one of them shows Brunelleschi offering him a model of San Lorenzo. There is also the large medallion, in the Salone dei Cinquecento, in which Vasari painted him seated in the midst of a group of artists.   P.-H. M.

MEDICI Lorenzo de' (Florence, 1449 - Careggi, 1492). Grandson of Cosimo the Elder, son of Piero and Lucrezia Tornabuoni, Lorenzo de' Medici, called 'the Magnificent' (Il Magnifico), was brought up and educated first by his mother, then by some of the most famous humanists of the time: Marsilio Ficino, Cristoforo Landino, Argyropoulos. After his father's death (1469), his supporters urged him to take up, at the age of twenty, 'the responsibility of city and state'. His wide culture had prepared him for patronage and his reign (for it was already a reign, in spite of the republican form of government) coincided with the golden age of Florence. The Medici palace became a meeting place for scholars and artists from all parts of Italy and all countries of Europe. We can see how much Lorenzo valued, from his youth, all forms of artistic creation by the number, over 250, and quality of the manuscripts to be found in his personal library, now kept at the Laurenziana, and by the building he undertook and the commissions he gave, among others, to the workshops of the Pollaiuoli and of Verrocchio. Unlike other patrons of the arts, Lorenzo gradually made his patronage into a real 'cultural propaganda'. To establish the supremacy of Florence, he encouraged Tuscan artists to go further afield, while still inviting foreigners to his own palace. Thus, in 1481, Leonardo went to Milan; the same year,

chapel was decorated by Benozzo Gozzoli with a *Journey of the Magi* (1459), a subject which remained especially dear to the Medici family until the end of the century. He collected a considerable amount of manuscripts, medals, statues and various artistic treasures. Painting was not forgotten either. The library he built near the Badia Fiesolana was decorated with a painting of Apollo and the nine Muses, each accompanied by one poet. He particularly valued Filippo Lippi.

No portrait of him was painted during his life. The most lifelike are, together with the anonymous medal struck shortly after his death, the portraits painted by Pontormo (Uffizi) and Vasari. In the halls of the Palazzo

Botticelli, Domenico Ghirlandaio and Cosimo Rosselli were called to decorate the Sistine Chapel; later Verrocchio left for Venice and took his workshop there: all this with Lorenzo's approval; on his advice, too, Filippino Lippi went to Rome in 1488. Lorenzo's policy also created or encouraged contacts between artists and scholars: thus the improved social standing of the artist which Alberti already considered desirable in his treatise *On Painting* in 1435 was at last fully recognised and the masters of the 16th century were to reap the benefit of it.

Among the direct achievements of Lorenzo's patronage are the Villa Volterra which Filippino Lippi decorated with paintings; the Villa Poggio a Caiano whose building he personally supervised and whose interior decoration, only executed after his death, he inspired; and above all the school in a garden at San Marco where some of the most famous painters and sculptors of the time were trained. The word 'school' used by Vasari is not exactly correct: no formal teaching was given in the garden of San Marco; the *scuola* was merely a museum of antiques, which had become the seat of an academy, the collection of a rich nobleman generously open to artists, a place where they could meet to exchange ideas and find models.   P.-H. M.

MELOZZO da FORLI Michelozzo degli Ambrogi, *called* (Forli, 1438 - Forli, 1494). At the end of the 15th century, the whole region that stretched from Rome to Ferrara, including the Marches, but skirting Tuscany, was a field for the activities of Piero della Francesca's followers. Melozzo was one of the most active among them; with a less aristocratic and less pure manner than his master, he carried his grand, monumental style to Rome and spread it to Urbino, took it to Loretto and was probably the link between Bramante,

MELOZZO DA FORLI. ANGEL MUSICIAN. FRAGMENT OF A FRESCO FROM THE SANTI APOSTOLI. ABOUT 1480. VATICAN, ROME.

who was decorating the House of the Philosophers at Bergamo in 1477, Urbino and Rome. He divided his time between these three centres on frequent journeys, which sometimes makes it difficult to follow him. At Rome, he worked in the church of San Marco *(The Redeemer, St Mark the Pope* and *St Mark the Evangelist)* possibly in 1465-1470. The fresco of *Sixtus IV opening the Vatican Library* (about 1475, Vatican) is an impressive and masterly feat in its spatial organisation, owing to the rising perspective and the forceful modelling of the figures. Melozzo's contribution to the church of the Santi Apostoli, which

189

was connected with the Cardinal della Rovere, was no less impressive. The *Ascension* and the *Angel Musicians* (Vatican) survived from it and a few other fragments have been recently added to them.

It is difficult to decide Melozzo's exact share in two cycles: *Illustrious Men* (part at Urbino, part at the Louvre) and the *Liberal Arts* (two pieces in Berlin were destroyed in 1945; *Music and Rhetoric*, London, National Gallery), since the Spaniard, Berruguete, worked on them and possibly the Flemish painter, Joos van Ghent. Anyway, it was one of the most important meeting points of northern technique and the spatial vision of the Italians, which is well illustrated by Giovanni Santi, Raphael's father.

Melozzo's work exercised a strong influence at Rome on painters like Antoniazzo. It spread still farther through his work on the Sacristy of St Mark at Loretto after 1477. The perfection of the dome is striking, but the plunging angels show the hand of assistants like Marco Palmezzano. He worked again with Melozzo at Forli on the Feo Chapel in San Biagio (destroyed in 1944). In conclusion, the artistic personality of Melozzo was a final expression of the Quattrocento principles of Piero della Francesca on the eve of great changes that were to give definition to Roman classicism.   A. C.

MEMMI Lippo (Siena, active between 1317 and 1347). A Sienese artist, son of Memmo di Filippucio and brother of Federico di Memmo, both painters, and grandsons of Filippuccio, the goldsmith. In 1317, he worked with his father in the Palazzo Comunale of San Gimignano on the decoration of the Sala del Consiglio where he painted, among other things, a signed and dated copy of Simone Martini's *Maestà*. In 1333, he worked with Simone Martini, completing his *Annunciation* with two

figures of saints, placed to the right and left of the central panel. In 1347, at Avignon, he painted, with Federico di Memmo, a *Madonna* for the Franciscan church.

His undated works include: the *Virgin and Child* in Santa Maria dei Servi at Siena, known as the *Madonna del Popolo* (about 1320); a diptych now shared by the Berlin and Augsburg Museums (about 1330); the *Madonna della Misericordia* in Orvieto Cathedral; the *Virgin and Child* in the Altenburg Museum; a fresco fragment representing the *Virgin Enthroned* with the Child, surrounded by St Peter, St Paul and St Dominic (cloister of San Domenico in Siena). A few other unsigned paintings are attributed to Lippo Memmi for stylistic reasons. They all reveal the influence of Simone Martini, but in Memmi's compositions, the outline is sharper, the colour more opaque and the size generally smaller.   P.-H. M.

MICHELANGELO Michelangelo Buonarroti, *called* (Caprese, near Arezzo, 1475 - Rome, 1564). The long career of Michelangelo illustrates more clearly than that of any other artist the marvellous fecundity and universality of genius and their counterpart of spiritual drama and solitude. This has been felt ever since his own time, when two rival biographies were published well before his death: that by Vasari at the end of the *Lives* (1550 edition) and the other by Condivi (1553). Michelangelo's time was fairly evenly divided between Rome and Florence, works of painting alternating with sculpture and, after 1541, with architecture. The stylistic periods are clearly distinguishable.

In his youth, Michelangelo was privileged to know the flower of the Medici culture on the eve of its disruption. Born at Caprese in the Casentino, he came of a family of Florentine notables with noble connections. His taste for the arts was precocious; in 1488 he

entered the studio of Ghirlandaio as an apprentice, where his friend, Granacci, also worked. However, he left the following year to work in the 'garden of San Marco' directed by the old sculptor, Bertoldo. It was during this time that Torrigiani hit his rival, Michelangelo, with his fist, breaking his nose and disfiguring him for life. The young artist attracted the attention of Lorenzo il Magnifico, who took him into the Medici palace in the via Larga. Michelangelo lived there from 1490 until the death of Lorenzo in 1492; it was there that he met the humanists, Poliziano, Ficino, Benivieni and Landino. He worked on the two bas-reliefs of the *Madonna of the Stairs* and the *Rape of Deianira*. After Lorenzo's death, he returned to his father's house and made

a *Crucifix* in wood for the Prior of San Spirito and also his first free-standing marble sculpture of *Hercules*. He studied anatomy. However, at the revolution of 1494, he fled from Florence to Venice and then to Bologna where he stayed until 1495, sculpturing two small statues for the tomb of St Dominic. He returned to Florence during the government of Savonarola, but left again in June 1496 for Rome where he stayed until 1501. He carved a *Bacchus* for Jacopo Galli and Cardinal Jean de Villiers de la Grolaye commissioned the *Pietà* destined for St Peter's. This masterpiece brought him much fame. He made the cartoon (lost) for *St Francis receiving the Stigmata* for San Pietro in Montorio.

Returning to Florence in 1501, where

MICHELANGELO. PIETÀ. DRAWING.
ALBERTINA, VIENNA.

the Pitti *Madonna* (for Bartolomeo Pitti), 1505 (Florence, Bargello), and the *Madonna with a Bird,* about 1505-1506 (London, Royal Academy) or painted, like the Doni *Holy Family* (for Angelo Doni, 1503, Uffizi). The pontificate of Julius II, during which the best artists in Italy were attracted to Rome, interrupted this activity; Michelangelo was invited there in 1505. Julius II commissioned him to make the papal tomb. The project having been suspended, Michelangelo left Rome, the day before the first stone of Bramante's design for St Peter's was laid. He returned to Rome at the end of 1507, having been reconciled with the Pope who entrusted him in May 1508 with the immense enterprise of painting the vault of the Sistine Chapel. It took Michelangelo five years to achieve this feat, which was to change the whole trend of painting and whose heroic quality is in contrast to the more tender and eclectic style of Raphael, who was simultaneously working in the Vatican Stanze. The rivalry of these two men of genius, one virile, the other feminine, was a central point of the Renaissance. The death of Julius II in 1513 was the source of countless vicissitudes in the making of his tomb. There were six successive projects which in the end meant the abandonment of the colossal dream of 1506. The figure of Moses, finished in 1516, became the centre of a mediocre arrangement in San Pietro in Vincoli, Rome.

The third period begins with the election of Pope Leo X, son of Lorenzo il Magnifico and childhood friend of Michelangelo. He commissioned sculpture for the sepulchral chapel of the Medici in San Lorenzo, Florence. Michelangelo therefore set about bringing marbles from Carrara and Pietransanta (1516-1519) to be used for the façade, but the contract was cancelled in 1520. However, he sculptured the remarkable tombs in the New Sacristy

he remained until 1505, he entered his first great creative period. He carved the *David* (1501-1504), which was set up in front of the Signoria, designed the figures of the twelve apostles for the Duomo of which only the *St Matthew* survives (Venice, Accademia) and undertook the large fresco of the *Battle of Cascina* (cartoon lost; painting by Aristotile da Sangallo at Holkham Hall, Norfolk, is supposed to be a nearly complete copy), which was to complement Leonardo's *Battle of Anghiari* in the Signoria. At the same time he made *tondi:* either sculpture like

MICHELANGELO. DECORATIVE FIGURES. DETAIL FROM A FRESCO. 1508-1512.
CEILING OF THE SISTINE CHAPEL, ROME.

and at the same time he designed the entrance, or *ricetto,* of the Bibliotheca Laurenziana, which is a perfect example of mannerist architecture. After the sack of Rome in 1527, seized with a fit of civic enthusiasm, Michelangelo put himself at the disposition of the Florentine republic and supervised the fortifications of San Miniato. At the fall of the republic, he received a pardon from Pope Clement VII and returned finally to Rome in 1534. He had, however, left his mark on Florentine art; Pontormo was directly influenced by him and developed Michelangelo's cartoons. Michelangelo gave Antonio Mini, one of his pupils, his daring *Leda.* He composed a *Noli me tangere* for the Marchese del Vasto in 1531 (cartoon by Pontormo only survives), and a *Venus and Cupid* (lost; copy by Pontormo in Accademia, Venice) for Bartolomeo Bettini.

After his arrival in Rome, Michelangelo executed a series of mythological designs for Tomaso Cavalieri: *Ganymede, Tityos, Phaeton, Arcieri,* a *Bacchanale of Putti.* He also did a portrait of Cavalieri (lost). Clement VII died in 1534. The pontificate of Paul III, humanist and patron of the arts, opens another productive period in Michelangelo's work which was dominated, for the last time, by painting. The chief work of this period was the *Last Judgment* for the wall behind the altar in the Sistine Chapel for which the cartoon was made in 1535; the fresco itself

193

MICHELANGELO. THE FLOOD (DETAIL). FRESCO.
1508-1512. SISTINE CHAPEL, ROME.

painted two more frescoes for the Cappella Paolina, the *Conversion of St Paul* (1542-1545) and the *Crucifixion of St Peter*. These violent compositions, full of movement, were his farewell to painting. Architecture engrossed him; he finished the Palazzo Farnese (1546), planned the Piazza del Campidoglio and completed St Peter's, including the dome. He further executed a project for San Giovanni dei Fiorentini for Pope Julius III (1550); offered to make the plan of the Gesù for Ignatius Loyola (1554) and erected Santa Maria degli Angeli within the Baths of Diocletian (1561). Under the pontificate of Paul IV the humanist spirit of the papal court disappeared; the nude figures of the *Last Judgment* were ordered to be covered. Michelangelo sculptured his last *Pietà* for himself. His religious drawings, the *Crucifix, Annunciation, Christ driving the sellers out of the Temple* (this last an allusion to the purification of the Church), bear witness to his isolation and to his suffering. He died on February 18th, 1564, and his corpse was taken by night to Florence and buried on the 14th March in Santa Croce, where it still reposes. The official funeral took place at San Lorenzo on July 14th, the city of Florence claiming before Rome the privilege of honouring this prodigious personality, who was venerated by all the academies and was imitated throughout Europe.

His work in painting consists of certain religious *tondi,* secular pictures and the great Vatican cycles. In the earlier works the forceful contours and bright colour indicate clearly his Tuscan inheritance; but his beginnings have not been altogether elucidated and Ghirlandaio's influence was purely technical. In sculpture, Michelangelo had two masters, Donatello and the antique. In painting, he reverted to the rigour and monumentality of Masaccio.

The works of 1501-1505 adapt motifs from Leonardo and Michelangelo's

was begun in 1536 and finished in 1541. The Counter-Reformation was at its height. Michelangelo, deeply preoccupied by religious problems, lived constantly in the circle presided over by Vittoria Colonna, Marchesa of Pescara. He conceived a noble attachment for this great lady which was closely connected with his mystical experiences. He executed a series of religious works for her: a *Crucifix,* a *Pietà,* etc. After the final version of the tomb of Julius II (1545), he

Battle of Cascina was to have been a companion to his *Battle of Anghiari*. If this picture of nudes and bathers had been realised, it would have been an unprecedented study of anatomy. The Doni *Holy Family* is notable for the powerful interlocking of figures, which creates a kind of undulating block of great plastic force, without subtleties of chiaroscuro. Michelangelo had already discovered the power of giant forms and envisaged their use in the tomb of Julius II. These forms, which haunted his imagination, appear again in the Sistine ceiling; the theme is both historic and symbolic, the great scenes from Genesis, the Creation, the Fall, the Deluge, complement the scenes of the Coming of the Messiah already painted on the walls. Their grandeur is magnified by the presence of the twelve Prophets and Sibyls, all types of inspiration, which, accompanied by their 'daemons', seem to uphold the tremendous painted architecture of arches and vaults which provide the framework for the ceiling. These figures, in which everything is coherent and defined, down to the pleats of drapery and the smallest of gestures, are the highest achievement of Florentine linear composition amplified by Roman monumentality. In the upper zone, framing the nine panels of Genesis, are seated the amazing adolescent figures, the *ignudi*, whose attitudes alone seem to express a quite different range of emotions. There is every reason to suppose that this organisation of the design in stages and this symbolism of the forces of the soul, directed by faith, is due to Michelangelo himself. It contains traces of the optimistic and conciliatory doctrines which he had assimilated in the Florentine circle of Lorenzo il Magnifico; that is, the neo-Platonic ideal, which postulates an accord between classical thought and Christian order as essential to the dignity of man. The ascending movement of the Sistine ceiling corresponds to the

MICHELANGELO. THE FALL OF THE DAMNED. DETAIL FROM THE 'LAST JUDGMENT'. FRESCO. 1536-1541. SISTINE CHAPEL, ROME.

tripartite schema of matter, reason, spirit, in 'Platonic theology'. This 'theology' considers the poet and the artist as belonging to the spiritual order. For the first time, ornamental figures are incorporated into the architectural composition in such a way as to form an integral part of the design. Quattrocento motifs dissolve into forms inspired by the antique and the whole comprises a decorative entity from which generations of artists were to draw instruction. Every part of the work

MICHELANGELO. STUDY FOR THE LEDA.
DRAWING. CASA BUONARROTI, FLORENCE.

vibrates with a vitality which testifies to the artist's capacity to depict human aspiration towards the divine nature.

Thirty years later, Michelangelo was drawn back again to painting by Paul III's commission for the *Last Judgment* on the end wall of the Sistine Chapel. He was at that time sixty years old. The composition is conceived as a tremendous gyration, ascending on the left side, descending on the right, centred on the figure of Christ who appears as a Hercules or an angry Jupiter. This is the world of *terribilità*. Unlike the ceiling, the composition has no architectonic frame. It takes shape in a visual space regulated solely by forces of attraction and repulsion. Those figures that ascend do so without the aid of supernatural beings, only by the power of faith. This leaping beyond bounds is also a symbol of renunciation of human restrictions. The brown bodies spin against an intense blue background, above the sinister redness of the infernal regions. If the ceiling represents the supreme moment of classic balance, the *Last Judgment* is the entry into the pulsing movement of baroque.

In the last work painted in the Cappella Paolina, the *Conversion of St Paul* and the *Crucifixion of St Peter,* all feelings of classic balance have disappeared. The astounded face of St Paul, the agonised face of St Peter, each appears in the midst of a furious mêlée. The style has become heavy, the masses compact; the statement of Christian truths is no longer made without 'fear and trembling'. The same anguish and profound need for penitence appear in the restrained drawings of Crucifixions,

MICHELANGELO. PROFILE WITH A BIZARRE HEAD-DRESS. DRAWING. ASHMOLEAN MUSEUM, OXFORD.

the last, moving *Pietà* and the poems of the same period.

As a painter, Michelangelo worked chiefly in fresco: the greatest fresco painter of all time in the breadth of his conception and the authority of his drawing. The Tuscan mannerists immediately drew on the example of his supple line and clear colour (pure yellows, airy mauves and delicate pinks appear constantly in the Sistine ceiling); but his influence was again apparent in 1600 in directing the 'classicism' of the Carracci. As for the *Last Judgment,* it is certain that it leads to the swirling eccentricities of the baroque. The art of Michelangelo both dominates all styles and cannot be defined as any one of them. Its distinguishing mark is undoubtedly the sublime quality integral to all work that seeks to uncover the mysterious life of the soul through the inexhaustible beauty of the human body.   A. C.

MICHELINO da BESOZZO (born in Lombardy, active between 1388 and 1445). From 1388 to 1445 numerous documents testify to Michelino da Besozzo's long period of activity at Pavia and Milan, emphasising his importance as the leader of a school and giving the reasons for his reputation. Among the very few evidences of his art which have come down to us are two paintings, a *Mystic Marriage of St Catherine* at Siena and a *Marriage of the Virgin* in the Metropolitan Museum of New York, a fresco at Viboldone, two miniatures for the *Funeral Oration of Gian Galeazzo Visconti* (1404, Bibliothèque Nationale) and several drawings for a *Book of Hours* (Avignon Library). A few drawings too have survived as examples of his art. They suffice to give us an idea of his extremely refined art. After Giovannino de' Grassi, Michelino emerges as one of the chief creators in Italy of the 'international gothic' style at the beginning of the 15th century. His influence was wide-

MICHELINO DA BESOZZO. MYSTIC MARRIAGE OF ST CATHERINE. PINACOTECA, SIENA.

spread in Lombardy where it determined the style of two generations of painters and miniaturists; it extended as far as the Veneto (Michelino is documented in 1410 at Venice, where possibly he met Gentile da Fabriano) and above all, to Verona.   M. L.

MILAN. Her privileged position at the intersection of the great routes from the Alps towards the Adriatic and the principal European centres explains the historical importance of Milan, one of the great cities of the Roman Empire. Little remains of this past, because Frederick Barbarossa had the entire city razed except for a few churches (1162). Only rare traces, often difficult to date, remain as memories of the times of St Ambrose and St Augustine; one of the most remarkable is the church of San Lorenzo. Subsequently the ambitions and genius of Lombard architects endowed the city with great architectural ensembles, which had such a grand effect that it became customary from the time of Charlemagne to crown the King of Italy at Milan. The Basilica di Sant'Ambrogio, the most original of these creations, is a perfect example of romanesque architecture. It was founded as far back as 386, but was twice transformed, in the 7th, then the 9th century and finally assumed the appearance, which we know today, at the end of the 11th century.

Painting, just as in the other centres in Italy, began with mosaic. The first examples of painting are often difficult to date: the most outstanding are to the north of Milan, in the church of Castelseprio where the rich Byzantine iconography is combined with a pronounced classicism. Specialists disagree on the dates (about 650-670 or 925-950) of this ensemble, which is difficult to place in Lombard art, although a mixture of oriental, asiatic and classical elements appears in its goldsmith's work. In sculpture, the ciborium of Sant'Ambrogio in Milan (10th century) and its famous gold altar leave us a similar impression of this taste for luxury and its strange mingling of classical and Lombard elements. During the gothic period, Lombardy found itself closely linked with northern France and the Rhine region. It was the age of the city and Milan, like Florence, Siena, Bologna and Perugia was assuming her own character. However, her pictorial development was slow: the works were impregnated with Tuscan influences and original personalities, like Giovanni da Milano, were rare. This influence also marks the miniature and what is called 'Lombard work', with its fine, pure style in which the outlines of animals alternate with piquant, realistic details. Giovannino de' Grassi and Michelino da Besozzo are

the outstanding names in this wave of prosperity that spread over the west. In sculpture, it was from the circle of Giovanni Pisano and Giovanni di Balduccio that the gothic inspiration came.

During the Renaissance, Milan was one of the great powers of the day. In 1447, a condottiere, Francesco Sforza, ejected the Visconti dukes, who had been masters of the town until then. It was on the full tide of expansion and the political rival of Florence when Francesco Sforza drew the Tuscan artists to it: Michelozzo, who worked at Sant'Eustorgio, and Filarete, the follower of Brunelleschi. The influence of Bramante, who came from Urbino and was in the service of Ludovico il Moro in 1481 was superimposed on the Florentine contribution and added a magnificent and monumental breadth. It was the period when Vincenzo Foppa dominated Lombard painting with the sumptuous gravity of his art. There flourished by his side a whole, original school of which the great names were Bramantino, Butinone, Zenale and Ambrogio Bergognone. Milan, like so many other Italian cities, was very open to Flemish influences and Petrus Christus, who revealed Van Eyck to it, lived in Milan.

The arrival of Leonardo da Vinci in 1482 transformed the centre; the fascination and breadth of his personality set off a movement parallel to the Roman classicism. The imitators of his painting or pupils, Ambrogio da Predis, Boltraffio, Gianpietrino, Marco d'Oggiono, Cesare da Sesto, Solario and Luini, adopted his technique without always understanding his delicate effects with light and his symbolism. Milan continued throughout the second half of the century to welcome artists from outside: Galeazzo Alessi from Perugia, Leone Leoni from Arezzo and Pellegrino Tibaldi from Bologna.

Political change in Milan and the decadence of the Duchy perhaps partly

MONSU DESIDERIO. THE DESTRUCTION OF SODOM. ABOUT 1624.
MARIO GIURLANI COLLECTION, ROME.

explains why so wealthy a town did not possess any great architects during the baroque period. Painting, however, held its own brilliantly with Giovanni Battista Crespi, called Il Cerano, P. F. Mazzuchelli, called Il Morazzone and G. C. Pracaccini in whose appealing art, with its violently expressive chiaroscuro, Roman and Bolognese influences appear. The painting of the next generation was an echo of Caravággism: Daniele Crespi, Tanzio da Varallo, Francesco del Cairo and Nuvoloni; to these could be added the names of Evaristo Baschenis, a painter of still-lifes, and Alessandro Magnasco, a Milanese by adoption.   s. b.

MONSU DESIDERIO (17th century). The name, transmitted by De Dominici, the historian of Neapolitan painters, has caused a great deal of speculation. *Monsù* was a prefix attached to names of artists who were not Italian. The painter has been identified with Didier Barat (or Barrat), a Lorrainer born in Metz in 1590, who supposedly left his native town for Rome in 1608, settled down in Naples about 1617, and signed as Desiderius Barra a view of Naples painted in 1647. But it is doubtful whether this artist, who seems to have specialised in perspectives, can be the author of the fairly large number of pictures, dispersed in various museums and collections, that are traditionally attributed to him: fantastic buildings decorated with outsize statues and standing out in white relief as though embossed on the leathery background. The subject is usually some disaster or other. Several of these works carry the signature of a certain François de Nome, also a Lorrainer, who was born in Metz in 1593, came to Rome in 1602 and to Naples in 1610. He may have had one or several imitators. The influence of theatre sets on these pictures is obvious.   p. c.

PIERO DELLA FRANCESCA. PORTRAIT
OF BATTISTA SFORZA. 1465-1466.
UFFIZI, FLORENCE.

MONTAGNA Bartolomeo (Orzinovi, near Brescia, *ca* 1450 - Vicenza, 1523). His career was typically provincial. Settled in Vicenza in 1480, Montagna lived there till his death, with short visits to Venice. In 1482, he was commissioned to paint two biblical compositions for the Scuola di San Marco, in 1483 he painted the Pala for the Venice Hospital and in 1487, *St Sebastian and St Roch* (Bergamo, Accademia Carrara). His productive period was at the turn of the century, with the *Madonna Enthroned between Four Saints* (Brera), the *Virgin between St James and St Philip* (1499, lost), the *Pietà* for the Madonna del Monte Berico (1500) and the *Nativity* for the church at Orgiano, which was completed in 1502. It is a sequence of monumental works, in which we see the

Paduan heritage in the firm placing of figures on the ground, the broken draperies, the rusty colours and leaden tones. Montagna was first and foremost a master of modelling and, in spite of his monumental groupings, was considered more and more old-fashioned at the beginning of the 16th century. He also worked at the Scuola del Santo, in Padua, and his career was prolonged by the painting of numerous village *Madonnas* in which he tried at the end to achieve lighter effects. His compositions are dominated by stone and rock: flagstone pavings, elaborate architectural backgrounds and solid rock foundations, which give them a powerful balance. As a colourist, he is less successful.   A. C.

MONTEFELTRE (The). Successors of the Counts of Carpegna, the Montefeltre, lords of Urbino since 1234, had not distinguished themselves in the course of two centuries otherwise than by excessive fierceness and a quarrelsome spirit when, as the family was almost extinct, it blossomed forth and produced two patrons of the arts: Federico and Guidobaldo. The former, nicknamed by Robert de la Sizeranne 'the virtuous condottiere', was one of the most remarkable figures of the Renaissance. Federico (1422-1482), first Count, later Duke of Urbino, succeeded in 1444 his brother Oddantonio who had been murdered by his rebellious subjects. Although of illegitimate birth, he soon commanded respect and love from all by his comparative urbanity, his culture and his organising ability. His second wife, Battista Sforza, helped him in his patronage. He is responsible for the building of the extraordinary palace of Urbino whose massive bulk stands, in parts, on the edge of sheer declivities.

Federico commissioned it from the Dalmatian architect, Francesco Laurana, as we learn from the letter he wrote to him in 1468. That precious document, discovered in 1838, was published in

1950 by P. Rotondi *(Il Palazzo ducale di Urbino)*. The work was supervised until 1472 by Laurana, then after he had left, by Francesco di Giorgio Martini.

The palace was profusely decorated with panelling, sculptures and various works of art, and Federico collected a library which was in its time one of the richest in western Europe. As for the paintings, particular mention must be made of the decoration of the *studiolo,* a private study where the Duke retired for solitary meditation. The upper part of the four walls of that little room were covered, in two tiers, with the portraits of twenty-eight famous men, illustrating the achievements of the human mind. On the top tier were holy characters, Old Testament figures, Fathers and Doctors of the Church (Moses, Solomon, St Ambrose, Albert the Great) and two secular poets (Dante and Petrarch); on the lower: philosophers, poets and ancient and modern scholars from Plato to Pietro d'Abano. Two painters worked on the decorations: Joos van Wassenhove (known as Justus of Ghent) on the upper tier and Pedro Berruguete on the lower. The *studiolo* portraits are now partly in the Galleria Nazionale, Urbino, and partly at the Louvre.

In the library were represented on seven panels the liberal arts, shown as seated women, with a servant at the feet of each one who was a near relative or intimate of Federico. Two of those compositions have survived and are now in the National Gallery in London; the others have been lost. The paintings in the library, later than those in the *studiolo,* are more Italian in character. The influence of Piero della Francesca is noticeable. Melozzo da Forlì also worked on the decoration of the Duke's palace

The striking figure of Federico has inspired painters and medal engravers. Notable among the paintings, is the miniature in the manuscript of Landino's

PIERO DELLA FRANCESCA. PORTRAIT OF FEDERICO DA MONTEFELTRO. 1465-1466. UFFIZI, FLORENCE.

Disputationes Camaldulenses (Vatican Library), the painting by Berruguete, where the Duke is shown with his son Guidobaldo, aged nine or ten, and the portrait by Piero della Francesca (Uffizi), painted in 1465/66. After Federico's death, Guidobaldo (1472-1508) succeeded him. When he grew up, he continued his father's work. The splendour of his court is described by Baldassare Castiglione in the famous dialogue of the *Courtier*. P.-H. M. .

MORETTO Alessandro Bonvicino, *called* (Brescia, *ca* 1498 - Brescia, 1554). He is, with Savoldo and Romanino, the leading painter of Brescia in the 16th century. Moretto was a pupil of the local painter, Ferranola, with whom he was working in 1516. He owed much to the Vene-

ALESSANDRO MORETTO. PORTRAIT
OF A LADY. KUNSTHISTORISCHES
MUSEUM, VIENNA.

tian tradition, but at the same time remained faithful to the Lombard tradition of Foppa. He was favoured with innumerable ecclesiastical commissions and he spent his career entirely at Brescia and its environs. His work tends to be monotonous. The large altarpieces are generally planned on the same classical composition of two stages, one occupied by the Virgin and Child, the other by a group of three or four saints, standing against a background of sky (*Virgin* and *Child with Saints,* Brescia, Santa Maria delle Grazie) or architecture (Bergamo, altarpiece in the church of Sant'Andrea). The types are repeated: austere old men realistically treated, saints with placid, heavy profiles (*St Justin,* Vienna, Kunsthistorisches Museum). Moretto did not, however, avoid the most complex compositions (*The Sorrowing Christ with an Angel,* Brescia, Pinacoteca Tosio Martinengo); he was capable on occasion of multiplying figures without disturbing the design of a large composition (*Adoration of the Child,* ibid.). The firmness of the faces is a reminder that he was a remarkable portraitist (*Portrait of a Gentleman,* 1526, London, National Gallery), who could play skilfully with the floral design of a fabric or a salmon pink satin (*Portrait of a Gentleman,* Brescia, Pinacoteca). The quiet strength of the outlines and the peaceful spirituality of an art that submitted willingly to traditional ideas represent a sort of serene counterpart to the vibrant experiment of Venice.   J. T.

MORONE Domenico (Verona, *ca* 1442 - Verona, 1517) *and* Francesco (Verona, *ca* 1471 - Verona, 1529). Domenico

GIOVANNI BATTISTA MORONI. PORTRAIT
OF AN OLD MAN. ABOUT 1565-1570.
ACCADEMIA CARRARA, BERGAMO.

Morone followed in the tradition set by Benaglio, practising and instituting from 1480 onwards at Verona a classical type of painting, very much after the style of Mantegna. The influence of Gentile Bellini and Carpaccio on the other hand explains the liveliness of his narrative in works such as the *Battle of the Gonzaga and the Bonacolsi* (1494, Mantua). After 1496 he worked in close collaboration with his son Francesco, in particular on the frescoes for the Convent of San Bernardino (1503). Francesco accentuated his father's tendencies, drawing his inspiration even more directly from the Venetians (*Samson and Delilah*, Milan, Museo Poldi-Pezzoli), and finally evolved an ingenuous and monotonous purist style, but based it on a streamlined definition of volume, visualised as smooth, round shapes with deep, full colours. Many painters were trained in the Morone workshop, notably Girolamo dai Libri, Cavazzola, Michele da Verona and Giovanni Caroto.   M. L.

MORONI Giovanni Battista (Albino, near Bergamo, *ca* 1520/1530 - Bergamo, 1578). Moroni was a pupil of Moretto at Brescia and Moretto's influence clearly remains in his work (*Dispute of the Doctors of the Church and the Triumph of the Virgin*, Trento, Santa Maria Maggiore); but the greater part of his career was spent at Bergamo, occupied mainly with commissions for altarpieces for churches in the town and its environs, where a fair number have remained (*The Virgin and Child with St Catherine and St Jerome*, 1576, Bergamo, Duomo). The long portrait gallery of Bergamo notables are quite distinct from these works with their traditional conception and rather monotonous feeling. These portraits earned the approbation of Titian himself for Moroni during his life-time and a justified reputation for the artist today: half-length figures (a fine collection in the Accademia Carrara at Bergamo; *Portrait of a*

GIOVANNI BATTISTA MORONI. THE TAYLOR. NATIONAL GALLERY, LONDON.

Man, Vienna, Kunsthistorisches Museum; *Portrait of a Sculptor*, ibid.) and particularly notable are the full-length portraits in which the simple, masterly composition is sufficient to convey the mobility of the model (portraits of *Bernardo Spina* and *Pace Rivola Spina*, Bergamo, Accademia Carrara; *Portrait of a Gentleman*, London, National Gallery). An execution free from all littleness lends distinction to a sober colouring with silvery tones and can draw fine effects from the black of a doublet (*Portrait of a Gentleman*, 1554, Milan, Ambrosiana) and the interplay of grey and whites (*Portrait of a Taylor*, London, National Gallery). The psychology remains superficial, but the expression, which is always restrained is naturally suffused with a delicate melancholy that imparts a genuine poetry to these portraits.   J. T.

N - O

NAPLES. Serried on the shore of its gulf the harmony of whose curve is almost proverbial, climbing the heights above, Naples has none of the charm of so many Italian towns in which the traveller leaves behind a part of his soul. Its distant origins—Neapolis-Parthenope dates back to the 8th century B.C.—and its Roman period, when the shore was dotted with luxurious villas, have left no trace except in the Museo Nazionale and in the towns, buried by Vesuvius, which were, in a way, its suburbs. Ruled in turn by the Byzantines, the Normans, and the Hohenstaufen, Naples became Angevin in 1294 and Aragonese in 1442. During the Middle Ages sizeable churches were built in the city almost invariably on sites drowned in the amorphous mass of houses pressing around them. One of the principal monuments of Naples, the Angevin Castel Nuovo was magnificently completed at the Renaissance by a triumphal arch designed by Laurana. But painting was for a long time imported: Cavallini and Giotto worked in Naples and with them the Tuscan manner dominated the 14th century. In the 15th, Flemish and, perhaps, Catalan painting come to the fore. Colantonio was undoubtedly a Neapolitan but Antonello da Messina, in spite of his southern origins, introduced an art inspired by the great Flemings.

Annexed by Spain in 1504 with the Kingdom of the Two Sicilies, Naples was well enough governed by its viceroys but not until the baroque did it come artistically into its own. Caravaggio arrived in 1607. The Certosa di San Martino, near the Castel Sant'Elmo, became a veritable Caravaggist sanctuary; painters like Ribera, Stanzioni, Caracciolo and Fracanzano contributing to its decoration. These artists, who followed Caravaggio in their predilection for sharp contrasts of light and shade and scenes of violence, formed an exclusive group jealous of its privileges and dominated by the Spaniard Ribera. Domenichino who came to Naples to decorate the Chapel of San Gennaro in the Cathedral, suffered severely from their hostility. However, other foreign artists, like the Parmesan Lanfranco or the Calabrese Mattia Preti, produced major works in Naples, while the great decorators, Luca Giordano and Solimena, inundated with their paintings the walls of Neapolitan churches whether newly built or renovated in an upto-date style. Artistically this was the most brilliant period, feebly continued by Salvator Rosa whose romantic landscapes achieved a wide success, while a debased Caravaggism lived on in the popular art of a Traversi, and the stilllifes of Ruoppolo and others like him luxuriated in the abundance of detail.

Naples has, throughout its history, remained an inarticulate cluster of buildings frequently ravaged by fire and epidemic. The Bourbons ruled from 1734 onwards—rather badly—but at least they contributed in a major way to the architecture of the city. Among their achievements in this field is the square in front of the cold but imposing structure of San Francesco di Paolo, and the Reggia di Capodimonte, the latter since admirably transformed into a museum of painting. The Bourbon domination saw the development of the fragile and specifically Neapolitan art of Christmas cribs. The Parthenopaean Republic and the kingship of Murat were, politically, no more than interludes.

Then, in 1860, Garibaldi entered the city which became part of the Kingdom of Italy.

Painting was actively pursued in Naples throughout the 19th century, but no great names emerged. In the landscape tradition the school of Posillipo may be noted. Giacinto Gigante and Palizzi interpreted the natural setting of Naples. Domenico Morelli and especially Antonio Mancini, a very prolific artist, achieved some prominence.

Naples suffered considerably in the last war. One of the effects of bombing has been to restore the church of Santa Chiara to its gothic appearance by destroying the baroque revetment that had obscured it.   P. C.

NARDO di CIONE (died at Florence, 1365/66). He was the brother of the Florentine painter, sculptor and architect, Andrea di Cione, called Orcagna (a third brother, Jacopo di Cione, was also a painter). In the middle of the 15th century, Ghiberti described the paintings in the Strozzi Chapel in Santa Maria Novella, Florence, as 'the Inferno that was painted for the Strozzi family' and ascribed it definitely to Nardo. The altarpiece in the chapel is signed by Orcagna and is not identical in style, so the Inferno fresco must be regarded as the touchstone for all attributions to Nardo. In the work of Orcagna there is a metallic hardness of form, combined with a non-illusionistic, flat treatment of space: in his brother's paintings there is a softer, less sculptural, feeling for plasticity and a very delicate sense of colour.   P. M.

NEGRETTI Jacopo di Antonio. *See* Palma.

NEROCCIO di BARTOLOMEO de' LANDI (Siena, 1447 - Siena, 1500). A painter and sculptor, trained by Vecchietta like Francesco di Giorgio Martini with whom he opened a workshop and

NARDO DI CIONE. A SAINT. DETAIL FROM THE 'PARADISE'. FRESCO. STROZZI CHAPEL, SANTA MARIA NOVELLA, FLORENCE.

remained associated until 1475, Neroccio, of noble birth but penniless, was quiet, unassuming and home-loving. While so many Sienese painters spread the field of their activities from Naples to Avignon, he only left his native town once, for a short stay in Lucca in 1481. The Virgin and Child between two saints is the subject of most of his paintings (gathered in the Siena Pinacoteca), from the *Virgin between St Jerome and St Bernardino* (1476, one of his early paintings, and the first to be dated) to the *Virgin between St Andrew and St John the Baptist* (about 1496). Keeping to a well established iconographic tradition, Neroccio paints all his Virgins in the same attitude:

NICCOLÒ DELL'ABBATE

the head leaning sideways, the eyes looking down; they always have delicate hands. His style, his subjects, varied little except for the use of soft colours in his first works and of more vivid tones in his last paintings.   P.-H. M.

NICCOLÒ dell' ABBATE (Modena, *ca* 1509 - Fontainebleau, 1571). His personality is first noticeable in his decorations at Modena (frescoes in the Palazzo Comunale, 1546) and Bologna (frescoes in the Palazzo Zucchini-Solimei and at the University): Dosso's influence and his close study of Correggio and Parmigianino are both equally evident in his taste for romantic subjects and his ideas on landscape, with its panoramic views of indented coastlines. In 1552 he was summoned to France, and it is here, where he acted as Primaticcio's brilliant second, that he demonstrated the full measure of his art: he supported Primaticcio's elegant style with his vigorous handling and vibrantly live figures (the *Continence of Scipio,* Louvre), and brings a hint of fantasy to his spirit of subtle sensuality (the *Rape of Persephone,* Louvre). Niccolò dell'Abbate had an im-

portant influence on the development of the Fontainebleau school.   J. T.

NICCOLÒ da FOLIGNO Niccolò di Liberatore di Giacomo Mariani, *called* Niccolò Alunno, *or* (Foligno, *ca* 1430 - Foligno, 1502). In 15th century Umbria, Foligno remained an artistic centre distinct from Perugia and characterised by a liveliness which has been called expressionistic. The starting point of this animated, but somewhat heavy, style is probably the art of Gozzoli who, between 1450 and 1452, painted frescoes in San Fortunato in Montefalco. Niccolò decorated a chapel in Santa Maria in Campis, but he painted mainly altarpieces with a gilt background: in 1461-1465, the Cagli polyptych (Brera), in collaboration with his father-in-law, Pietro Mazzaforte; in 1466, the panels in the Trittico di Camerino and Polittico di Montelpare (Vatican). While working in the Marches, Niccolò met Crivelli whose influence probably contributed to make his work more emphatic and sometimes more precise: we find this new manner in the Nocera Umbra altarpiece (1483) and even more at

San Nicolò in Foligno (1492) in the *Virgin of Mercy* (Rome, Galleria Colonna) which is characteristic of this robust devotional painting, somewhat gaudy and naïve.　　　　A. C.

NICCOLÒ di PIETRO (Venice, active between 1394 and 1430). The son and grandson of painters, he is sometimes called Niccolò Paradisi because his house in Venice was next to the Ponte del Paradiso. He does not treat colour with the concise technique of the 14th century. His figure grouping is less crowded than that of his predecessors. He can be considered as the representative of the Venetian transitional style. Although he broke completely with the gothic-byzantine style, he was unaffected, however, by the new tendencies which appear in Gentile da Fabriano. Three works by him exist, whose authenticity is not contested: a *Virgin with the Child in her Arms* (1394, Venice, Accademia); a *Crucifix* surrounded by the symbols of the Evangelists (1404, Palazzo Comunale in Verucchio, near Rimini) and a *Madonna* preserved at Santa Maria dei Miracoli (1409, Venice).　　　　A. L.

NUZI Allegretto da Fabriano, *called* Allegretto (Fabriano, *ca* 1315 - Fabriano, 1373). He was one of the intermediaries who helped to spread Giotto's art towards the Marches, where the Byzantine influence was still very strong (and after all, in and near Ravenna, we find the most remarkable early Christian mosaics). Allegretto, a fresco-painter, is mentioned in 1346 as a member of the Guild of Painters of Florence and must have been Bernardino Daddi's pupil. After 1350, he worked in Rimini and in Fabriano. From Giotto, he took somewhat squarish shapes, a strong composition flavoured with archaic Byzantine features, which we notice in the frescoes of the San Domenico sacristy in Fabriano *(Crucifixion* and

Story of the Virgin). If we compare him to Pietro da Rimini and other important painters from the province, Allegretto strikes us as rather provincial in his stiffness and overbright colours. The altarpieces on a gilt background, the *Vatican Triptych* (1363), the enthroned *Madonnas* (Sanseverino and Urbino Museums) show a delicate Sienese touch with a hint of preciosity, which we often find at the end of the 14th century.　　　　A. C.

ORCAGNA Andrea di Cione, *called* (Florence, active from 1344 to 1368). Painter, sculptor and architect, he is considered the most versatile and best artist of the mid-century generation to which his three brothers, Jacopo, Matteo and Nardo di Cione belonged. From 1354 to 1357, he was engaged on the altarpiece of the Strozzi Chapel in Santa Maria Novella, in Florence, where there seems a partial tendency to forget the tradition of Giotto and return to the hieratic manner of Roman and Byzantine painting: Christ in majesty reappears, a theme abandoned since the beginning of the Trecento. As the principal artist of the great Tabernacle of Or San Michele in Florence (1352-1359), he employed several assistants, including his brother, Matteo. The general grouping of the Tabernacle holds the attention, although it is rather masked by the excessive profusion of ornaments. The eye is first attracted to the incrustations of polychrome marbles and sculptures. With its entases and innumerable pinnacles, the structure as a whole belongs to the late gothic style enlivened, however, by the new spirit. It is characteristic of a transitional art between the Middle Ages and the Renaissance. In 1359, Orcagna, accompanied by his brother, Matteo, went to Orvieto to supervise the work on the Duomo. He stayed there till 1362 and contributed personally to the mosaics on the façade. When he returned to

ORCAGNA.
ST LAURENCE
SAVING THE SOUL
OF HENRI II.
DETAIL FROM
THE PREDELLA
OF THE STROZZI
ALTARPIECE. 1357.
SANTA MARIA
NOVELLA, FLORENCE.

Florence, he helped in the designs for the new cathedral, begun in the last years of the 13th century under the direction of Arnolfo di Cambio and radically modified in the 14th century by Francesco Talenti. In 1368, he was commissioned by the 'capitani' of Or San Michele to paint a Madonna (lost); the one that now decorates the Tabernacle is by Bernardo Daddi.

His varied activities have placed Orcagna in the ranks of the 'universal artists'. Nevertheless he always described himself as a painter and his architectural work should be considered as of secondary importance. The Tabernacle of Or San Michele is really a piece of architecture, reduced to a small scale. At the Council for the Works at Santa Maria del Fiore, as at Orvieto, he seems to have been particularly interested in the preparations of the interior and the decoration of the façades. His painting, which was influenced by Giotto and the Sienese masters, is distinguished by its original flavour and also by its abundance, if the works that have vanished are taken into account, particularly the frescoes at Santa Croce admired by Ghiberti. Orcagna's fame was considerable during his life-time and after his death a certain number of paintings, sculptures and mosaics were attributed to him that have since been taken away and some restored to the real artists. Among these spurious works are the *Nativity of the Virgin* of Orvieto Cathedral (the mosaic of the façade is signed with Orcagna's name, but the inscription has been tampered with); the Loggia of the Piazza della Signoria in Florence; two large frescoes in the Camposanto at Pisa, the *Triumph of Death* and the *Last Judgment* (an attribution accredited by Vasari). These mistakes indicate Orcagna's profound influence on Florentine art, particularly on the painting at the end of the 14th century.   P.-H. M.

P - Q

PACCHIAROTTO Giacomo (Siena, 1474-Viterbo, *ca* 1540). A group of artists kept up the traditional style and iconography of the Sienese Quattrocento and even Trecento until the middle of the 16th century. One of them was Pacchiarotto, whose excellent technique was highly thought of, although his inspiration was far from original. We find in his work distant reminiscences of Francesco di Giorgio Martini, of Benvenuto di Giovanni, of Pietro di Domenico, and also Florentine and Umbrian influences. The choice of subjects was as unimportant to Pacchiarotto as that of his models, and, in spite of his notorious bad living, he specialised in religious painting: *Coronation of the Virgin* (Asciano, Chapel of San Sebastiano a Montalboli); *Virgin and Child,* 1520 (Casole, Palazzo Comunale); two pictures of the *Visitation* (Siena, Pinacoteca), etc. The small scenes on his predellas have a great charm. He was the last of the Sienese.   P.-H. M.

PADUA. Until the beginning of the 15th century, while under Venetian domination, Padua was the gateway to the mainland for Venice, which was then the capital of a maritime empire turned towards the East. Padua University was famous for its teaching of law and the humanities and the town soon became a centre of archaeological interest and even a market for 'antiques'; but with the arrival of Giotto (Scrovegni Chapel) at the beginning of the Trecento, then the activities of Giusto de' Menabuoi (Baptistery) and Altichiero (San Giorgio Chapel), it became an important artistic centre. About 1400, it was well known for its medallists who imitated Roman coins. In 1413, the discovery of the so-called tomb of Livy created a sensation. During the second quarter of the 15th century, there were again important contacts with Florence. In 1434, Palla Strozzi, a Florentine exile, surrounded himself with scholars and spread a new artistic fashion, very different from the 'late gothic' which reigned at the Palazzo Ducale with Gentile da Fabriano, and in the whole of northern Italy with Pisanello. In 1444, Donatello settled in Padua for ten years and was a complete success; he made among other things the Gattamelata Monument. Then Paolo Uccello caused a stir with the decoration of the Casa Vitaliani. The conjunction of the hard Tuscan style with the passion for 'antiques' explains the part traditionally attributed to Squarcione who trained— for a short time, admittedly—most of the young painters with new ideas, Mantegna first of all. A complete decorative style, rich in Roman motifs used in a fantastic manner, thus spread towards Lombardy (Vincenzo Foppa), Ferrara (Cosimo Tura) and Venice itself. It taught Mantegna to fill his compositions with pilasters, inscriptions and armoured warriors. In any case, most northern painters had some contact with Padua where Mantegna soon imposed an precise style, such as neither Tuscany nor Umbria ever knew. He influenced the Verona painters, such as Domenico Morone, the Paduans such as B. Parenzo, Venetian art generally through the Bellini and Bartolomeo Vivarini, and the art of the Marches through Crivelli. At the beginning of the 16th century Titian was in Padua, at the Scuola del Santo (1511); then the architect Falconetto da Verona was commissioned by Alvise Cornaro to build the gates of the town, where the school of painting was no longer of any importance. A. C.

PALMA GIOVANE Jacopo di Antonio Negretti, *called* (Venice, 1544 - Venice, 1628). Among the followers of Tintoretto and Veronese, the most important is Palma Giovane, son and pupil of Antonio Palma, and great-nephew of Palma Vecchio. He was a history painter with mannerist leanings and worked, when he was still very young, in the Venetian circle, particularly with Titian. During an eight year stay in Rome, he came in contact with the work of Michelangelo and Raphael. When he returned to Venice in 1568, he was therefore attracted by Tintoretto's manner which combined Roman forms with Venetian effects of light. He went on imitating that manner in his decorations of the churches and palaces of the town: San Francesco della Vigna, Santa Maria Gloriosa dei Frari and the sacristy of San Giacomo dall'Orio (1575). After the fire in the Palazzo Ducale in 1577, he took part in the decorating of the Sala di Gran Consiglio with the Bassani, Zuccaro and Veronese, and became famous through his large decorative compositions such as the *Last Judgment* in the Sala dello Scrutinio, which is a medley of figures in action. His most typical work is probably the narrative cycle in the Oratorio dei Crociferi in Venice (about 1590) in which we find the cleverness and dynamic confusion of Venetian mannerism between 1500 and 1600. A. C.

PALMA VECCHIO Jacopo Negretti, *called* (Serina, near Bergamo, *ca* 1480 - Venice, 1528). He is mentioned for the first time in 1510. The inventory of his studio in 1528 revealed sixty-two works, mostly unfinished: his only signed work is the Berlin *Madonna*. He arrived young in Venice and probably, never really was Bellini's pupil; his art hints at contacts with the Bergamo school, which set him apart from the Bellini circle. Nevertheless he followed the new trends: he was one of the first to be interested in Giorgione, whose influence is found in some of his Madonnas (Rome, Galleria Colonna). About 1505-1508, he painted a group of small pictures with mythological subjects, one of which (Philadelphia) is a sort of variation on Giorgione's *Tempest*. He concentrated on studies of the nude: *Adam and Eve* (Brunswick, Landesmuseum), *Two Nymphs* (Frankfurt), *Venus* (Dresden). Rather pale tones are characteristic of the years 1512-1515. He then began to paint pastoral compositions reminiscent of Giorgione: *Three Sisters* (Dresden). But his church paintings remained numerous, including large ambitious altarpieces such as the *Virgin between two Saints* in San Stefano at Vicenza, with its still Giorgionesque types and effects, or the robust and typical *St Barbara* (about 1522-1523, Venice, Santa Maria Formosa). A. C.

PALMEZZANO Marco (Forlì, 1456/59 - Forlì, 1539). The are few documents about him before 1489, when he visited Rome, probably with Melozzo da Forlì. A protégé of Catarina Sforza, Palmezzano left the town when it changed its master and went to Matelica, then to Faenza where he was in 1505. Between 1490 and 1495, he completed the decoration of the Feo Chapel in San Biago at Forlì. The *Crucifixion* fresco, the *Annunciation* and the bust of the *Virgin and Child* (1492) still observe the square shapes and perspective effects of Melozzo. The *Madonna and Child with Four Saints* and the *Madonna* (Forlì, Pinacoteca, 1497-1500) are more reminiscent of Mantegna and the Ferrara school. The second part of the artist's career is less interesting, more repetitive, and through his visits to Venice he lost much of the vigour of his touch. A. C.

PANNINI Gianpaolo (Piacenza, 1691/92 - Rome, 1765). A painter and architect trained in the school of the Bologna stage designers (the Bibiena), he later painted *vedute* which were then produced in great numbers in Rome. In 1718, he decorated the Villa Patrizi and began to be offered important commissions which made him specialise in pictures commemorating official parties, public festivals or historic events: *The Preparations for Fireworks in the Piazza Navona* (Dublin); *Interior of St Peter's, with Cardinal de Polignac* (1729, Louvre); *Benedict XIV receiving Charles III, King of Naples* (Naples), etc. He still conceived them as *vedute* and used urban perspectives, bathed in light and cut by strong diagonals, very much in the Roman baroque taste which, thanks to him, remained popular till the middle of the 18th century. But the ruins in his landscapes also link, in a way, with the more romantic art of Hubert Robert and Piranesi.   A. C.

PAOLO di GIOVANNI FEI (Siena, active from 1372 to 1410). This painter is first mentioned in 1372, as a member of the Siena Town Council, and for the last time in 1410. Paolo di Giovanni Fei painted in a style similar to that of his contemporaries, Andrea Vanni and Bartolo di Fredi. His talent was slight, but his technique sound, and he left numerous works: frescoes, large altarpieces, small paintings. In one of his first pictures, the *Virgin Nursing the Child* (Siena Cathedral), the sinuous folds of the Virgin's dress are reminiscent of Simone Martini's style. His most famous work, the triptych of the *Birth of the Virgin* (Siena, Pinacoteca), was obviously inspired by Pietro Lorenzetti; but the austere setting of the original has been replaced by a rich interior with a rose garden in the background. These secondary motifs are rendered more elegantly still by the Master of the Osservanza.   P.-H. M.

PAOLO DI GIOVANNI FEI. NATIVITY OF THE VIRGIN (DETAIL). PINACOTECA, SIENA.

PAOLO VENEZIANO (Venice, end of the 13th century - Venice, *ca* 1362). He was the most important of the Veneto-Byzantine painters. Berenson described his style as 'nearly as Byzantine as if trained and working at Constantinople. Influenced somewhat by Italian art'. The *Coronation of the Virgin,* in the National Gallery, Washington, is dated 1324 and is attributed to him. This is the earliest date for his activity, the latest being 1358, on another *Coronation* (New York, Frick Collection) which he signed together with his son, Giovanni. His son Luca was also a painter and all three signed the cover which they painted for the *Pala d'Oro* in San Marco in 1345. Two other paintings are

PAOLO AND GIOVANNI VENEZIANO.
THE CORONATION OF THE VIRGIN. 1358.
FRICK COLLECTION, NEW YORK.

signed by Paolo alone—a polyptych in Vicenza of 1333 and a *Madonna* of 1347 in the parish church at Carpineta, near Cesena. Among the dated panels ascribed to him are the parts of a dismembered polyptych (1353), in the Campana Collection, of which the central panel, representing the Madonna, is in the Louvre. Apart from his sons, Lorenzo Veneziano was probably also his pupil.   P. M.

PARMA. Now an important agricultural centre of the province of Emilia,

Parma long enjoyed the glamour of a capital city. Though little remains of the Roman colony, the Cathedral and Baptistery of pink marble (12th and 13th centuries) recall the city of the Middle Ages with its violent internal strife. During the Renaissance, Parma passed backwards and forwards between the Visconti, the Sforza, the Pope and the King of France. This period endowed the city with magnificent churches such as the Santa Maria della Steccata. The ambitions of the Farnese (1545-1731) live on in their splendid theatre and the immense Palazzo della Pilotta. French influence, so active during the reign of the Spanish Bourbons and of Marie-Louise, wife of Napoleon, survives in the somewhat chilly elegance of the town.

For many years painting in Parma was under the influence of neighbouring cities. Jacopo Loschi (died before 1503) was inspired by Cremonese models; Filippo Mazzola (died in 1505), Cristoforo Caselli (died in 1521) and Josafat Araldi (died about 1520), brought from Venice a reflection of Giovanni Bellini, whilst Alessandro Araldi was directly inspired by Costa and Francia. It was only with the appearance of Correggio (about 1518/19) that Parma suddenly contributed a new voice to the chorus of Italian art. This awakening was as dazzling as it was unforeseen. Parmigianino, adding his own seduction to the art of Correggio, assured it a widespread influence and a whole constellation of painters benefited from this twin example: Michelangelo Anselmi (about 1492 to about 1554), Francesco Maria Rondani (1490-1550), Gerolamo Bedoli Mazzola (about 1500-1569) with his romantic subtleties, Giorgio Gandini del Grano (1489-1538), tormented in his inspiration, and above all, the strange Lelio Orsi (1511-1587). Parma became synonymous with the subtlest of art, uniting elegance with sensual grace and a refined vision. Its influence was immense and lasting, but the School of Parma was short lived. In the 17th century painters such as Schedoni, Lanfranco or Sisto Badalocchio, natives of Parma, however profoundly affected by its lessons, nevertheless belong to the School of Bologna. In spite of possessing excellent artists such as Giovanni Battista Tagliasacchi (1697-1737) or Giuseppe Baldrighi (1723-1802), a pupil of Boucher, and in spite of the foundation of the Accademia di Belle Arti by the Infante Don Filippo, Parma never recovered the transient burst of inspiration of the 16th century whose memory alone survives on the walls of the city's churches and in its fine gallery.   J. T.

PARMIGIANINO   Francesco Mazzola, *called* (Parma, 1503 - Castelmaggiore, 1540). Parmigianino was a precocious genius influenced by Correggio, but this first and decisive influence did not prevent him from turning his attention to other matters, such as the light effects peculiar to Beccafumi (apparently passed on through Michelangelo Anselmi's works) or the violent, forceful style of Pordenone. He went to Rome at the beginning of 1524 (having probably passed through Mantua) and this was not only an opportunity to make direct contact with Tuscan mannerism (his meeting with Rosso), but also offered the young artist a tempting diversity: first and foremost Raphael's grace, and also Michelangelo's power, Sebastiano del Piombo's colour and Pierino del Vaga's decorative elegance. He succeeded in fusing these various elements (the *Vision of St Jerome,* London, National Gallery) and made out of them a highly personal art, delicately fashioned yet powerful, where the virtuosity he acquired early in life and had ostensibly cultivated (*Self Portrait in a Convex Mirror,* 1523/24, Vienna, Kunsthistorisches Museum), follows the dictates of his imagination, which grows ever more divorced from reality. He

PARMIGIANINO. THE MADONNA WITH THE LONG NECK. 1534-1540. UFFIZI, FLORENCE.

fled to Bologna after the Sack of Rome (1527) and as he already commanded a tremendous reputation in spite of his youth, he demonstrated his ability there in a powerful and elegantly rhetorical style (*St Rocco with a Donor,* Bologna, Basilica of San Petronio). He uses contrasting rhythms and figures in *contrapposto* (the *Madonna of the Rose,* Dresden) and mingles subtle and sensual evocations with ancient ruins or withered leaves (*Madonna with St Zachariah, Mary Magdalen and St John,* Uffizi). On returning to Parma (1531), he consolidated his style and developed it further, but he did not give up any of his freedom to pursue new ideas. The

PARMIGIANINO. THE COURTESAN ANTEA.
MUSEO NAZIONALE, NAPLES.

frescoes in Santa Maria della Steccata (1531-1539), that gorgeous ornamental frieze where he fails to meet the requirements of religious illustration and relegates the figures to a very inferior position, undermines the conventions of church decoration. With the strange, seductive *Madonna with the Long Neck* (1534-1540, Uffizi) he takes long, tapering and elegant lines and unorthodox forms to the extreme. He lived the same number of years as Raphael, and death interrupted his artistic career when he seemed to be developing towards a greater austerity, a style with more solid forms and more accentuated rhythms (the *Madonna with St Stephen*

and St John the Baptist, Dresden).

As a portraitist, Parmigianino left behind some wonderful likenesses, where he stresses only the most aristocratic aspect of his model (*Gian Galeazzo Sanvitale,* Naples, Museo Nazionale; the *Lady in a Turban,* Parma, Pinacoteca), and, of the total psychology, only the melancholy and alluring secret of an inner reverie remains (*Portrait of a Young Boy,* Hampton Court; the *Lady with a Fur,* called *Antea,* Naples, Museo Nazionale): yet there is so much vitality in these figures that they have become inseparable from our general idea of his century. As a religious painter, he shunned crowd effects, preferring compositions with few figures, where gracefulness is the chief and enchanting feature; neither did he lack the courage to outdo Correggio in voluptuous sensuality: yet his is an entirely different atmosphere of intellectual abstraction, where, through its own imagination, he deliberately distorts his figures and abolishes anything which does not directly serve his purpose. Some very fine etchings (the *Entombment*) quickly brought widespread prestige for his style; both Primaticcio and Niccolò dell'Abbate carried it abroad to France. In Parmigianino we may see Raphael's true successor. His graceful elongated silhouettes, his harmonious, rippling lines, and the aristocratic allure of his facial expressions seemed to be the feminine equivalent of Michelangelo's art, and the clash between these two temperaments and these two styles was later to be found at the heart of all mannerist works.   J. T.

PAUL III Alessandro Farnese, Pope (Canino or Rome, 1468 - Rome, 1549). From his election as a Pope (1534) to his death, Alessandro Farnese who had been educated in the humanities first in Rome, then in Florence, later at the court of Lorenzo il Magnifico and finally in Pisa, spent a large part of his income on the patronage of the arts and letters. He restored the University of Rome, gave new catalogues to the Vatican Library, undertook important building work, made Bembo a cardinal and appointed Michelangelo directing architect, sculptor and painter at the Vatican. During his pontificate, Michelangelo completed the decoration of the Sistine Chapel (*Last Judgment*, 1536-1541) and decorated the Pauline Chapel (1542-1549). The subtlety of the scholar and the diplomat, prudence even wiliness are revealed in his portrait by Sermoneta (Rome, San Francesca Romana) and even more in Titian's painting (1546) where he is attended by his grandson, Ottavio, and the Cardinal Alessandro Farnese (Naples, Museo di Capodimonte). P.-H. M.

PERUGIA. Towards the middle of the 15th century, Perugia, through the visits of Fra Angelico, Domenico Veneziano and also Gozzoli, became a very active artistic centre and gave birth to a school which was to be famous for its suavity, sweetness and elegance. The first important workshops were those of Bonfigli, Giovanni de' Boccati, Caporali, then that of Fiorenzo di Lorenzo, which produced charming, somewhat mannered panels, the outcome of a flowery Renaissance still in contact with Siena and its gentle art, while giving its due to the majesty serenity of Piero della Francesca. To Perugia we owe the delightful series of the *Life of St Bernardino* (1470), the combined work of Pinturicchio, Bonfigli and Perugino himself; on the other

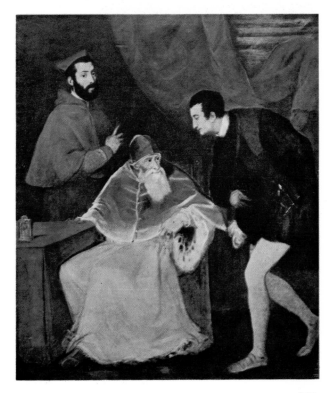

TITIAN. PAUL III AND HIS GRANDSONS, OTTAVIO AND THE CARDINAL ALESSANDRO FARNESE. 1546. MUSEO DI CAPODIMONTE, NAPLES.

PERUGINO. MARY MAGDALEN. 1496-1500.
PALAZZO PITTI, FLORENCE.

peaceful rhythm, the soft warm light, the feeling of spaciousness cannot be explained without taking into account the influence of Piero della Francesca. It is a restrained art, which avoids contorted forms and aims at a feeling of lightness and ease: these qualities are in evidence in the hall of the Collegio del Cambio in Perugia, and in numerous altarpieces throughout the province. This new 'relaxed' tone, popularised by many Madonnas, was going to be a decisive element of classical beauty in the art of Raphael who kept the careful harmony and the freshness of Perugino. But Umbria is also represented by Pinturicchio who imposed his style first in Rome, under Alexander VI Borgia, then in Siena: he always retained his taste for anecdote and the meaning of the narrative, rejected a balanced composition and impressionistic effects of light and made every effort to elaborate the picturesque and richness of effect.

Thus, from 1490 to 1505, between the Florentine crisis and the flowering of Rome under Julius II, Umbria held an important place, no doubt justified by its past; but its school did not survive the territorial division which finally submitted Umbria to Rome and the rule of classical art.   A. C.

PERUGINO Pietro Vannucci, *called* (Città della Pieve, *ca* 1445 - Fontignano, near Perugia, 1523). Pietro came from Umbria but in 1472 he was listed on the roll of St Luke's Congregation in Florence. He learnt the modern technique of oil painting under Verrocchio. In fact, we know little about his youthful production. He did some work on several panels of the *Life of St Bernardino,* which consists of eight charming little pictures painted in Perugia in 1473; the *Adoration of the Magi,* also in Perugia, may date back to 1475. His first properly dated work is the *St Sebastian* of 1478, which he painted in the church of Cerqueto (south of Perugia), the still

hand, an Umbrian master, influenced by the art of the Marches, painted the famous Barberini panels in which we find the same taste for architecture and decoration.

Between 1460 and 1480, there were constant exchanges between Siena, Perugia and Urbino, which by-passed Florence. Francesco di Giorgio Martini, a pupil of Vecchietta, did some important architectural work in Umbria. Siena's links with Umbria were unbroken and created a sort of capricious Renaissance next to the earnest Florentine art. The two main streams of the 'Umbrian sweetness' are represented by Perugino and Pinturicchio. The origins of Perugino's art are complex, as we have seen. But in the *Delivery of the Keys to St Peter* (Sistine Chapel, 1481), the

impressive remnant of a larger composition. In 1481, he was well enough
known to be commissioned with Rosselli,
Ghirlandaio and Botticelli to decorate
the walls of the Sistine Chapel. Pinturicchio was his assistant; the *Delivery of
the Keys to St Peter* made his reputation.
It marked the beginning of a feverishly
productive period and already in 1500
he was ridiculed for his facile 'sweetness'.
Perugino had a workshop in Florence
and one in Perugia and never refused
a commission. Among his too numerous works, we must mention the
Louvre tondo: the *Virgin and Child
enthroned between St Rose and St Catherine*;
in 1488/89 the *Annunciation* in Santa
Maria Nuova at Fano; in 1489, the
Vision of St Bernard (Munich); the triptych at the Villa Albani, dated 1491.
Between 1493 and 1497, he did a series of
Madonna and Child pictures which
established a sweet type, which was
very characteristic; we find them in
Vienna, at the Uffizi, in Sant'Agostino

in Cremona, at the Vatican, in Fano
where there is a predella representing five
remarkable little scenes from the *Life of
the Virgin*. During the same period
were painted *Christ in the Garden of
Olives* (Uffizi), the *Pietà* (Pitti) and the
Louvre *St Sebastian*. In 1496, he painted
the *Crucifixion* fresco in Santa Maria
Maddalena dei Pazzi, Florence, with a
wonderful feeling for spaciousness and
atmosphere, and, at the same time, the
Virgin and Child with Saints (Bologna).
In 1499, he painted a triptych (London,
National Gallery) for the Certosa di
Pavia; in 1500, the Uffizi *Assumption*.
'He is the best painter in Italy', Agostino
Chigi wrote. Nobody seemed to doubt
it. At that time, Perugino worked
mainly in Florence, in Rome and Perugia
where, in 1500, he decorated with
Raphael the Audience Chamber of the
Collegio del Cambio. He also worked
for Isabella d'Este and painted for her
in Mantua a few laboured pictures,
among which the *Love and Chastity* in

PERUGINO.
ARCHERS. DRAWING.
MUSÉE CONDÉ,
CHANTILLY.

the Louvre. But soon, both in Rome and Florence, he was considered old-fashioned. He spent the last years of his life in Perugia, copying his own manner in pictures commissioned by small Umbrian towns. He had many pupils, among whom were Pinturicchio and Raphael.

Perugino started from a high level of achievement. In Cerqueto and at the Sistine Chapel, his mastery is startling. Vasari may give us the key to the enigma when he writes that Vannucci started from Piero della Francesca, whose influence was always strong in Umbria. But—probably after a period in Verrocchio's workshop—he acquired a feeling for a more 'naturalistic' technique—which allows us to attribute the *Madonna* in the Musée Jacquemart-André, Paris, to him rather than to the Umbrian Fiorenzo da Lorenzo. On that solid basis, Perugino gradually developed a most influential style: peaceful, pleasant almost to the point of prettiness, harmonious, exquisitely original at times, but verging on sentimentality, all the more because of the repetition of motifs. In the eyes of his contemporaries, he represented the summit of religious art: the rich Francesco del Pugliese, convert-

ed by Savonarola, longed to acquire the *Dead Christ* (Pitti) of Santa Chiara Convent, painted in 1495. The fresco in Santa Maria Maddalena dei Pazzi, where three arcades frame three compositions remarkable in their simplicity, shows us what he could do and what Raphael learnt from him. But already then, his manner lacked the necessary authority for large compositions. At the Cambio, he was unable to put life into a solemn, somewhat boring pictorial scheme which lacks the leaven of imagination. About 1505-1506, when he was asked to complete the main altar of the Servites, begun by Filippino, the Florentines were censorious about his mannered style ('ridotto a maniera'), as is shown by numerous anecdotes, and by a scornful remark of Michelangelo's. The 19th century glorification of Perugino and the supremacy given him by the Pre-Raphaelites, are therefore excessive. But nevertheless, we must not underestimate the historical importance of his serene, relaxed style which the whole of Europe imitated, of his feeling for a clearly organised picture space, for a harmonious symmetry of masses through a subtle use of colour—in a word, the grandiose beauty of his *Delivery of the*

PESELLINO.
ST COMO
AND ST DAMIAN
VISITING
A SICK MAN.
LOUVRE, PARIS.

PIAZZETTA.
ELIEZER
AND REBECCA.
ABOUT 1740.
BRERA, MILAN.

Keys to St Peter, the charm of his *Apollo and Marsyas* (Louvre) and the inspiration of his *Wedding of the Virgin,* which is close to Raphael.   A. C.

PESELLINO Francesco di Stefano, *called* Francesco (Florence, 1422 - Florence, 1457). In Florence, artisans followed closely the main stylistic developments, as in the decorative panels for wedding or presentation chests *(cassoni),* which consisted of a carved framework surrounding painted panels, which represented contemporary scenes or—more often—romantic episodes in a charming fairylike manner. Pesellino was particularly skilled at painting those colourful, delicate creations which are the equivalent in painting of courtly poetry, and often take up the same themes: the *Story of Griselda* (Bergamo), the illustration of Petrarch's *Triumphs* (Boston, Gardner Museum), the *Story of David* (Wantage, Loyd Collection). The influence of Filippo Lippi and Fra Angelico is noticeable in the scene painted after Petrarch's *Triumphs,* in which light figures play against a stylised rocky landscape. This flowery manner

suited profane themes and pleased the Florentine taste. The art of the *cassoni* prepared the way for the dancing silhouettes and the graceful scenes of Botticelli and Filippino Lippi.   A. C.

PIAZZETTA Giambattista (Venice, 1682 - Venice, 1754). Giuseppe Maria Crespi, of Bologna, seems to have exercised a considerable influence on 18th century Venetian painting. Piazzetta who began, like his father, as a wood-carver, and then worked in the studio of Molinari, came across the works of Crespi when he went to Bologna to complete his artistic education. The attraction of Crespi's painting was its realism and its treatment of colour learnt from the Carracci, with Caravaggio as the ultimate source. Piazzetta returned to Venice in 1711 and was soon working on a number of commissions *(Virgin Appearing to St Philip Neri,* about 1725, Venice, Santa Maria della Fava). In 1727 he finished a very large canvas for Santi Giovanni e Paolo representing the *Glory of St Dominic.* Unlike so many of his compatriots he did not paint frescoes. The work, featuring

PIAZZETTA. THE FORTUNE-TELLER. 1740.
ACCADEMIA, VENICE.

and in the light parts one finds clear blues, straw yellows and pinks. In 1750 Piazzetta became director of the Accademia di Belle Arti in Venice. But now a decline into banality set in and, eclipsed no doubt by the younger generation, he died in Venice in 1754, a somewhat forgotten man.

It would be unjust to neglect his drawings. Piazzetta composed numerous and pleasing vignettes. He illustrated the *Gerusalemme Liberata* (1745). His particular excellence was nudes drawn in charcoal heightened with chalk; the soft modelling anticipates Prud'hon. His self-portrait done in this medium is at the Albertina in Vienna.   P. C.

PIERO di COSIMO Piero di Lorenzo, *called* (Florence, 1462 - Florence, 1521). He was a pupil of Cosimo Rosselli, to whom he owes his name, and was his assistant in the Sistine Chapel in 1481. He then returned to Florence where he spent the rest of his life. He was a strange character, lived alone, in dirt and squalor, and worked frenziedly; he worshipped nature, we are told, and had a neurotic aversion for bells, fire and meat. He was influenced in turns by Pollaiuolo, Leonardo, Signorelli, Raphael and Flemish artists, but none the less was one of the most original masters of the Florentine school through the freshness of his imagination, his feeling for nature and for intimate scenes, his interest in colour. He was attracted by evocative, somewhat strange mythological themes: the *Death of Procris* (London, National Gallery), *Prometheus* (Strasbourg). His masterpiece, *Venus, Mars and Love sleeping* (Berlin), is full of delightful details of animals, flowers, butterflies in a dream landscape. *Andromeda freed by Perseus* (Uffizi) belongs to a later period in which the grouping, the *sfumato* are inspired by Leonardo, and the landscape by Flemish art. We find the same characteristics in his religious paintings: the Florence and

an open sky with airborne figures seems to anticipate Tiepolo.

In the years following Piazzetta, influenced by Liss and Feti, developed a somewhat different manner with a predilection for strong contrasts, though even here the lights, with their rich texture confidently laid on, offer delicate chromatic effects (*Assumption*, 1735, Musée de Lille). At Santa Maria del Rosario dei Gesuati for which he did an altarpiece, he was in company with Tiepolo, his pupil. He was at his most brilliant between 1740 and 1750. Among the best works from this period are the *Fortune-Teller* at the Accademia in Venice, somewhat enigmatic in subject-matter and truculent in form, the *Standard-Bearer* at Dresden and *Eliezer and Rebecca* at the Brera. The tonality of these paintings is not far from what later prevailed in Venice in the 18th century: the contrasts have grown softer

Berlin altarpieces, the Madonnas in Strasbourg, Stockholm and Paris and, according to a recent attribution, the *Virgin with the Child and St John* (Venice, Cini Collection), a composition remarkable both for its feeling and its technique. A taste for down-to-earth subjects allied to a love of the fantastic account for his successful visions of primitive man and wild life: *The Hunt* (New York), *Lapiths and Centaurs* (London, National Gallery). His portraits are taken straight from life: *Giuliano Sangallo* (Amsterdam, Rijksmuseum), *Francesco Giamberti* (ibid.), *Simonetta Vespucci* (Chantilly, Musée Condé). The Carnival of Death which he organised in Florence in 1511 has remained famous as a macabre fancy. A restless, bizarre temperament, Piero acquired a reputation for strangeness and misanthropy. A. C.

PIERO della FRANCESCA (Borgo San Sepolcro, *ca* 1410 - Borgo San Sepolcro, 1492). Forgotten outside his own province after the 16th century, Piero

PIERO DI COSIMO. ST JOHN THE BAPTIST. METROPOLITAN MUSEUM, NEW YORK.

PIERO DI COSIMO. HYLAS ABDUCTED BY THE NYMPHS. THE WADSWORTH ATHENEUM, HARTFORD.

della Francesca was rediscovered by modern art historians who gradually pieced together the details of his career, revealed the scope of his influence and taught us to appreciate his noble, poetic style; nowadays, he is considered as the greatest Quattrocento painter. Born at Borgo San Sepolcro, in a valley of the Tuscan Apennines, he was the son of Benedetto dei Franceschi, a cobbler, and of Romana di Pierino di Carlo who came from the neighbouring village of Monterchi. His name appears for the first time, on September 7th, 1439, next to that of Domenico Veneziano, in the accounts of the hospital of Santa Maria Novella in Florence, against a sum paid for frescoes in Sant'Egidio (now destroyed). We therefore assume that he was in Florence between 1435 and 1445. But he left the town about 1445, never to return.

From then on, he travelled widely and was active in the villages of his native district where he ruled supreme, and in the cities of the Adriatic side of the Apennines: Ferrara, Rimini, Urbino, whose generous and enterprising princes were early to appreciate his majestic style. On January 11th, 1445, the Compagnia della Misericordia of Borgo San Sepolcro commissioned from him a polyptych which, according to the contract, had to be painted by his own hand and completed by 1448. In fact, Piero employed assistants and only received his payment in 1462, which probably means that he worked for over ten years on the painting. During the same period, he painted the *Baptism of Christ* (London, National Gallery) for the priory at Borgo San Sepolcro, and *St Jerome with Donor* (Venice, Accademia). Called to Urbino by Federico da Montefeltro, Piero may have painted then the remarkable *Flagellation* (Urbino) which, however, art historians now tend to ascribe to a later period. From Urbino, the master went to Ferrara where he worked, before 1450, for Lionello d'Este.

He met the brothers Lorenzo and Cristoforo da Lendinara, intarsia workers for whom he made some designs. Unfortunately, the frescoes of the Castello Estense and of the Augustine church of Sant'Andrea have been destroyed. In 1451, he was in Rimini where he painted the portrait of the awe-inspiring Sigismondo Pandolfo Malatesta with his patron saint, signed and dated 'Petri de Borgo opus 1451'. His most considerable work was the decoration of the church of San Francesco in Arezzo; it had been begun by Bicci di Lorenzo and remained unfinished when he died. Luigi Bacci, possibly on the advice of Domenico Veneziano, engaged Piero who spent the years between 1452 and 1459 working on the enormous *Legend of the True Cross,* which was to be the most important work in his career. The date of his first visit to Rome is unknown: he was there in 1459, according to an order from the Pope, dated April 12th, 1459, to pay the artist for work done in the chamber of Pius II. He also worked in Santa Maria Maggiore where a *St Luke the Evangelist* is still extant, in a chapel. Soon after 1460, Piero left Rome to return to Umbria. He may have stopped at Perugia to paint the *Virgin and Child between Saints* (Perugia, Galleria Nazionale). Between 1460 and 1470, he visited Borgo, Urbino and Arezzo. From that period date the *Madonna del Parto* in the chapel of the small churchyard in Monterchi, near Borgo, and the *Resurrection of Christ* (Borgo, Palazzo Comunale). He also painted then the Polyptych commissioned on November 14th, 1454 by the Augustine Convent in Borgo and paid on November 14th, 1469, and the *St Julian* fresco discovered in 1954 in the deconsecrated church of Sant'Agostino, which may have been part of a larger composition. A visit to Urbino about 1465 allows us to date the famous double portrait of *Federico da Montefeltro and Battista Sforza* (Uffizi). In 1466, he was back in Arezzo where

PIERO DELLA FRANCESCA. LEGEND OF THE TRUE CROSS: THE QUEEN OF SHEBA AND HER SUITE. FRESCO. 1452-1459. CHURCH OF SAN FRANCESCO, AREZZO.

the Brotherhood of the Annunziata commissioned from him a banner which was completed in 1468, in a neighbouring village where Piero had fled from the plague. Between 1474 and 1478, he paid his last visits to Urbino. During that period, he painted the *Sinigaglia Madonna* for the Duke (Urbino), the *Nativity* (London, National Gallery) and finally, about 1475, the *Pala di Montefeltro* (Brera). He then wrote his treatise *De prospectiva pingendi,* inscribed to the Duke of Montefeltro and, after a last visit to Urbino, a small *Treatise of Arithmetic and Geometry* (manuscript in the Laurenziana Library) and a small

booklet *De quinque corporibus regularibus,* which Pacioli took up again as his own and published together with his *De divina proportione* in 1509. On July 5th, 1487, Piero wrote his last will and testament; he died blind five years later, on October 12th, 1492.

His artistic training took place between 1430 and 1440, during a period rich in artistic innovations of which Piero could take full advantage. Before his coming to Florence, he had no known master and there is no proof that, in Florence, he was Domenico Veneziano's pupil before becoming his assistant. But his childhood had been

223

spent in a Sienese atmosphere: in 1437, Sassetta painted the main altarpiece in the church of San Francesco at Borgo. In Arezzo, Piero must have seen the polyptych of Pietro Lorenzetti (1320), which he remembered in his *Resurrection* fresco. He never forgot that colour must be applied lightly and with gem-like effects. When he arrived in Florence, Masaccio had been dead ten years; but he had left the *Trinity* at Santa Maria Novella and the unfinished frescoes of the *Story of St Peter* at the Brancacci Chapel in the Carmine church. Piero found himself among devotees of 'space' painting and of wide perspectives. In Ferrara, he exerted a marked influence on painters, illuminators, marquetry workers, but he must also have been influenced himself by artists he met, for instance by Mantegna, who never forgot him, and above all by Rogier van der Weyden and by Flemish painting; in

that way, he strengthened his own naturalistic tendencies, which are apparent in *St Jerome* and the *Baptism of Christ* through the interest in detail, the linking of landscape and characters, the noting of slight irregularities of form and light —all those characteristics are even more noticeable in the *Nativity*. An original adaptation of Flemish techniques can be found throughout his work: the *Sinigaglia Madonna* is the first Virgin in Italian art to be represented in a domestic interior. We know that Piero frequented the court of Urbino at the same time as Alberti; he shared the latter's mathematical and rational ideals and may have inspired some of his architectural and decorative schemes. His prestige was so great, in matters of geometry and proportions, that in the *Summa aritmetica* published in Venice in 1494, Pacioli called his master, Piero de' Franceschi, 'the Monarch of Painting'. We under-

PIERO DELLA FRANCESCA. LEGEND OF THE TRUE CROSS: THE QUEEN OF SHEBA RECEIVED BY KING SOLOMON. FRESCO. 1452-1459. CHURCH OF SAN FRANCESCO, AREZZO.

PIERO DELLA FRANCESCA. THE VIRGIN AND CHILD SURROUNDED BY SAINTS AND ANGELS;
FEDERICO DA MONTEFELTRO KNEELING BEFORE THEM. ABOUT 1475. BRERA, MILAN.

stand more clearly nowadays why he towered so high above his own time.

The Arezzo cycle and the Urbino panels show a modern 'synthesis' of space and colour which is the basis of his art. The *Flagellation* owes its overwhelming clarity to the harmonious network of architecture and tiling; the influence of Alberti is particularly obvious in the use of the Corinthian order, the elegant entablature, the marble inlays; the portico is similar to that of San Pancrazio by Alberti, and the importance given to architecture suggests that the date may be as early as 1460. The characters are part of the spatial

PIERO DELLA
FRANCESCA.
THE RESURRECTION.
ABOUT 1460.
PALAZZO
COMUNALE, BORGO
SAN SEPOLCRO.

rhythm, and the group in the foreground on the right helps to give depth to the left half of the picture. Thus, everything contributes to the solemnity and the slight feeling of mystery: the group of three 'oriental characters' may suggest Judas giving back the pieces of gold to the priests.

Hidden symbolism is an integral part of Piero's art: in the Montefeltro altarpiece in the Brera, the Virgin and Child are enthroned between saints, angels, and Federico da Montefeltro kneeling in the foreground (some of the details are by another hand); the characters are placed under a huge shell-shaped apse from which is suspended a giant egg. It is an ostrich egg, the traditional allegorical motif of the Immaculate Conception, which is also part of the Montefeltro arms, and is moreover connected with cosmological symbolism. Piero knew how to create his own impressive iconography.

The artist was a thinker and spent a long time on compositions like the Misericordia Polyptych. His creative process involved a silent, slowly-maturing meditation which gave his works a calm, majestic tone—particularly the wonderful Arezzo frescoes. They are probably connected with the crusade projected during the pontificate of Pius II. The theme is the story of the wood of the Cross, which we find in the *Golden Legend* by Jacopo di Voragine. The subject was popular with Franciscan churches. Piero masterfully balanced the scenes which stand opposite each other on each level, without following the iconographic order too closely: there is a very dramatic contrast between the naked figures of the first men and the splendid costumes of Solomon's court, between Constantine's dream during the night and his victory in full daylight; the attitudes, the gestures, the composition are powerfully expressive. Each sequence has its own marked rhythm: it is divided by a clear, vertical line into two unequal parts, one square, one rectangular. Light floods into these exactly measured sections and creates a pale, clear colour, with exquisite nuances, which filters into the regular network of spaces as if they were the sections of a coat of arms.

Piero's style was universal in scope. We can see his mastery and his sense of order in the way he reacted to Flemish formulas, for instance in the London *Nativity,* which for a long time was considered unfinished, but which in fact has suffered from bad restoration. The Child is not unlike Hugo van der Goes' newborn child, and in the landscape the contrasts between light and shade are reminiscent of the *Baptism of Christ ;* but the round trees and bushes remind us of Rogier van der Weyden, as they also do in the Apennine background behind the portraits of Federico da Montefeltro and his wife. Such a methodical assimilation of northern innovations allows us to compare Piero's development with that of Antonello da Messina, who was also interested in colour and monumental effects. Piero combines both extremes remarkably and is at the same time bold and sensitive in his use of light and the first of the geometrical painters: for instance he inspired the brothers Lendinara, whose marquetry work in Modena Cathedral and in San Martino in Luca is beautifully abstract. His art has been compared to archaic Greek sculpture because of the impersonal, mysterious quality of his characters and the importance given to accidental or ephemeral features. But Piero's art is even more striking if you

PIERO DELLA FRANCESCA. MADONNA DEL PARTO (DETAIL). CHAPEL IN THE CAMPO SANTO, MONTERCHI.

consider it within his period whose enormous vitality he sums up in a dual style, at the same time rustic and courtly, earthy and heroic, which explains the epic nature of his works.   A. C.

PIETRO da CORTONA Pietro Berrettini, *called* (Cortona, 1596 - Rome, 1669). Between 1620 and 1630, this Tuscan evolved a very personal style which was partly due to his apprenticeship under Andrea Commodi (in Cortona and Rome), but mainly, during the first years in Rome, to his studies which embraced classical art as well as Raphael, Titian, and Carracci, and the influence of moderns like Lanfranco and Bernini. Once created, he never modified his style and it deeply impressed his contemporaries (Romanelli, Bourdon, Baldi, Gaulli, Giordano, etc.). Cortona very soon obtained the patronage of the Sacchetti family for whom he painted

PIETRO DI GIOVANNI. THE INFANT JESUS. DETAIL FROM THE 'ADORATION OF THE SHEPHERDS'. 1446-1448. MUSEUM OF SACRED ART, ASCIANO.

in the Palazzo Pitti in Florence, where he stayed several times). His colours were light and delicate, and there is a nostalgia for a happy world, all charm and sensuality; these qualities provide an intensely poetic complement to his perfect mastery of rhythm and arrangement of subject matter. As an architect, however, Cortona was also responsible for working out some of the earliest baroque formulas (façade of Santa Maria della Pace, 1655-1657).   J. T.

PIETRO di GIOVANNI d'AMBROGIO *also known as* Pietro di Giovanni Pucci (Siena, *ca* 1410 - Siena, 1449). During his all too short life, partly devoted to public works, Pietro di Giovanni produced a small number of works of high quality. The combined influences of the old Sienese masters, of the Sienese artists of his generation, who were strongly influenced by Florence, and of the Florentine painters themselves (Uccello, Masaccio, Angelico) fostered the development of his very original personality. We only know a few paintings by his hand: a banner (dated 1433) with a *St Catherine of Alexandria* on one side and a *Crucifixion* on the other (Paris, Musée Jacquemart-André), several pictures of *St Bernardino,* one of which (Siena, Pinacoteca) may have been painted before the death of the saint (1444), and a remarkable *Adoration of the Shepherds* (Asciano, Sant'Agostino) which has been attributed to the master's last years (about 1446-1448).   P.-H. M.

his first masterpieces (the *Triumph of Bacchus,* about 1624, Rome, Museo Capitolino, the *Rape of the Sabine Women,* about 1630, ibid). He also found patronage with the Barberini family who commissioned him to decorate the vast ceiling in the Great Hall of the Palazzo Barberini (1633-1639): it was a successful gamble, a starting-point for baroque decoration in the grand manner, and one of the key works of the century. Although he had to concede mastery in easel pictures to Poussin, for thirty years Cortona held first place in Rome for altarpieces (*Nativity of the Virgin,* Perugia, Galleria Nazionale), large-scale mythological paintings (*Remus and Romulus,* about 1643, Louvre), huge decorations on sacred subjects (frescoes in the Chiesa Nuova, Rome, 1647-1665) and profane decorative works (Palazzo Pamphili in Rome, apartments

PINTURICCHIO Bernardino di Betto, *called* (Perugia, *ca* 1454 - Siena, 1513). Slightly younger than Perugino whose collaborator, rather than pupil, he was in Rome, Bernardino, nicknamed 'the Dauber', occupied at the end of the 15th century his own place between the painters of Perugia and of Siena. He worked with Perugino on the small panels of the 1473 *Miracles of St Bernardino of Siena* (Perugia, Galleria Nazionale):

in the two panels he painted *St Bernardino and the Cripple* and *The Freeing of a Prisoner,* his bright colours suggest a miniaturist's training. From 1481 to 1483, in the Sistine Chapel, he again worked with Perugino; through this contact, his own style became lighter (the *Circumcision of Moses' Son;* the *Baptism of Christ*). Later, perhaps as early as 1485, he came back to Rome to work on numerous decorations which show his popularity: decoration of the palace of Cardinal Domenico della Rovere, now Palazzo dei Penitenzieri (remains), frescoes in the Palazzo Colonna, and decoration of the apartments of Innocent VIII at the Belvedere (remains), decoration of the Bufalini Chapel at Santa Maria in Aracoeli with the *Story of St Bernardino.* His style had become more personal, richly coloured; he used all the fashionable techniques, even in his *Madonnas,* such as the *Madonna della Pace* for the church of San Severino in the Marches. Alexander VI appreciated the rich, ornate, spicy style of Pinturicchio; he commissioned from him the decorations of the Borgia apartments in the Vatican, which the artist painted quickly from 1492 to 1494 with the help of many assistants. In Umbria, he painted a polyptych for the church of Santa Maria dei Fossi in Perugia, but his main work was the fresco decoration of the Baglioni Chapel in Santa Maria Maggiore in Spello, where he painted a fine self-portrait, in the form of a wall tablet at the side of a large *Annunciation.* In Siena, after the St John the Baptist frescoes in the cathedral, he painted a cartoon for the *Fortuna,* one of the designs for the pavement (1506), and decorated in his lively style the Piccolomini Library of the cathedral with the *Story of Pius II.* Finally, still in Siena, Pinturicchio painted for the palace of Pandolfo Petrucci il Magnifico, where the old Signorelli was working, the *Story of Ulysses and Penelope* (London, National Gallery).

Pinturicchio's development is utterly different from that of Perugino. He was influenced in his youth by Benozzo Gozzoli and even more by Bartolomeo Caporali. He prolonged into the 16th century the fashion for a rich, golden, picturesque art which we find at its best, after the more restrained Sistine frescoes, in the apartments of Alexander VI in the Vatican. From that time, Pinturicchio was at the head of an important workshop where precious and bizarre effects were cultivated. The stuccoes, gilding and embellishments which he often used to hide the banality of the forms and the weaknesses of the draughtsmanship, provoked ironic criticism, echoed by Vasari. His inventions are none the less original: he was the first to make a

PINTURICCHIO. PORTRAIT OF A YOUNG BOY. GEMÄLDEGALERIE, DRESDEN.

PISANELLO. MADONNA WITH A QUAIL.
CASTELVECCHIO, VERONA.

PISA. The history of Pisa is similar to that of Siena and several other Italian towns in one respect: its great artistic period coincided more or less with its period of political power, which came to an end with the victory of the Genoese fleet at La Meloria in 1284. During the 13th century, painted crosses inspired by Byzantine models, with paintings at the end of each arm and sometimes along the sides as well, were very popular in central Italy and particularly in Pisa and Lucca. The many extant examples can be divided in two different types: at the beginning of the century and until 1250, we find mainly impassive Christs with open eyes; Giunta and his followers introduced the sorrowful Christ figure with closed eyes, painted at the moment of death.

In the 14th century, Pisa remained a great artistic centre visited by numerous Sienese and Florentine artists, while the local painters (the most original is Francesco Traini) were content to accept their influence. In 1320, Simone Martini went to Pisa where he painted the polyptych on the main altar of the church of Santa Caterina; later, other Sienese artists like Luca di Tommè, Cecco di Pietro, etc. also visited Pisa. The Florentines (Taddeo Gaddi, Andrea da Firenze and with them Antonio Veneziano, Spinello Aretino) worked, from 1350 onwards, on the grandiose decoration of the Camposanto, most of which was destroyed by an incendiary raid on July 27th, 1944. During the 15th and 16th centuries, one can no longer talk of Pisan art, but visiting artists were still working in Pisa: Masaccio (polyptych for Santa Maria del Carmine), Benozzo Gozzoli (a fresco made up of twenty-three scenes from the Old Testament, on the north wall of the Camposanto, 1468-1485), Andrea del Sarto, Pierino del Vaga. Finally, among the Pisan painters of the 17th and 18th centuries, we must mention Riminaldi, Orazio Gentileschi, Aurelio Lomi

systematic use of 'grotesques' to frame fairylike and noble scenes. For instance Catherine of Alexandria is represented in a flower-studded frock, among Oriental characters (Prince Djem on horseback on the right of the picture) or hermits, surrounded by palms; in the spandrels are added strange fantasies heightened with gilt, the story of Osiris, the emblematic Borgia ox referring, as an exotic allusion, to the fable of the bull, Apis. The Spoleto Duomo shows more simplicity and sincerity. But Pinturicchio's talent had a lively, amusing charm, even at the cost of seriousness, as in the Piccolomini Library in Siena, or of narrative coherence. His manner was completely untouched by humanism and by the grand style.   A. C.

PISANELLO.
LUST. DRAWING.
ALBERTINA,
VIENNA.

PISANELLO.
STUDY
OF MONKEYS.
DRAWING.
LOUVRE, PARIS.

PISANELLO. HORSEMEN. DETAIL FROM 'ST GEORGE RESCUING THE PRINCESS
OF TREBIZOND'. ABOUT 1436. FRESCO FROM SANT'ANASTASIA, VERONA.
CASTELVECCHIO, VERONA.

and last, but not least, Giuseppe Melani (1673-1747), brother of the architect Francesco Melani, who decorated with baroque paintings, in the manner of Pietro da Cortona, many palaces and churches in Pisa and its surroundings.   P.-H. M.

PISANELLO Antonio Pisano, *called* (Pisa, *ca* 1395 - . . ., *ca* 1455). Born at Pisa, Pisanello lived as a young man in Verona and there received his early training in which Stefano da Verona probably took a hand. From 1415 to 1420 he worked on the decoration (now destroyed) of the Sala del Maggior Consiglio in the Palazzo Ducale at Venice, under the direction of Gentile da Fabriano whom he may possibly have followed afterwards to Florence. Later

on, after other travels, he continued Gentile's unfinished frescoes in San Giovanni in Laterano (1431-1432). From then onwards Pisanello became famous (in 1432 he drew the Emperor Sigismondo's portrait) and while still retaining the contacts made in Verona, he was sought after and welcomed by the courts of Milan (1440), Rimini (1445), Naples (1449) on several occasions Mantua, and especially Ferrara where he made lengthy visits. A series of portrait medallions (which he started in 1438 with the famous medallion of John VIII Paleologus, Emperor of the East, who had come to Ferrara for the Council) illustrates the different stages in his career as a court artist.

In spite of a huge collection of drawings (many of them in the Louvre) which enable us to reconstruct certain aspects of his pictorial activity, and in any case to get an idea of his exceptional versatility, both as a draughtsman of genius and a connoisseur of many interests, we know Pisanello's paintings today only in part. There exist for certain four or five small panels and two frescoes at Verona. The more important panels show portraits of Lionello d'Este (about 1441, Bergamo) and one of a *Princess of Este,* possibly Ginevra (1433 ?, Louvre). These portraits stand out from a floral background that resembles tapestry and has an air of fantasy that brings to mind the whimsical decoration of international gothic. Yet the precision in the modelling of the faces, seen in profile as on the medallions, proves how earnestly Pisanello tried in his way to reproduce the realistic, third-dimensional quality of his model. This artist was the last and undoubtedly the most brilliant Italian representative

PISANELLO. PORTRAIT OF A PRINCESS OF THE HOUSE OF ESTE (GINEVRA D'ESTE ?). ABOUT 1443. LOUVRE, PARIS.

PISANELLO. STUDY FOR THE HEAD OF THE PRINCESS IN THE FRESCO OF 'ST GEORGE AND THE PRINCESS'. DRAWING. LOUVRE, PARIS.

of the courtly, ornate style which had swept the whole of gothic Europe from the end of the 14th century, but he was by no means a retrograde. He came at first under the influence of Stefano da Verona (works considered by some historians to be by the latter have often been attributed by others to the young Pisanello) but he is the undisputed heir to Gentile da Fabriano; the elegant and graceful *Annunciation* painted about 1426 in fresco in San Fermo at Verona bears testimony to this, as, in a more general way, does the finely drawn delicacy of his pictorial technique. Yet he differs from his predecessor in his search for characterisation and his penetrating analysis of reality. He studiously avoids the double pitfall of abstract stylisation and picturesque superficiality, striving with an intense and often fierce concentration to get an insight into every tiny particle of natural life, but without burdening this vision with a unified moral intent or logical composition in perspective, and it is in this respect that he takes sides with the Tuscan innovators; he portrays every facet of life in detail—animals, flowers, men, outlandish pieces of architecture— all with the same fanatical precision and based on the same plan. His masterpiece, *St George and the Princess,* painted in Sant'Anastasia at Verona between 1433 and 1438, is a wonderful epitome of the odd yet rich mixture of this style with this kind of poetry: here in the twilight of the Middle Ages he recreates those dreams of chivalry and fantasy

SCHOOL OF PISA. PIETÀ. COMPARTMENT OF A DECORATED CRUCIFIX. ABOUT 1230-1240. MUSEO NAZIONALE, PISA.

with a light-hearted and romantic imagination, but with a vitality in his forms and a thirst for knowledge that are the mark of a 'modern' man.   M. L.

PITATI Bonifacio de'. *See* Bonifacio Veronese.

PITTONI Giambattista (Venice 1687 - Venice, 1767). A pupil of his uncle Francesco and of Balestra, Pittoni rose to such eminence that, in 1756, he was appointed, together with Giambattista Tiepolo, to select the first members of the Academy of Painting in Venice, and was its president from 1758 to 1761. His painting is light, graceful and luminous. Like the older Bolognese painter Creti, who influenced him, Pittoni excelled in providing landscape settings for gentle mythological scenes which have curious affinities, especially in their female types, with similar pieces by French artists like Boucher. Pittoni worked for a number of foreign courts. He is regarded as a typical representative of Venetian rococo (*Multiplication of Loaves,* Venice, Accademia). Towards the end of his life Pittoni's manner became colder under the influence of neoclassical painters.   P. C.

PIUS II Aeneas Silvius Piccolomini, Pope (Corsignano, near Siena, 1405 - Ancona, 1464). First bishop of Trieste, then papal legate in several countries of central Europe, Aeneas Silvius became Pope in 1458 and scholars rejoiced as they thought the very name of Pius—an allusion to Virgil's Pius Aeneas—was a good omen. They were disappointed. From then on, Pius II was absorbed by religious and political problems, particularly by the scheme of a great crusade against the Turks, and he neglected his old friends. But he helped artists, as we see from the building work he undertook at the Vatican and in Siena. His greatest achievement as a patron was the creation, on the site of

ANTONIO (OR PIERO) POLLAIUOLO.
PORTRAIT OF A GIRL. MUSEO POLDI-
PEZZOLI, MILAN.

his native *castello,* of a town which he called Pienza. The work began in 1459 and painters were also called upon. The best known masters of the Sienese school: Vecchietta, Sano di Pietro, Giovanni di Paolo, Matteo di Giovanni, painted frescoes on the walls of the new cathedral.

The main episodes in the life of Pius II are commemorated by the decoration of the *Libreria Piccolomini* (frescoes by Pinturicchio, 1505-1508) in Siena Cathedral. 　　　　　　　　　P.-H. M.

POLLAIUOLO Antonio (Florence, 1432 - Rome, 1498) *and* Piero (Florence, 1443 - Rome, 1496) di Jacopo Benci, *called.* The two brothers, who worked almost continually together after 1460, are fairly representative of a busy Florentine workshop with varied activities, in which a sort of division of labour was practised under a common signature. Respective attributions are therefore very uncertain. Both brothers were trained as gold-

smiths, and both used a technique combining vigour with accuracy of detail. Soon after 1464, Antonio decorated the Villa Arcetri for a member of the Medici family with extraordinary dancing figures which have been likened to those in Etruscan frescoes. He executed for Piero de' Medici three large compositions of the *Labours of Hercules* which we know through smaller copies and which were probably close to the *St Michael* (Museo Bardini) painted at the same time.

Apollo and Daphne (London, National Gallery), which may date from 1470 or thereabouts, shows an assimilation of Flemish techniques through the handling of colour, and so does the *Rape of Deianeira* (New Haven, U.S.A.) through the unusual importance given to landscape. The brothers Pollaiuolo were then among the best known artists in Florence. They took part in the preparations for the 'Giostra' in 1468. In 1469 and 1470, Piero was asked to paint the *Six Virtues* (Uffizi) for the court chamber of the Tribunale di Mercanzia in Florence; he also painted the *Coronation of the Virgin* (1483) for the Collegiata of San Gimignano. Antonio had produced a masterpiece, in his harsh and precise style, with the impressive *Martyrdom of St Sebastian* (1475) for the Pucci chapel in the Annunziata in Florence (London, National Gallery). Portraits seem to have been Antonio's work (Berlin; Milan, Museo Poldi-Pezzoli; Florence, Uffizi). We must set apart the engravings like the *Battle of the Nudes,* not to mention embroidery cartoons for Santa Maria del Fiore, numerous commissioned pieces of jewelry mentioned in the accounts, and small bronzes like *Hercules and Antaeus* (Florence, Uffizi). The two brothers were called to Rome in 1484 to work on the tomb of Sixtus IV, and from then on, devoted all their time to sculpture.

All critics agree that, while the pre-

ANTONIO POLLAIUOLO.
DAVID TRIUMPHANT.
KAISER FRIEDRICH
MUSEUM, BERLIN.

vious generation had introduced tactile values, Antonio added to Florentine art two fresh elements: anatomy and landscape. The feeling for sculpture was more than ever the basis of Florentine draughtsmanship. But after Donatello and the Flemish artists, anatomic accuracy and the language of gestures and mimicry were used more and more to express movement and violence, in fact, the very opposite ot Masaccio's stately humanity. The embroideries for the cathedral (1466-1480, Florence, Opera del Duomo) are full of nervous, jerky motifs. On the other hand, new problems of perspective harmony arose through the elaboration of the landscape which is noticeable in the panels of the *Labours of Hercules* and of the *Rape of Deianeira*. This dual interest in anatomy and nature culminated in the *St Sebastian* in which, without the brilliant compositional devices, the excessive detail in the human body would for the first time reveal the limitations of naturalism. As the Florentines, after 1460, were interested above all in liveliness and movement, the popularity of the brothers Pollaiuolo is understandable. It is confirmed by the success of their engravings in which Antonio circumscribed and characterised form by a firm contour; the famous *Battle of the Nudes* (about 1470) impressed Mantegna and, through him, Dürer. Connected with the humanist circles, introduced by Lorenzo de' Medici in 1489 as the 'principale maestro della città', Antonio directed with his brother a workshop which used all the techniques and knew all the innovations. Around 1480, at the peak of the Florentine period, the only corresponding 'bottega' was that of Verrocchio.   A. C.

PONTORMO Jacopo Carucci, *called* (Pontormo, near Empoli, 1494 - Florence, 1557). Jacopo Carucci, called Pontormo after his native village, was the most sensitive and the most characteristic artist representing the trend which, from 1520, led the disciples of Florentine and Roman masters beyond or even against the norms of 'classicism': that reaction is usually called 'mannerism'. Jacopo may have known Leonardo and was trained by Albertinelli before he became, in 1512, the disciple and assistant of Andrea del Sarto; we can see those influences in his *Visitation* in the porch of the Annunziata, and in the *Madonna with Four Saints*. His artistic personality had developed by the time he painted the *Pala dei Pucci* and the three panels of a 'cassone' for the wedding of Pier Francesco Borgherini and Margherita Acciaiuoli, in 1515: the *Story of Joseph* (Henfield, Grey Walls, Salmon Collection). The influence of Leonardo and Piero di Cosimo reinforced his natural taste for elegant contour and for unusual motifs and attitudes.

Thanks to the protection of Cardinal Ottaviano de' Medici, he was asked to decorate the great hall of Poggio a Caiano, which had remained unfinished at the death of Lorenzo (1520-1521). On one of the side lunettes, whose theme, *Vertumnus and Pomona,* must go back to the original project, Pontormo painted a very elegant and lively pastoral scene in which the rustic figures are treated in scarely tinted greys and yellows.

Between 1522 and 1525, at the

Certoso del Galluzzo, south of Florence, Pontormo painted in the cloister a large cycle depicting the Passion (badly damaged): the composition is full of

PONTORMO. 'PORTRAIT OF UGOLINO MARTELLI. NATIONAL GALLERY OF ART, WASHINGTON.

technical innovations, the figures are elongated and the draperies have unexpected lines; but there are also many features borrowed from German engravings, particularly from Dürer. Vasari claimed later that the artist had betrayed the Tuscan manner. Pontormo's intentions become clear in his *Deposition* in Santa Felicità (1526), which is a masterpiece of its kind painted in light cool tones of mauve, pink and green with undulating figures effectively arranged in a composition built up of sinuous tiers. As a portrait painter, he created a new type with his smooth, elongated, uneasy looking models: *The Gem Engraver* (Louvre), *Alessandro de'*

PONTORMO. THE VISITATION. ABOUT 1530.
PARISH CHURCH OF CARMIGNANO.

Medici (Lucca), and the Portraits of Women (Frankfurt and Vienna) are all remarkable through their clear colours, the emphasis on the hands, and the detailed draughtsmanship.

Pontormo had a worried, unsettled temperament and left a Diary which gives us details about his last years and the work he undertook. In the Carmignano *Visitation* (about 1530), he made the central group stand out through a strong foreshortening, and, instead of the two traditional characters, gathered four figures in one block of faded yellow and red draperies. Finally, under the influence of Michelangelo who gave him cartoons to work up, he tried to give more volume to his compositions and the contrast grew more marked between the delicate faces of his models and their huge muscular bodies. In the choir of San Lorenzo, in Florence

(1546), the frescoes have been painted over, but the artist' sketches allow us to imagine the gigantic bodies and twisted forms, uncontrolled by any decorative design. No possible balance could be achieved and the result was generally considered a failure.   A. C.

PORDENONE Giovanni Antonio de' Sacchis *or* Sacchiense, *called* (Pordenone, *ca* 1484 - Ferrara, 1539). Of Lombard origin, but born in Friuli, in the village which gave him his name, the artist was trained by local masters such as Gianfrancesco da Tolmezzo, and the confident vitality he learnt from them survived all other influences. His discovery of Giorgione is echoed in the Susegana *Madonna* by a combination of harmonious colours with clear forms. A stay in Rome, beginning in 1520 and perhaps even in 1516, confirmed his taste for monumental figures, which we notice in his large compositions in the Malchiostri Chapel in Trevisa (1520) and in Cremona Cathedral (1521) where he painted dramatic and tempestuous scenes from the Passion. After 1525, however, an elegance, which is reminiscent of Parmigianino and of other influences, appears, for instance, in the outlines of *St Gothard between St Roch and St Sebastian* (Pordenone). But in his work in the choir of San Rocco (1528-1529) and in the cloister of San Stefano (1532) architectural backgrounds became more important and a new style developed: the figures had become gigantic and more lively and already anticipated Tintoretto. In that way, Pordenone represents a reaction against Titian, which continued and amplified that of Lotto; he represents a type of mannerism that had some success in the provinces.   A. C.

POZZO Andrea (Trento, 1642 - Vienna, 1709). After studying under the Jesuits, he began painting first at Trento, then Como. On the 23rd December, 1665, under the influence of a sermon he joined the Order of Jesuits, but did not give up his art. In 1676, he painted the Missione church of the Jesuits at Mondovì. Father Gian-Paolo Oliva, the General of the Jesuits, summoned him to Rome in 1681 and, in 1685, he began to decorate San Ignazio, his most celebrated work. The vertiginous effects of illusionist perspective in the ceiling of the nave open into the infinity of the heavens: daring architectural perspectives of columns, arcades and airborne porticoes fling into the space, above the real church, an imaginary church where sacred figures float like birds. Father Pozzo was a great organiser of religious festivities and he wrote a treatise on perspective, *Prattica della Perspettiva* (1692), which had an enormous success and was translated into English and German. In this he makes the art of painting dependent on perspective alone, which is in keeping with the personal tastes of a painter of illusionist architecture, while elsewhere he forces himself to justify the details of style by reasons that are as often religious as archaeological. In 1702, Pozzo went to Vienna. There he decorated the Jesuit church, the Universitätskirche (1703), and in the Gartenpalais Liechtenstein he painted figures in mid-flight against sumptuous porticoes seen in perspective (1704-1708). At Vienna, where he died, his influence was considerable and in Italy his art had its effect on Solimena in Naples and Tiepolo in Venice. S. B.

PREDIS Giovanni Ambrogio da (Milan, ca 1455 - Milan, 1517). He had two brothers, also painters. In 1482, he was appointed court painter to the Sforza. In 1483, he and his brother, Evangelista, worked with Leonardo for the Confraternity of the Immaculate Conception in Milan, on an altarpiece which included the *Virgin of the Rocks* (London, National Gallery), his most famous work in collaboration with the

AMBROGIO DA PREDIS. PORTRAIT (PRESUMED) OF BEATRICE D'ESTE. AMBROSIANA, MILAN.

master. He painted two wings for it, depicting angels, of which only one remains. He became Leonardo's most faithful disciple and was particularly successful as a portrait painter. Some of his works are so close to Leonardo that a few of his portraits have been attributed to his master, for instance, the *Gentleman* in the Brera. Sometimes, on the other hand, he went back to the old Lombard tradition of profiles, as in the portrait of *Francesco Brivio* (Milan, Museo Poldi-Pezzoli). His position at the court of the Sforza provided him with famous sitters: he painted the portraits of Ludovico, of the Marchesa Catarina and Bianca Maria Sforza and, after the latter's marriage, he accompanied her to Austria and painted in 1502 the portrait of her husband Emperor *Maximilian I* (Vienna), his only signed and dated work. In his work, the influence of Leonardo is still combined with the spirit of the Quattrocento.   S. B.

PRETI Mattia, *called* il Cavaliere Calabrese (Taverna, Calabria, 1613 - Malta, 1699). Preti's work always has a foundation of realism, as he may well have been influenced by early contact with Caravaggism in Naples, then by the neo-Caravaggism fashionable in northern European circles in Rome (where he probably arrived about 1630), but his taste for movement and colour is accentuated by the knowledge he gained in Venice and the influence of both Ludovico Carracci and Guercino. He was a great traveller (visits to Spain, Paris) and evolved a style which is on the surface eclectic, but reveals a fine intensity of feeling: dark or warm colours with glinting highlights fill his canvases (the *Raising of Lazarus,* Rome, Galleria Nazionale d'Arte Antiqua), and the composition of his frescoes is compact yet at the same time full of movement (Rome, Sant'Andrea della Valle, 1650-1651). Preti's return visit to Naples, about 1656-1660, when he discovered the work of the young painter, Luca Giordano, and then his long period of activity in the distant province of Malta contributed to the perfunctory, purely decorative element in his art which is often careless and often superficial, yet it still contains some fine flashes of poetry (the *Baptism of Christ,* Valletta, Museum).   J. T.

PRIMATICCIO Francesco (Bologna, 1504 - Paris, 1570). He was trained at Mantua under Giulio Romano, with whom he worked for six years in the Palazzo del Tè, developing his talent as a great decorator, but he was also

PRIMATICCIO. THREE NYMPHS. DRAWING. 1545-1547. LEHMAN COLLECTION, NEW YORK.

fascinated by Parmigianino's work, with its long tapering forms and subtle colouring. He was called to the service of Francis I, and executed large-scale fresco decorations at Fontainebleau and Paris (Galerie d'Ulysse, 1541-1570, destroyed; Salle de Bal, 1551-1556, mostly restored); after Rosso's death (1540) he became Director of Works to the King and supplied designs for sculptures, enamels, architecture and decorations for festivities. Unfortunately whole works of his have been destroyed or damaged, but the stuccoes (Chambre de Madame d'Étampes at Fontainebleau) and a set of superb drawings testify to his sensual, elegant genius, his skill in tackling complicated problems of space (*Cupola for the Chapelle de Guise,* drawing, Paris, École des Beaux-Arts) and exploiting all the magical appeal of the ancient myths (the *Masquerade of Persepolis,* drawing, Louvre). He had a positive and lasting influence on the development of French art.   J. T.

QUATTROCENTO. The 15th century in Italy ('Quattrocento', meaning the century of the years 1400) has a character of its own. The peninsula had neither political nor cultural unity; it was divided into rival states, each longing to conquer the others (Milan and Florence were enemies until the battle of Anghiari in 1440; then Florence and Rome; then Venice and all the others), but some sort of equilibrium had at last been achieved through those very rivalries when the arrival of the French army led by Charles VIII and Louis XII created a new situation and involved Italy with European conflicts. By then, Italian culture had reached its maturity and made a lasting impact on the rest of Europe.

One of the main events of the century was the swift revival of papal power, under Nicholas V and Sixtus IV, which brought Rome both a material restoration and a renewal of prestige; from then on, the old capital of the Roman Empire again took the lead in the arts. That development, however, took place chiefly at the beginning of the 16th century; during the 15th century, the scholars worked mainly in Florence and the archaeologists in Padua and in the north. The 'return to the antique' was only one of the causes of the cultural and artistic revolution which happened in Italy, but an important one because it made artistic circles more and more clearly aware of their unique ancient heritage; thus Italy was to lead western Europe back to Mediterranean forms. But it was a slow process and we must take into account the various artistic centres all attempting to maintain their originality and their own traditions: Florence, Milan, Venice launched great building schemes and developed distinct 'schools' which still clung, at least the two former, to 'gothic' features while trying to assimilate the new style for the sake of prestige. Siena alone kept up for a long time its own delightful style and remained aloof from the general evolution. The Quattrocento saw the blossoming of small centres like Rimini, Urbino, Ferrara, Perugia, little towns in the Marches which, by the following century, would no longer be able to compete.

A reaction against a courtly gothic, the so-called international style, had started in Tuscany, as in Flanders, in the name of a more lively rendering of nature and of religious feelings. But the domination of Florence did not last, except for sculpture; her painters made important discoveries about the handling of space and the use of draperies, around 1430; colourists and draughtsmen vied with each other in exploiting those discoveries until about 1470. Their influence spread towards Umbria, the Marches and the northern provinces. A subsidiary centre developed in Padua, where Squarcione forged a lasting link between the study of antiques and the new interest in form, a link which Mantegna took up and imposed on the whole of northern Italy, in Venice (with Jacopo Bellini and Giovanni's first manner), in Milan (with Foppa), in Mantua (with Mantegna himself), and in Ferrara (with Ercole de' Roberti). The latter town became at the time of Borso, then of Ercole d'Este, one of the most important centres of the Quattrocento, and one which gave its best then: the influence of Squarcione was combined with that of Piero della Francesca who worked there towards the middle of the century.

Piero della Francesca undoubtedly dominated the 15th century with his personality: beside Florence, where he did not return after 1445, his activity linked the valleys of the Tuscan Apennines with the Adriatic side (Rimini, Urbino, Ferrara) and with Rome. He made a synthesis of perspective, which he conceived as the introduction of mathematical rhythms into space, and colour, which he conceived as a continuous pattern of clear, solid shapes. This dual preoccupation, reinforced by the complementary influence of Antonello da Messina who arrived in Venice in 1475, directed Venetian masters towards 'tonal' painting, which was already foreshadowed at the end of the Quattrocento in the work of Bellini and Carpaccio and which allowed a new development of the picturesque and of the exotic elements both so popular in Venice.

Another interesting development, which did not survive the Quattrocento, took place in Umbria. The influence of some Florentine artists who liked bright cheerful pictures, like Gozzoli, of Sienese artists like Sassetta, and of Piero della Francesca, led to the birth of a 'school' at the same time sophisticated and naive, from which emerged Perugino, who also happened to be Piero della Francesca's pupil. Admittedly, like his rival Signorelli, he combined Florentine draughtsmanship and tactile values with Piero's sense of order; but unlike Signorelli who sacrificed everything else for the sake of dramatic effect and monumentality, Perugino made subtle use of cool, light tones, of soft landscape and peaceful rhythms. The 'aria dolce' of his compositions may be artificial and exaggerated; but this suppler style played a decisive part in the evolution towards a stricter, more coherent organisation of forms.

Such an evolution was one of the possible conclusions of the Quattrocento, along the path of classical art. Perugino's school met with formidable competition from Leonardo who triumphed in Milan after 1482 and was known everywhere by the end of the century. Starting from Verrocchio and trained in the Florentine tradition, Leonardo, as a Quattrocento man, had an unlimited confidence in human achievement and believed that painters were alone capable of expressing the hidden rhythm, as well as the outward beauty, of the universe. He wanted to abolish clear outlines and harsh modelling and to create a style of the utmost sincerity and realism. A clash with the 'neo-gothic' style of Botticelli or of the Venetian Crivelli, and with the 'all'antica' style of Mantegna, was to be expected: we notice it throughout Italy, in Milan, in Rome, in Naples. But the 'aria dolce' and the 'sfumato' triumphed almost everywhere in the 16th century. The word 'primitive' invented by the Romantics to describe Italian painting before Raphael, wrongly lumps together the innovations of the Quattrocento and the works of the Trecento. There is, however, a noticeable shade of difference between the works of the 15th century and those of the High Renaissance in which we no longer find the freshness and the intensity of the sometimes fruitless experiments of Quattrocento artists. A. C.

R

RAIBOLINI Francesco. *See* Francia.

RAPHAEL Raffaello Sanzio, *called* (Urbino, 1483 - Rome, 1520). Raphael's irresistible charm and meteoric career fascinated his own contemporaries. The son of Giovanni Santi, painter at the court of Urbino, he lost his mother at the age of eight, and his father four years later; he had already started painting, and pursued his training under Timoteo Vitti who had come back to Urbino in 1495. The Marches were always artistically dependent on Umbria and, in 1500, Raphael was with Perugino at the Cambio in Perugia, where he probably painted *Fortitude* and *Justice*. The same year, he worked with a pupil of his father's, Evangelista di Pian di Meleto, on an altarpiece for Città di Castello (fragments) in Naples and in Brescia. His somewhat unassertive, delicate treatment was already evident in the small mythological and allegorical compositions of that period: the *Three Graces* (Chantilly), the *Knight's Dream* (London, National Gallery). Between 1500 and 1504, he developed his personal style in large-scale religious works: the *Marriage of the Virgin* (Brera), signed and dated 1504, intended for Città di Castello, and a series of Madonnas: the *Madonna Conestabile* (Hermitage), the *Virgin with the Pomegranate* (sketch in Vienna) and large altarpieces: the *Coronation of the Virgin* for the church of San Francesco in Perugia, and the serene 1503 *Crucifixion* (London, National Gallery). Already, he was no longer just Perugino's pupil: the compositions were as clear and well balanced as those of his

RAPHAEL, VIRGIN WITH THE POMEGRANATE. DRAWING. ALBERTINA, VIENNA.

Umbrian master, but the draughtsmanship was more subtle. At that time, he painted the *Portrait of a Man* which has been definitely attributed to him since the overpainting was removed in 1911 (Rome, Galleria Borghese), the *Christ Blessing* (Brescia), and above all the portraits of the Urbino family: *Guidobaldo da Montefeltro, Elisabetta Gonzaga* (both in the Uffizi) and *Emilia-Pia,* their sister-in-law (Baltimore).

The *Virgin surrounded by Saints* (New York, Metropolitan Museum), once

243

RAPHAEL. MARRIAGE OF THE VIRGIN. 1504. BRERA, MILAN.

belonging to the Colonna family, was commissioned by the nuns of the Convent of St Anthony of Padua in Perugia; the predella has been dispersed. The panels balancing each other on both sides of the high throne represent female figures: St Cecilia and St Catherine; and amply draped male figures: St Peter

and St Paul. Raphael may already have visited Florence at that time. At the end of 1504 at the latest, he went there and discovered the work of Leonardo; his awakened interest is obvious in works like the *Madonna del Granduca* (Pitti), the *Virgin in the Meadow* (Vienna) and the numerous Madonnas painted with increasing originality and gentle feeling. The delightful *Belle Jardinière* (Louvre), the monumental *Madonna del Baldacchino* (Pitti) show the painter's range, which widened considerably with his dramatic *Entombment* (Rome, Galleria Borghese), commissioned in 1507 by Atalanta Baglioni for the church of San Francesco in Perugia.

Towards the end of 1508, Julius II invited him to decorate the old apartments of Nicholas V in the Vatican, the Stanze. A group of Umbrian painters including Perugino, Signorelli, Bramantino, Sodoma, had started working there; but the Pope, fascinated, soon discarded them all in favour of the young artist. He first decorated the Stanza della Segnatura, whose grandiose theme deals with the whole of spiritual life. Its completion in 1511 was a triumph for Raphael who was then asked to decorate the next room, called the Stanza d'Eliodoro, in which the great events of the Pope's reign are commemorated. He naturally painted the Pope's portrait. He then began to be given commissions by Roman noblemen: by Sigismondo de' Conti, the *Madonna di Foligno* (Vatican), meant for the main altarpiece of Santa Maria in Aracoeli on the Capitol; and above all by the Sienese banker, Agostino Chigi, the decoration of the Farnesina (from 1511) with the *Triumph of Galatea,* which was followed by the scenes from the *Story of Psyche* for the Loggia (sketches by Raphael, painted by Giulio Romano and Penni). His most remarkable Madonna pictures belong to that period: the *Madonna della Sedia* with its very effective 'tondo' shape (Pitti); the *Sistine Madonna* (Dresden), shown as an apparition between St Sixtus and St Catherine (or St Barbara). Raphael was not yet thirty.

Leo X's pontificate brought some important changes to his career. After Bramante's death in 1514, Michelangelo's departure and the failure of Leonardo,

RAPHAEL. VIRGIN WITH THE GOLDFINCH (DETAIL). ABOUT 1506. UFFIZI, FLORENCE.

Raphael was the only one left of the great artists called to Rome by Julius II. He was in charge of all artistic work: the supervision of the architectural work at the Vatican, the Loggie and their decoration, a series of tapestries—ten cartoons—for the Sistine Chapel, together with private commissions, not to mention the care of the ancient monuments of Rome. During the last seven years of his life, Raphael feverishly produced a series of masterpieces. In June 1514, he had hardly completed the decoration of the second Stanza when he started on the third, called the Stanza dell'Incendio: the frescoes were finished in 1517. The work was handed over to pupils, particularly to Giulio Romano, as the master was busy designing cartoons for the tapestries intended for the lower

RAPHAEL. PORTRAIT OF TOMMASO INGHIRAMI.
ABOUT 1515. PALAZZO PITTI, FLORENCE.

grotesques). The following year, the decoration of the fourth Stanza, called the Sala di Costantino, was begun, to be finished only after the death of the master, by Giulio Romano and the workshop. Raphael succeeded Bramante as architect of St Peter's and had to provide a new plan. He built the Palazzo Branconio dell'Aquila (destroyed) in Rome and designed a large villa for Giuliano de' Medici, the future Clement VII, on the slopes of Monte Mario (now the recently restored Villa Madama). At the height of his glory, happiness and productivity, the young genius died at the age of thirty-seven. Rome gave him a splendid funeral and mourned him like a demi-god.

Trained in one of the most sophisticated centres of humanist culture, Raphael remained faithful to its ideals. Perugino's art, which was an early influence, suited his temperament and suggested the light tones and open, peaceful landscapes of the *Three Graces* and the *Knight's Dream*. The end of that period was marked by the *Marriage of the Virgin*, a brilliant, refined adaptation of the Perugino's *Delivery of the Keys to St Peter* in the Sistine Chapel. The elements are the same: a central temple lit up by a shaft of light, a wide perspective giving a feeling of space; but everything has acquired at the same time more subtlety and more strength. The forms are elegant without affectation, the colour balance is perfect. It is a triumph of clear tones. In the *Madonnas*, Raphael's touch was more lively and more realistic, a double preoccupation which drew him quite naturally to Leonardo. With the *Madonna del Granduca* (Pitti), the Umbrian tradition was replaced by the secret, harmonious world revealed by Leonardo in which mathematical principles coincided with an intuitive feeling for nature. He adopted the *sfumato* technique as well as a pyramidal composition in the *Belle Jardinière*, the linking of figure and

part of the Sistine Chapel. The cartoons were made during the years 1515-1516, and the tapestries woven from 1517 to 1519 in Brussels and delivered at the end of 1519. Those monumental tapestries illustrating the *Acts of the Apostles* were so well received that the cartoons (London, Victoria and Albert Museum) were borrowed by the Duke of Mantua to have a second set made, then by the Duke of Urbino who had them woven for the third time.

In the Loggie, Raphael's contribution was limited to general instructions: he introduced the use of 'grotesques', which Giovanni da Udine was to develop. In 1516, he sketched for Cardinal Bibiena the decoration of his Stufetta, that is, his bathroom at the Vatican (mythological scenes, framed by 'Pompeian' landscape in the portrait of *Maddalena Doni* (Pitti). At first conceived as busts, his portraits became half-figures according to Leonardo's practice.

In the same way, he exploited the innovations of Michelangelo, who resented it, and assimilated Michelangelesque forms already in the *Entombment,* and the Michelangelesque nudes and sense of drama in the *Fire in the Borgo* at the Vatican and in the *Sibyls* of Santa Maria della Pace. Raphael was also influenced by some aspects of Venetian tonal painting and even by Titian himself whom he knew through Sebastiano del Piombo; this influence is noticeable in the *Mass of Bolsena,* in the second Stanza, in the *Madonna with the Fish* (Prado) and in a few portraits like the *Donna Velata* (Pitti).

We can follow these developments and the emerging of the school which prolonged the artist's activity in the Vatican Stanze. The four 'storie' in the Stanza della Segnatura (the *Disputà* or the *Disputation concerning the Holy Sacrament,* the *School of Athens,* the *Parnassus* and the *Decretals*) illustrate, together with the allegories on the vault, the four aspects of a Platonic and Christian doctrine. The symbolism is at the same time humanised by the use of typical figures and made significant by making the group, which illustrates the theme, into the centre of the perspective composition. Thus Raphael put his genius at the service of ideas. After the 'mirror of doctrine', followed the 'mirror of history'; in the Stanza d'Eliodoro the artist has represented dramatic episodes from the history of the Church: *Heliodorus driven from the*

RAPHAEL.
SWISS GUARDS.
DETAIL FROM
THE 'MASS
OF BOLSENA'.
FRESCO.
1511-1514.
STANZA
D'ELIODORO,
VATICAN, ROME.

RAPHAEL. DONNA VELATA. ABOUT 1514.
PALAZZO PITTI, FLORENCE.

the artist's death, completes the decorative scheme with a rhetorical style which was to provide models for churches and palaces throughout Italy; the *Battle of Ponte Molle* illustrating Constantine's victory over Maxentius is reminiscent of the *Battle of Anghiari* and must have been painted after a cartoon of the master's.

The essence of Raphael's classic style is found mainly in his representations of the Virgin. From the *Madonna di Foligno* with her queenly grace to the *Madonna della Sedia* with her humanity and motherliness and the *Sistine Madonna,* a supernatural theophany, he elevated to sublime heights the most hackneyed theme in Christian art. The fusion of Christian and antique elements is also remarkable in the *Vision of Ezekiel* (Pitti), the master's last composition. The world of fable is treated with an equally subtle understanding in the Farnesina frescoes, particularly that of *Galatea* in which nature seems in harmony with the amorous themes which the artist liked.

Raphael's art was passionately admired by the humanist circles to which he belonged. The portrait of *Baldassare Castiglione* (Louvre) for instance, with its restrained and sure touch, shows how close the understanding must have been between fastidious intellectuals and this sensitive master. What they appreciated above all in his work was the 'mirabile giudizio' which governed the composition and his power to express characters through drawing. After his death, his pupils unashamedly exploited his discoveries, keeping mainly the composition and the imitation of antiquity. His genius provided the Italian Renaissance with its classical framework. 'He always did what others dreamt of doing', Goethe said of him, and Taine, comparing him to Mozart, found in his natural generosity and deep humanity the secret of an art so learned, but so true, that one can only praise it for its simplicity. A. C.

Temple, the *Liberation of St Peter, Leo I halting Attila before Rome,* the *Mass of Bolsena:* we can follow the whole pontificate of Julius II through these solemn evocations. Such a grand conception demanded a grand style. The combined influences of Michelangelo and of Venetian light effects are apparent; the light effects are particularly noticeable in *The Liberation of St Peter.* The last two rooms are hardly by the master's hand: busy with other commissions, he merely gave general instructions to Giulio Romano and the workshop. In the third Stanza, whose theme is the glorification of the Pope's power, called the Stanza dell'Incendio because the first painting is the *Fire in the Borgo* which was miraculously stopped by Leo IV, the first fresco may be entirely by Raphael's hand, but it is the only one. The Sala di Costantino, finished after

RENAISSANCE (The). Among the theories explaining the Renaissance, one of the oldest—and most charming—makes it spring from the cultural developments which took place in Italy at the end of the 13th century and connects those developments with the spreading of Franciscan doctrines (St Francis died in 1226, Dante was born in 1265, Petrarch in 1304). With Giotto in Assisi, we are told, mystic 'naturalism' came in contact with the rebirth of the great monumental style and Italian art was set on the road which, with gradual softening and enriching, would lead to Masaccio, Piero della Francesca, Raphael and Titian. Thus, a deeper and more human religious feeling, a return to original Mediterranean forms are, according to that theory, the deep meaning and secret impulse of the Renaissance.

By analysing this sentimental and specious interpretation, we can introduce more accurate factors and reach a more convincing historical picture. Franciscan ideas are not sufficient to account for the 'rebirth' of the 13th century: the movement started by the Ghibelline circle around Frederick II, the influence of Rome and the work of a Niccolò Pisano are equally important. Moreover, the proto-Renaissance of the 13th century coincided with the acceptance of gothic forms: painting, emancipated by Giotto from the Byzantine tradition, was soon to be engulfed in the gothic wave which dominated the 14th century, with the exquisite Simone Martini, the rough Barna, the clever Orcagna. And we can only place the beginning of the Renaissance at the time of the reaction, after 1400, against the jewelled, precious, conventional style of altarpieces and frescoes: such was the part played by Masaccio, who was determined to do for painting what Donatello had done for sculpture, that is to give it more reality, to stress effects of space, the movement of

RAPHAEL. LA FORNARINA. ABOUT 1515. GALLERIA NAZIONALE, ROME.

draperies and intensity of expression. This had nothing to do with the rendering of nature or of human tenderness: it was a calculated step towards a grander, more dramatic style. The most marked change of outlook took place in architecture, with Brunelleschi and Leo Battista Alberti. It became the science of measuring and dividing space, of creating strict and harmonious volumes. The change was slower in painting; at least, the impulse given by Masaccio's revolution often led, as had already happened after Giotto, to the new development of unreal, ornate settings (Benozzo Gozzoli) or to a linear gothic style (Botticelli). Everywhere, there was an opposition between, on one side, the colourists, interested mainly in brightness and light effects (Domenico Veneziano, Fra Angelico) and, on the

LEONARDO DA VINCI. SELF-PORTRAIT. DRAWING.
ABOUT 1512. ROYAL LIBRARY, TURIN.

other side, the draughtsmen, preoccupied with space and plastic values (Uccello, Andrea del Castagno); alone, Piero della Francesca, who dominated the first phase of the Renaissance, combined both approaches. His 'synthesis' of volume and colour started a new *ars poetica* of painting. This new set of rules could —and soon did—incorporate more and more learned knowledge: Mantegna introduced archaeology; Perugino treated rhythm and space with less strictness and used a suppler style; Antonello da Messina and Giovanni Bellini enriched the colour range. And finally Leonardo used *sfumato* to intensify suggestive effects and to react against overstressed

outlines, harshness and loose composition. His influence was decisive.

During the second phase of the Renaissance, the problems of the end of the 15th century and the sometimes unruly or extreme ways in which they had been solved were left behind. The period was dominated by Bramante for architecture, Jacopo Sansovino and Michelangelo for sculpture, Raphael, Perugino's heir, and Giorgione, successor, with Titian, of Giovanni Bellini, for painting. A suppler, more harmonious style triumphed, but it was conditioned by a strictly balanced composition and a set of rules as rigid as in architecture. Ornaments and draperies had become to a certain extent standardised, like architectural orders. All arts were now in unison. And all were capable of transforming contemporary civilisation, the civilisation that emerged from the heroic pontificate of Julius II and the epicurean reign of Leo X, by lending it the rediscovered setting of the antique world and unfolding huge, powerfully organised artistic conceptions. These sublime creations were marked by a spirit of optimism. The Vatican Stanze and the Loggie, the ceiling of the Sistine Chapel, were soon recognised as masterpieces. Artistic life was very active; each centre adopted with conviction the latest discoveries, which found unexpected developments with the voluptuous art of Correggio, the delicate, melancholy style of Andrea del Sarto and Sodoma, both influenced by Leonardo. Large compositions, a strong cohesion of multiple elements and the depicting of a heroic humanity were found at the same time in Titian. The authority of these masters spread to the whole of Europe. The Renaissance was going to transform western art in depth.

The principles of composition common to all painters are often considered as the main contribution of the Renaissance at its best. The importance of clear, well defined forms had never been stressed so much: everything was seen in sculptural terms. Although in the work of great artists, genuine feeling still came through this solemn style, their numerous pupils and imitators often produced more artificial works: this trend towards academicism already appeared in Raphael's workshop, became worse with the next generation and dominated the third phase of the Renaissance, usually called 'mannerism', which was to influence the French school through Fontainebleau, the Flemish school through Antwerp, the Spanish school through the Escorial and the Bohemian school through Prague. The same process took place in sculpture with Benvenuto Cellini, Ammanati, in architecture with Giulio Romano who, at the Palazzo del Tè, in Mantua, provided an example of a new style, anti-classical in some ways, in spite of the exclusive use of classical elements. Wall painting ranged from the rather restless subtleties of Pontormo to the brutal outspokenness of Cambiaso. Feats of skill were fashionable, and so were Bronzino's coldness and Parmigianino's elegant sophistication. All artists used surprise effects, even in Venice where Tintoretto developed to the utmost a new pathos of scene painting and light effects never achieved before, while Veronese, on the contrary, used a clear, restrained technique and gave a new life to Roman and classical models. Decadence had set in, as the Academies were beginning to codify formulas. Numerous treatises dealt with artistic knowledge, that is, with the legacy of the masters interpreted according to philosophical principles usually borrowed from Aristotle ('mimesis') or Plato (the 'Idea'), from iconology to perspective, from 'physiognomy' to the theory of draughtsmanship. There was an awareness of belonging to an exceptional age now on the wane, which was expressed through historical studies of famous men and their works, the

RAPHAEL. PRESUMED TO BE A SELF-PORTRAIT OF THE ARTIST AS A CHILD. DRAWING. ASHMOLEAN MUSEUM, OXFORD.

sign of a closing cycle. The stimulating 'myth' of the Renaissance became for three centuries the legend of an exemplary golden age in which art reigned for ever.   A. C.

RENI Guido (Bologna, 1575 - Bologna, 1642). Trained first in Calvaert's workshop and then in the Carracci Academy, he later divided his time between Bologna and Rome where he openly competed with Caravaggio (*Crucifixion of St Peter,* 1603, Vatican), but soon took up again the tradition of Raphael and the Cavaliere d'Arpino in his first masterpieces, the fresco of *St Andrea walking to his Execution,* 1608-1609 (Rome, San Gregorio

GUIDO RENI. ATALANTA AND HIPPOMENES. 1625. MUSEO NAZIONALE, NAPLES.

Magno) and especially with the decoration in the Paolina Chapel at Montecavallo, 1610 (Rome, Palazzo del Quirinale). In spite of the fashions set by Caravaggio, he was very soon successful in promoting his elegant style with a faintly abstract, lyrical charm, though it always bears traces of sensuality. His compositions are deliberately complex (*Triumph of Jacob,* Paris, Notre-Dame) and he always avoids the extremist baroque styles, striving for light tones and fresh skin colouring. As the years pass his touch becomes lighter, his outlines softer, and his tones more silvery, resulting in the astonishing freedom of his later figures (*Young Girl with Crown,* Rome, Museo Capitolino). Guido's religious inspiration often degenerates into an insipid charm (*Ecce Homo,* Louvre), which was responsible first for his tremendous reputation and then his long period of disfavour, but its proper aesthetic balance is restored by the fluid colouring and delicate execution (*Baptism of Christ,* 1623, Vienna, Kunsthistorisches Museum). The mythological scenes, however (the famous *Aurora* ceiling, 1613-1614, in the Palazzo Rospigliosi, Rome, and the four *Deeds of Hercules,* 1617-1621, Louvre) or the scenes of historical legend (the *Rape of Helen,* 1627-1632, Louvre) show a sturdiness and strength of spirit that justify his present re-instatement (Exhibition at Bologna, 1954).   J. T.

RICCI Marco (Belluno, 1676 - Venice, 1729). Marco Ricci was Sebastiano's nephew and pupil. Obliged to leave Venice after a brawl, he took refuge for several years in Dalmatia where perhaps he studied landscape painting. He accompanied his uncle in some of the latter's peregrinations. Back in Venice in 1717, he collaborated with Sebastiano in *Moses Striking the Rock* (Venice, Accademia), He committed suicide in

1729. Like his uncle but to a greater degree, Marco was influenced by the Neapolitan landscapists and by Magnasco. He is in a sense an ancestor of the Romantic landscape (*The Cascade,* Venice, Accademia). He also etched, particularly in his last years.   P. C.

RICCI Sebastiano (Belluno, 1659 - Venice, 1734). Sebastiano Ricci began in Venice under Cervelli and Mazzoni, but before long he left the city. In 1682 we find him in Bologna working in the studio of Giovanni Gioseffo dal Sole and studying the great local painters, in particular the Carracci and Guido Reni. He travelled further and became one of the most widely travelled of Italian painters. Patronised by Ranuccio II Farnese, he stayed in Parma and Piacenza. In Rome he acquainted himself with the decorators, Pietro da Cortona and Baciccia. He went on to Milan, Modena, Bergamo and Vienna. He was twice in Florence where he took part in the decoration of the Palazzo Pitti *(Diana and Actaeon),* in London in 1712, then, probably, in Holland. During his stay in Paris in 1716 he was elected to the Académie Royale de Peinture et de Sculpture. In 1717 he finally returned to Venice to share with Canaletto the patronage of the consul, Smith.

As an artist he is difficult to pin down on account of his eclecticism, the result of the many influences he absorbed. He seems often to be in a direct line with Veronese. At other times he is close to Pellegrini. About 1710 he shows himself very receptive to the nervous art of Magnasco (the Dresden *Ascension*). Then, towards the end of his life, he developed a polychromatic palette and a differentiated lighting which were to be a source of inspiration to Venetian decorators and landscape painters (*St Gregory Releasing the Souls from Purgatory,* Bergamo, Sant'Alessandro). The Royal Collection at Windsor possesses two albums of his drawings; they are full of fantasy.   P. C.

SEBASTIANO RICCI. BACCHANALIA. DRAWING. ACCADEMIA, VENICE.

ROBERT of ANJOU (1275/78 - 1343).
He was the third son of Charles II, King
of Naples, and succeeded his father in
1309. He surrounded himself with a
brilliant court, frequented by Petrarch
and Boccaccio. Because of his interest
in philosophy, literature and the arts, he
was called Robert the Wise and his reign
marked the beginning of the Renaissance
in Naples. Even before he became
king, he called many artists to the
Campania. In 1305, Montano d'Arezzo
decorated two chapels in the new royal
palace. In 1308, Cavallini directed the
decoration of the Church of Donna-
regina, and in the *Last Judgment* one
can recognise among the just several
members of the royal family. Around
1317, Simone Martini painted, for the
church of San Lorenzo, a large altarpiece showing on one panel Robert
receiving the crown from the hands
of his brother St Louis of Toulouse, who died in 1298 and had
just been canonised. P.-H. M.

ROBERTI Ercole de' (Ferrara, *ca* 1450 -
Ferrara, 1496). Ercole de' Roberti, the
third artist of genius of the Ferrarese
15th century, after Tura and Cossa,
owed a great deal to his forerunners.
The metallic harshness of their manner
and the strange lyricism of their fanciful
ornamentation are the source of his
artistic personality. From its very first
manifestations the latter is strongly
marked with originality. Thus, in the
series of the Months in the Palazzo di
Schifanoia, *September* (particularly in
the *Forge of Vulcan* and the *Love of Venus
and Mars*) seems to show the irony, the
fantasy and the vehemence of the young
artist, then barely twenty (about 1469/
70). For some years Ercole seems to
have worked in close collaboration with
Cossa. He helped him paint the huge
Altarpiece of San Lazzaro in Ferrara
(Berlin, destroyed in the last war),
then followed him to Bologna where he
carried out, probably about 1476, the
predella and the pilasters with *Saints* of
Cossa's *Griffoni Altarpiece*. In this
predella, now in the Vatican, he depicted
the *Miracles of St Vincent Ferrer* with
stupendously inventive brio, next to a
strange, cruel crowd of frantic silhouettes
weighed down with heavy drapery or
caparisoned with metal, amidst weird
buildings. There is the same uneasy
lyricism in the *St John the Baptist* of the
Berlin Museum, who stands like an
emaciated insect against the distant,
silent background of a seascape. This
rather bitter sharpness is relieved in the
admirable altarpiece painted in 1480
for Santa Maria in Porto in Ravenna
(now in the Brera). Confining his
extravagant manner to ornamental details and his lyrical outbursts to the

ERCOLE DE' ROBERTI. PORTRAITS OF GIOVANNI II BENTIVOGLIO AND
HIS WIFE, GINEVRA. NATIONAL GALLERY OF ART, WASHINGTON.

landscape, the artist carried out his composition (the *Virgin and Child with Four Saints*) with a new effort towards colour harmony and balance of light to form a synthesis. Henceforth he joined the most modern and classical manner of the great Italian painting of the period, that of Piero della Francesca, Antonello da Messina and Giovanni Bellini. But such concern for stylistic and moral unity did not compromise his rarest qualities: the excessively nervous elegance of his design, the refinement of his colouring, the almost 'cubist' firmness of his crystallisation of form. The major work of his mature period, the frescoes painted towards 1480-1485 as a continuation of Cossa's work in the Garganelli Chapel of San Pietro of Bologna, have unfortunately disappeared. Only partial copies are known. But his contemporaries' admiration and the later fame of these frescoes (Michel-

angelo paid great tribute to them) attest their importance.

Now famous, Ercole returned to Ferrara for good in 1486. In Bologna he had already worked for the court of the Bentivoglio, painting in particular the incisively elegant portraits of *Giovanni II Bentivoglio* and his wife *Ginevra* (Washington, National Gallery). On his return to his native city, he entered the service of the Este, becoming, after Tura, the official artist. His decorative works, like Tura's, have disappeared. However, the mastery of his style and the depth of his inspiration can be judged after 1480 thanks to a series of little panels among which mention must at least be made of the *Harvest of the Manna* in the National Gallery, London, and above all of a predella painted for San Giovanni in Monte in Bologna. On either side of a *Pietà* (Liverpool) could be seen the *Prayer in the*

Garden of Olives and the Arrest of Christ and the *Way of the Cross* (Dresden), scenes of an almost unbearable tragic cruelty, vibrant with an intensely dramatic dynamism, but which an amber light, a colouring borrowed from the tints of autumn, seems to bathe in melancholy. Ercole here attains a combination of ferociousness and bitter serenity of which the Italy of the period can offer no other example.   M. L.

ROBUSTI Jacopo. *See* Tintoretto.

ROMANESQUE (Period). From late antiquity to the Renaissance, the tradition of pictorial art in Italy was uninterrupted and therefore it is difficult to isolate romanesque painting. The 11th and 12th centuries were its peak and the middle of the 13th century was the latest date of its survival in belated examples. Italian romanesque painting had a double source: Byzantine art by which Italy was the first to be influenced, and a local, early Christian art born in the catacombs; it was later characterised by the combination of these two elements, of unequal importance but always recognisable. Northern influences, on the other hand, remained negligible: until the 13th century, it was Italy which influenced western countries (France, Spain, Germany, even England). The amount of painted decorations which have been

THE CREATION
OF EVE.
DETAIL
FROM A FRESCO.
END OF THE
12TH CENTURY.
ABBEY OF
SAN PIETRO,
FERENTILLO.

THE CHOSEN. DETAIL FROM THE 'LAST JUDGMENT'. FRESCO. END OF THE 11TH CENTURY. SANT'ANGELO IN FORMIS.

preserved, at least in part, and which are listed today is, in Italy as everywhere else, very much smaller than the amount of lost or unknown works. It would be rash, therefore, to generalise about the characteristics of regional schools whose scope may be changed by new discoveries. It is better to consider each of the existing groups of paintings by itself. However, to make matters easier, art historians divide romanesque Italy into three main zones: south, central and north. In the former, we may with some justification speak of a 'school' because of the historical part played by the Abbey of Monte Cassino, and in particular by Abbot Desiderius who, after a journey in the East (1065), brought Greek painters back with him to Campania. They trained pupils and started the school of Monte Cassino which had a wide influence, one of its most remarkable examples being the church of Sant'Angelo in Formis, near Capua (last third of the 11th century). The share of Byzantine influence and local tradition in this important cycle has been disputed. In central and northern Italy there are similar problems, but they are less clear cut because of the greater diversity of existing works. In some Roman paintings, or paintings by Roman artists, the local element is predominant (Rome, vestibule and nave of the Lower Church of San Clemente; Castel Sant'Elia, 11th century). Other important examples are: San Giovanni a Porta Latina, Rome (12th century); Abbey of San Pietro, Ferentillo (end of the 12th century); and Anagni Cathedral (about 1255) in central Italy. In the north: Galliano (early 11th century); SS Pietro ed Orso, Aosta (11th century); Civate (11th or 12th century). P.-H. M.

ROMANINO Girolamo di Romano, *called* (Brescia, ca 1484 - Brescia, after 1562). Little is yet known of the career of this felicitous and fertile artist, but it seems to have been spent entirely at Brescia and its environs, Trento and Cremona. His formative period was without any doubt influenced by Giorgione and Titian (*Altarpiece of St Justina,* Padua, Museo Civico) and there remained with him a taste for subtle colouring and a fondness for silvery and rose tones, but unexpected touches, reminiscent of Lotto and German painters, mingle with the Venetian flavour of his work. A sort of romantic disquiet invests his portraits (*Portrait of a Man,* Brescia, Pinacoteca Tosio Martinengo; *Portrait of a Man,* Bergamo, Accademia Carrara) and imparts a real pathos to the religious scenes (*Pietà,* Berlin; *Christ at Emmaus,* Brescia, Pinacoteca). Dramatic incidents, heightened to the point of expressionism, as well as the most sensual associations appear in the large decorative paintings. The scenes of the Passion at Cremona Cathedral (1519) are treated with a violence of gesticulation that seems inspired by the engravings from northern Europe, while the frescoes in the Castello del Buon Consiglio (Trento, about 1530-1532) enliven the walls of that austere palace with beautiful mythological figures or familiar incidents of everyday life (*Ladies and Gentlemen, singing and playing Music,* Loggia of the Magno Palazzo). Bold experiments, like the candlelight in *St Matthew and the Angel,* painted for the Chapel of the Holy Sacrament in San Giovanni Evangelista at Cremona, which seem to lead directly to Caravaggio, are again drawing attention today to a painter whose more sombre last works have caused his personality and inventiveness to be underestimated. J. T.

ROME. The 13th century which had started with the taking of Constantinople by the Crusaders (1204), ended, in Rome, with a triumphant Jubilee proclaimed by Boniface VIII in 1300. The Popes' capital had, for a while, recovered her prestige. During the first half of the century, the influx of Greek decorators and mosaic workers still imposed on Roman art a strong Byzantine imprint (mosaics in San Paolo fuori le Mura, in St Peter's, in Santa Maria in Trastevere; fresco in the St Sylvester Chapel in SS Quattro Coronati). But at the end of the century, a purely Italian school of mosaic workers and fresco painters developed, when artists like Jacopo Torriti and Pietro Cavallini softened the stiff 'Greek manner' through their knowledge of Early Christian art. Torriti made, in the apse of San Giovanni in Laterano, the *Pantocrator* mosaic (1291) which already showed his mastery of the grand style, and in the apse of Santa Maria Maggiore, a *Coronation of the Virgin* (1295) in which he used motifs from antiquity. Cavallini, in the *Life of the Virgin* mosaics in Santa Maria in Trastevere (about 1291), realised an even better synthesis between a Byzantine iconography and a modern interpretation; classical formulas are dominant in the frescoes, unfortunately badly damaged, in the Convent of Santa Cecilia in Trastevere (*Last Judgment* in the Nuns' Choir) and in the destroyed frescoes in the atrium of St Peter's. This new style soon spread to central Italy: the Florentine Arnolfo was working in St Cecilia at the same time as Cavallini. Roman and Tuscan masters met while working in Assisi.

But the Pope's power was soon to fade. The Papacy was in conflict with Philippe le Bel and, between 1309 and 1376, the Popes went into exile in Avignon: then from 1378 to 1417, the Great Schism shook the Church's foundations. The Trecento was a century without either Pope or Emperor. Rome was empty and no Roman gothic emerged. It is only after the end of the Great Schism, the final return of the Pope to Rome and the restoration of the town by Nicholas V (1447-1455), symbolised by the brilliant and fruitful Jubilee of 1450, that the Holy City began to revive. With Pius II Piccolomini, the humanist who became Pope (1458-1464), an important development of the Renaissance became apparent: the Holy See formed an alliance with the new cultural and artistic currents and, on the other hand, the supremacy of Rome was attacked more and more violently by Italian and foreign preachers.

During the Quattrocento, the town was rebuilt, modernised and at the same time became a centre for archaeological research. Already a political capital, it became a cultural centre. Nicholas V encouraged a vast rebuilding project, including St Peter's, the forty pilgrimage churches and whole quarters, under the supervision of Bernardo Rosselli (whose choice suggests that the scheme was inspired by Alberti). The Tuscan style was dominant in architecture and the Lombard style in sculpture. Sixtus IV was most concerned with the embellishment of the town, which won him the title of 'restaurator urbis'. Among the new buildings were the hospital of Santo Spirito and above all the Palazzo Riario, later called the Palazzo della Cancelleria. Artists found their way back to Rome: Fra Angelico visited the Vatican in 1440, then from 1447 to 1450, and painted for Nicholas V the chapel of St Lawrence and St Stephen (the chapel of Nicholas V); Jean Fouquet painted a portrait of Eugenius IV; Piero della Francesca was in Rome in 1459. Umbrian and Florentine artists in turn worked for Sixtus IV. Melozzo da Forli composed in his honour the *Opening of the Vatican Library* (about 1470). The Pope's most fortunate venture was to invite, in 1481, renowned painters, such as Signorelli and Botticelli, to decorate the new Vatican chapel which was to be named after him. But those painters did not yet constitute a coherent artistic school. Such a school only emerged at the end of the century with Pinturicchio, who completed in 1494 the decoration of the Borgia apartments and with Antoniazzo Romano who worked in Santa Croce in Gerusalemme and many other churches.

With Julius II, everything changed. In 1505 Michelangelo, then in 1508, Raphael, came to Rome: in ten years, the town assumed a unique importance. Artists rushed there, building schemes thrived and masterpieces were created. Under Cardinal Giovanni de' Medici who took the name of Leo X (1513-1521), the Roman School was born. It was formed around Raphael, who acted as a director of the arts, and its ideals, its culture and its enthusiasm were to leave a lasting mark on modern art. Nothing is more impressive than this grandiose meeting of antiquity and Christianity in a city which had once been the centre of the Mediterranean world and was now again a religious and imperial capital. The 'Grand Style' or 'Grand Manner' became the law of a culture, confident both about its past and about its mission. The design of the new St Peter's, begun in 1506 and completed only in 1626, was symbolic of this proud style which integrated the antique Rome with the new world: the building was started and interrupted again and again until Michelangelo finally took over in 1547 and returned to Bramante's original plan, which shows that the execution of the scheme was not always clearly visualised. But finally, the Roman school worked out its own rules when the 'naturalism' of the Renaissance was restrained by the imitation of classical antiquity. We find the conception of an ideal model in Raphael's workshop, where the pupils developed the master's 'ideas'. Mannerism was not far away.

The Sack of Rome in 1527 appeared to the people as a punishment from Heaven. The Spanish rule weighed heavily over Italy: the religious crisis stimulated feelings of fear, of doubt, of repentance which, particularly under Paul III, transformed the Roman atmosphere: art had to justify its existence. Michelangelo's *Last Judgment* was hardly finished (1541) when the Council of Trent (1545-1563) imposed a new catechism and some simplifications in the liturgy; through its recommendations, religious art had to be expurgated and controlled. This new attitude favoured doctrinal books and the vulgarisation of the classics, particularly in Rome. As a result, during the second half of the century, when the city became artistically alive again, there was a constant struggle between a classicist 'purism' and an elaborate 'mannerism'. Vignola, who later published the *Five Orders of Architecture* (1562), met Ammanati at the villa of Julius III, the Villa Giulia whose main façade he designed; but in 1568 he built the Gesù, which was originally conceived as an austere building. The Piazza del Campidoglio, planned by Michelangelo and finished by Giacomo della Porta, was once again a monument to the glory of Rome and St Peter's, a monument to the glory of world Christianity. Under Sixtus V, and thanks to Domenico Fontana, the town began to take on its final character. Great architectural schemes were planned and executed and artists returned to Rome to seek the examples of both antique and modern art.

The Carracci, who founded the Bologna Academy, worked in Rome in 1595. Later, they were asked to decorate the gallery of the finally completed Palazzo Farnese: they did it with brio, turning to the great models of the beginning of the 16th century. Soon, young Caravaggio, coming from Lombardy, began an artistic revolution: he worked in the chapel of St Matthew at San Luigi dei Francesi on strong compositions simplified by an intense light, which brought him sudden fame. The Bolognese decorators and the 'luminist' followers of Caravaggio helped to create a new taste. For over a century, Rome was to be the capital of European art. Artists from Florence, Venice and even from the Tessino (Serodine), from the Rhine valley (Elsheimer) and Lorraine (Leclerc) came to work there. Rome became a cosmopolitan centre where new artistic fashions were born: for instance the genre painting called *bambocciata*. While this realism was thriving, the classical ideal kept alive by Guido Reni and Domenichino attracted to Rome the French painter Poussin. Meanwhile, builders and decorators had started work again on a large scale after the triumph of the Counter-Reformation; Bernini was working on St Peter's, Pietro da Cortona in SS Luca e Martina, Borromini in Sant'Ivo. The new emphasis on form resulted in a generalised use of monumental sculpture and ceiling decorations (Pietro da Cortona, Andrea Sacchi, Pozzo) and brought about the birth of the baroque style.

Rome remained the privileged place where amateurs and artists came to discover the great styles; but those styles gradually fell into disregard. Stricter masters were honoured again, mainly the 16th century artists who were closer to their antique models, like Raphael. In spite of the success of the 'vedutisti', like Pannini, the classical stream lost its impetus. But Rome was to become, once more, the head of the European school: when 'neo-classicism' introduced a return to antiquity, Winckelmann, David, Canova and the authors of numerous books of prints found their inspiration in Rome. Piranesi is the sublime conclusion of that 18th century Rome, dominated, fascinated and finally exalted by its own ruins. A. C.

ROSA Salvator (Arenella, near Naples, 1615 - Rome, 1673). Salvator Rosa was born into a family of artists. His father was an architect and he received his first training from Domenico Greco, an obscure artist, and his brother-in-law, Francesco Fracanzano. He was particularly influenced by Cerquozzi, the painter of battle scenes, and Ribera. In 1635, he was in Rome, then Viterbo. He was again in Rome in 1639, when he caused something of a scandal by his improvisations, inspired by Neapolitan masks, and his violent criticisms of the all-powerful Bernini. For nine years, from 1641 to 1649, he lived in Florence and worked for the Medici (*Cavalry Battle, Forest of the Philosophers,* Pitti) before finally settling in Rome. He was a restless person, with astonishing imaginative gifts and a romantic fancy. He was a satirical poet and engraver as well as a painter, who turned from battle scenes to *bambocciata* and particularly landscapes, which were always picturesque, haunted by brigands and gods. He painted too hastily and his works, which once earned him an enormous reputation, have turned dark and are less esteemed than in his day. P. C.

ROSSELLI Cosimo (Florence, 1439 - Florence, 1507). This pupil of the humble Neri di Bicci and of Benozzo Gozzoli was no great painter, but he popularised a calm, clear style, for instance in the somewhat lifeless groups of *St Anne with the Virgin and Child* surrounded with saints (1471, Berlin), of the *Annunciation with Four Saints* (1473, Louvre) and of

ROSSO FIORENTINO. MARS AND VENUS. DRAWING. LOUVRE, PARIS.

the frescoes relating the story of *San Filippo Benizzi,* about 1475, in the small cloister of the Annunziata in Florence. In 1481, Cosimo was, with Botticelli, Ghirlandaio, etc., one of the team of artists commissioned by Sixtus IV to decorate his chapel; his share of the work: *Moses destroying the Tablets of the Law,* the *Sermon on the Mountain* and the *Last Supper,* is far from being the best. The characters, their grouping and even the colours are very close to Ghirlandaio. Back in Florence, Rosselli painted frescoes in the monastery of St Ambrosius (lost) and in the church, where the scene of the *Miracle of the Holy Sacrament* —clear, but rather overcrowded, in the Gozzoli manner—is still extant. He also painted a *Madonna and two Saints* (Florence, Accademia), a *Virgin in Glory* and a *Coronation of the Virgin.* Fra Bartolomeo and Piero di Cosimo were his pupils. A. C.

ROSSO FIORENTINO. DESCENT FROM THE CROSS.
1521. PINACOTECA, VOLTERRA.

ROSSO FIORENTINO Giovanni Battista di Jacopo, *called* (Florence, 1494 - Paris, 1540). He was the most striking case of the sophisticated, elaborate approach called 'mannerist', which finally contributed to the creation of an international style. Rosso probably worked with Andrea del Sarto, but the Florentine workshops where he was trained left no deep impression on him. In 1517, he was asked to paint the *Assumption of the Virgin* for the small cloister of the Annunziata, which Andrea had no time to paint, and in 1518 the *Madonna with Four Saints* (Uffizi) for

Leonardo Buonafede, Rector of Santa Maria Novella. His strange, somewhat gaudy composition was refused by his client. None the less, Rosso's activity increased: in 1521, the *Madonna with Two Saints* (Villamagna) and the *Descent from the Cross* (Volterra); in 1522, the pala for the Dei family in San Spirito; in 1523, the *Marriage of the Virgin* for Carlo Ginori in San Lorenzo in which his weird, faded manner became more marked. He then went to Rome (about 1524): there, he painted in Santa Maria della Pace the mediocre frescoes of the *Creation of Eve* and *The Fall of Man* and was able to study the works of Michelangelo and Raphael. Fleeing from the Sack of Rome in 1527, he moved to central Italy: he worked at Perugia, in the San Sepolcro; painted the so-called *Transfiguration* (Città di Castello, 1528); stopped in Arezzo where he left a *Jesus bearing his Cross*; met the young Vasari; visited Aretino in Venice and drew for him *Mars and Venus* which Caraglio engraved. There, in 1530, he received an invitation from Francis I. He settled in France at the end of that year and began working on the decoration of the Grande Galerie in Fontainebleau, the most important and coherent work in his whole career. He painted a *Pietà* (Louvre) for Anne de Montmorency. He is believed to have committed suicide in 1540.

A born revolutionary, Rosso first stood out against the subtleties of Andrea del Sarto by using large draperies with broken facets of harsh colour and tortured, haggard faces, a sort of conscious 'diabolism'. Stimulated by his stay in Rome and the assimilation of a whole repertory of ornaments, this tormented style triumphed in France: the originality of the Grande Galerie at Fontainebleau comes from the artist's use of stuccoes and insets, his gusto and his unusually vivid imagination. This lively, capricious style was to become a model for his time.   A. C.

S

SALVIATI Francesco de' Rossi, *called* Cecchino (Florence, 1510 - Rome, 1563). Francesco de' Rossi was a pupil of Andrea del Sarto in whose studio he worked in 1529. He owed his nickname of Cecchino Salviati to Cardinal Salviati, who took him into his service in 1531. This stay in Rome, which was essential to his development, brought him into touch with the work of Pierino del Vaga and the movement that grew out of the work of Michelangelo and Raphael. He also got to know there the art of Parmigianino whose elegant and flexible grace he imitated. He was invited to Venice in 1539 by Cardinal Grimani to decorate, with Giovanni da Udine, a ceiling (now lost) with the story of Psyche. After a visit to Bologna, he went to Rome in 1541 to decorate a chapel in Santa Maria dell'Anima (1541-1544). On his return to Florence in 1544, he was commissioned to paint the important cycle in the Sala dell'Udienza of the Palazzo Vecchio, illustrating the story of Camillus. He had been invited to France as far back as 1542, but it was not till 1554-1555 that he made this journey. He was received at the court of Francis I and worked for the Cardinal of Lorraine in the château of Dampierre. Unfortunately, nothing remains of his work in France, except a *Descent from the Cross* at the church of Sainte-Marguerite and the *Incredulity of St Thomas* (Louvre) which he painted for the Chapel of the Florentines at Lyons. When he returned to Rome in 1555, he decorated one of the rooms in the Palazzo Farnese. During the last period of his life, Salviati's work did not develop further and was completely dominated by the influence of Michelangelo, as the frescoes in the Palazzo Farnese already show.   s. b.

SANO di PIETRO Ansano di Pietro di Mencio, *called* (Siena, 1406 - Siena, 1481).

SANO DI PIETRO. ANGEL MUSICIAN. DETAIL FROM THE 'VIRGIN AND CHILD WITH ANGELS'. PINACOTECA, SIENA.

CARLO SARACENI.
JUDITH.
KUNSTHISTORISCHES
MUSEUM, VIENNA.

Like several other painters from his generation, Sano di Pietro came, as a young man, under the influence of the Osservanza Master and of Sassetta. Lacking the great poetic and imaginative gifts of his models, he was nevertheless famous for his talents as a decorator. Popular in his day, and highly valued at first by modern critics who called him 'the Angelico of Siena', he has now fallen from favour. His works, so numerous that their list would be tedious, lack variety; he paints the same subjects again and again (for instance, the many portraits of St Bernardino painted after the saint's death in 1444). His main works are in Siena: altarpieces, predellas, panels from polyptychs (Pinacoteca);

a *Coronation of the Virgin* (Palazzo Pubblico); the *Sermon of St Bernardino* (chapter house of the cathedral). In France: *St Francis receiving the Stigmata,* fragment of a predella (Nantes). P.-H. M.

SANTI Giovanni (Coldarbolo, near Urbino, 1435 - Urbino, 1494). Raphael's father deserves to be mentioned, not only because he contributed to his son's training, but also because he created in Urbino an artistic centre. His Chronicle in verse to the greater glory of Duke Federico da Montefeltro (who died in 1482) is bad poetry, but reveals a kind, faithful nature. Only his very last works are known: the 1489

Urbino *Madonna* and the large 1490 *Annunciation* (Brera) with the Virgin appearing under a portico. The composition is serene, the style very supple with shadowy effects, particularly in the series of the *Muses* painted in collaboration with Timoteo Viti for the palace at Urbino. Reminiscences of Melozzo and even Mantegna are softened by a somewhat facile gentleness.   A. C.

SARACENI Carlo (Venice, 1585 - Rome, 1620). Carlo Saraceni settled down in Rome at the beginning of the 17th century and became one of the best of the Caravaggisti while following closely the explorations of light and landscape of the German, Elsheimer, and Domenico Feti. Some of his pictures painted in oils on copper used to be attributed to Elsheimer. Of a somewhat extravagant disposition, Saraceni dressed according to French fashions, although he had never been to France. He collaborated frequently with his pupil, the Lorrainer, Le Clerc, who accompanied him to Venice and engraved several of his works. The two painters are difficult to tell one from the other and it is possible that a third artist, anonymous and probably French, further complicates the situation. Among Saraceni's principal works is his *St Cecilia* at the Galleria Nazionale d'Arte Antica, and the very curious *Denial of Peter* (perhaps with Le Clerc's collaboration) with its Chinese shadows, at the Galleria Corsini in Florence. Saraceni returned to Rome shortly before his death which, according to Fiocco, occurred in 1620. The German, Johann Liss, was a pupil of his.   P. C.

SARTO Andrea del. *See* Andrea del Sarto.

SASSETTA Stefano di Giovanni di Consolo, *called* (Asciano or Cortona, *ca* 1392 - Siena, 1451). His life is little

SASSETTA. MYSTIC MARRIAGE OF ST FRANCIS. 1437-1443. MUSÉE CONDÉ, CHANTILLY.

known but at least we can be sure of his activity in Siena between 1425 and 1450, which is recorded by many contracts. Sassetta kept alive, in the 15th century, the religious ideals of the Trecento masters, while giving free rein to his own imagination and mystic fervour. Following in the footsteps of Paolo di Giovanni Fei, he maintained the tradition of Sienese gothic, which from then on developed on such original lines that we can hardly call it gothic any more. Sassetta's sources were many: we find in his painting reminiscences of Simone Martini, Lippo Vanni, the French or Franco-Flemish miniature painters, Masolino, Uccello and contem-

SASSETTA.
ST MARTIN
DIVIDING
HIS CLOAK WITH
A POOR MAN.
1433. PALAZZO
CHIGI-SARACINI,
SIENA.

porary Florentine works; but these varied influences contributed to make up his personal and coherent style.

Among the surviving works of Sassetta, the earliest are fragments of a broken up and partly destroyed altarpiece painted between 1423 and 1426 for the Arte della Lana chapel. The architectural backgrounds with perspective effects are reminiscent of those of the Lorenzetti. On the other hand, in a panel like the *Last Supper* (fragment from the predella, Siena Pinacoteca), we notice, as it was noticed as early as the 18th century, that the architectural background is no longer gothic, but consists of semi-circular arcades, revealing a knowledge of Brunelleschi's innovations which is surprising in Siena at that time.

Between 1430 and 1432, Sassetta painted for the Siena Cathedral the

Madonna delle Nevi altarpiece (Florence, Contini Bonacossi Collection). During the same period until 1437, he painted numerous works, including the polyptych in San Domenico at Cortona, the *St Thomas Aquinas Praying* (Budapest) and the *Vision of St Thomas* (Vatican).

In 1437, Borgo San Sepolcro commissioned from Sassetta a polyptych for the main altar of the cathedral which was being built (the contract was signed on September 5th). This large work, his masterpiece, comparable in breadth to Duccio's *Maestà,* was only finished seven years later. It was a polyptych with a predella and pinnacles, painted on both sides. In 1752, it was taken from the altar and dismembered. The central panel *(Virgin and Child)* and two wings with figures of saints are now in Bordeaux (Private Collection); the other two wings and the central panel from the back *(St Francis in Ecstasy)* in Settignano (Berenson Collection); seven out of the eight scenes on the back are in London (National Gallery) and one in Chantilly (Musée Condé). We only know of one scene from the predella (Berlin). In the Chantilly painting *(Mystic Marriage of St Francis)*, three women are floating in the air without wings, defying all laws of gravity. This work is one of the most charming of the declining Sienese style; it holds all the poetic feeling of the end of the Middle Ages and seems specially designed for the romantic interpretation of the 19th century.　　　P.-H. M.

SAVOLDO Giovanni Girolamo (Brescia, *ca* 1480 - probably Venice, after 1548). The small number of his surviving works and their refined lyricism, which is in strong contrast to the grand manner of Venetian painting, set Savoldo in a place apart. Much of his career is obscure. His inscription among the painters of Florence in 1508 proves that he stayed in Tuscany and another document that he was in Venice in 1521, where he spent most of his life. The protection of Duke Francesco II Sforza would suggest that he lived in Milan during the years 1529/1535 and a will drawn up in 1526 reveals that he was married to a Dutch woman and, because of this, probably had connections with northern Europe. A few works, which are dated exactly *(The Nativity,* 1527, Hampton Court; an altarpiece, 1533, in Santa Maria in Organo, Verona), are landmarks in an output which was always slender and only won a modest reputation for the artist. A tribute is paid to it, however, by the writings of Paolo Pino, his pupil *(Dialogo di Pittura,* 1548) and Aretino (letter of the same year). Instead of large altarpieces in churches *(Virgin in glory with the Saints,* Brera), Savoldo seems to have preferred smaller pictures, painted slowly, to

which he attempted to bring his own personal solution to problems left by Giorgione: the so-called *Gaston de Foix* (Louvre), whose reflection in a double mirror illustrates the famous 'paragone' or parallel between painting and sculpture, dear to the artists of the time; the meticulous detail of bright light reflecting on silvery satin drapery in the *Magdalen* (London, National Gallery) may show a debt to Flemish models; the *Adoration of the Shepherds* (Brescia, Pinacoteca, and Venice, San Giobbe) attempts a skilful nocturnal effect by framing a moonlit shepherd in a window. His painting is often heavy with dense shadow *(Adoration of the Shepherds,* Turin, Galleria Sabauda); or is sometimes shot with great bursts of light *(Transfiguration,* Uffizi); or an amber atmosphere envelops realistically treated figures and landscapes; and sometimes it seems to reach back beyond Giorgione to Van Eyck, with a subtle lyricism that makes one easily forget the rather limited vision of their creator.　　　J. T.

SCANNABECCHI Dalmasio, *called* Lippo di Dalmasio, *or* Maso da Bologna (second half of the 14th century). We know little about this painter who must have been born about 1352, and died before 1421. There is a series of documents recording his activity between 1376 and 1410. Lippo was a nephew of Simone de' Crocefissi, and extended his Bolognese training with a knowledge of Tuscan art, which he probably studied on the spot. This might account for his giving such graceful outlines to his solid figures, a combination rare in Bologna at that time, and in it lies the appeal of the best of his works that have been preserved, such as the small *Coronation of the Virgin* (Bologna, Pinacoteca), a *Madonna* signed and dated 1397 (Bologna, Chiesa della Misericordia), or the *Virgin and Child with Angels* in the National Gallery, London, which shows a simple, delicate feeling.　　　J. T.

SEBASTIANO DEL PIOMBO. DOROTHEA.
KAISER FRIEDRICH MUSEUM, BERLIN.

SCHIAVONE Giorgio Chiulinovich, *called* (Scardona, in Dalmatia, *ca* 1434 - 1504/05). Nothing is known of his training, but in his early works, the *Madonnas* in the Museo Correr, Venice, and in Amsterdam, the influence of Filippo Lippi can be felt. This Dalmatian (or 'sclavone') was one of the young painters belonging to Squarcione's circle in Padua and his somewhat sugary manner remained close to that of his strange, learned master; for instance in small elaborate compositions such as the *Virgin and Child* (Turin and National Gallery, London). He left Padua after five or six years' work for the *bottega* and, in 1462, he was in Zara. He was bold enough to compete with other Squarcione followers, not only Zoppo with whom he had much in common, but even Mantegna (Polyptych, National Gallery, London). His contorted figures fit in with the whole

Paduan archaeological repertory of decorations with its accumulation of marbles, cameos and archways in religious paintings.   A. C.

SEBASTIANO del PIOMBO Sebastiano Luciani, *called* (Venice, *ca* 1485 - Rome, 1547). He was the friend and pupil of Giorgione and, at first, one of the closest disciples of his master, whose melancholy gentleness he imitated in his *Death of Adonis* (Uffizi). But the influence of Giorgione's last manner and of the monumental style of the Fondaco dei Tedeschi is even more marked in the large figures he painted in the shady niches of the church of San Bartolomeo. Another interesting work from that period is the *St John Chrysostom* pala (Venice, San Giovanni Crisostomo), painted in a typically Venetian style with a landscape in the background and a group of three young women on the left. But as soon as Sebastiano arrived in Rome, his style started developing. In 1511, Agostino Chigi asked him to take part in the decoration of the Farnesina where he painted *Polyphemus,* among other frescoes, and the lunettes in the loggia. He was a member of Raphael's circle as we can see from his subtle portraits: the *Fornarina* (Uffizi), the *Violin Player* (Paris, Rothschild Collection), *Cardinal Carondelet* (Lugano, Rohoncz Collection), the poet *Tebaldeo* (Budapest) and *Dorothea* (Berlin). He in his turn influenced Raphael who borrowed from him some Venetian features, in the *Mass of Bolsena* in the Vatican Stanze, for instance.

But Sebastiano's art became heavier later: in Rome, he came under the strong influence of Michelangelo who confided in him in a series of very interesting letters and gave him sketches and cartoons to work out; for instance the *Flagellation* in San Pietro in Montorio, the *Raising of Lazarus* (London, National Gallery), *Christ in Limbo* (Madrid), the *Birth of the Virgin* (Rome, Santa Maria del Popolo). The results are not very good and the general effect is lost because the treatment is so laboured. Sebastiano was at his best in his portraits—for instance those of *Andrea Doria* (Doria Collection) and of *Clement VII* (Naples). After the Sack of Rome, he wandered through Italy, spent some time in Mantua working for the Gonzaga family, then in Venice; back in Rome, he was given a Papal sinecure with the title of 'il Piombo'; hence his nickname. From then on, he only painted a few rather cold portraits; they were his safest ground. Those dark portraits, almost Giorgionesque in feeling, have a classical discipline and austerity. We can therefore conclude regretfully, but without doing him an injustice, that 'Sebastiano Veneziano'— as he was called—introduced through his grand manner the monumental art and ample style of the new century, but did not succeed in making a synthesis between Venetian colour and Roman forms. A. C.

SEGNA di BONAVENTURA (Siena, active between 1298 and 1326). Sienese painter whose existence is documented between the dates 1298 and 1326. Notable among his numerous works, four of which are signed, is a polyptych in the Siena Pinacoteca, entirely by the master's hand except for the central panel which is by Duccio. This collaboration confirms the strong links which must have existed between Segna's workshop and Duccio's. Segna, and later his sons, Niccolò and Francesco, and his other pupils remained faithful to Duccio's formulas. But his work also shows other influences, the elongated figures of Ugolino di Neri and above all, the imprint of Simone Martini whose new manner was already gaining influence. P.-H. M.

SEMITECOLO Niccolò (active at Padua and Venice between 1353 and 1370). A document, which he signed as a witness in 1353, proves that he was then painting in Venice in collaboration with his father, Donato. The only important works of his that we know are the six panels preserved in the Biblioteca Capitolare in Padua. They represent the *Trinity*, a *Virgin* and four scenes from the *Life of St Sebastian* of which one is dated 1367. Historians differ considerably in their appreciation of his style. Some find great resemblances with that of Guariento, and in this respect Semitecolo would be more Paduan than Venetian; Van Marle compares him with Giotto: according to him he took his popular, narrative style from Giotto, but all historians insist on the skill with which Niccolò Semitecolo painted architectural subjects and rendered the effects of perspective. Altichiero and Avanzo seem in this respect to have been influenced by him. A. L.

SFORZA (The). In the 14th century, the Sforza were only an obscure family of soldiers from the Romagna; by the 15th century, they had supplanted the Visconti and were ruling over the Duchy of Milan. At the death of Francesco, the first Duke of Milan, his eldest son, Galeazzo Maria (1444-1476), then in France, hastily returned to Milan. Sumptuous living now replaced the austerity maintained by the previous generations. One of Galeazzo's great schemes, which he partly realised, was the transformation of Milan castle, the Castello Sforzesco. New buildings were erected, all the rooms were to be decorated with frescoes and teams of painters worked day and night, but before they were let into the fortress, they had to show they were not armed. Even as a patron, the Duke was distrustful and probably with good reason, since he was murdered in 1476.

His son Giovanni Galeazzo, aged eight, succeeded to the title, but the real ruler was Ludovico il Moro (1451-

SIENESE SCHOOL.
THE NATIVITY.
COMPARTMENT FROM
THE 'PALIOTTO'
OF SAN PIETRO
IN BANCHI.
ABOUT 1280-1285.
PINACOTECA, SIENA.

1508), brother of Galeazzo Maria. Lodovico Mauro (those were his Christian names) had nothing African about him as his portraits prove, notably in a Lombard altarpiece, painted at the end of the 15th century (Milan, Brera) and Paolo Giovio, who knew him, says his complexion was not dark. He has been compared to Lorenzo il Magnifico, and with some justification. A great Renaissance nobleman, he surrounded himself with scholars and artists. Bramante and Leonardo worked together on the decorations of the Sala delle Asse (Milan, Castello Sforzesco). He gave his patronage to Leonardo, who had offered his services to him in a famous letter (1481). He appointed him organiser of his fêtes and commissioned from him, among other things, his equestrian statue, the portrait (now lost) of his mistress, *Cecilia Gallerani,* and the *Last Supper* (Convent of Santa Maria delle Grazie, Milan). As an art lover who was interested in everything, he kept himself informed about Florentine paint-

ing: a report addressed to him about the most famous Florentine painters (about 1484) mentions Botticelli, Ghirlandaio, Perugino and the young Filippino Lippi, who were then working on the decoration of the Villa Spedaletto for Lorenzo il Magnifico. Ludovico's war with Louis XII, his emprisonment and death at Loches in France, put an end to this brilliant period of the Milanese Renaissance. P.-H. M.

SIENA. Built on a hill and easily defendable, Siena, like Venice, was a place of refuge during the period of the great invasions and enjoyed an enviable prosperity through the difficult times of the late Middle Ages. The city became a bishopric in the 7th century, grew under the protection of the Church and, in the 12th century, asserted its independence; but in 1555 it became part of the Grand Duchy of Tuscany and, while retaining some autonomy, fell under the authority of Florence.

There is a striking and obvious con-

SIENESE SCHOOL.
ANNUNCIATION.
COMPARTMENT
FROM THE
'DOSSALE' OF
SAN PIETRO
IN BANCHI.
ABOUT 1280-1285.
PINACOTECA,
SIENA.

nexion between the political and artistic history of the city: the period of political freedom coincides with the great period of Sienese art which, heralded by the work of the miniature painters in the Benedictine abbeys, began in the 13th century, was at its best in the 14th and 15th centuries and went on until the middle of the 16th century. During this long period, Sienese painting developed, but always maintained its distinctive style, in particular a remarkable sense of decoration and a fondness for bright colours, more marked than in Florentine art, a predilection for sharp outlines, which isolated figures in an absolutely pure space and left them unsoftened by the technique of *sfumato*. The conditions determining Sienese painting were those of all medieval painting in the gothic age, but whether they were established more forcefully, or whether they were more congenial to the aspirations of the native genius, the fact remains that they were accepted more readily and with greater felicity

than anywhere else. This probably explains the long continuance of an art, which as far as its essential features are concerned, seemed impervious to the vicissitudes of history.

A small panel dated 1215, but still rather romanesque (Siena, Pinacoteca) shows in the centre Christ in a mandorla with the symbols of the evangelists, and on each wing three scenes from the life of St Helena and from the story of the True Cross. This first example of Sienese painting was followed, shortly after, by the works of Guido da Siena whose *Virgin and Child* (1221, Siena, Palazzo Pubblico) already shows a fairly free interpretation of the Byzantine style. This painting is a long way from the archaic panel of 1215, but from Guido da Siena to Duccio the evolution was, on the contrary, surprisingly slow. That is why the clearly legible and authenticated date of 1221 has been questioned by several art historians. We have to accept it, however, while remembering that parts of the picture,

MASTER OF THE CODICE DI SAN GIORGIO. NOLI
ME TANGERE. 14TH CENTURY. BARGELLO,
FLORENCE.

the face of the Virgin, for instance, were
touched up at the end of the 13th and
beginning of the 14th century, that is to
say, at the time when Duccio, with his
masterly work, was giving the Sienese
school its individual character and
founding a tradition.

Without abandoning the 'Greek manner', Duccio gave life to his characters
and glow to the colours. He, more
than Cimabue, softened the rigid Byzantine conventions and opened a golden
age which was to last over half a century.
The artists who followed him, Simone
Martini, the brothers Lorenzetti, played
their part in the stylistic evolution not
only by assimilating the gothic style more
thoroughly, but by creating a specific
Sienese gothic with its own style, settings
and iconography. In Siena, during the

first half of the Trecento, all painters
came more or less under the influence of
Duccio, Simone and the Lorenzetti: the
variety of the great models was echoed
by the richness and diversity of an
artistic flowering.

During the second half of the 14th century, new paths opened up in front of
artists because of the growing influence
of a style which was spreading throughout western Europe and which we now
call by the doubly incorrect but conve-
nient term: international gothic. Without abandoning their own tradition, the
Sienese looked for new inspiration
outside their city and outside Tuscany;
they were attracted by the style of
Lombard, French and Franco-Flemish
miniature painters. Gentile da Fabriano, a painter from Umbria trained
in Verona and Padua, played a large
part in spreading this new style; but
even earlier, Bartolo di Fredi, in his
old age, had introduced it to Siena.

In the Quattrocento, Sienese artists
remained faithful to a glorious artistic
past whose prestige was growing, and
they sometimes give the impression of
being behind the times, in an age of
rapid artistic progress. But, with Florence so near, they could not ignore the
fascinating innovations of the first
Renaissance, and they began to assimilate
them around 1430 (Domenico di
Bartolo). The tradition of their old
masters, the attraction of gothic, the
sudden flowering of the great Florentine
art (Masaccio, Uccello) formed a complex combination of influences, but
Sienese painting retained its originality,
through the hesitations, the reservations,
the passing enthusiasms of individual
artists, from Sassetta to Vecchietta, and
in spite of various temptations.

It changed little until the end of the
Quattrocento. But with each new
generation, outside influences (from
Florence, Umbria or the north) became
stronger and the last of the Sienese gave
way either to monotony—a symptom of

the exhaustion of their tradition, like Sano di Pietro, or to a pathetic melancholy, the sign of an art on the wane, like Matteo di Giovanni. A few rare artists still had a strong enough personality to overcome this decadence (Francesco di Giorgio).

In the 16th century, the decline was even faster. A few painters clung to a dying tradition and prolonged it through a perfected technique (Pacchiarotto), but the more gifted artists gave up the old manner and followed the teachings of the great Renaissance masters (Beccafumi). For a long time, Siena remained an artistic centre for the whole of Italy: after Sodoma, Guido Reni and Guercino decorated its churches. In the 18th century, it was the birthplace of the Nasini, then of Giuseppe Collignon. But what we call 'Sienese painting' nowadays is limited by the two dates of 1220 and 1540.   P.-H. M.

SIGNORELLI Luca (Cortona, *ca* 1450 - Cortona, 1523). According to reliable witnesses such as Pacioli and Vasari, Luca da Cortona was a pupil of Piero della Francesca. We find additional evidence of that training in the fresco he painted in 1474 for the Bishop's Palace in Città di Castello and three *Madonnas* (Boston; Oxford, Christ Church; Rome, Villamarina Collection) which, through their firm, noble style, seem to belong to his early manner. But already Luca, unlike his master, depicted his characters in action. It was the main preoccupation of Florentine art at the time of Pollaiuolo. The figures became more animated, the contrasts more pronounced in the *Annunciation* in Casa da Monte (now in San Francesco in Arezzo), in the *Madonna lactans* (Brera) and the sharply drawn *Flagellation* (ibid.). Signorelli obviously met Pollaiuolo and saw the frescoes by Filippo Lippi in the Prato Duomo. His Florentine leanings became more marked in the frescoes in the

SIGNORELLI. LIFE OF ST BENEDICT. DETAIL FROM THE FRESCO 'TWO BENEDICTINES BREAKING THEIR FAST'. 1497. CLOISTER OF MONTE OLIVETO.

vestry of the Loreto basilica, painted between 1476 and 1479 with a very personal feeling for contre-jour effects and shadows. In 1481, he was one of the painters invited by the Pope to decorate the Sistine Chapel; his contribution was the masterful *Testament and Death of Moses*. He had a gift for strong compositions, as for instance the *Adoration of the Magi* (1482, Louvre) for the church of Sant'Agostino, in Città di Castello, or the Pala in Perugia (1484). From that time, he was given commissions all over central Italy: in 1488, he painted a banner representing the Virgin for Città di Castello and was given honorary citizenship; in 1490, he was one of the artists asked to submit a

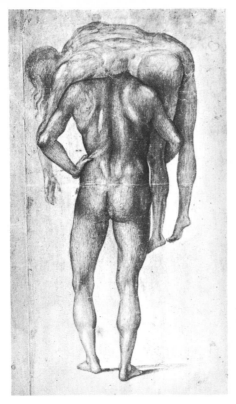

SIGNORELLI. NAKED MAN CARRYING A CORPSE.
DRAWING. LOUVRE, PARIS.

Magi for Sant'Agostino in Città di Castello, a *Nativity* for the church of San Francesco and the *Martyrdom of St Sebastian* for San Domenico; he was also working on the *Visitation* tondo (Berlin); all these works are characterised by their well organised composition and the great number of characters. But he was at his best in monumental decoration: from 1497, he painted in the cloister of Monte Oliveto Maggiore eight frescoes illustrating the *Life of St Benedict,* which soon became famous, and in 1499 he was invited by the Chapter in Orvieto to complete the decoration of the vaults in the chapel of San Brizio, which had been started by Fra Angelico half a century before. The contract described him as 'famosissimus pictor in tota Italia' and stipulated that all the figures had to be painted by his own hand. Satisfied with his work, the Opera Pia also commissioned from him in 1500 the decoration of the walls. In 1508, almost thirty years after his first visit to Rome, he was asked by Julius II to take part in the decoration of the Vatican Stanze; but the Pope soon sent him and the other artists away, and handed over all the work to Raphael. Between 1508 and 1513, he was at the Palazzo Petrucchi in Siena, with Pinturicchio. In 1513, when Leo X became Pope, he went back to Rome. But fashions had changed, so he retired to Cortona as a provincial master producing uninspired compositions. In 1523, Cardinal Passerini, who had built a palace near Cortona, asked Signorelli to paint the *Baptism of Christ* in the chapel, but the artist died without completing this work.

Signorelli was not inspired by Piero della Francesca's open treatment of space, but rather by his sculptural rendering of figures and his dramatic feeling. Already in his *Flagellation* (about 1475), he used a strong, oblique lighting, which was to become more noticeable still in the sacristy of Loreto

design for the façade of the Duomo in Florence. He painted in quick succession for Lorenzo de' Medici the Uffizi *Madonna* and the *Triumph of Pan* (Berlin, destroyed in 1944). Such a large work on such an unusual theme must have been composed for a specific purpose. In fact, we know through several writings that Pan was one of the Medici divinities who inspired much occasional verse and numerous epistles. At the same time, he painted the *Holy Family* now in the Uffizi (1491), the Volterra *Annunciation* and the *Circumcision* (London, National Gallery). In 1493, he painted another *Adoration of the*

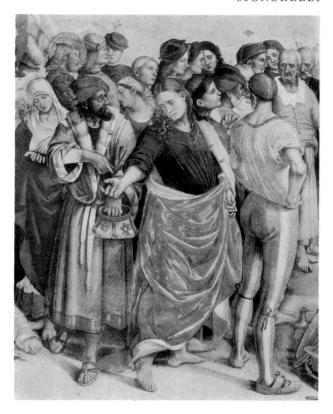

(about 1478), and interesting contrasts: fair haired angels dance lightly all over the eight sections of the cupola while the Evangelists and the Doctors look suitably grave. Signorelli exploited such contrasts and used symmetrical compositions with somewhat stereotyped oppositions of colours and facial types, as for instance in the group of saints around the Perugia *Madonna*. His predilection for nudes, or for draperies which reveal the movements of the human body, is obvious in the Sistine Chapel fresco; he used contemporary costumes with striking ease and dignity. He left some of his numerous works in most towns of Tuscany and Umbria.

His powerful *Pan* is one of the most original and daring compositions of the end of the Quattrocento, with strongly modelled nudes, and it has been interpreted as a learned meditation on the hidden forces of the universe, inspired by humanist sources. The work is presented as a Sacra Conversazione with characters grouped round a central throne, and with a gravely religious atmosphere. The style is similar to that of his other works of the same period; for instance, the static composition, with the main lines following the direction of the characters' glances, is also used in the *Madonnas* in Perugia (1484) and in Volterra (1491). The landscape with dark rocks and an architectural motif is very reminiscent of the Uffizi *Madonna* (about 1490) in which a round temple, a ruined archway and shepherds constitute an evocation of the Pagan world; it also reminds us of the background of the Berlin *Portrait of a Man* and of the plain, strewn with buildings, of the Urbino *Crucifixion*. Signorelli seems to have been the first to depict ephebes in a sort of timeless Arcadia perpetuating the antique world. He stressed the plastic values of the old Florentine school; the nude body was for him the main element of an artistic language which led directly to Michelangelo.

Through his impetuosity his *terribilità*, Signorelli was—apart from Michelangelo—the last of the great fresco painters of 15th century Tuscany. But it was not in Florence that he found the opportunity of triumphing over the colourless style which was fashionable at that time. The lively frescoes of Monte Oliveto Maggiore had made him popular and he won, over Perugino and Pinturicchio, a commission from the Orvieto Chapter for the Chapel of San Brizio. Once he had been accepted, he suggested a complete scheme for the six walls of the chapel on a theme which was unusual in Italy at that time: the Last Judgment. He spent four years over it and, to stress that he had only completed the work begun by Fra Angelico, he placed a representation of the Blessed next to his portrait, in the left-hand corner of the first fresco. On the vault, he painted the choirs which completed his predecessor's work; he covered the lower part of the walls, under the frescoes, with picturesque motifs surrounded by arabesques and grotesques. In the panels, nudes and dramatic foreshortenings are predominant: the Anti-Christ—probably an allusion to Savonarola—is represented in a picturesque scene. But the Resurrection of the Dead is painted in a different style;

the Judgment Scene shows demons with membraned wings, towering over tormented naked bodies, under a sky torn apart by the trumpet call of the angels.

Signorelli re-established for a while the links between Umbria and Florence, but in a way diametrically opposed to that of Fra Angelico. From Piero della Francesca, he had learnt to paint static groups of characters with restrained gestures, but his figures have a nervous energy alien to the impassive master of Borgo. He was more Tuscan than Umbrian and he surprises us by his powerful, harsh realism and his bold mastery in the use of movement. The hard, dry, often reddish colour which he had already used in Loreto is emphasised by a dramatic use of light which, at times, gives us a foretaste of Giulio Romano. The grand style of 1460, as practised by Piero della Francesca, had started two opposed developments illustrated by Perugino and Signorelli who gradually enriched them with innovations going beyond the preoccupations of the Florentines. The *terribilità* of the one and the gentle manner of the other were to find a final expression in Michelangelo and Raphael for whom they respectively prepared the way by their concern with form and with grouping.   A. C.

SIMONE MARTINI. *See* Martini, Simone.

SIXTUS IV Francesco della Rovere; elected Pope in 1471 (Cella Liguria, 1414 - Rome, 1484). From his first year as Pope, Sixtus IV started large scale works in Rome (improvements to the city and building of churches), founded the Museo Capitolino, welcomed or called back the scholars whom his predecessor, Paul II, had sent away from his court. He was the second founder (Nicholas V being the first) of the Vatican Library whose collections he enriched and which he decorated with paintings by Antoniazzo Romano, Domenico and Davide Ghirlandaio and Melozzo da Forli. A fresco by the latter shows the Pope making Platina his librarian (1474). But his main claim to glory is undoubtedly the founding of the chapel which bears his name. Built by Giovannino de' Dolci, the Sistine Chapel was decorated by Botticelli, Domenico Ghirlandaio, Signorelli, Rosselli, Pinturicchio and Perugino (1481-1484). Facing each other on the lateral walls, stretch the *Story of Moses* and *Scenes from the Life of Christ*. This admirable ensemble still survives, but Perugino's three frescoes *(The Nativity, Assumption of the Virgin, Finding of Moses)*, which decorated the far wall behind the altar, have disappeared to make way for Michelangelo's *Last Judgment* (1534-1541). In the central fresco *(The Assumption)*, Sixtus IV is represented kneeling, in the traditional attitude of the donor.   P.-H. M.

SODOMA Giovanni Antonio Bazzi, *called* (Vercelli, Piedmont, 1477 - Siena, 1549). On November 28th, 1490, he began his training in Vercelli, in the workshop of Giovanni Martino Spanzotti, where he studied for seven years. He came under the influence of Umbrian painters, particularly Signorelli and Raphael, and, in Milan, he probably worked with Leonardo whose art left its mark on his work. About 1501, he settled in Siena, but often worked outside that city. In 1503, he painted the frescoes in the refectory of the Olivetan monastery of Sant' Anna in Campana (or Sant' Anna in Creta), near Pienza. Shortly afterwards, he painted one of his most famous works: the decoration of the cloister in the monastery of Monte Oliveto Maggiore; from 1505 to 1508, he worked there on thirty-one frescoes continuing the *Life of St Benedict* begun by Luca Signorelli between 1497 and 1501. These light,

open compositions show a remarkable gift for the grouping of characters and an almost morbid beauty in the faces and attitudes. On October 13th, 1510, he signed a contract for the decoration of the Stanza della Segnatura at the Vatican, for a fee of fifty ducats. In 1512, in Siena, he decorated the façade of the Palazzo Agostino Bardi and, the same year, went to Rome to paint, at the Villa Farnesina, *Alexander and Roxana* whose formal beauty, nudes, architecture and putti are typical of the Renaissance style. But these frescoes suffer from being juxtaposed to those by Raphael and it is hardly surprising if Julius II gave up his original idea of asking Sodoma to decorate the Stanza della Segnatura. In 1518, he was paid for the frescoes of the Brotherhood of San Sebastiano in Siena, which were painted under his supervision by Girolamo del Pacchia and Domenico Beccafumi. The decoration of the chapel of St Catherine in San Domenico in Siena, in 1526, is one of his masterpieces. During the same period, he painted the touching and graceful *St Sebastian* (Uffizi). He also worked in Volterra and in Pisa. His numerous works are all characterised by a very personal style: a pleasant technique, beautiful colour, subtle light effects, gentle faces and a poetic feeling for landscape. Unfortunately, these qualities are often spoilt by affectation.   S. B.

SOLARIO Andrea (Milan, *ca* 1460 - . . ., 1520). He was born in an artists' family and his brother Cristoforo, who was a sculptor and an architect, was probably his first master. In 1490, he accompanied him to Venice and his *Virgin between St Joseph and St Jerome* (Brera) shows how much he was influenced by Venetian art. The two brothers returned to Milan when Cristoforo was appointed court sculptor to replace Mantegazza. From 1507 to 1509, Andrea worked in Gaillon, in

Normandy, for the Cardinal of Amboise. In 1514, he was in Rome; in 1515 he was back in Milan and painted the *Rest during the Flight to Egypt* (Milan, Museo Poldi-Pezzoli). There is no reliable information about his later career. His most famous works are: *Christ with a Crown of Thorns,* the *Madonna with the Green Cushion* and the *Head of St John the Baptist* (Louvre). According to Vasari, he died while he was finishing the *Assumption* in the vestry of the Certosa di Pavia, in 1520.

Trained in the manner of Alvise Vivarini, he was also influenced by Antonello da Messina, by the Bellini and by Flemish artists. A complex personality, with a remarkable feeling for colour, he was one of the most gifted followers of Leonardo.   s. b.

SOLIMENA Francesco (Nocera, near Naples, 1657 - Nocera, 1747). Solimena was taught at first by his father, who settled in Naples in 1674, then he followed Luca Giordano almost exclusively. He executed commissions at Monte Cassino, in Rome, and went to Spain three years after Luca. But most of his work was done in Naples and its environs. There are ensembles by him at Santa Maria di Donna Regina (1684), San Paolo Maggiore (*Fall of Simon Magus,* 1689) and especially at the Gesù Nuovo, which houses his masterpiece, *Heliodorus driven from the Temple* (1725). His sketches, filled with numerous figures, are dashingly done (*Massacre of the Giustiniani in Chios,* Naples, Museo Nazionale). He is more luminous than Luca Giordano, and on this account he was much admired by 18th century decorative painters, particularly the French.   p. c.

SPINELLO ARETINO Spinello di Luca Spinelli, *called* (Arezzo, *ca* 1346 - Arezzo, 1410). Orcagna's influence can be seen in his early works: the Arezzo *Annunciation* (Church of the Annunziata), the *Trinity* (Arezzo, Pinacoteca) and the

St John (Florence, Santa Croce). Later, Spinello returned to Giotto's narrative style in his wall paintings and, together with Agnolo Gaddi, he kept up the great Florentine tradition until the end of the century. But he was also open to other influences: the Lorenzetti and particularly Traini, who was responsible for the increasing gothic flavour of his late works. His main frescoes are in Florence (*Scenes from the Life of St Benedict,* Sacristy of San Miniato, about 1386, now restored), near Florence (Antella, Chapel of St Catherine, 1387-1388), in Pisa (Camposanto, *Legend of St Ephesus and St Potitus,* 1391-1392, badly damaged in 1944), and Siena (Palazzo Pubblico, *Scenes from the Life of Pope Alexander III,* 1407). His numerous altar paintings are scattered in various European and American museums. There is an *Annunciation* in Paris (École des Beaux-Arts).   p.-h. m.

SQUARCIONE Francesco (Padua, lived between 1397 and 1474). A strange character, not always honest according to documents (his pupils complained of being exploited and some of them started legal proceedings against him), whose workshop seems to have played a vital part between 1440 and 1460. Mantegna and Cosimo Tura were among his followers. We do not know if he had any theoretical knowledge, but he collected antique busts, statues, bas-reliefs, architectural fragments and even mouldings which he used for his teaching. He was a mediocre artist as we can see from the polyptych painted between 1449 and 1452 for Lione de Lazzara and intended for the family chapel in the Carmine (Padua, Museo Civico). Squarcione started a fashion for garlands of fruit and wrought decorations: he knew how to use for his own purposes the art of Donatello and Filippo Lippi, as for instance in the Berlin *Madonna.* His reputation as an innovator, which is now questioned by some art historians,

GHERARDO STARNINA. THE THEBAID (DETAIL). UFFIZI, FLORENCE.

was probably due less to his own merits than to a clever use of the latest Florentine discoveries. Although he may not always have kept his promises to his pupils, none the less, his workshop was an original meeting ground for archaeology and art, and the focus of the strange 'romanticism of the antique' which flourished in the 1460's.   A. C.

STARNINA Gherardo (Florence, *ca* 1354 - Florence, 1409/13). The scant knowledge we possess of this artist we owe to Vasari, who gives his date of birth as 1354. He is said to have been taught in Antonio Veneziano's studio. In 1378 after the Ciompi conspiracy he went into exile in Spain. Back in Italy, he executed his most famous work: the frescoes in the Castellani Chapel at Santa Croce in Florence. He is thought to have died between 1409

and 1413. There are reminiscences in him of Agnolo Gaddi and in particular of Giotto, whom he even copied in one of the Santa Croce frescoes. Under the name of Starnina works have been grouped which may well not be by him. Among his works are the *Virgin surrounded by Saints* (Berlin), *St Julian* (Munich) and the *Madonna* in the Parry Collection in Gloucester.   A. L.

STEFANO FIORENTINO (Florence, beginning of the 14th century). The early historian, Ghiberti, professed great admiration for this disciple of Giotto and called him 'grandissimo dottore'. It is through him that we know that Stefano Fiorentino decorated the ambulatory of the Convent of Sant'Agostino in Florence with three frescoes. At Santa Maria Novella, also in Florence, he painted in the cloister of the Convent

279

STEFANO DA VERONA. MADONNA IN THE ROSE
GARDEN. ABOUT 1405-1410. CASTELVECCHIO,
VERONA.

international gothic style, taking his lead
from the Lombard artists, Michelino da
Besozzo in particular. Following on
from them, he produced a very elegant,
resolutely unrealistic and free interpretation of that worldly mannerism in his
masterpiece: the *Madonna in the Rose
Garden* (Verona, Castelvecchio). Here
he takes up the gothic theme of
the 'enclosed garden' and the ornamental
part of the background of little flowers,
with such a delicate fantasy that it borders
on the whimsical and defeats all logic of
perspective. There are also several
frescoes of his extant, but in a bad state
of preservation, at Verona and Mantua,
and a superb series of drawings (Louvre, Albertina, Uffizi.)   M. L.

STROZZI Bernardo (Genoa, 1581 - Venice, 1644). After the death of his
father, who had planned literary studies
for him, Strozzi took up painting and
worked in the studio of the Sienese, Sorri.
At seventeen he became a Capuchin
monk and was ordained, which explains
why he was called 'Il Prete Genovese'.
Given temporary leave from his religious
duties to help his family, he was employed from 1615 to 1621 as harbour
engineer in Genoa. After his mother's
death and his sister's marriage, he refused
to return to the Capuchins. In 1631, he
fled to Venice and settled down there
after obtaining a dispensation from his
vows. The components of his work
are mannerism, a rather superficial
Caravaggism and, above all, considerable northern influences, Rubens and
Rembrandt (*The Cook,* Genoa, Palazzo
Rosso). Venice conquered him and his
palette became so light that he seems at
times to anticipate Tiepolo. The few
portraits by Strozzi, which exist, are of
pre-eminent quality and remind one
of Velasquez.   P. C.

the *Navicella,* the *Transfiguration* and the
Healing of a Possessed Man, as well as a
figure of *St Thomas,* which it was said
seemed to be 'stepping out from
the wall'. Unfortunately, none of the
above mentioned works remain and the
attributions suggested by the historian,
Siren, have all been contested.   A. L.

STEFANO da VERONA (Verona, 1374 -
Verona, after 1438). Although his
activity is only documented between
1424 and 1438, and his sole dated work
(*Adoration of the Magi,* Brera) is of 1435,
Stefano had certainly been at work
right from the end of the 14th century
in Verona. Here he introduced the

T

TADDEO di BARTOLO (Siena, *ca* 1362 - Siena, 1422). Like most Sienese painters of his generation, Taddeo followed the masters of the first half of the century. This tradition was passed on to him by Bartolo di Fredi whom Vasari, through the similarity of names, mistakenly believed to be his father. He was a very productive painter. He worked in Genoa (1393), then in San Gimignano, Pisa, Triora in Liguria, Perugia, Volterra, but mainly in his native town where he returned after every journey. During his first period, until about 1400, he kept to the usual subjects of religious painting; for example, the 1395 triptych with *Virgin and Child* (Grenoble). Later, his choice became freer and he was considered an innovator, less because of his style than because of his subjects: the *Articles of Faith* (Siena, Opera del Duomo), or classical gods and heroes (Siena, frescoes in the Palazzo Pubblico).   P.-H. M.

TIBALDI Pellegrino, *or* Pellegrino de' Pellegrini (Puria di Valsolda, 1527 - Milan, 1596). Having completed his first training in Emilia (under Girolamo da Carpi and Girolamo da Treviso) Tibaldi went to Rome and there developed a great admiration for Michelangelo (*Adoration of the Christ Child,* 1549, Rome, Galleria Borghese; fresco in the San Dionigi Chapel of San Luigi dei Francesi). This influence persisted throughout the different stages of his roving career; we see notable examples of it at Bologna, where he gives an ingenious interpretation of the ancient myths (Palazzo Poggi frescoes 1554-1555); at Milan, where he is almost exclusively concerned with architecture (works at the Cathedral); and in Spain

TADDEO
DI BARTOLO.
REGISTER OF THE
BICCHERNA. 1388
STATE ARCHIVES,
SIENA.

(1587-1596) where his typically mannerist attempt to break form down into geometrical shapes reaches the extreme in the Escorial Palace decorations.　　j. t.

TIEPOLO Giambattista (Venice, 1696 - Madrid, 1770) *and* Giandomenico (Venice, 1727 - Venice, 1804). There were Doges of Venice in the Tiepolo family and Giambattista came of pure Venetian stock. He began life in modest circumstances and was taught by Gregorio Lazzarini. His early paintings show the influence of Piazzetta from which he soon freed himself. In particular he discarded the contrasts which Piazzetta had learned in Bologna from Giuseppe Maria Crespi. These contrasts did not suit Tiepolo whose chosen medium was the fresco. Tiepolo took up, if not directly, the heritage of Veronese in Venice, the brilliant palette of that artist, his appreciation of women and their clothes, his lightness and his festive air. In 1717, Giambattista Tiepolo was enrolled in the guild of painters. In 1719, he married Cecilia Guardi, Francesco's sister, who gave him nine sons. By 1725, he was the most celebrated artist in Venice and thenceforth he went from success to success. Count Tessin, Swedish Minister in Venice, described him a few years later as 'full of wit, willing to please, like Taraval, and astonishingly quick'. No more than a bare mention of his main decorative pieces is possible here, beginning with Venice. In churches: Santa Maria del Rosario dei Gesuati (1737-1739), with more illusionistic architecture than is usual for him; the Scuola dei Carmini (1740-1744); Santa Maria degli Scalzi whose vast ceiling (1743-1744), destroyed by shells in 1915, represented the Translation of the House of the Virgin to Loreto. In palaces: the *Meeting of Antony and Cleopatra* and the *Banquet of Cleopatra,* the most Veronesian of his works, at the Palazzo Labia (about 1745-1750); the *Apotheosis of Quintiliano Rezzonico* (about 1758), with the help of Giandomenico Tiepolo, at the Ca' Rezzonico. Outside Venice: the *Reception of Henry III* at the Villa Contarini (now at the Musée Jacquemart-André, Paris); the ballroom in the Villa Pisani at Stra on the Brenta Canal (1761-1762).

Tiepolo went to Bergamo to decorate the Colleoni Chapel with scenes from the life of John the Baptist (1733). One of his most complete and most attractive works is the cycle at the Villa Valmarana outside Vicenza (1757), with scenes taken from Homer, Vergil, Ariosto and Tasso in the main building, and decorations full of fantasy with chinoiseries in the *foresteria* (guest house) of

GIAMBATTISTA TIEPOLO. A GENTLEMAN.
DRAWING. MUSEO CORRER, VENICE.

GIAMBATTISTA TIEPOLO. NYMPH. DETAIL FROM A FRESCO. 1740. PALAZZO CLERICI, MILAN.

which a large part was painted by the artist's son, Giandomenico. Giambattista was also commissioned to paint frescoes in Udine where one of his earliest works is to be found in the chapel of the Sacrament, in the cathedral (1726); in Milan, at the Palazzo Clerici (1740); in Verona, at the Palazzo Canossa (1761). His reputation had become universal. In 1750, the Prince-Bishop of Würzburg summoned him with his sons, Giandomenico and Lorenzo, to decorate the Residenz. Tiepolo decorated with frescoes the Kaisersaal and the gigantic ceiling of the Grand Staircase, where the *Four Continents* is perhaps his most enthralling work. In answer to an invitation from the King of Spain, he arrived in Madrid in 1762 and proceeded to devote five years to the decoration of the royal palace.

It can be said that, but for very small differences, all his works deserve equally high praise. Painted in fresco with luminous tones his ceilings are suffused with an even clarity. They are filled, but not overcrowded, with fresh complexioned women and angels. Tiepolo is the master of airborne figures. He was no doubt a good perspectivist, but his knowledge was instinctive and not a matter of pedantic learning as with Andrea Pozzo. Thus he avoided giving too much importance to architectural ensembles that collapse when viewed from the wrong angle. The female type he created is fleshy and plump, but its nudity has none of the equivocalness of the goddesses of Boucher. Tiepolo's women disport themselves with innocence and enjoy moving their limbs in a sort of celestial dance. Stories were current in his time about a model dear to his heart whom he apparently took with him to Spain. His imagination, his effortless ease make him the greatest decorator of his century, and certainly the most attractive, blond or silvery, sparkling with a divine gaiety, inexhaustible in formal invention.

Even though done in oils, his ceiling sketches have something of the lightness of his frescoes. The same is true of his pictures with subjects taken from myth or fable or everyday life in Venice. Although such themes suited Giambattista best he was an all-round artist— witness his portrait of the *Procurator Querini* (Venice, Galleria Querini-Stampalia), ugly and cunning, and the scenes from the *Passion* (Venice, Sant'Alvise) in which he achieves genuine emotion. The draughtsman in him admirably prepared the way for the painter. On paper, with a pen, he indicated a nude elliptically by a contour traced in downstrokes and upstrokes, with only a touch

of bistre or a sepia wash to heighten it. As an engraver he has other surprises in store. His *cappricci* and *scherzi di fantasia,* done with very fine strokes sometimes so close together as to fuse into blacks without any heaviness, reveal a mysterious side in him: one sees a serpent, a dead man, a tomb, a punchinello. The word *cappriccio* is wellchosen; there are no logical connexions but the effect is not tragic.

This unrealistic aspect of Tiepolo provides a link with his son, Giandomenico, who was his faithful collaborator at the Villa Valmarana as well as at Würzburg and Madrid. In 1780 Giandomenico was elected President of the Venetian Academy. In the difficult role of the son of a genius, he succeeded in keeping his independence. He was the painter and designer of punchinellos. In the family house at Zianigo he portrayed them engaging in various exercises and these frescoes, now at the Ca' Rezzonico,

GIANDOMENICO TIEPOLO. YOUNG SWINEHERD WITH TWO PEASANT WOMEN.
DRAWING. MUSÉE DE BAYONNE.

are in nowise undistinguished besides those of Giambattista. As a draughtsman he was very different from his father: he treated his personages individually and liked to caricature them. Affinities have been found between Giambattista and Goya. Giandomenico, who drew a great deal in Madrid while Goya was there, anticipated the great Aragonese more directly. Occasionally his drawings strike a rather unexpected macabre note.   P. C.

TINTORETTO Jacopo Robusti, *called* (Venice, 1518 - Venice, 1594). Jacopo was a pure Venetian, the son of Battista Robusti, a dyer, which was the rather malicious reason for his nickname. The evidence for his birth in 1518 is the entry in the burial register of San Marciliano at Venice, where it is noted that he died in May 1594, at the age of

seventy-five years and eight months. It is thought that he worked under Titian, but he also had mannerist painters for his masters. In 1539, he was an independent artist, living in the parish of San Cassiano and known as 'mistro Giacomo depentor'. In 1545, he painted for Aretino the ceiling decoration of *Apollo and Marsyas* (Hartford, Wadsworth Atheneum) and *Mercury and Argus* (lost). The following year he was occupied with frescoes for the Arsenal. The first works, dated with certainty, are the *Last Supper* (1547) for San Marcuola and *St Mark rescuing a Slave* (1548) for the Scuola di San Marco (Venice, Accademia). The following year, he painted an altarpiece for San Marziale. About 1550, he was working for the Procurators and married Faustina dei Vescovi from whom he had several children; Marietta, Domenico and

Marco, all followed their father's profession. He had already been to Rome (1545) and a little later he went to Mantua. In 1552, he painted two Saints for the Magistrato del Sale (Venice, Accademia) and four Evangelists for Santa Maria Zobenigo. The following year, he painted the excommunication of Frederick Barbarossa for the Sala del Maggior Consiglio in the Palazzo Ducale, which disappeared in the fire of 1577. *Susanna and the Elders* (Vienna) dates from the 60's. In 1561, he painted the *Marriage at Cana* for Santa Maria della Salute. He worked from 1562 to 1566 for the powerful Confraternità di San Marco, which had commissioned three pictures illustrating the *Miracles of St Mark* (two are now in the Accademia, Venice, the third is at the Brera, Milan). In 1562, he painted another scene from the life of Frederick Barbarossa, the *Coronation,* for the Sala del Maggior Consiglio, in the Palazzo Ducale, which also disappeared in the fire. In 1563, he was a member of the commission responsible for examining the mosaics of Zuccati at St Mark's. He was undaunted by the immensity of the task when, in 1564, he was given the commission for the huge cycle of the Scuola di San Rocco, which was not completed till 1587. The following year, he became a member of the Scuola himself and painted a *Crucifixion* for it. During 1566-1567, he completed the decoration of the church of San Rocco and painted a *Last Judgment* for the Sala dello Scrutinio in the Palazzo Ducale (burned). In 1568, he signed a contract with the Scuola de San Marco for a large picture representing the translation of the body of St Mark to Venice. The same year, he designed his first cartoon for the mosaics in St Mark's and painted a *Christ in Limbo* for the church of San Cassiano. During 1571-1572, he did work for the Old Library. From 1572 to 1574, he was occupied with a picture of the *Battle of Lepanto* for the Palazzo Ducale (burnt in 1577). In 1574, he painted a portrait of *Henry III of France* (disappeared; copy in the Palazzo Ducale). In 1564, he began work on the ceiling of the Scuola di San Rocco and continued work on it until 1581. Meanwhile he signed a permanent contract with the Scuola.

TINTORETTO.
SUSANNA
AND THE ELDERS.
ABOUT 1560.
KUNSTHISTORISCHES
MUSEUM, VIENNA.

The *Temptation of St Anthony* for the church of San Trovaso belongs to 1577. The same year, the fire in the Palazzo Ducale destroyed a considerable amount of his work. The following years were spent on decorating it. His visit to Mantua took place about 1580 and he painted eight scenes there illustrating the history of the Gonzaga family (Munich). From 1583 to 1587, work on the Palazzo Ducale in Venice alternated with work on the main hall of the Scuola di San Rocco. He painted the *Battle of Zara* for the Sala dello Scrutinio. In 1588, he painted, again for the Sala del Maggior Consiglio reconstructed after 1577, his *Paradise*, which has been considered one of the greatest pictures in the world. In 1592, he became a member of the Scuola dei Mercanti. From 1592 to 1594, he worked at San Giorgio Maggiore. March 30th, 1594, he made his will and died on May 31st.

According to Ridolfi (1642), the young Tintoretto was apprenticed to Titian. The story even relates that he only stayed a few days with him, because his exceptional gifts roused the jealousy of the master. In fact, he is more more likely to have been placed with Bonifacio dei Pitati, Schiavone or Bordone. The influence of the first artist does not appear in his early works, but in those of his maturity. On the other hand, it is easy to see how the fevered palette of Schiavone and the rather artificial traits of Bordone appealed to him. His first works, the *Last Supper* and *St Mark rescuing the Slave,* are well in the Venetian tradition, with its fondness for a composition in which elements of equal importance are crowded into the foreground. *St Mark rescuing the Slave* is directly inspired by Michelangelo's *Conversion of St Paul;* there is the same contrast in both between the prostrate and standing figures. The *Last Supper* shows the attraction of Titian and at the same time a rejection of his art. But

TINTORETTO. CHRIST WITH MARY AND MARTHA. ALTE PINAKOTHEK, MUNICH.

what appears above all is a new sense of drama with a sweep and authority that are rare. The carefully drawn buildings are still in the tradition of the Bellini and Carpaccio. There is already a change in *Christ washing the Feet of the Disciples* (Prado), which comes from San Marcuola, and where there is a striking perspective effect. With the large painting of *St Augustine healing the Plague-striken* (Vicenza), Tintoretto displayed his virtuosity in producing dramatic effects: space rhythmed by colourless forms, often set against the light alternating with areas of intense colour; figures, placed obliquely or in diagonals with astonishing foreshortenings, punctuate

287

TINTORETTO.
VENUS, ARIADNE
AND BACCHUS.
ABOUT 1578.
PALAZZO DUCALE,
VENICE.

the scene in every direction. Tintoretto is closer to Titian in the later *Fall of Man* (Venice, Accademia) and even Veronese in the admirable *Susanna and the Elders* of Vienna in which a huge, translucent nude stands out against a deep, luxuriant garden. From that point, his style developed the characteristics of mannerism with an inconceivable energy and speed. He revealed its prodigious powers of invention for the first time: the long, sinuous figure, oblique composition and a discolouring light that accentuates the dramatic effect of the scene. His art became a refined instrument of narrative that could create a vibrant, tense, emotional world. His colossal conception of the human form is given full expression in the three *Miracles of St Mark,* where the figures in movement swing in a shadowed perspective shot with light. This prodigious effect is particularly noticeable in the *Finding of the Body of St Mark* (Brera) in which the figures occupy space in every direction with a dazzling facility.

The immense cycle in the Scuola di San Rocco, which he worked at for twenty-three years, is the peak of his achievement, the testament of a visionary. Tintoretto began with the upper floor. There, light and colour give a direct emphasis to the figures; for example, the white form of *Christ before Pilate.* The visual orchestration reaches the limits of possibility in huge paintings like *Christ on the Road to Calvary* and the *Crucifixion,* where a swirling crowd eddies on the fringe of the central action, yet drawn into participation with it by the strange, insinuating light. The involvement of heaven and earth is indescribable in the *Ascension* and the *Baptism of Christ,* but the contrast between the colourless, silvery silhouettes and the purple and orange garments is sufficient to indicate distance and scale. His most lyrical and inventive paintings are to be found in the lower hall (1584-1587): the *Flight into Egypt,* with its astonishing landscape of darkness and palms and the complex scene of the *Magdalen in the Wilderness.* The whole sacred story is swept into swirling movement, which still gives full importance to the striking, realistic detail, like the chair of the Virgin in the *Annunciation,* or the straw of the crib in the *Nativity.* The touch of the painter's brush had never shown greater virtuosity or power, nor greater freedom. The beginnings of mannerism have been left far behind.

This immense work was followed by the paintings in the Palazzo Ducale, where Tintoretto had secured a certain number of important commissions. He took on enormous projects in the Sala del Collegio; the Sala del Senato, where the ceiling is decorated with the famous glorification of Venice, as queen of the seas; and the huge painting of *Paradise* in the Sala del Maggior Consiglio, a masterpiece of orchestration, where the colours, some violent, others subdued, hollow or thrust into space, without however avoiding a feeling that sheer compositional virtuosity has harmed the work and made it inferior to the preparatory sketch (Louvre).

It was in the art of portraiture that Tintoretto kept closest to the Venetian tradition. His portraits are as numerous as his decorative paintings. Titian could not satisfy the needs of his Venetian clientèle. Tintoretto added a greater brilliance and a more studied intensity to Titian's fine composition. The faces and dresses contrasted with the sombre background, and the intense life of the sitter are a pleasure to the eye as in the portraits of *Jacopo Soranzo* (Milan, Castello Sforzesco), *Vicenzo Morosini* (London, National Gallery) and *Alvise Cornaro* (Pitti).

Tintoretto was a keen and regular worker, eager for every commission, which meant that he had to take on the execution of huge cycles. His passionate, dramatic feeling is clearly revealed in the charcoal drawings, where the figure is strongly modelled by hatchings, even when one feels that they are from little clay models, intended as studies in muscular relief.

TINTORETTO. PORTRAIT OF JACOPO SORANZO. CASTELLO SFORZESCO, MILAN.

He lived nowhere except at Venice and only wanted to know Venice. He was the sum of its energies and extended its horizon far beyond reality and the probable. His manipulations of human types, perspectives and draperies were innumerable. But a feeling of irresistible power, drawn from Michelangelo, bears along his humanity. Everything contributed to heightening his grandeur, but it was projected and sometimes lost in a dark, flickering universe in movement, which no longer belonged to the Renaissance and which the baroque no longer kept within bounds.   A. C.

TITIAN Tiziano Vecellio, *called* (Pieve di Cadore, *ca* 1485 - Venice, 1576). The long reign of Titian, who was famous even in 1512/13, lasted for more than sixty years. He ruled supreme in Venice, then in Italy and even western

TITIAN. YOUNG WOMAN AT HER TOILET.
ABOUT 1512-1515. LOUVRE, PARIS.

TITIAN. FLORA. ABOUT 1515.
UFFIZI, FLORENCE.

Europe, leaving his mark on the development of painting for ever. This long career can be divided into four or five major phases. He was born in the lower Alps of Cadore and, when he was nine or ten years old, was taken to Venice with his brother, Francesco, and apprenticed to Sebastiano Zuccato, who later sent him to Gentile Bellini. Titian soon went on to Giovanni Bellini and finally to Giorgione. He helped his master with the frescoes on the façade of the Fondaco dei Tedeschi (lost, but known from drawings). They were disturbed times and the young painter left the city, perhaps on account of political events. He was at Padua in December 1510, which was shortly after the death of Giorgione. In 1511, he was paid—still at Padua—for three frescoes of the *Miracles of St Anthony of Padua,* executed for the Scuola del Santo. The drawing for the large woodengraving, *The Triumph of Faith,* belongs to this period. When he returned to Venice in 1513, he was welcomed as a master and the heir of Giorgione. The field was free for him and he could claim the first place in it. This was the period of the first Sacre Conversazioni and of *Sacred and Profane Love* (Rome, Galleria Borghese). In May 1513, the Venetian humanist, Pietro Bembo, offered him an opportunity of working for Leo X in the Vatican. But Titian refused and, at the same time, he requested the commission for a battle scene in the Sala del Maggior Consiglio from the Council of Ten. His suggestion was accepted (the painting, which was to be on the subject of the *Battle of Spoleto,* was not completed for twenty years, after various objections and hindrances) and from that moment Titian made Venice his home. He opened an atelier and in 1516 received the commission for an *Assumption* for the church of Santa Maria Gloriosa dei Frari. His relations with the court of Ferrara began in the same year. He

completed Giovanni Bellini's unfinished painting, the *Feast of the Gods,* with a landscape. In 1518, the *Assumption* was presented to the Frari and was such a success that the commissions flowed in. The *Virgin appearing to St Francis, St Aloysius and a Donor* (Ancona, Pinacoteca) was painted in 1520 for San Francesco at Ancona and two years later the polyptych of the *Resurrection* for Santi Nazaro e Celso in Brescia, which was a commission from the papal legate, Altobello Averoldo. In 1523, his connexions with the court at Mantua began and he painted some religious pictures for Duke Federico II, the *Virgin and Child with St Catherine,* known as the *Virgin with the Rabbit* (about 1530, Louvre) and, after 1537, the representations of the *Twelve Caesars* to decorate a hall in the palace. He still continued working for Venetian churches: between 1519 and 1526, he did the altarpiece of the *Madonna of Pesaro,* to commemorate, at the Frari, Jacopo Pesaro's victory over the Turks at Santa Maura; in 1530 the huge altar-piece of *St Peter Martyr* for San Zanipolo (destroyed by a fire in 1867), which was commissioned after a competition that Titian won against Jacopo Palma and Pordenone.

His fame was such that he became the acknowledged painter of princes and popes. He became acquainted with Pietro Aretino, who, according to Vasari, acted as his intermediary in 1530, when Ippolito de' Medici invited him to Bologna to paint his first portrait of Charles V (lost). During a further visit to Bologna in the winter of 1532-1533, the Emperor sat a second time for the master (Prado). The same year, 1533, Titian was appointed court painter and made a Count Palatine, with the dignity of Knight of the Golden Spur. The most eminent figures of the day solicited his services: *Cardinal Ippolito de' Medici* (1533, Pitti), *Isabella d'Este* (1534, Vienna), *Francesco Maria della Rovere,* the Duke of Urbino, and his wife, *Eleonora di Gonzaga* (1536-1538, both at the Uffizi), *Alfonso d'Avalos, Marchese del Vasto* (1536, Paris, de Ganay Collection).

Meanwhile, he also painted, for Guidobaldo II, the *Venus of Urbino* (1538, Uffizi) one of the finest achievements of his maturity.

At the same time, he continued to work at Venice and, between 1534 and 1538, executed the huge painting of the *Presentation of the Virgin* (now in the Accademia, Venice) for the Scuola della Carità. Titian, Jacopo Tatti and Aretino formed a sort of triumvirate, which was the arbiter of artistic matters in Venice. He was passionately fond of music and painted the portrait of *Andrea degli Organi* in return for one of his instruments. He was indefatigable and there is some difficulty in giving an account of his activities. It was the period when he painted the ceilings of Santa Maria della Salute (1543-1544) with biblical subjects and the portraits

of *Cardinal Pietro Bembo* (about 1542, Washington, National Gallery), *Clarissa Strozzi as a Child* (1542, Berlin), *Paul III* bareheaded (about 1543, Naples), which was probably painted when the Pope went to Emilia for his meeting with Charles V at Busseto, *Pietro Aretino* (1545, Pitti). In 1545, Titian left for Rome, passed through Pesaro, where he had a sumptuous reception from Guidobaldo, and was welcomed at Rome by Cardinal Alessandro Farnese and Pietro Bembo. He was the guest of Paul III at the Belvedere and visited the Sistine Chapel and Stanze with great interest. During his stay in the Vatican, he painted a group of portraits for the Farnese family (*Paul III and his Grandsons*, Naples, Museo di Capodimonte and the *Danaë* (Naples). He received the title of Citizen of Rome in March, 1546, and

TITIAN.
TWO YOUTHS
IN A LANDSCAPE.
DRAWING.
ALBERTINA,
VIENNA.

TITIAN. THE VENUS OF URBINO. 1538. UFFIZI, FLORENCE.

then took the road to the north, after a brief visit to Florence.

His style changed: his manner grew freer and his activity more widespread. After completing the altarpiece for the parish church of Serravalle (1547), he went to Augsburg at the invitation of Charles V, to paint a number of portraits, among others that of the Emperor himself, seated (1548, Munich, Alte Pinakothek) and on horseback, in armour, on the battlefield of Mühleberg (Prado), *Nicholas Perrenot, Cardinal Granvella* (Musée de Besançon), *Isabella of Portugal* (1548, Prado) and *Ferdinand of Austria*. During his second visit (1550-1551), he worked at different portraits, notably those of *Philip II* (Madrid and Naples) and of *John Frederick, Elector of Saxony* (1550, Vienna), then he painted

for the Emperor '*La Gloria*', which he took to the monastery of Saint-Juste, with the *Ecce Homo* of 1547 and the *Mater Dolorosa* (all three are now in the Prado). Titian was now sixty and he was honoured everywhere. Lucas Cranach was eager to paint his portrait. A more intimate tone appeared in official communications. Philip II admired him so much that for twenty years, beginning in 1553, he was the eminent patron of the painter, who executed sacred paintings and mythological compositions for him. The old master worked for other clients too, who were less illustrious, but who paid him more promptly: *Appearance of Christ to the Virgin* (1554) for the parish church of Medole; three ceiling decorations for the Palazzo Comunale of Brescia (1564);

293

his last *Pietà* (1573-1576) which he never finished. He outlived everyone; Aretino died in 1556, Tatti in 1570. The last illustrious visitors to his atelier were Henri III, the King of France, and Giorgio Vasari. He died in Venice on 27th August, 1576, during an epidemic of plague. In spite of special laws forbidding this for a victim of the plague, he was solemnly buried in the church of Santa Maria dei Frari.

Titian was the heir of Giorgione. He was perhaps less sensitive to the gentle modelling of his master than to his poetry, less to the nuances of *sfumato* than to his aspiration to monumental form, which finally appeared in the frescoes of the Fondaco dei Tedeschi. In any case, as early as the Paduan frescoes, his forms are stronger and colour areas more clearly defined. The picture soon depended on the interplay of luminous colour tones alone. Some problems of attribution to the two painters have still not been satisfactorily solved (did Titian paint the *Orpheus and Eurydice* of Bergamo and the two panels of the *Birth of Adonis* and the *Forest of Polydorus,* at Padua?) the influence of Giambellino, Carpaccio and Cima da Conegliano is evident in the altarpiece of *Jacopo Pesaro presented to St Peter by Pope Alexander V* (Antwerp). The superb *Sleeping Venus* of Dresden can be described, as was once said, as a 'Giorgione in the manner of Titian'. Titian was soon sufficiently esteemed to be entrusted with painting in the background landscape of Bellini's *Feast of the Gods.* He completed it successfully.

The painter created the models for Venetian beauty in a series of variations on themes from Giorgione: the *Vanitas* (Munich), *Flora* (Uffizi) and *Young Woman at her Toilet* (Louvre) are the finest and most lasting examples, as well as the as in the series of paintings, which Poussin admired so much in the 17th century: the *Offering to Venus* (1518-1519), the *Bacchanale* (1520, Prado) and *Bacchus*

TITIAN. DANAË. 1552-1554. PRADO, MADRID.

least touched with melancholy. There is something impressive in the development of his religious painting, from the *Madonna of the Cherries* (Vienna) to his masterpiece of dramatic style, the *Assumption* of the Frari, where groups of figures, without any architecture, are the only means he uses for organising space, while the colour range of the painting is both heightened and dependent on the harmony of red and blue in the figure of the Virgin. After that, Titian was a master who could be measured against Raphael and Michelangelo. The *St Sebastian* of the Brescia polyptych has a little of both of them. The *Entombment* (Louvre) is classical splendour at its finest. But Titian could also recreate just as well the world of classical myths, *and Ariadne* (1523, London, National Gallery).

Until about 1530, Titian was not so concerned with portraiture as he was later on, but already in the *Man with a Glove* (Louvre) his characteristic clarity and refinement appear. Between 1530 and 1540, his portraits are numerous and varied; the colour becomes richer, more sumptuous and is varied by a fine gradation of tones. Three portraits of the same woman belong to this period: *La Bella* (Pitti), the *Girl in a Fur* (Vienna) and the *Venus of Urbino* (Uffizi). Titian preserved his sturdy, serene attitude for a long time. However, after 1535-1540, even he became aware of the crisis of preciousness and refinement, called 'mannerism', which at last arrived at

Venice, and, impressed by Michelangelo, he began to simplify even further. His colour became more vibrant and the last portraits of *Charles V* and *Paul III* and the *Annunciation* (about 1565) for San Salvatore at Venice possess a new warmth. In his last works, like the *Pietà* (Venice, Accademia), pathos added a personal and poignant accent, which was new, to their grandeur. Never had a painter expressed himself in a pictorial world that was so vast and so coherent, so full of poetry and so certain. Painting could never be the same after him. A. C.

TOMMASO da MODENA (Modena, 1325/26 - before 1379). His family originated in Modena, but he worked primarily at Treviso where his most important mural works are preserved, the *Dominican Saints and Men of Learning* in the chapter of San Niccolò (1352), and the scenes from the *Life of St Ursula,* now in the Galleria Estense. His feeling for individual characterisation, which he drew from Bolognese models, and his own naturalistic ideas of narrative caused him to play a leading part in the development of northern Italian painting which, from a conventional idealism, gradually gave way during the second half of the 14th century to a more objective description of reality, bordering on the anecdote. Several small portable altarpieces (Baltimore, Bologna, Modena, Verona) and miniatures also reveal the subtlety of his pictorial technique. M. L.

TORRITI Jacopo, *or* Jacopo da Torrida (active in Rome, end of the 13th century). He was a painter and mosaicist about whom we know only that he worked in Assisi and in Rome, where three great works are the result of his activities between 1280 and 1295.— *a)* About 1280, in Assisi, he worked with Cimabue on the paintings in the Upper Church of the Basilica of St Fran-

cis. It is often difficult to date and attribute the various parts of this large composition, as work went on until the 15th century and there were many later restorations. The collaboration of Torriti, whom Cimabue may have met in Rome in 1272, is none the less established.—*b)* In 1291, in Rome, Torriti, together with Jacopo da Camerino, made the mosaic in the apse of San Giovanni in Laterano. Under a bust of the Pantocrator, the heavenly Jerusalem is represented, with the four rivers of Paradise springing from it; below, a row of saints among whom, next to the apostles, St Francis, St Anthony of Padua and, kneeling at the Virgin's feet, the reigning Pope, Nicholas IV, ex-General of the Franciscans. Franciscan elements are thus mixed with a Byzantine iconography. The style is impossible to assess as the mosaic was entirely remade in the 19th century.—*c)* The mosaic in the apse of Santa Maria Maggiore, Rome, which is signed and dated 1295 and is in a good state of preservation, is the only work which gives us a reliable idea of Torriti's art. It is a *Coronation of the Virgin*. In a star sprinkled circle representing the heavens, Christ and Mary are sitting on the same throne, surrounded by angels; below, saints and a portrait of Cardinal Jacopo Colonna; in a lower register, several scenes from the life of the Virgin. This is a masterful work, with rich colour and subtle composition. The artist has given a Roman flavour to eastern iconography. He deserves to rank with Cavallini, among the direct forerunners of Giotto. P.-H. M.

TRAINI Francesco (Pisa, 14th century). Traini's existence is first authenticated in a legal document dated 1321. His origins are unknown, but he always worked in Pisa. Half forgotten, not mentioned by Vasari, he was reinstated by modern critics and is now considered as the greatest Pisan painter of the

14th century. In 1340, he decorated a banner for the Fraternità delle Laudi of the Cathedral. In 1344/1345, he painted an altarpiece, *St Dominic,* for the church of Santa Caterina (now in the Museo Nazionale, Pisa); and in 1363 a *Triumph of St Thomas Aquinas* (church of Santa Caterina). This remarkable allegorical painting of Dominican inspiration celebrates the victory of Thomist thought, in other words, the victory of Christian Aristotelianism over the Arabian Aristotelianism of Averroes. The *Triumph of Death* fresco in the Camposanto, painted about 1350, was attributed in turn to Orcagna, to Pietro Lorenzetti, to Vitale da Bologna, before it was finally given back to Traini. This austere composition is more obviously didactic than the simple narrative frescoes of Giotto's followers, imbued with the Franciscan spirit, it is an exhortation to penance. It was destroyed by the 1944 raid, but as the painting came off, it left on the wall the preparatory sketches, the *sinopie.*   P.-H. M.

TURA Cosimo (Ferrara, *ca* 1430 - Ferrara, 1495). Throughout his entire active life Tura seems to have been the official painter of the Ferrarese princes, Duke Borso d'Este and his successor, Ercole. From 1451 to 1485 numerous documents mention portraits of princes, decorative paintings at Belfiore, or religious paintings at Belriguardo, that he carried out for the court, as well as designs he provided for tapestries, furniture, gold and silver ornaments and robes for state occasions or tournaments. Time has obliterated almost the whole of these creations and today Ferrara possesses only two examples of his activity in the city: the shutters painted for the cathedral organ, and, in the Museum, two fragments of the reredos of *St Maurelius,* formerly at San Georgio fuori le Mura. Elsewhere some thirty paintings are attributed with certainty to him, distributed among the museums of Europe

COSIMO TURA. PORTRAIT OF A MEMBER OF THE ESTE FAMILY. METROPOLITAN MUSEUM, NEW YORK.

and America, and often deriving from polyptychs, split up during the course of centuries. Documents enable us to date with some certainty three of these works: the shutters on the cathedral organ, already referred to *(St George,* the *Annunciation)* 1469, the great *Roverella Polyptych* painted for San Giorgio about 1474 (now divided between the National Gallery in London, the Louvre, the Galleria Colonna in Rome and four American museums), the *St Anthony of Padua,* 1484, painted for San Niccolò of Ferrara (now in Modena). But it is often difficult to date precisely the other pictures not mentioned in documents: the beautiful *Madonna with St Jerome and a Saint* in the Musée Fesch at Ajaccio has been placed by some historians at the

COSIMO TURA. ST GEORGE AND THE DRAGON.
1469. CATHEDRAL OF FERRARA.

Moreover works, like the *Pietà* in the Museo Correr at Venice, show that he had understood the dramatic naturalism of Rogier van der Weyden. The diversity of the curious paintings link him with the followers of Squarcione, whom he probably knew personally in Padua. Fascinated like them by the power or the strangeness of matter, he contrived a passionate transmutation of the real into an imaginary world of fantastic rocks, metal, precious stones and translucent enamels; like them he arrived at a gothic, anti-classical interpretation of the Renaissance. Yet he excels all of them, except Mantegna, in the power of his poetic inventions, the intensity of his expressionism, now savage (and there is no better example of this than the *Pietà* in the Louvre), now tender, invariably feverish and anguished. His superiority is clear too in the exceptional mastery of his style; if he still seems linked to the medieval spirit in his lyrical and decorative imagination, he places his figures with sculptural authority, worthy of the Florentine innovators, emphasises forcefully relief effects and knows how to compose his most elaborate compositions (like the *Madonna with Angels* in London) with a most modern conception of spatial cohesion. For all these reasons Tura appears as the founder of the Ferrarese school whose strangeness and rather disturbing poetry owes him a great debt. M. L.

beginning of the artist's career and by others at the very end. Such uncertainty is due to the consistency of his artistry and the unity of his work.

Benefiting from the extraordinary multiplicity of influences in Ferrara at mid-century, Tura created a most original style in which graphic sharpness and the fantasy of courtly gothic are fused with the plastic strength of the Donatellian milieu of Padua and the ornamental clarity of Piero della Francesca.

TURONE (Verona, 14th century). Turone signed and dated a polyptych of the *Trinity* (now in the Castelvecchio, Verona) in 1360, and this distinguishes him as the first outstanding personality of the 14th century in Verona prior to Altichiero. His work is powerfully constructed, in the Giottesque tradition, but the air of anecdote about it proves that the artist was in touch with the innovators of the day, especially Tommaso da Modena. M. L.

U - V - Z

UCCELLO Paolo di Dono, *called* Paolo (Florence, 1397 - Florence, 1475). Uccello, prettily nicknamed the Bird probably because of his love of winged creatures (as Vasari maintains), was an unusual and slightly eccentric figure of the Florentine 15th century. He was not only a painter, but also a mosaicist, worker in marquetry, decorator and one of the most skilled and conscientious craftsmen of his time. This explains his preoccupations with geometry, which earned him the amusing story recounted by Vasari. ('What a wonderful thing perspective is !' he is supposed to have exclaimed to his wife, who had suggested that he should go to bed.) He was the son of Dono di Paolo, a barber-surgeon of Pratovecchio, who became a Florentine citizen in 1373. Uccello is mentioned in 1407 as a 'garzone di bottega' in Ghiberti's atelier, where he remained until about 1414/15. Ten years later, in 1425, he was in Venice, where he was employed at St Mark's as a master mosaicist; a *St Peter* on the left corner of the façade was by his hand, but it is difficult to decide his share in the mosaics inside. Uccello returned to Florence in January, 1431. He probably began the frescoes in the Chiostro Verde of Santa Maria Novella before receiving the commission for the equestrian portrait, in the cathedral, of *John Hawkwood,* called Giovanni Acuto, signed and dated 1436. (He may have restored it himself twenty years later, when Andrea del Castagno was painting the portrait of Niccolò da Tolentino as a companion piece.) In 1443, again for the cathedral, he decorated the clock on the west wall and then provided three stained glass cartoons for the *oculi* in the dome, representing the *Ascension, Resurrection* and *Nativity,* followed in 1444 by a fourth cartoon, the *Annun-*

UCCELLO.
ST GEORGE
AND THE DRAGON.
NATIONAL GALLERY,
LONDON.

UCCELLO. THE ROUT OF SAN ROMANO. 1456-1458. NATIONAL GALLERY, LONDON.

ciation. The only design rejected was the *Ascension ;* a cartoon by Ghiberti on the same theme was preferred. The work, mentioned by Vasari, *Scenes from Monastic Life,* fragments of which have been recently discovered on the wall of the cloister of San Miniato al Monte, probably belongs to the same period. Towards the middle of the century, Paolo Uccello's most notable work, which made his reputation, was the cycle in the Chiostro Verde, the *Flood,* the *Drunkenness of Noah,* etc. The five portraits in the Louvre, a typical product of the cult of great men at Florence, probably also belong to the same period. Unfortunately, they have been considerably repainted.

When he stayed in Padua between 1445 and 1448, Uccello introduced the virile, monumental style of Tuscany into the north with a series of large figures, called the *Giants,* at the Casa Vitaliani, which impressed Mantegna

(lost). The three panels, illustrating Niccolò da Tolentino's victory over the Sienese at San Romano in 1432, or the *Battles* (Uffizi; Louvre; London, National Gallery), are contemporary with the equestrian portrait of the victor by Andrea del Castagno, in the cathedral at Florence (1456). Their success must have been considerable; the three panels were hung in the great hall of the Medici palace, via Larga. Other scenes, painted at the Casa Bartolini at Valfonda (lost) represented, according to Vasari, horses, armed men and portraits of warriors. Uccello's experiments in painting animals on the panels of *cassoni* are just as interesting. *St George and the Dragon* (Paris, Musée Jacquemart-André; London, National Gallery) gives us an idea of the *Battle of the Dragons and Lions* (lost), which was in the Medici palace, and the *Four Elements,* represented as animals, a fresco on the ceiling of a hall in the

UCCELLO. THE ROUT OF SAN ROMANO. 1456-1458. UFFIZI, FLORENCE.

Palazzo Peruzzi. Uccello reappears in 1465 at Urbino, where he was commissioned by the Confraternity of the Corpus Domini to paint the panels of the *Desecration of the Host,* but he was getting old and the altarpiece was finished by Joos van Ghent, after Piero della Francesca had refused. The astonishing *Hunt* (Oxford, Ashmolean Museum), which is sometimes thought to be a fragment of a decoration commissioned by Federico da Montefeltro, is one of Uccello's last works. He returned to Florence at the end of October, 1468, died there in 1475 and was buried on December 12th in his father's tomb in Santo Spirito.

Uccello was above all a decorative artist whose aim was to give a more vigorous plastic quality to all the ornamental techniques, but there is a complexity in his painting that gives it an original flavour. His point of departure was the monumental style developed after 1424 on the walls of the Brancacci Chapel by Masaccio, but he went beyond this. The new manner of composition was for Uccello the vehicle of forms as varied and unusual as possible. He was, from this point of view, a master of the northern naturalism, which depicted a wealth of natural forms, trees, plants, grass, horses and birds, with an elegant draughtsmanship. He was influenced by Pisanello's style, which gave them a vital, modern flavour. At Venice he discovered the decorative painting that Gentile da Fabriano had just finished in the Palazzo Ducale and his *Battle of Salvore* may have inspired Uccello's *Flood.* When he returned to Florence, Uccello produced his masterpiece, the frescoes of the Chiostro Verde, under the shock of Masaccio's art. We can feel in them both his delight in the powerful monochrome of 'terra verde' (the ground in 'terra verde' has given its name to the cloister) and a style

UGOLINO LORENZETTI

UCCELLO. THE SERPENT. DETAIL FROM THE
FRESCO OF 'THE FALL'. SANTA MARIA NOVELLA,
CHIOSTRO VERDE, FLORENCE.

grounds in the style of the Urbino predella. His animal battles were spread abroad through engravings and his geometrical drawings have come to be regarded as expressions of the fine intellectuality, belonging to a generation of artists, who had a lasting influence on modern art.   A. C.

UGOLINO LORENZETTI (Siena, 14th century). The imaginary name of Ugolino Lorenzetti has been given to an anonymous master whose style is akin to that of Ugolino di Nerio and of Pietro Lorenzetti. In any case, he was a Sienese living during the first half of the 14th century. Among the works attributed to him are a polyptych now in the museum of Santa Croce in Florence and a *Madonna* (Lucca, Pinacoteca) in which the outstanding feature is the lively movement of the Child who seems to be embracing his mother. It is believed that this group of works belongs to a first period of the artist and shows mainly the influence of Ugolino di Neri. The influence of Lorenzetti is more obvious in a second group of pictures, with more sumptuous backgrounds (for instance, the *Madonna* in San Pietro a Ovile, in Siena). Some critics believe them to be by another hand.   P.-H. M.

UGOLINO di NERIO (Siena, *ca* 1317 - *ca* 1349). Sienese painter, also known as Ugolino da Siena, active between 1317 and 1327. According to Vasari, he died in 1349, ' grown old'. He worked in various parts of Italy, particularly in Florence where, among other things, an altarpiece for Santa Croce was commissioned from him. This large polyptych was dismantled in 1847 and the central part has been lost. The existing panels are scattered in various museums (Berlin; London, National Gallery) and private collections. Apart from this signed and dated work, other paintings attributed to Ugolino are the polyptych

with an unprecedented plastic strength, which possesses as much affinity with sculpture as with painting. The equestrian portrait of Sir John Hawkwood, intended to take the place of a marble statue, is like the demonstration of an optical exercise. The interest of the San Miniato frescoes (greatly altered) lies in their construction. There are traces of astonishing perspectives and the artist's feeling for abstraction and ornament was so strong that, to everyone's surprise, he painted the fields red and the towns blue. The system of perspective is just as important in the three panels of the *Battles,* but Uccello's genius expressed itself above all in the profusion of details, the curious forms and marvellously fanciful back-

302

at the Ricasoli castle in Broglio and the *Virgin of Mercy* at San Casciano. Other works are attributed to him with less certainty. Vasari blames Ugolino for having obstinately clung to 'the Greek manner', that is the Byzantine style; but we also find in his work the liberating influences of Duccio and Pietro Lorenzetti. P.-H. M.

VANNI Andrea (Siena, *ca* 1332 - Siena, *ca* 1410). He was a Sienese painter born during the first half of the 14th century and trained in the circle of Lippo Memmi. His long career stretched from 1353 to about 1410. He took part in the religious and political activities of his birthplace; he was a fervent disciple of St Catherine and was sent as envoy to Naples, Florence and Avignon. Of the works he painted in Naples, only a signed triptych has survived (now in the National Gallery, Washington). But he worked mainly in Siena where the following works are still kept: in the church of San Domenico, the moving picture of *St Catherine* holding a lily and allowing a woman to kiss her hand; in the Pinacoteca, a *Crucifixion* (about 1390); in San Francesco, a *Madonna* (fragment of a triptych, 1398-1400); in San Stefano alla Lizza, a large polyptych (1400).

For a long time, Andrea Vanni worked with Bartolo di Fredi. His manner derives from the style of the Sienese masters of the beginning of the century, especially Simone Martini, whose sinuous lines he straightens out, but from whom he borrows a few characteristic features (compare the half closed eyes of St Catherine with those of Martini's *St Clare,* in the Lower Church at Assisi). P.-H. M.

VANNI Lippo (Siena, 14th century). He was a Sienese artist whose works were painted between 1341 and 1375. Lippo Vanni is known mainly as a miniaturist, but also left a small number of frescoes

and altarpieces: a triptych, signed and dated 1358, in the church of San Domenico and San Sisto in Rome. The wings each consists of two panels, one above the other. The central panel shows the Virgin and Child surrounded by two angels and two saints and at her feet, Eve and the serpent, a fairly unusual motif. Eve is seated and is represented on a very small scale. At Siena the following works survive: the fragment of a fresco, an *Annunciation* (cloister of San Domenico, 1372); the *Battle of Val di Chiana* (Palazzo Pubblico, 1372); a fresco, imitating a polyptych, in the Seminario Arcivescovile; the fresco of the *Virgin* in San Leonardo al Lago, near Siena. They show the influence of Pietro Lorenzetti. P.-H. M.

VANNUCCI Pietro, *called* Perugino. *See* Perugino.

VASARI Giorgio (Arezzo, 1511 - Florence, 1574). Vasari can be described as a genial art historian, a fair decorative architect and a bad painter. But he was an important figure. He knew Michelangelo and Andrea del Sarto, then at Arezzo, his home town, he met Rosso Fiorentino in 1529 and painted the *Descent from the Cross* from his cartoons. In 1532, he entered the service of Cardinal Ippolito de' Medici at Rome. There he made the acquaintance of Salviati, then later at Florence of Alessandro de' Medici. These connexions led to the painting of a certain number of portraits, among which were those of *Alessandro* and *Lorenzo de' Medici*. His other works include a *Virgin and Saints* for the Camaldolesians of Arezzo (1538), an *Assumption* at Monte Sansovino, the decoration for the convent refectory at San Michele in Bosco, with the help of Gherardi, in 1540 the *Allegory of the Conception* for the church of the SS Apostoli, then in 1541 a *Leda* for Francesco Rucellai and a *St Jerome*. In 1542, he decorated his

VASARI.
PERSEUS AND
ANDROMEDA.
DECORATION IN
THE STUDIOLO
OF FRANCESCO I
DE' MEDICI. 1573.
PALAZZO VECCHIO,
FLORENCE.

own house at Arezzo with frescoes. In 1546, the decoration of Florence for the visit of Charles V began a long period of activity as the official 'organiser of festivities'. He travelled all over Italy, gathering a prodigious amount of information, which he published in 1550 in the first edition of his *Lives of the most eminent Painters, Sculptors and Architects*. In 1555, he entered permanently into the service of Cosimo de' Medici and began decorating the Palazzo Vecchio: the Apartment of Leo X, the Sala dei Cinquecento and the Quartieri degli Elementi. Their heavy, pompous style, of historic interest only, dated badly. The work occupied him for ten years and in 1573 he added the

over-refined decorations for Francesco de' Medici's *studiolo*. Meanwhile, the Uffizi was reorganised according to his plans and the Academy of Painting founded in 1562. He partly rewrote and enlarged his *Lives* in 1568. His theories had an extraordinary popularity, but not his painting, which is academic and combines the energy of Michelangelo with a rather decadent version of Raphael's manner. His portraits sometimes have an air of melancholy seriousness: his allegories are complicated. Through his innumerable assistants he spread an official style all over Italy. It was prolific and facile and is now considered a rhetorical form of art. A. C.

VECCHIETTA Lorenzo di Pietro, *called* (Castiglione di Val d'Orcia, *ca* 1405 - Siena, 1480). He was a sculptor, an architect, a military engineer, but above all a painter since he spent the best years of his life painting. Vecchietta belonged to the generation who, in the course of the 15th century, either led or followed the artistic evolution from gothic to the new Florentine style. This historical position makes his enthusiasms and his reticences of particular interest to us. While still young, between 1433 and 1439, he worked with Masolino at the Collegiata of Castiglione d'Olona, in Lombardy, where, in the two scenes attributed to him, his Florentine tendencies are made obvious. Back in Siena, he worked for nearly ten years on various decorations in the Ospedale di Santa Maria della Scala: frescoes in the *Pellegrinaio* (three scenes from the *Story of Tobias,* 1441); in 1445, paintings for the *Arliquiera,* a depository where the relics were kept (now in the Siena Pinacoteca); in 1446-1449, frescoes in the sacristy. In the *Arliquiera,* we notice a return to medieval ideas and in the badly preserved sacristy frescoes a mixture of gothic and Renaissance elements which, far from hindering the feeling for decoration, seems on the contrary to enhance it. Between 1450 and 1453, Vecchietta painted on the vault of the Baptistery another series of frescoes illustrating the *Articles of Faith,* a favourite subject with the Sienese. After 1461, he gave up fresco painting altogether, but he went on painting altarpieces; the most remarkable is the *Assumption* in Pienza cathedral (1461-1462). P.-H. M.

VECELLIO Tiziano. *See* Titian.

VENICE. Under barbarian pressure that

VECCHIETTA.
MARTYRDOM
OF ST BIAGIO.
DETAIL
FROM A PREDELLA.
MUSEO CIVICO,
PIENZA.

lasted from the 5th to the 7th century the inhabitants of the Adriatic coast retreated to the islets of the lagoon formed by the mouths of the rivers of Venezia and built a city which remained for a long time under the nominal rule of Byzantium. Geographical determinism should not be invoked too freely, but the situation of Venice, open towards the east, isolated by the lagoon from the west, became a major factor in her history. By the year 1000 the Doge Pietro Orseolo II was conducting a naval expedition to Dalmatia and already in the 10th century the marriage of the

Republic with the Adriatic was commemorated in an annual feast with the doge throwing a golden ring into the sea. After the capture of Constantinople by the Crusaders in 1204 the Doge Dandolo extracted a handsome reward for his assistance by annexing a large part of Greece. In the west Venice could afford to ignore the quarrels of the Italian mainland and strike out on her own, not that she did not acquire possessions on the mainland; in the 15th century she held Bergamo, Udine, Brescia, Padua, Vicenza and Verona and, among other things, many of her artists came from one or other of them. Venice itself remained inviolable and inviolate until 1797. Finally, the easiest road from the north found its natural outlet in Venice bringing across the Brenner people from the other side of the Alps, especially Germans. These as well as Turks had an establishment of their own in the city (Fondaco dei Tedeschi, Fondaco dei Turchi).

The Republic evolved a political system of some originality: from 726 onwards an elective doge with limited powers, the Great Council (Maggior Consiglio), the Council of Ten (set up in 1310) and the Senate. The prevalent trend was towards oligarchy, but the leading families checked each other and subordinated their interests to the state. Another characteristic feature distinguishing Venice from other Italian cities was the relative absence of private patronage in art. The two chief patrons were the Church and the State, the latter often rewarding artists with rich sinecures. Thus Giovanni Bellini and Titian became brokers at the Fondaco dei Tedeschi: others were given the farm on salt.

The art of Venice remained Byzantine well into the Middle Ages, like the Cathedral of Torcello on one of the islets of the lagoon. The years 1043 to 1094 saw the erection, on the site of two earlier churches, of the Basilica of

CARPACCIO. A GONDOLIER. DRAWING
ISABELLA STEWART GARDNER MUSEUM, BOSTON

St Mark in honour of the apostle whose body had been brought from Alexandria in 828. The Basilica was modelled on the Church of the Holy Apostles in Constantinople and workmen were partly recruited from that city. The mosaic decoration was still in progress in the 14th century and, in fact, went on until the 19th. The persistent practice of mosaic in Venise was a delaying factor in the development of her painting.

Gothic struck root in Venice much more easily than in a number of other regions of Italy. The two major churches of the city after St Mark, Santa Maria Gloriosa dei Frari and Santi Giovanni e Paolo, with the doges tombs in the latter, were founded towards the middle of the 13th century by the Franciscans and the Dominicans, but were both rebuilt in the 14th and 15th centuries, which are the two great centuries of Gothic architecture in Venice. The Palazzo Ducale near San Marco was built between 1301 and 1442 and became a sanctuary of Venetian painting. A number of other palaces date from this period, their style present-ing a typically Venetian mixture of mature gothic and oriental influences; the Ca' d'Oro is the most striking example.

Painting lagged behind. No local artist could be found to paint the Sala del Maggior Consiglio and Guariento had to be called in from Padua, which had much livelier contacts with the rest of the Peninsula and could boast of having had Giotto in its midst. Later, Gentile da Fabriano and Pisanello came to work on the Sala. In Venice itself two families, roughly contemporary, stood for two different conceptions of painting: the Vivarini, who combined Byzantine traditions with Germanic ele-ments (Antonio Vivarini, the earliest of the line, was associated with a certain Giovanni d'Alemagna), and the Bellini, no less stoutly Venetian but more open to novelty, who established links with Padua by the marriage of the daughter of Jacopo, the head of the family, to the great Mantegna. While the Vivarini persisted in an archaic manner that one finds even in Crivelli, Giovanni Bellini, or Giambellino, the exact contemporary

VENETIAN SCHOOL: PALMA VECCHIO OR
TITIAN (?). VIOLANTE. KUNSTHISTORISCHES
MUSEUM, VIENNA.

of Crivelli, had a sufficiently flexible talent to learn in old age from the work of his juniors. The curiosity of Venice about the east also appeared in her painters: Gentile Bellini was summoned to Constantinople by Mehmet II and made a bey. Carpaccio, the most gifted of these artists and akin to Gentile, though with a sharper sense of light and grouping, shows medieval reminiscences in his descriptiveness and his taste for narrative.

The first half of the 15th century marks the apogee of Venetian power. The city had nearly 200,000 inhabitants and commanded a fleet of 3,300 vessels. But the first signs of decline were not long in appearing. After the capture of Constantinople by the Turks in 1453 Venetian possessions in the east began to melt away. The discovery of America altered trade routes to the detriment of the Republic. The War of the League

of Cambrai in 1508 brought her to the brink of disaster. But the effects of these reverses were not immediately felt and to the triumphs of prosperity succeeded the triumphs of art. The 16th century is for everyone the great century of Venice. The printing press was introduced in 1499 and the splendid plan of Venice, showing her as she then was, was engraved in 1500 by that curious artist, Jacopo de' Barbari (Jacob Walch) who acted the part of an intermediary between the Germanic world and Venice. Albrecht Dürer stayed in the city at least once and the Fondaco dei Tedeschi housed other visitors from the north. But, most important of all, Giorgione and Titian, followed by a whole school, inaugurated an entirely new kind of painting. They replaced definition by contour with a freer treatment, allowing their forms to integrate themselves in the atmosphere and giving primacy to colour which they set down on the canvas with a new boldness and assurance. This rich and sensual painting met with immediate success and held its own against other schools. Titian became the portraitist of princes. His fertility was incomparable. He was surrounded by a constellation of pupils and imitators like Palma Vecchio, Paris Bordone, later Pordenone, Sebastiano del Piombo who, to his detriment, switched his loyalty to the Roman school, and Lorenzo Lotto who combined Titian's influence with northern elements and worked mainly outside Venice. Tintoretto, a true-born Venetian, as against Titian who came from the mountains of the Cadore, was the painter of Venice par excellence, of her Palazzo Ducale for which he executed the vast *Paradise,* of her churches, of one of the most important of her *scuole,* the Scuola di San Rocco, charitable institutions of a local type belonging to a confraternity and including a hospital. Veronese, a magnificent decorator, came from the mainland, as did the family of

FRANCESCO GUARDI. THE RIALTO BRIDGE AT VENICE. DRAWING. MUSÉE DE BAYONNE.

da Ponte which derived from its native town the name of Bassano. Several Bassani lived well into the 17th century.

Sansovino's Libreria Vecchia di San Marco and the Procuratorie Nuove added the final touch of splendour to the Piazza di San Marco and the Piazzetta. In Vicenza, Palladio created a severely classical architecture at a time when the rest of Italy was on the point of moving in an entirely different direction. He built for the Vicentini, as well as for Venetian nobles, villas of refined proportions. One of the most beautiful of these, the Villa Maser, was decorated with frescoes by Veronese.

Continuing in her isolation, Venice did not take up the baroque in any major way but she had her revenge in the 18th century. Her political structure and her way of life were now irremediably decadent. She became the pleasure resort of all Europe, famous for her carnival and for the easy virtue of her women. But the setting changed. The city palaces, as well as those along the Brenta, were given a delicate stucco decoration moulded and coloured with delicious tones. Their furniture, in spite of the extremely complex forms, were generally graceful. The Ca' Rezzonico, now a museum of applied art, gives a good idea of them. The theatre had never been more brilliant. Venetian rococo, more elaborate than French, had a witty charm. In painting, Venetian decorators were unequalled anywhere else in Europe. Piazzetta, with his use of strong contrasts, had considerable influence in Austria and Germany. But the enchanter is the heavenly Tiepolo. The painters of townscapes, *vedutisti,* moving in the wake of Canaletto and Guardi, have left a charming record of the city, and Pietro Longhi a truthful chronicle of its daily life.

VERONA. The few surviving frescoes at San Fermo and San Zeno are not enough to provide much information about painting in Verona before the middle of the 14th century. The impetus given to the arts by Cangrande della Scala (he brought Giotto to Verona) and his successors is well known, but nothing is known about the first paintings produced. It was not till 1360 that a Veronese school of painting took shape with Turone. The great figure of Altichiero dominated this school till the end of the century. His influence was as much felt in Padua, where he worked for a long time and gathered round him his compatriots (Jacopo da Verona) as in Verona itself. It can be seen too in Martino da Verona, whose creative period ran roughly from 1390 to 1415, a clever artist even if somewhat old fashioned; several of his frescoes are to be seen in the churches of Verona.

Verona became once more a vital and intensely creative centre with Stefano da Verona and later with Pisanello. The outstanding success of these artists in the luxurious, extravagant and refined manner known as the international gothic style, have long suggested to historians that Verona was the first Italian home of this style and that from here it spread throughout north Italy and as far as central Europe. If today it seems more reasonable to ascribe this historic mission to Lombardy, as hitherto (Verona had in any case fallen under the political domination of Milan from 1387 to 1402), it is none the less true that this city was one of the privileged centres of this style, fine examples of which are to be found as far apart as Paris, Cologne, Valencia, Prague and Dijon. Side by side with Stefano, Giovanni Badile (born in 1379) developed it in less vigorous form. Constant exchanges with Venice, which had been since 1405 the suzerain of Verona, also characterise this productive period:

whilst Pisanello worked on the Palazzo Ducale, the Venetians, Niccolò di Pietro, Giambono and Jacopo Bellini lived in turn for a period in Verona. After these thirty years of glory (1410-1440), the Veronese painters fell back into routine and discovered only much later the Paduan revolution, despite the proximity of this city. Francesco Benaglio (1432-about 1492) also imitated with a certain crudeness Mantegna, one of whose masterpieces, the triptych of San Zeno, was brought to Verona in 1459. The same influence, coupled with that of Alvise Vivarini, is discernible in the work of Francesco Bonsignori (1455-1519), who was also a clever portraitist.

Towards 1475-1480, the arts took on a new lease of life, enriched by close contact with Mantua and Venice. For about fifty years the Veronese studios were to produce frescoes and pictures, which if not strikingly original, show remarkable technical qualities. Two trends may be distinguished in this enormous output. The only outstanding figure of this period, Liberale da Verona, led the first group of artists, among whom mention may be made of Giovanni Francesco Caroto, Francesco Torbido (1482-1562), an excellent portraitist influenced by the Venetians, and particularly Niccolò Giolfino (about 1476-1555), an unequal painter whose mythological compositions reveal a strange fantasy. At the opposite pole to this group, the Morone and their friends, Cavazzola, Michele da Verona, and Girolamo dai Libri (1474-1555) practised a more relaxed classicism. Yet the common element in these two tendencies is a taste for brilliant and subtle colour effects, which the next generation was to inherit; but the latter hardly constitutes a school in the true sense. Despite the stimulating visit of a Moretto, a Romanino or a Savoldo to Verona, the young painters had to seek new ideas elsewhere. After some

VERONESE. THE FEAST AT LEVI'S. 1573. ACCADEMIA, VENICE.

time spent with Antonio Badile (1516-1560), Paolo Veronese settled permanently in Venice, and the eclecticism of Domenico Brusasorzi (1516-1567) or Paolo Farinati (1524-1606) no longer owed much to local traditions, except to Veronese. Among later artists of Veronese origin mention must be made of at least three, who, without forming a school, show evidence of similar original research: Pasquale Ottino (1580-about 1630), Alessandro Turchi (about 1588-1650) and particularly Marc'Antonio Bassetti (1588-1630), all three influenced to various degrees by Caravaggism, with which they came into contact in Rome and which gives, especially to the work of the latter, deep human sympathy. M. L.

VERONESE Paolo Caliari, *called* Paolo (Verona, 1528 - Venice, 1588). When Verona was conquered and absorbed by Venice in the 15th century, as an artistic centre she became of secondary importance, but with Paolo Caliari she made a major contribution to Venetian painting in her turn. He was the son of a sculptor and the nephew of a local painter, A. Badile. He remained at Verona until he was twenty-five years old, and received lessons from the humble but sensitive Giovanni Caroto. A certain transparency in his colours and a taste for bright tones was part of his Veronese heritage. Titian's *Assumption* (taken to the cathedral about 1525) came to him as the great revelation of Venetian painting; but in the middle of the century, Verona was particularly receptive to the examples of mannerism and the achievements in the Palazzo del Tè, Mantua, of Giulio Romano, the pupil of Raphael—and they left their imprint on him. He never lost this bond with the artists of Emilia and, through them, with the culture of Rome. Among his first known works are the Pala of Bevilacqua (Verona, Museo Civico, 1548), the Pala of Cardinal Gonzaga (Mantua, 1552) and the *Temptation of St Anthony* painted for the cathedral at Mantua (1553, Musée de

Caen). A Veronese architect, Michele Sanmicheli, procured for him the work of decorating the Villa Thiene and the Villas Soranzo and Fanzola in Castelfranco. He settled in Venice in 1553 and hardly left the city, except to go to Rome in 1560. He was entrusted with painting three ceilings in the Palazzo Ducale by the Council of Ten: *Jupiter striking down the Vices* (Louvre), *Juno scattering her Gifts over Venice* (Louvre) and *Age and Youth*. The prior of the convent of San Sebastiano commissioned from him in 1555 a *Coronation of the Virgin,* surrounded by the Evangelists. The trompe-l'œil was treated with such ease that he was commissioned the following year to paint a cycle of the *Life of Esher* (1556) and finally in the choir a *Life of St Sebastian* (1558). The foreshortening in the *Triumph of the Madonna* is a marvellous piece of virtuos-

ity; a great festive crowd invades the space and the colour is in light, bright tones, very different from those of Titian.

In 1560, the Procurator, Girolamo Grimani, took him to Rome. It was the only big journey in this hard working life. Veronese could not fail to have found in the work of Raphael and Michelangelo a strong encouragement to continue in the grand manner. On his return, official commissions never ceased to flow in: the Sala del Maggior Consiglio in the Palazzo Ducale, in collaboration with Orazio Vecellio, the son of Titian (1562); and notably the large paintings of sacred festivals: the *Marriage at Cana* (Louvre), commissioned by the monks of San Giorgio Maggiore, for their refectory (1562); the *Feast at Simon the Pharisee's* (Louvre) for the Servites (before 1573); the *Banquet of St Gregory*

VERONESE.
MARS AND VENUS.
GALLERIA SABAUDA,
TURIN.

the *Great* for the sanctuary of Monte Berico (1572); the *Feast at Levi's* (Venice, Accademia) for the Dominicans of Santi Giovanni e Paolo. The last painting led to the famous proceedings by the Inquisition from which he extricated himself by pleading the licence granted to poets and madmen and by retouching the painting a little. The decorations at the Villa Barbaro at Maser (1563) are treated with a sort of intoxicated illusionism: buildings, landscapes, false doors cover all the walls as well as a procession of mythological figures. The accents of light, pale colour, according to Ridolfi, 'add to the gaiety of the laughter'. Veronese, who had become the great 'impresario' of painting, resolutely set himself against the dramatic effects of Tintoretto. In the large religious compositions, a crowd of figures is highlighted and stretched across the canvas: Pala of San Zaccaria (about 1562); *Adoration of the Magi* (signed 1573, London, National Gallery) for San Silvestro in Venice; the *Martyrdom of Justina* for the church of the saint in Padua (1575) and the *Mystic Marriage of St Catherine* (about 1575, Venice, Accademia), conceived as a marvellous 'social event'. As early as 1560, Veronese had painted several of the allegorical *tondi* for the large hall in the Old Library. He was given the task of glorifying Venice in one of the finest and best contrived works of the time, which clearly anticipated the baroque: the ceiling of the Sala del Maggior Consiglio or *The Triumph of Venice* in which Venice is depicted between Justice and Peace, who are attended by Juno and Ceres and other allegorical figures, Fame, Honour and Liberty. The delivrance of Smyrna in 1471 and the defence of Scutari against the Turks in 1474 are also celebrated in it. Voluptuous mythological scenes like *Mars and Venus* (1576-1584; New York, Metropolitan Museum), also date from this period. But sometimes his tone becomes more serious: *Calvary* (Louvre), with its greys and its jagged expanse of sky, possesses a feeling of pathos that was increasingly noticeable in the final manner of the painter, for example, in San Pantaleone (1587), a year before his death. He left an enormous atelier and several pupils. His brother, Benedetto, and his two sons, Carlo and Gabriele, put the final touches to his works.

Possibly his slightly old fashioned training in the beginning in the provincial centre of Verona, which was still faithful to Bellini and Mantegna, was a great benefit to Veronese in the end. He saw the work of Correggio and Parmigianino at Parma and of Giulio Romano at Mantua, without losing his instinctive attachment to clarity of colour and form. He learned from them facility of draughtsmanship, an unconventional treatment of the rules, the solidity of figures and the painting of rumpled draperies. When he confronted Venice at a time when Tintoretto and Titian were at the height of their reputations, he was rather like Palladio, with his fundamentally classical notions. He was, of course, influenced by them, but he used his own palette with its personal characteristics, without sacrificing his taste for a cold atmosphere and a less concentrated, more transparent light in which the forms stood out against a lighter shadow. Consequently, his contribution to painting was a sumptuous,

balanced, rather superficial decoration for a city, frightened by the tormented cycles of Tintoretto. The great Venetian scenes were no longer stirred by an inner drama. While Tintoretto combined Titian and Michelangelo, the style of Veronese was tempered by the memory of Correggio. It is easy, but nevertheless necessary, to compare the compositions of Tintoretto, torn by oblique movements, with Veronese's porticoes, colonnades and genial décors of landscapes and outlines that are in harmony with the forms of Palladio. With a gift for scenography, which was only equalled by Tiepolo, Veronese organised his teeming compositions, which, although they were full of figures and little episodes, still remained under control, because he possessed in the highest degree the art of representing huge spectacles without any confusion and without any apparent sacrifice; for example, the *Family of Darius before Alexander* (London, National Gallery), where the masses converge to emphasise the essential in the scene. In the large paintings of the Last Supper, the interplay of vanishing points, the hidden symmetries, the equilibrium of masses and other devices all show an unequalled virtuosity. In spite of their apparent liveliness, these compositions remain as firm as though they were actually static; the rising perspective does not swing at all. Veronese possessed a second register, more dynamic than this, which directly anticipated the baroque, with its broken planes and obliques. Thus the *Annunciation* in the Rosary Chapel, in San Zanipolo at Venice, or in the *Martyrdom of St George* (San Giorgio in Braida, Verona), the unity is held by the tonality of the brilliant colours; the play of deep greens, transparent oranges, pinks, greys with accents of silver, which all tend to harmonise the garments and flesh tints of the women, the sky and the marbles in a kind of pure and scintillating tissue. His resources were so

VERONESE. CALVARY. ABOUT 1570. LOUVRE, PARIS.

varied that he could forget or even compromise the light and felicitous harmonies, which are characteristic of his work. *St Menna* and *St John the Baptist,* painted for the organ of San Gemignano of Venice (about 1565, Modena, Galleria Estense) reveal a change; the atmosphere is almost 'Giorgionesque' and, after 1570, his colour loses some of its limpidity, so that the *Adoration of the Magi* (Vicenza, Santa Corona) and the *Agony in the Garden* (Brera) acquire the more muted tones, the more sombre emotions of the nocturnal world of Bassano and Tintoretto.

Veronese has long been praised as the representative of Venetian classicism. He has also won the reputation of being superficial. His artistic personality is never other than brilliant. The observer is invited to a festivity and its noise sometimes becomes wearisome. The vast orchestration of his paintings, which astonishes because it always seems on the point of disintegrating, is made up of true, vital elements and is organised round a centre that is generally well constructed and conceived. The gravitation of forms in space is impressive, even though it sometimes gives the impression of being contrived,

VERROCCHIO. VIRGIN AND CHILD.
METROPOLITAN MUSEUM, NEW YORK.

and natural talent, which may only have lacked the culture and disquiet of the greatest geniuses of the Renaissance to have equalled them, and which possessed all the decorative potentialities of painting.   A. C.

VERROCCHIO Andrea di Michele Cioni, *called* (Florence, 1435 - Venice, 1488). It was usual at Florence for an artist to be proficient in several techniques, but there is something exceptional in Verrocchio's versatility, which anticipated as early as 1460 the universality of Leonardo da Vinci. He painted banners for the 'giostra' of Lorenzo de' Medici in 1468 and Giuliano de' Medici in 1475. He designed ceremonial helmets and the embellishments for fountains and organised festivities. After his superb sarcophagus of the Medici at San Lorenzo (1472), he received the commission for the marble funeral monument for Cardinal Forteguerri at Pistoia, which had first been given to the Pollaiuoli. In 1482, he gave the full measure of his powers with the sculpture of *Christ and St Thomas* for a niche in Or San Michele. In sculpture, he reinterpreted, with more refinement and complexity, the two great themes of Donatello: the nude youth, as in his *David,* and the equestrian statue. In 1483, he went to Venice to execute the equestrian statue of the condottiere of Bergamo, *Bartolommeo Colleoni.* The work was not completed until after his death. His stature can be gaged by the number and quality of the artists who passed through his studio: the sculptors, Francesco di Simone, Benedetto Buglioni and Francesco Rustici; the painters, Perugino, Lorenzo di Credi, Leonardo da Vinci and Francesco Botticini.

It is difficult to establish an exact catalogue of his paintings, particularly for the *Madonnas* (Berlin; London, National Gallery), which have been attributed to his studio. The height of Verrocchio's activity falls into the

as in the *Annunciation* (Uffizi) or of preciousness, as, for example, in *Mars and Venus* (Turin, Galleria Sabauda) where the painter introduces ironically the animal motif that he was fond of, the head of a horse. The strength and inventions of his art are like the compensation for a dying world in which his painting flourished, where the strain of paganism had partly dissolved the religious spirit and which the genius of art would soon abandon. Nevertheless, Veronese left an immense heritage. Poussin and Claude Lorrain learned from him the value of architecture in a landscape. Rubens and Le Brun learned the secret of composition. After influencing the 17th century in France, he inspired the fêtes galantes and voluptuous mythology of all the 18th century. Veronese had a genuine period 1470-1480. The *Baptism of Christ* (Uffizi) was begun after 1470. Leonardo da Vinci's hand can be recognised in the curly headed angel on the left, whose refined figure is a contrast to the hard outlines of those beside it. His style appears to better advantage in the *Madonna with St Donatus and John the Baptist,* with its new simplicity in composition and the remarkable strength of the figures. It was commissioned for the cathedral at Pistoia, but was only completed after 1483 by Lorenzo di Credi. In the classical taste of his harmonious and balanced compositions, clothes and flesh tints, treated with Flemish precision, acquire an unusual emphasis. Verrocchio was an active, cultivated and accomplished director of his studio. He was not only the master of Leonardo, but, as Verino put it, 'of nearly all those whose names fly through the cities of Italy today [about 1490]'. His departure for Venice in 1483 and his premature death deprived Florence of a strong personality at a time when new tasks were increasing. His reputation has suffered from Vasari's disparagement, who tried to lessen his importance by emphasising the extent of his activities and the inadequacies of his talents. He lived, however, at an interesting turning point in the development of Floretine art. He elaborated new types of composition, defined new themes, like the affronted captains (cast in bronze for Mathias Corvino and known today through drawings and engravings) or the 'angelic' boy. He imparted a greater richness to technique and seems to have helped in enhancing the idea of the artist, his universal vocation and intellectual dignity, which was in keeping with Florentine culture at the time of Lorenzo il Magnifico, and the new awareness of the value of art, which found its ultimate expression in Leonardo da Vinci's conception of painting.   A. C.

VITALE da BOLOGNA Vitale d'Aimo de' Cavalli, *called* (first half of the 14th century). This painter is regarded as the founder of the Bolognese school, and nicknamed during his life-time Vitale of the Madonnas, but, despite the efforts of modern scholars, it is really difficult to establish his position. Documentary evidence proves he was active in Bologna between 1334 and 1359; works such as the *Madonna de' Denti,* signed and dated 1345 (Bologna, Galleria Davia Bargellini), the *Madonna de' Battuti* (Vatican), the San Salvatore polyptych finished in 1353 (Bologna, Pinacoteca), in addition to the remains of various frescoes (Bologna, San Francesco Refectory), show the importance of his workshop. They do not enable us, however, to make a very accurate reconstruction of his career or his art, in which it seems the influence of miniatures and the Umbrian and Sienese style of painting are merged in the graceful precision of his line, his taste for decoration and his efforts to breathe life into his rather cumbersome and freely modelled figures.   J. T.

VIVARINI Alvise (Venice or Murano, *ca* 1446 - Venice, 1503/05). He was the son of Antonio Vivarini and probably the pupil of his uncle, Bartolomeo, judging at least from the rather strained style of the *Montefiorentino Polyptych* (1475, Urbino, Galleria Nazionale) which is his first known work. He learned tonality in painting from Antonello da Messina, as can be seen from the Sacra Conversazione, with St Louis of Toulouse and St Anthony of Padua (1480, Venice, Accademia). In the end, Alvise became the most careful and precise exponent of the crystalline, luminous style, which dominated the end of the century. The panels of *St Anthony and St Clare* possess an unusual clarity of conception, less rich in manner, but sometimes more pure, than that of the Bellini. The *Madonna with four Saints,*

ALVISE VIVARINI. ST CLARE (DETAIL).
ABOUT 1480-1485. ACCADEMIA, VENICE.

with its architectural superstructure, (Berlin, destroyed in 1945), and *St Ambrose* (Venice, Santa Maria dei Frari), which his pupil, Basaiti, completed, show fairly close affinities with Giovanni. Some portraits (1497, London, National Gallery) in a smooth, restrained style, have been attributed to him.   A. C.

VIVARINI Antonio (Murano, *ca* 1415 - Venice, between 1476 and 1484) *and* Bartolomeo (Murano, *ca* 1432 - Murano, 1499). The Vivarini family included Antonio the eldest, Bartolomeo his younger brother, and Alvise, Antonio's son. From about 1440 to the years around 1490, the pseudo-gothic forms of their painting steadily became more flexible until they acquired clarity of outline and greater plasticity. Their atelier, which began at Murano, had more the character of a workshop than that of the Bellini, which was more or less its rival for over half a century. Its characteristics were a feeling for fine materials, enamel-like colour and a carefully balanced composition. It was a style that was supplanted by the innovations of Giorgione.

From 1440 to 1450, Antonio worked regularly with Giovanni d'Alemagna: the *Coronation of the Virgin* (1444, Venice, San Pantaleone) is typical of their taste for rich and congested composition. Antonio's *Madonna* at San Tomaso in Padua, in spite of all the flowers and flourishes of gothic decoration, is more elegant. In 1448, the two companions were invited to decorate the Ovetari Chapel at the Eremitani in Padua, but in the end Pizzolo and Mantegna's team was preferred, because it was considered more modern in spirit. Antonio, nevertheless, had been touched decisively by that spirit; his space became more articulated, his outlines more vital and a solemn grace appeared in his paintings. The panels of the *St Catherine casting out a Pagan Idol* (Washington, Kress Collection) and of *St Peter Martyr* (New York, Milan, etc.) have led to Antonio's being considered as a sort of 'Venetian Masolino' (R. Longhi).

Bartolomeo's artistic personality has more energy. He began in the shadow of his brother (1450-1462), but he reacted strongly to Mantegna's example and developed a polished, but rather sharp style, which often had contradictory strains in it: the *Madonna with Saints* (1465, Naples) is florid; a sense of volume characterises the *Madonna della Misericordia* (1475, Venice, Santa Maria Formosa); and at times a sort of gothic linearism reappears, as in the painting at San Giovanni in Bragora (1478) and also *St George* (1485, Berlin; destroyed in

1945). There is a greater simplicity, but a colder feeling, in the large polyptych of 1490 (Florence, Contini Bonacossi Collection), but the hand of assistants, who became more and more numerous, appears in it and also in *St Martin between St Sebastian and St John the Baptist,* where the clear, dry forms stand out against a rocky landscape (1491, Bergamo, Accademia Carrara). Alvise Vivarini, the last representative of the 'glassy' painting of the Muranesi, was trained in this atelier.   A. C.

VOLTERRA Daniele Ricciarelli, *called* Daniele da (Volterra, *ca* 1509 - Rome, 1566). He was a painter, sculptor and worker in stucco and, in the middle of the 16th century, was the link between the imaginative mannerism of Siena and the grand style of Rome. In fact, he trained at Siena under Sodoma and went on later to the atelier of Beccafumi, who gave him a certain taste for effects of light. After varied work in his own region (*Justice,* Volterra, Palazzo dei Priori), he soon settled in Rome and immediately came under the influence of Michelangelo, as can be appreciated in his works in the Chapel of the Crucifixion in San Marcello (1541-1546) and particularly at Santa Trinità dei Monti, where in the *Descent from the Cross* (1541) an extraordinary intensity is imparted by its size and strength that owes something to Sebastiano del Piombo. It was one of the most admired works in Rome by the young generation. The *Beheading of John the Baptist* (Turin, Galleria Sabauda) is a good example of his bold composition and provocative manner. In 1547, Daniele decorated the Sala Regia in the Vatican with stucco and frescoes among which was the *Massacre of the Innocents.* In 1557, after a brief stay in Volterra, he was indicted as a result of a prudish controversy, inspired by Aretino, on whether the nudes of Michelangelo in the *Last Judgment* should be covered up. This earned him the

BARTOLOMEO VIVARINI. ST MARTIN DIVIDING HIS CLOAK WITH A POOR MAN. 1491. ACCADEMIA CARRARA, BERGAMO.

nickname of Braghettone and an unpleasant reputation, which was quite unjustified.   A. C.

ZAMPIERI Domenico, *called* Domenichino. *See* Domenichino.

ZENALE Bernardo (Treviglio, 1436 -

Milan, 1526). He often worked with Bernardo Butinone and their partnership produced one of the most significant works of Lombard art: from 1485 to 1500, they painted together the large polyptych in the church of Treviglio, which is one of the richest and most imposing in north Italy. They worked afterwards on the *tondi* in the nave of Santa Maria delle Grazie in Milan and joined forces again, after 1490, for the frescoes in the large hall of the Castello Sforzesco, Milan, and the frescoes in the Grifi chapel of San Pietro in Gessate, also in Milan, which they both signed. Zenale ended his career as architect in the Duomo of Milan. His artistic personality is less clearly defined than Butinone's: he differs from him in a less expressive, less strained style. Like Butinone, he was influenced by Foppa and Bramante, but he tended to construct his paintings more carefully and emphasise the perspective, a characteristic that his activities as an architect would probably explain. At the end of his life, he was slightly influenced by Leonardo da Vinci. His work has often been confused with that of other artists, particularly Civerchio and the pseudo-Civerchio.   S. B.

ZOPPO Marco (Cento, *ca* 1432 - Bologna, 1478). 'Adopted' by Squarcione at Padua in 1452 and, like so many others, exploited by him, Zoppa left his master in 1455 to establish himself in Venice. From then onwards he divided his time between that city and Bologna. Throughout his life, however, he bore the stamp of the Paduan culture that had first stimulated his art, and was often linked with the great Ferrarese artists in his frenzied efforts to achieve a powerful plasticity and expression. His best personal qualities come to light in his most complete work, the polyptych in the Collegio di Spagna at Bologna: here we see a freedom of movement in his flowing, sinewy lines, and a luminous,

transparent quality in his colour which owes much to the examples of Piero della Francesca and the Venetians. In his subsequent paintings the latter influence shows still more clearly.   M. L.

ZUCCARO Taddeo (1529 - 1561) *and* Federico (1542 - 1609). Both artists were born at Sant'Angelo in Vado, near Urbino. After working with Vasari on the cupola of Santa Maria del Fiore in Florence, Taddeo went to Rome in 1542, where he and his brother ornamented the ceilings of the Villa Giulia with several stucco decorations for the future Pope Julius III. In 1562, Annibale Caro dictated to him in a celebrated letter the allegorical cycle of the Palazzo Farnese in Caprarola where they gave the full measure of their unrealistic art. The two brothers also painted together the frescoes of the Sala Regia in the Vatican. After the death of Taddeo, Federico pursued his brilliant career of decorative painter until the end of the century: at Venice in the Sala del Maggior Consiglio of the Palazzo Ducale and at Milan. He travelled to France (1572-1574) at the invitation of the Cardinal of Lorraine. He was called to England and then Spain in 1585 to decorate the high altar in the Capilla Major of the Escorial. Federico was a theorist and he transformed his house in the via Gregoriana, with a façade that was a sort of manifesto of the new mannerist tendencies, into an academy of painting. In 1607, his treatise, *Idea,* gave a summary of his teaching and principles at the time. The Zuccari brothers belonged to the last generation of the mannerists. They liked to use their skilful, often excessive art, which anticipates baroque, in vast cycles with learned allusions. At the same time they elaborated an academic theory to justify it. This was handed down to the next generation; in 1768, Federico Zuccaro's treatise was successfully reissued.   S. B.